Borderland Generation

Modern Jewish History
Henry Feingold, *Series Editor*

Select Titles in Modern Jewish History

Assimilated Jews in the Warsaw Ghetto, 1940–1943
Katarzyna Person

Between Persecution and Participation: Biography of a Bookkeeper at J. A. Topf & Söhne
Annegret Schüle and Tobias Sowade; Penny Milbouer, trans.

The Children of La Hille: Eluding Nazi Capture during World War II
Walter W. Reed

Horace Kallen Confronts America: Jewish Identity, Science, and Secularism
Matthew J. Kaufman

Jewish Libya: Memory and Identity in Text and Image
Jacques Roumani, David Meghnagi, and Judith Roumani, eds.

One Step toward Jerusalem: Oral Histories of Orthodox Jews in Stalinist Hungary
Sándor Bacskai; Eva Maria Thury, trans.

"We Are Jews Again": Jewish Activism in the Soviet Union
Yuli Kosharovsky; Ann Komaromi, ed.; Stefani Hoffman, trans.

"What! Still Alive?!" Jewish Survivors in Poland and Israel Remember Homecoming
Monika Rice

For a full list of titles in this series, visit https://press.syr.edu/supressbook-series/modern-jewish-history.

Borderland Generation

Soviet and Polish Jews under Hitler

Jeffrey Koerber

Syracuse University Press

The views or opinions expressed in this book, and the context in which the images are used, do not necessarily reflect the views or policy of, nor imply approval or endorsement by, the United States Holocaust Memorial Museum.

Syracuse, New York 13244-5290

First Edition 2020

20 21 22 23 24 25 6 5 4 3 2 1

∞ The paper used in this publication meets the minimum requirements of the American National Standard for Information Sciences—Permanence of Paper for Printed Library Materials, ANSI Z39.48-1992.

For a listing of books published and distributed by Syracuse University Press, visit https://press.syr.edu.

ISBN: 978-0-8156-3619-9 (hardcover)
978-0-8156-3637-3 (paperback)
978-0-8156-5465-0 (e-book)

Library of Congress Cataloging-in-Publication Data

Names: Koerber, Jeffrey, author.

Title: Borderland Generation : Soviet and Polish Jews under Hitler / Jeffrey Koerber.

Other titles: Soviet and Polish Jews under Hitler

Description: First edition. | Syracuse, New York : Syracuse University Press, 2020. | Series: Modern Jewish history | Includes bibliographical references and index. | Summary: "Borderland Generation: Soviet and Polish Jews under Hitler" explores the Holocaust in eastern Poland and the western Soviet Union under German occupation during World War II. Drawing upon written and oral sources recorded in the multiple languages of the region, many never before examined by scholars, the book follows the trajectories of individuals too often portrayed in the historical literature as faceless victims."— Provided by publisher.

Identifiers: LCCN 2019042562 (print) | LCCN 2019042563 (ebook) | ISBN 9780815636199 (hardcover) | ISBN 9780815636373 (paperback) | ISBN 9780815654650 (ebook)

Subjects: LCSH: Jews—Belarus—History—20th century. | Jews—Poland—History—20th century. | Belarus—Ethnic relations. | Poland—Ethnic relations. | Holocaust, Jewish (1939–1945)—Belarus. | Holocaust, Jewish (1939–1945)—Poland. | Soviet Union—History—German occupation, 1941–1944. | Holocaust survivors. | Hrodna (Belarus)—History—20th century. | Vitsebsk (Belarus)—History—20th century.

Classification: LCC DS135.B38 K643 2019 (print) | LCC DS135.B38 (ebook) | DDC 940.53/1809478—dc23

LC record available at https://lccn.loc.gov/2019042562

LC ebook record available at https://lccn.loc.gov/2019042563

Manufactured in the United States of America

Contents

Illustrations

Figures

TABLE

Acknowledgments

With deep gratitude, I thank the many scholars, colleagues, family, and friends who helped bring this work to completion.

I thank Debórah Dwork for her perceptive advice and tireless encouragement at all stages of this project. It was my great privilege to have been among her graduate students and advisees at the Strassler Center for Holocaust and Genocide Studies at Clark University. She also generously offered her time and guidance during the development of the manuscript. On nearly every page, I tested the many interpretations and concepts that I learned from Dr. Dwork.

When I was still considering research topics during my first semester of graduate work, visiting professor Yehuda Bauer suggested to me, "You should go to Belarus." He made the recommendation knowing that the region offered new avenues for Holocaust research. I followed up on his suggestion and made my first research trip to Belarus in the summer of 2005. In subsequent journeys, I uncovered extraordinary documents in the archives. Dr. Bauer had indeed offered good advice.

I received similarly formative guidance from many other visiting and resident faculty and staff at the Strassler Center. Visiting professor Barbara Harff influenced my interpretation of the unfolding nature of events on the eve of the Holocaust through her seminar analyzing the preconditions of genocide. Simon Payaslian introduced me to the transnational dimensions of the Armenian Genocide, circumstances that paralleled the experiences of Jews living across the Polish–Soviet borderlands. Thomas Kühne imparted foundational analysis of the actions of Nazi perpetrators and their collaborators. Tatyana Macaulay offered much appreciated counsel that helped to transform me into an engaged and enthused scholar. Without the early endorsement of visiting professor Robert Jan van Pelt, I might never have had the opportunity to pursue Holocaust studies. A special place in my mind and heart is held by Holocaust-era rescuer and psychoanalyst Marion Pritchard, who cotaught Professor Dwork's seminars. Sitting at the seminar table with Dr. Pritchard definitively shaped my understanding of the Holocaust as human experience.

The scholars who offered their time and expertise during the research and writing of this book are numerous. Wendy Lower (Claremont McKenna College) and Kate Brown (University of Maryland, Baltimore County) provided insightful comments as readers on my dissertation committee. I had the unique opportunity to study the Yiddish-language works of historians Emmanuel Ringelblum, Isaiah Trunk, and Raphael Mahler with Samuel D. Kassow at Trinity College. Cynthia Hooper at College of the Holy Cross guided me through the intricate history of the Great Terror in the Soviet Union. In recent years, Richard Hovannisian has further expanded my understanding of the memory of genocide through his discussions of how it pertains to the Armenian Genocide. Anika Walke offered her counsel on the experiences of Soviet Jews before and during the Holocaust. Natalia Aleksiun (Touro College) provided encouragement at a key stage in the preparation of the manuscript. I owe a special debt of gratitude to my teachers of Yiddish language and literature, Ellen Kellman at Brandeis University and Rebecca (Rivke) Margolis at the University of Ottawa.

I also offer thanks to my fellow graduate students at the Strassler Center for their advice and encouragement, including Cristiana Andriani, Betsy Anthony, Stefanie Fischer, Tiberiu Galis, Michael Geheran, Adara Goldberg, Naama Haviv, Alexis Herr, Rachel Iskov, Stefan Ionescu, Ümit Kurt, Natalya Lazar, Ilana Offenberger, Jody Russell Manning, Raz Segal, Joanna Sliwa, and Dottie Stone. Their friendship and support were particularly important during the preparation of the manuscript.

The Strassler Center at Clark University exists because of the generous support from its many benefactors, and I extend my profound thanks to them as well. I am grateful to the Conference on Jewish Material Claims against Germany and to Albert M. Tapper, who funded my five years of graduate study and dissertation research at the Strassler Center. Additional support for my research and writing came from a Fulbright Student Fellowship to Belarus and Poland, 2007–8; the Corrie ten Boom Research Award from the USC Shoah Foundation at the University of South California, Los Angeles, 2007; a Tauber Institute Award from the Tauber Institute for the Study of European Jewry, 2006–7; a Peter Hayes Research Fellowship Award from the Holocaust Educational Foundation, 2009; and a Kagan Claims Conference Academic Fellowship for Advanced Shoah Studies, 2009–11.

At Chapman University, where I have taught Holocaust history since 2011, I owe profound thanks to Marilyn J. Harran, Stern Chair in Holocaust Education and director of the Rodgers Center for Holocaust Education. This project reached completion because of Dr. Harran's encouragement and persistence. I greatly appreciate the support of Chapman University, particularly from Jennifer D. Keane, chair, Department of History; Glenn M. Pfeiffer, provost; and Daniele C. Struppa, president. I thank the benefactors of the Rodgers Center for the many community engagement and education opportunities they make possible. I have befriended many Holocaust survivors through my work with the Rodgers Center, including Zelda Gordon *z"l* (of blessed memory), whose story is told on these pages, and Curt Lowens *z"l*, survivor, rescuer, and brilliant character actor. The ever energetic Jack Pariser continues to challenge me with questions on how to preclude genocide in the future. In addition, I feel a special gratitude to my students because it is on their behalf that I have labored to develop clear and concise explanations of complex events, a skill that benefitted the creation of this work.

The patient staff at numerous archives and libraries warrant my deep appreciation and thanks for their help during the course of my research: in Belarus, the Belarusian State Archives branches in Vitebsk and Grodno; in Poland, the Jewish Historical Institute and the National Library; in Israel, Yad Vashem; and in the United States, the United States Holocaust Memorial Museum Library and Archives, the Library of Congress, the National Archives and Records Administration, the YIVO Institute for Jewish Research, and the American Jewish Joint Distribution Archive. I extend a special thanks to scholars Agnieszka Haska and Jakub Petelewicz in Warsaw for their assistance in accessing archives at the Jewish Historical Institute and the National Library.

My parents, Bill and Renee, taught me the values and ethics that made me the person able to do this work. I also thank my siblings—Steve, Mike, Jim, Kathy, and Peter—who have given me much moral support these many years. My friends Nick, Mike, and Kevin have also been understanding and helpful as I shuffled from one locale to another during the course of my research and writing.

I extend additional thanks to colleagues in my previous career as a historic preservation architect, in particular Deborah Slaton, who set me on the road to be a better writer, a thorough researcher, and an observant investigator.

At Syracuse University Press, I thank my editor, Deborah Manion, for her guidance and encouragement as this book approached completion.

I first turned to Holocaust studies nearly twenty years ago when I was awarded the Francis J. Plym Traveling Fellowship from my undergraduate alma mater, the School of Architecture at the University of Illinois at Urbana-Champaign. Over the course of four months through Poland, Germany, Czech Republic, Belgium, and France, I first encountered the historical sites of the Holocaust. I came away with more questions than I had at the start, primarily about the European Jews targeted during the Holocaust. What were the features of their lives, cultures, and traditions? How did they respond to unfolding threats to their societies, families, and individual lives? With this project, I hope I have begun to find some answers.

Principal Historical Figures

Belarusian Soviet Socialist Republic

Vitebsk

Elena Choukmazova, born 1930
Lev Fleish, born 1922
Raisa Gendelev, born 1932
Vera German, born 1927
Dmitri Khvat, born 1928 in Białystok, Poland
Grigorii Lesin, born 1921
Fivel Markelis, born 1927
Stepan Zavgorodnev, born 1926

Chashniki

Hirsh Reles, born 1913, writer and teacher, later migrated to Vitebsk, Minsk, Slutsk, and Novogrudok

Minsk: Soviet Yiddish Writers

Zelik Akselrod (1904–1941), poet
Izi Kharik (1898–1937), poet
Moishe Kulbak (1896–1937), poet, dramatist, and novelist

Second Polish Republic

Grodno

Batya (last name unknown), born early 1920s
Leib Bialo, born 1923
Chasia Bielicka, born 1921
Alexandre Blumstein, born 1930
Lisa Chapnik, born 1922
Elka Fomin, born 1928
Zelda Grodzienska, born 1923
Hirshl Grodzienski, born 1930
Bella Ilin, born 1937
Anna Kaletska, born
Sima Kapulska, born 1919
Daniel Klovsky, born 1928
Moishe Kremer, born 1918
Ann Lewin, born 1924
Fenia Muller, born 1922
Mina Muller, born 1927
Yehuda Rabinovich, born 1922
Leib Reizer, born 1910
Vichna Sidranska, born 1927
Sidney Sisun, born 1924
Bronia Winicka, born 1924

Second Polish Republic

Grodno (continued)

Feliks Zandman, born 1927
Iosif Zbar, born 1906

YIVO autobiographical essay authors (1930s):

Hanan L., born 1916
"Yankl," born 1916
Lev Zhubov (pseud.), born 1921

Białystok

Chaika Grossman, born 1919

Rubiezewicze

Sarah Fishkin, born 1923

Refugees from Western Poland

Sheyne Miriam Broderzon (Warsaw)
Joseph Ceder (Łódź)
Hanna Davidson (Warsaw)
Alexander Dimant (Warsaw)
Lucien Feigenbaum (Warsaw)
Liliana Goldsopl (Warsaw)
Moishe Grosman (Warsaw)
Rozalia Hollander (Warsaw)
Dora Huze (Łódź)
Anna Kaletska (Kielce)
Elias Rubinstein (Łapy)
Avraham Zak (Warsaw)

Borderland Generation

Introduction

A Generation Divided

In September 1921, a group of young Jews posed for a photograph, shown in figure 1. The First Jewish Workers' Artel "Hehalutz" (Pioneers) in the eastern European city of Vitebsk gathered at their communal garden on the southeast edge of the city, then in the territory of the Russian Soviet Federative Socialist Republic.[1] These *halutzim* (pioneers) preparing for agricultural work in Palestine met to celebrate their bountiful harvest. A year or two later and a few hundred kilometers to the west, a different group of *halutzim* in Grodno, Poland, looked into the camera while taking their lunch break, shown in figure 2. Both groups of young, idealistic Jews shared the common goal of establishing a Jewish state.

Closer examination of the photographs reveals small but significant differences. In Vitebsk, some of the young men wear Red Guard or Red Army uniforms, attire evidently suitable for the festive occasion. Many of the young women wear dresses, one with a lace collar. The labels *worker* and *artel* (communal association) in the group's name indicates ties with the new Soviet system. Hehalutz functioned legally in the Soviet Union because it would not be until 1927 that Zionism was banned.[2] As the image suggests, in 1921 the Vitebsk pioneers maintained a vibrant presence.

Fewer people populate the photo from Grodno, perhaps because the scene is an ordinary work day and not a celebration. As these pioneers presumably returned to the fields after their meal, their manner of dress is suited to the work that lay ahead. Some of the men wear

1. First Jewish Workers' Artel Hehalutz, Vitebsk, 12 September 1921. Photograph in the author's collection.

uniforms, although none is readily identifiable as belonging to active-service branches in Poland or Russia at the time. More noteworthy are the hats. Three young men in Grodno sport straw boaters, a bourgeois hat style unsurprisingly out of fashion in revolutionary Vitebsk. Given the urban origins of both sets of pioneers, they have apparently adapted well to the rigors of farming. Although both scenes are embellished by banners announcing the organization's name in Hebrew, the ornamental gate in Grodno is adorned by a small portrait of Theodor Herzl. Such Zionist iconography is either not visible or was already out of favor in the Communist world.

Labels, uniforms, hats—small but significant identity markers differentiating these youth-group members. As documented by appearance alone, distinct allegiances and cultural symbols had already emerged under newly established political systems, marking the distance that each group had traveled in only a few short years. When

2. Hehalutz members in Grodno, circa early 1920s. Photograph used by permission of Yad Vashem Photo Archive, Jerusalem, archival signature 1366/505.

these *halutzim* in Vitebsk and Grodno were born, they shared residency in the "Pale of Settlement," the western districts of Imperial Russia where the regions' Jews were authorized to make their residence (figure 3). By the time each group sat for the camera in the early 1920s, control over these regions had changed hands several times during the tumult of World War I, the Russian Revolution, and the Polish–Soviet War of 1919–21. The Pale's five million Jews, emancipated from the discriminatory restrictions imposed by the tsar, fell into separate political realms (figure 4). Belarus, the Slavic region spanning between Russia and Poland to the east and west and Lithuania and Ukraine to the north and south, was divided as well, placing its population under both Polish and Soviet sovereignty.

Events during the 1920s and 1930s accelerated this cultural drift. Young Jews in Vitebsk and Grodno married and raised families under vastly different political systems. Despite a common heritage, children born and raised on opposite sides of the Polish–Soviet border acquired

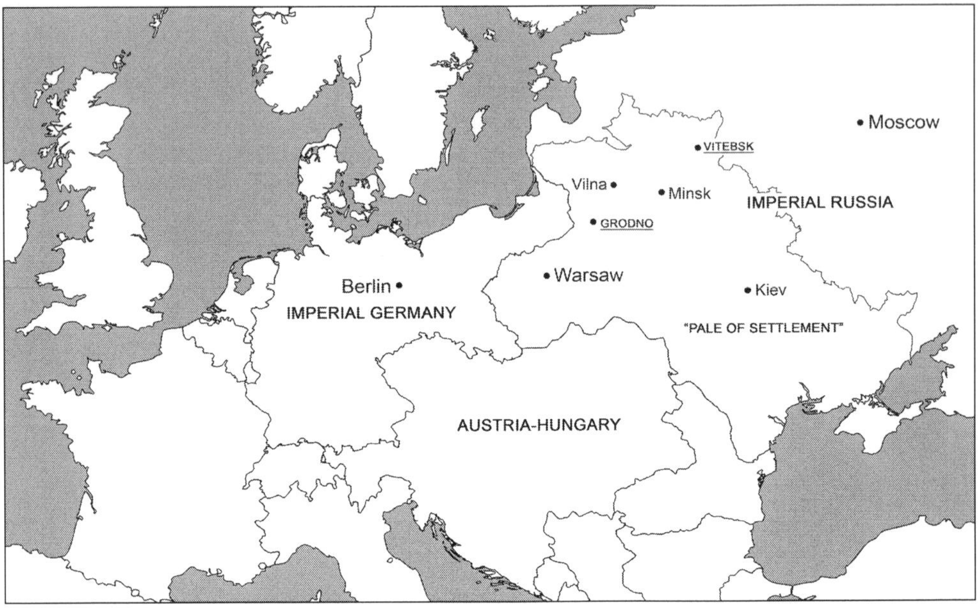

3. Map of Europe, 1914. Before World War I, Vitebsk and Grodno lay within the "Pale of Settlement," the region of Imperial Russia where Jews were permitted permanent residence.

distinct beliefs, values, and attitudes. Variances in civic commitment, school lessons, youth activities, religious observance, housing arrangements, and perceptions of security shaped the social education of the interwar generation of Soviet and Polish Jews.

These divided populations merit study within several disciplines: Jewish history, Soviet and Polish history, eastern European history, and transnational contexts such as borderland studies. Yet it is what happened two decades after the two photos were taken that defines their story. In the wake of the German invasion of the Soviet Union in June 1941, the Polish–Soviet borderlands became the epicenter of the genocide of Jews. When we examine how Polish Jews and Soviet Jews struggled to survive during the Holocaust, we find unique reactions and responses. Many young Jews from the western Soviet Union pursued opportunities to take on Slavic identities as a means of survival. Their counterparts across the border in Poland typically tried

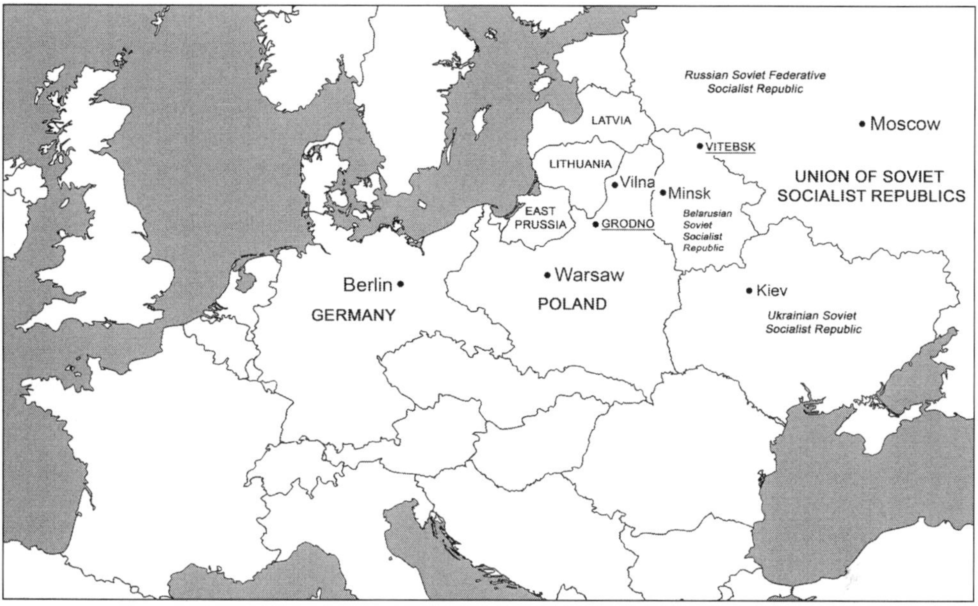

4. Map of Europe, 1929–38. The violence of World War I, the Bolshevik Revolution, and the Polish–Soviet War of 1919–21 redrew the map of eastern Europe. Vitebsk became a western borderland city of the Union of Soviet Socialist Republics. Grodno was an urban center of the Kresy Wschodnie (Eastern Borderlands) of the Second Polish Republic.

to "pass" as Gentiles only when they had exhausted all other options. Most of them instead banded together with other young Jews in their attempts to withstand the Nazis' murderous assault.

This book analyzes these contrasting responses. Examining the lives of young Jews of the Polish–Soviet borderlands, it looks at how the knowledge and skills attained during the 1930s shaped their attempts at survival during the violence and destruction of the Holocaust. Vitebsk and Grodno, cities flanking the interwar Polish–Soviet border, provide the context. Vitebsk, a city of about 100,000 (one-third Jews), sat within the borders of the Belarusian Soviet Socialist Republic, one of the Soviet Union's federation members. Grodno, located in the eastern border regions of the Second Polish Republic, had a population of 60,000, half of whom were Jewish. Communism in Vitebsk and nationalism and capitalism in Grodno shaped the lives of newly emancipated Jews in distinct ways.

The generation born between the world wars had no notion of the tragedy and violence that lay ahead. In the Soviet Union, young Jews found advocates among the Bolsheviks, who saw all youth as the future (chapter 1). Investing in children and adolescents, the Communist Party in Soviet Belarus sanctioned schools in each national language. Jews, whom the Bolsheviks considered a nationality and not members of an ethnicity or religion, had access to education in Yiddish. Many welcomed the opportunities for social advancement opened by the Soviet system. "Now we are strong, young, resolute," wrote the twenty-year-old poet Hirsh Reles in a verse published while he attended the teachers' training academy for Yiddish schools in Vitebsk.[3] Outside of school, in Soviet youth organizations and in the streets and parks of the Red city of Vitebsk, children of all nationalities enjoyed a social familiarity largely unknown across the western border in Poland. Then, too, the Bolsheviks had declared ethnic harmony to be a Soviet virtue. To be antisemitic was to be "anti-Soviet." As Vitebsk native Lev Fleish recalled of his youth during the 1930s, "We were all friends, we all went to school and went in for sports and there was absolutely no antisemitism."[4]

Jews were purportedly one of Bolshevism's success stories, an oppressed people liberated to stand beside other Soviet nationalities. But what was this Soviet Jewish identity? With the suppression of Jewish community functions in the 1920s, young Jews seldom learned much about their religious or cultural heritage. Jewish parents, realizing that the best chances for their children's advancement lay with the Russian- or Belarusian-language education system, showed little enthusiasm for the officially sanctioned Yiddish-language schools. Jewish children and adolescents adapted to these circumstances, acquiring knowledge of Slavic languages and cultures in schools and in communal living environments.

Concurrent with these developments within Jewish life, the Great Terror of the late 1930s shook Soviet society. Although primarily targeting perceived "class enemies," Communist Party cadres, and the Red Army's officer corps, the Great Terror also attacked Poles, Germans, and other national minority groups residing in the Soviet borderlands in the "national operations" conducted by the Narodnyy komissariat vnutrennikh del (NKVD, People's Commissariat for Internal Affairs). Jews were not specifically pursued because of their "nationality" during the purges. Nevertheless, thousands of them fell victim, including several leading Jewish cultural figures in Belarus. The turmoil filtered into young people's lives. Families feared the middle-of-the-night knock at the door by the NKVD. Fear divided friends and neighbors, undermining public and private trust. Antisemitism also intensified in Soviet society based on the false impression that Jewish NKVD agents led the purges. The Great Terror also spurred changes in policies toward minorities, hastening the acculturation of younger Jews. Party leaders in Soviet Belarus closed the Yiddish-language schools in the summer of 1938 and reopened them in the fall as Belarusian-language institutions.

Jewish young people in Grodno lived in very different circumstances from their counterparts across the eastern Polish border (chapter 2). By the 1930s, reborn Poland had become a hostile climate for ethnic minorities, in particular Jews. A pogrom in Grodno in June 1935 underscored the volatile atmosphere. But the problems facing Jewish youth extended beyond discrimination and violence. Economic opportunities were few, and the Jewish community was powerless to improve the situation. Many young Jews joined Zionist or Bundist groups to address their problems by shaping their own future. The desire for social interaction fostered youth-group development as much as ideological affinity. Writing in her diary in midsummer 1935, a Grodno teenager names Batya exulted, "I belong to an organization, I pursue an ideal, I am surrounded by people who understand me. I am no longer alone."[5] Young people who avoided official group affiliation bonded with friends to form their own cliques composed almost exclusively of other Jews. Whether in formal or informal group settings, such connections reinforced each individual's sense of Jewish identity.

The Molotov-Ribbentrop Pact of 23 August 1939 decisively shifted the destinies of young Jews in both cities. Within a month, the

Germans conquered western Poland, and the Soviets occupied and later annexed the eastern Polish provinces, including Grodno (chapter 3). Rapid sovietization of these new western Soviet oblasts toppled existing community structures. Zionist and Bundist youth groups were banned. The new rulers lured young Jews into the Soviet program with opportunities unknown in prewar Poland. Some joined the Pioneers and the Komsomol and heeded the messages disseminated by the party. Many others merely followed their friends into these authorized organizations because of the activities and benefits on offer. A few continued to meet in secret with fellow Zionist or Bund members. Regardless of the avenue they took, the Jewish youth of Grodno continued to maintain close connections with their peers exclusive of the young people from other ethnic groups.

While war raged in Europe, displays of Soviet power reinforced perceptions of invincibility (chapter 4). In the newly annexed regions, the NKVD rounded up hundreds of thousands of former political and community leaders, ethnic Poles, refugees from German-occupied Poland, and other potential "enemies" and deported them to labor camps in the Soviet interior. If the Bolsheviks could organize such operations, didn't the Soviet Union also have the means to repel any threat? The Soviet press reinforced such notions. Nazi aggression was a European affair, and the vigilant Red Army defended the border. Many in the Soviet Union maintained their faith in Soviet security even after hearing that German forces had crossed the frontier on 22 June 1941.

The collapse of Red Army defenses in the face of the German invasion shattered these illusions of Soviet invincibility (chapter 5). Grodno fell the first day of the offensive, making escape nearly impossible. The Wehrmacht captured Vitebsk two and a half weeks later, but flight necessitated recognition of danger and prompt action. Soviet Jews had been shielded from most reports of Nazi persecution in Poland, and the Germans' intent on Soviet territory emerged only in stages. Vitebsk and Grodno fell into separate zones of German occupation, flanking the rough continental divide of German annihilation policies based on imperial and local priorities, with murder by bullets to the east and murder by gas to the west. As the summer of 1941 waned, most Vitebsk Jews were dying of malnutrition, disease, or exposure in the ghetto set up by the Wehrmacht occupation authority. Renewal of the German assault on the Soviet capital triggered the elimination of the perceived hazard presented by a ghetto full of typhus-ridden captive Jews, a hell of the Nazis' own making. An Einsatzgruppe (Special Task Group) detachment shot the remaining Jewish population outside the city in early October. Escape before this final massacre meant accepting the painful abandonment of older or less-mobile family members and flight into the unknown. Young Jews who fled Vitebsk often used their prewar socialization in Slavic cultures to pose as Russians, Belarusians, Tatars—anyone but themselves. Some maintained the pretense for a few days or weeks, others for years.

Such choices were alien to young Grodno Jews (chapter 6). Cooperation among peers outweighed notions of individual impersonation as an instinctive response to adversity. Jews in Grodno had been confined to a ghetto in November 1941, becoming part of a forced-labor pool to support German interests in the Białystok District. Yet their "value" as workers was eventually trumped by Nazi SS demands for their destruction. As deportations to annihilation camps began in November 1942, small Jewish resistance groups accelerated their plans for an uprising. One young woman who took part in these activities in the Grodno ghetto was Zelda Grodzienska. "So we got a few guns and other homemade things," she remembered decades later.[6] But only a tiny, bungled revolt occurred during the last series of roundups from the ghetto.

Following the separation from their home cities, survival for Vitebsk and Grodno Jews led through the contrasting environments of concentration and forced-labor camps, hiding places, and underground movements (chapter 7). Cooperation among Grodno Jews did not end with the ghetto liquidation. Former group members continued to draw upon ties of solidarity in concentration camps, forming new bonds with young Jews from other towns. Some ties were based on communal solidarity as Jewish prisoners from the Grodno region looked to aid one another's survival. Others were political. Daniel Klovsky and his father, David, were helped by Communist prisoners out of respect for David's brother, an activist in prewar Grodno. Vitebsk survivors, by contrast, shunned close connections with their fellow prisoners until liberated by Soviet forces. "I tried to be absolutely unnoticeable," Lev Fleish later recalled, speaking of his time in a German forced-labor camp, where he posed as an ethnic Tatar.[7]

No two survivors experienced the same conditions, and differences in the Germans' genocidal policies restricted possible trajectories. Luck and opportunity proved to be the most crucial factors in survival in all cases. At the same time, chance and fortuitous circumstances opened small windows for individual agency. Within these limits, Jews from Soviet Vitebsk and Polish Grodno pursued different paths.

After liberation, many young Grodno Jews searched for relatives. Few were successful. Makeshift families formed between fellow survivors as new community structures emerged. Some remained in the western Allied zones of occupied Germany, site of their liberation. From there, America or the promise of a Jewish state in Palestine beckoned. Others returned to Grodno or at least made it as far as the Polish–Soviet border. As former Polish citizens, they could reclaim that passport. Many survivors did so as a springboard to the West, ultimately establishing new lives in a new land.

Vitebsk Jews faced compulsory repatriation to the Soviet Union. A few located surviving family members; the longer interval between the onset of the Germans' invasion and their arrival in the city allowed a greater number of Vitebsk Jews to flee compared to those in Grodno. Vitebsk survivors once again demonstrated flexibility by adapting to the economically austere and openly antisemitic conditions of the postwar Soviet Union. In this repressive atmosphere, most waited decades to tell their story.

• This "lost world" of eastern European Jewry was a polyglot one. Multiple languages as well as archival collections spread across the globe are necessary to reconstruct it. All translations in this work are mine unless noted otherwise.

Although American and Israeli repositories proved to hold much valuable material, I looked to the present-day Republic of Belarus for unexplored sources. Many archives in that country were lost during the fierce fighting of World War II. I discovered, however, that abundant collections of local institutions survived in the state archive branches in Grodno and Vitebsk, which lie within the borders of Belarus. The Jewish *kehilah* (communal administration) in Grodno provided funding for schools, organizations, and other facets of life that encompassed young Jews' daily lives. The Vitebsk Jewish Pedagogical Tekhnikum trained instructors for the Soviet Yiddish-language schools. The Vitebsk archive also contains wartime documents from the German occupation administration and the local collaborationist municipal authority.

Collections outside of Belarus address other significant themes and time frames. The United States Holocaust Memorial Museum Archives contain microfilm copies of German civilian administration documents for several cities in occupied Belarus as well as Soviet investigation reports prepared after liberation. The YIVO Institute for Jewish Research (YIVO, New York) holds autobiographies and diaries of adolescent Jews from Grodno and surrounding towns dating from the 1930s, and the American Jewish Joint Distribution Committee (also in New York) maintains records of its interactions with the Grodno *kehilah*.

Regional Yiddish-language newspapers from prewar Poland and the Soviet Union reveal perspectives of local events and international news. Literary sources have also informed my research. Soviet Yiddish writer Hirsh Reles (1913–2004) was a student at the Vitebsk Jewish Pedagogical Tekhnikum. He published verses in the local Vitebsk newspaper while he was a student and later mingled with the cream of Soviet Yiddish literati in Minsk. Many of these writers were executed during the Great Terror, tragedies that shaped Reles's subsequent actions.

Although these primary sources helped to define much of the where of this study, I turned to eyewitness accounts to determine the who. The stories of individuals provide essential human dimensions in an account of Jewish youth and serve as a thread spanning the moments on the timeline obscured by extant document collections. Some of these stories, such as witness statements collected by the Central Historical Commission in Warsaw after the war, were in written form. Yet it is videotaped oral-history testimonies, the majority recorded in the 1990s by the USC Shoah Foundation, that serve as the core of this study. These Holocaust survivors were between ten years old and their early twenties during the war, with the late teen years as the median.

Oral histories present certain interpretive challenges. To ground these eyewitness accounts in the known timeline of events, I triangulated spoken memories from videotaped testimonies with archival documents, diaries and autobiographical essays by contemporaries, and scholarly interpretations. The small number of survivors relative to the total number of those killed raises the question of how representative these witnesses are of the communities they came from. Yet, as Debórah Dwork notes in *Children with a Star*, those who survived were no more exceptional than those who did not,[8] and I agree with her. In this study, I assess the survivors' experiences as also representing their peers' experiences and perceptions. And I analyze the actions that individuals took against persecution, looking for the patterns common among contemporaries and trying to understand where that response originated. That some efforts were successful and some were not is not the point because the Germans' genocidal policies closed most paths to survival. This book seeks to analyze what young Jews did in the face of destruction and why they did it, and it traces their backstory to understand the basis for their acts.

In some cases, eyewitnesses gave statements at different times, or their narrative voices are also represented in different vehicles. Zelda Grodzienska, for example, recorded at least four videotaped testimonies from the early 1980s to the early 1990s. She also gave a deposition and witness testimony in 1968 at the Cologne trial of Grodno ghetto commandant Kurt Wiese. Grodno native Felix (Feliks) Zandman also sat for multiple recorded interviews, and he published a written memoir. My approach differed when analyzing testimonies of Jews born in Soviet Vitebsk because these accounts are not supported by additional retellings and often must stand on their own. To discern what responses and actions these stories hold in common, I compared the experiences of Vitebsk survivors with those from surrounding towns and cities in Soviet Belarus.

Seeking this convergence of evidence, I could not represent all points of view. Many families in Polish Grodno observed Jewish religious law, but similarly devout Jews in Soviet Vitebsk became much less conspicuous after the Bolsheviks dismantled the Jewish community institutions in the late 1920s. With the limited presence of the remaining observant Jews in Vitebsk in the historical record, I could not include their perspective in this study.

I seek, as a philosophical approach, to reconstruct the open-ended perspectives available to those living within the historical moment. Historical actors possess agency in response to unfolding events; action follows based on decisions meant to shape possible destinies. The British historian Hugh Trevor-Roper addressed this concept when he noted that in order to see history as a reality, scholars must "restore to the past its lost uncertainties, to reopen, if only for an instant, the doors which the *fait accompli* has closed."[9] Vitebsk and Grodno Jews confronted each development, each catastrophe without knowing with certainty the ultimate consequences and acted according to the information at hand and within the boundaries of what was possible.

At the heart of this book stand the stories of many individuals. From an early age, Hirsh Reles wanted to be a writer in his native Yiddish language; by the mid-1930s he was recognized as one of the promising young literary figures of Soviet Jewish culture. Fivel Markelis attended a Jewish house of prayer, one of the last of its kind in Soviet Vitebsk, when his grandmother tried to teach him about his Jewish heritage. Vera German, also from Vitebsk, played with paper dolls while her mother made her homemade dresses. Batya from Grodno found consolation for her teenage angst and loneliness in a Zionist youth group. Lev Zhubov, Batya's contemporary, was inspired by a teacher at his Talmud Torah school to form a group of *zamlers* (collectors) to record stories told by community members. Each of these witnesses also lived through oppression and violence. Hirsh Reles watched in horror as first one Yiddish writer, then another and another disappeared during the Great Terror. Fivel Markelis's family received a visit from the Soviet secret police solely because his grandmother corresponded with a brother in America. Although nobody was arrested, many of the Markelis household belongings were confiscated. During the Grodno pogrom of June 1935, attackers broke the windows of Batya's house and beat Lev as he made his way home. Vera German seemed to have experienced no traumatic incidents in the years leading up to war, but her parents did house a family of Jewish refugees from Poland. These experiences shaped their character, and they carried these experiences forward when ever greater challenges loomed.

1

Raised in the Red City

Vitebsk, 1933 to 1939

Hirsh Reles, a twenty-five-year-old Jewish writer and schoolteacher, entered a local Soviet reading room to find a librarian tearing pages out of a book. The year was 1938, the height of the Great Terror in the Soviet Union, when the arrest and disappearance of well-known individuals prompted suppression of their public presence. Still, Reles was shocked by the sight. He pleaded, "What are you doing?" "These writers are all arrested," the librarian replied, not looking up from her task. "I must get rid of their works." A poetry collection she pulled out included the works of several writers. Among them were verses by Izi Kharik and Moishe Kulbak, Hirsh Reles's literary mentors.[1]

Although the librarian's act was disturbing, there was little Reles could do. To object too strenuously might prompt the librarian to report him to the Soviet secret police, the NKVD. Because the encounter occurred in Slutsk, the town where he had recently accepted a teaching position, at the very least he would lose his job. His security at that moment required silence, one of an arsenal of survival skills he had acquired under Joseph Stalin's rule. Reles was tested many times. He survived the purges, unlike some falsely accused of espionage and subversion, such as Kharik and Kulbak. As a Red Army soldier, he succeeded in fleeing from advancing German forces in their invasion of the Soviet Union in June 1941. Reles's wife and daughter, however, were trapped and later murdered by the Nazis in the Holocaust. Finally, during the postwar Stalinist antisemitic campaigns, he evaded arrest with the help of supportive colleagues. Hirsh Reles endured all

5. Map of the Belarusian Soviet Socialist Republic (BSSR) and neighboring regions, 1926–39. Soviet Belarus, a federation member of the Soviet Union, grew from a small border region with the transfer of territory in 1924 and 1926 from the Russian Soviet Federative Socialist Republic. Vitebsk lay within the zone handed over to the BSSR in March 1924.

this to become, as one scholar dubbed him in the 1990s, the "patriarch of Jewish writers in Belarus."[2] He even outlived the Soviet Union, dying in his bed in 2004 at the age of ninety-one.

What Hirsh Reles survived is remarkable. How he and many of his generation survived is a central issue of this book. Although luck weighed heavily in anyone's chances to survive oppression, war, and genocide, Reles's instincts and initiatives shaped his fate as well. He demonstrated this during the encounter with the reading-room librarian. To understand his responses and actions, we need to examine the world that he and his fellow Soviet Jews inhabited before World War II.

The Jews of Imperial Russia received emancipation in the wake of the February and October Revolutions of 1917. Although the Bolsheviks repressed Judaism in tandem with other religions, they declared

Jews a nationality and supported a new Soviet Yiddish-language culture. Jewish children attended Yiddish-language schools to receive thorough indoctrination as future leaders for the revolution. Yet advancement of a distinct Jewish identity declined during the mid-1930s as the Communist Party looked to integrate Jews ever more tightly into the Soviet community. Language and cultural assimilation in exchange for educational and employment opportunities further distanced young Jews from their heritage. The Great Terror of the late 1930s upended the political and cultural consciousness of young Jews, and their cultural heroes disappeared even as their families feared a late-night knock on the door by the NKVD. In this atmosphere, young Soviet Jews developed not only flexibility of identity but an alertness to fluid situations, skills that aided their survival years later during war and genocide.

From Shtetl to City

Like many of his generation, Jew and Gentile, Hirsh Reles migrated from village to city in pursuit of opportunities. He was born in 1913 in Chashniki, a shtetl (Yiddish for "village" or "small town") located southwest of Vitebsk (figure 5). His father, Leib, a teacher in a *kheder*, a school for male Jewish children, and his mother, the daughter of a prosperous merchant family, exemplified an ideal Jewish marriage of stability and tradition: intellectual father and affluent mother.[3] This picture soon shattered as young Hirsh witnessed the impact of World War I and the Russian Revolution on his family. Although the German advance in 1914 and 1915 never reached Chashniki, Russian military commanders ordered the forcible expulsion of whole Jewish communities within the war zone. The Reles family and the Jews of Chashniki were spared this fate but not the economic chaos of war and revolution. The Russian Civil War and the Polish–Soviet War continued the turmoil into the first years of the new decade, with Chashniki incorporated within the borders of the Russian Socialist Federative Soviet Republic established in mid-1918. In March 1924, most of the Vitebsk *gubernia* surrounding Chashniki was transferred to the neighboring Belarusian Soviet Socialist Republic (BSSR), one of the territorial units making up the Union of Soviet Socialist Republics (USSR). These political changes served as the backdrop for the Reles family drama. After his wife's death in 1919, Leib Reles needed more lucrative work to support his children. In any case, the growing Bolshevik presence in the shtetl meant his work as a *melamed* (teacher) in a traditional Jewish religious school fell under increasing scrutiny.

During the times Leib was away seeking work, young Hirsh stayed with his maternal grandfather. Under his grandfather's tutelage, the boy developed an interest in Yiddish literature, reading and rereading Sholem Aleichem and other Jewish writers.[4] Chashniki was a typical eastern European multiethnic town, and Hirsh picked up the languages of the Belarusian and Russian neighbor children during playtime.[5] Many of his older relatives also spoke multiple languages, including Russian, which was not unusual given the region's 130 years under imperial rule. His formal education was multilingual as well. He began at a Soviet state Yiddish-language school, an institution made possible for young Jews by the Soviet system, yet this was only a four-year institution, so for the next three years he studied at the local Belarusian-language school.[6] Under Soviet guidance, Belarusian developed fully from a regional yet distinct Slavic language spoken mostly by peasants to a formalized linguistic culture manifested by state institutions, including schools. Outside of his formal lessons, Hirsh began to write poems. He initially composed in the Belarusian he learned in the classroom, but Leib Reles advised his son to employ Yiddish, the language of his heritage.[7]

In practice, Hirsh divided his literary development between Yiddish and the Slavic languages. He found avenues to develop his literary talents at his Belarusian school, joining its afternoon literary circle and writing pieces for the publicly displayed wall newspaper. In 1930, he published a poem dedicated to the Soviet Five-Year Plan in a regional Yiddish-language youth journal, *Der yunger arbeter* (The Young Worker), in which he also published several short articles.[8] His early poems dealt with Chashniki's encounter with socialism, its buildings and streets renewed ("Shtetele" [Little Village][9]), and its residents laboring in the surrounding fields, ready to confront spring planting

("Zunen signaln" [To the Sun's Motion][10]). An untitled poem mixed images of a bucolic summer night with Bolshevik optimism. Its closing lines extolled the youth as the bearers of the future:

> Now we are strong
> Young, resolute,
> To carry on youthful shoulders
> The abundant future, unwavering and vigilant.[11]

The Bolsheviks offered young Jews opportunities that their parents never enjoyed. As Hirsh Reles remembered decades later, "You could go to school, you could be what you wanted to be, you could realize all your talents."[12] Hirsh's own family was caught up in this youthful optimism: one sister wanted to be an actor; another aspired to be a painter. Chashniki was no place for such high ambitions, so they moved to the nearest city—Vitebsk. After Hirsh finished school in June 1931, he followed them.[13] He decided to enroll in the Vitebsk Jewish Pedagogical Tekhnikum, an institution to train instructors for the Soviet Yiddish-language schools. Possibly owing to more of his father's practical advice, Hirsh knew he would have to make a living at something until he could support himself as a writer, and teaching seemed a suitable profession.

The Multiethnic Soviet City

Vitebsk was in the midst of the first Five-Year Plan (1928–32) when Hirsh Reles arrived there. Rapid industrialization accelerated migration of the youth, Gentile and Jewish, from rural areas and villages to larger urban centers. From Reles's home shtetl Chashniki alone, the Jewish population seventeen to twenty-three years of age dropped by more than half between 1926 and 1935.[14] Even with this influx, the percentage of self-identified Jews in Vitebsk declined during the interwar years. In the Soviet census of 1926, 37.5 percent of the Vitebsk population (37,017) claimed Jewish "nationality" (as the Bolsheviks identified Jews), compared to the city's Belarusians (29.5 percent), Russians (26 percent), Poles (3.7 percent), Latvians (1.2 percent), and others.[15] Besides Jews, Belarusians presented a sizeable presence in Vitebsk, all the more significant when the bulk of the Belarusian population still lived in rural areas.[16] The growth of urban populations with the migration of peasants to the cities in the 1930s tended to reduce the Jewish population percentages. Nevertheless, when the ratio of Jews dropped to 22.2 percent as recorded by the Soviet census of 1939, this percentage totaled 37,095 Jews.[17]

With a population of 160,000 by the mid-1930s, Vitebsk was just one city where the Communist Party sought to forge a multinational community. A focal point of this new Soviet world was the factory, such as Vitebsk's Banner of Industrialization, where Belarusian flax was used to manufacture all types of brushes. The factory's "shock workers"—a propaganda device to prompt engagement with the first Five-Year Plan—numbered 2,500, including Belarusians (52 percent); Jews (39 percent); Russians (5 percent); and Poles, Lithuanians, Germans, and Romani (4 percent).[18] In early 1933, the local Belarusian-language newspaper, *Vitsebski praletarii* (Vitebsk Proletarian), showcased the largely female workforce at the Banner of Industrialization on its periodic Yiddish-language page.[19] Ten million women went to work outside the home during the 1930s, most of them out of necessity to support their families. Few held managerial positions.[20]

Outside the factories, the new stood alongside the old in this Red city. Workers made their way to the bright factories through the narrow, dirty, and poorly illuminated streets of the former imperial regional capital (figure 6). Facades of older buildings needed repair, and trees lining the streets wanted tending. Some thoroughfares lacked street lighting and proper sidewalks. The latter meant inhabitants trudged through the customary regional *blota* ("mud" in Yiddish) whenever it rained.[21] The homes they had just left often proved inadequate. The arrival of new workers led to scarcity of apartments, and what was available grew overcrowded. Many later remembered the living environments of their childhood years with spatial qualifiers: "three rooms" or "a shared house." Some lived in an archetypal Soviet *kommunalka* (communal apartment), with its associated spatial limitations, social structures, and psychological impact. Construction to alleviate the overcrowding, such as the new worker housing on

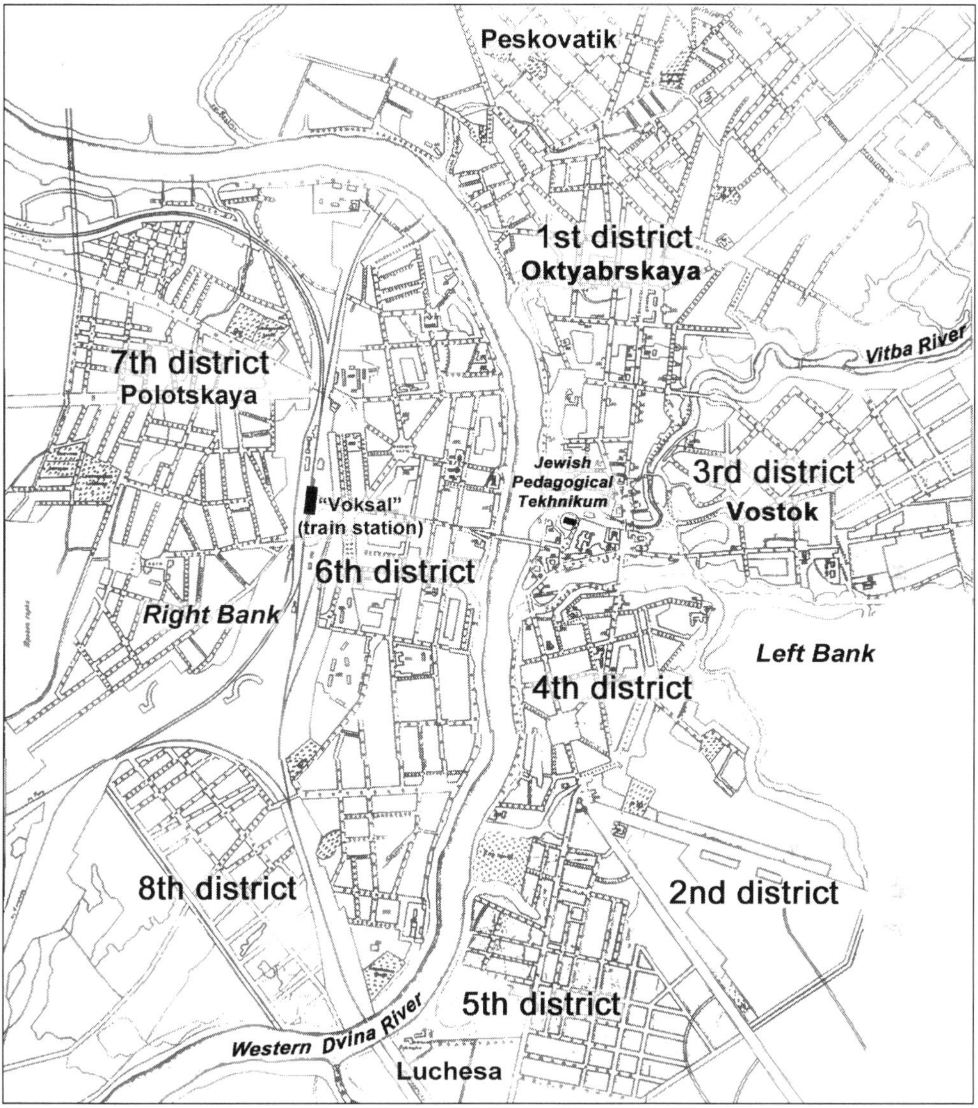

6. Map of Vitebsk with city districts, based on a historical map dated 1905. The Jewish Pedagogical Tekhnikum, founded in 1921, lay on the east side of the Western Dvina River near the city center.

Volodarskaya and Leninskaya Streets heralded in the pages of *Vitsebski praletarii*, failed to keep pace with demand.[22] Lack of sufficient goods also was a common complaint. Periodic food shortages during the first Five-Year Plan meant that valued factory workers went hungry.[23]

Despite the crowded living quarters and shortages, witnesses remembered generally good relations between people of different ethnicities. Elena Choukmazova, born in 1930, grew up among the Jews, Belarusians, and Russians who populated Polotskaya District west of the train station. "You see, there was no hostility like after the war," she told an interviewer, referencing the antisemitism of the post–World War II years.[24] Many others who grew up in Vitebsk held similar recollections of the 1930s. When asked if there was any division or any feature of difference between Jews and non-Jews, Lev Fleish (born 1922) declared, "There wasn't, wasn't, wasn't, wasn't, wasn't. . . . We all used to live together."[25] Stepan Zavgorodnev (born 1926), who had Jewish and Russian friends, recalled Vitebsk as a place where it was not important who was Jewish and who wasn't.[26]

Jewish children may have remembered little antisemitism in communal living environments and on the street in Vitebsk, yet it still passed among adults. The historian Arkadii Zeltser has traced the continuity and development of antisemitic attitudes in eastern Belarus in the interwar period.[27] In addition to the Christian anti-Judaism prevalent among Belarusian peasants, new stereotypes emerged with the rapid social and political advancement of Jews in urban areas.[28] The place of Jews in selected positions of authority did not go unnoticed, leading, for example, to the belief that these figures held particular responsibilities in the suppression of Orthodox Christianity.[29] Even the heightened presence of Yiddish elicited negative responses.[30] The scholars Sheila Fitzpatrick and Sarah Davies have documented similar patterns among the Soviet populace during the 1930s, particularly in cases of Jews or those perceived to be Jews in positions of authority and privilege.[31]

Some young Gentiles developed a range of antisemitic attitudes, despite pressure to conceal them. "We couldn't call them 'Zhid,'" recalled a young Belarusian male from Minsk, a former teacher trainee born in 1923. He meant the observation as a lament and went on to declare how Jews in the Komsomol, the youth section of the Communist Party, enjoyed special privileges and access to power. "All roads were open to them."[32] He felt open to express his bias against the Soviet system because of his status as a post–World War II refugee outside the scrutiny of Soviet power. That he felt as comfortable expressing his antisemitism reveals its genuineness.[33]

Some antisemitic incidents were reported in the contemporary press, part of the campaign to expose the anti-Soviet actions of offenders. One of the most sensational occurred in 1928, when six young men were placed on trial, convicted, and sentenced to prison for antisemitic verbal abuse and physical attacks against a Jewish female worker at the October glassmaking factory in Svisloch.[34] Even using the Russian word *Zhid*, "Jew," as a pejorative merited public condemnation. In a case the following year, a group of art academy students in Minsk, the Belarusian capital, requested the dismissal of two instructors for failing to punish a student who used the term.[35] Party newspapers also sought to combat Jewish chauvinism. For example, a Jewish worker at the Banner of Industrialization factory used a fellow worker's nationality as a pejorative when he screamed, "Oh, you Belarusian!"[36] In another instance, Jews harassing Belarusians at the Vitebsk Profintern sewing factory faced acts of "hooliganism" in retaliation. Both sets of offenders were publicly admonished for their "counterrevolutionary" behavior.[37]

Ethnic prejudice denounced with polemical arguments did little to address the myths underlying ethnic discord. Nor did such well-publicized cases reflect ordinary acts of cross-cultural engagement, often occurring outside the bounds of approved Bolshevik manifestations. This was the era in which young Jews such as Fivel Markelis (born 1927) received Purim gifts from his Russian neighbors.[38] Elizaveta Gurevich (born 1914) had many Russian Orthodox friends and went to church with them because the Christian service interested her.[39] Elena Choukmazova's family celebrated Christian as well as Jewish holidays because of her ethnic-Russian father, Nikolai. Elena remembered, "We painted eggs and baked small loaves at Eastertide."[40]

Fivel Markelis came into contact with Belarusian culture because of his mother's work schedule. Sofia Markelis took a job in a brush factory to support her three children after the death of her husband in 1937. Despite the presence of Sofia's mother in the home to cook and clean, much of Fivel's after-school time went unsupervised. He risked becoming, in his words, a "desperate hooligan." Fivel's older brother initially took him to a boxing club to vent his adolescent energy. When all he got was a beaten mug, his sister took him to a dance school. There he learned Belarusian folk dancing and participated in a children's song-and-dance ensemble. The troupe was rather successful, twice winning second place in all-republic competitions. Fivel learned Belarusian cultural customs, but not alongside many members of this ethnic group. Most children in the Belarusian dance troupe were Jews, as were the instructors.[41]

Jewish Family Life

The revolution reshaped all aspects of life, not least of all the family. After supporting liberally granted divorce and so-called free unions (essentially common-law marriages) during the previous decade, Soviet policy refocused on traditional family structures in the 1930s.[42] Even so, single-parent families remained fairly common through the loss of a parent from divorce, abandonment, or death. Others remarried and thus constructed blended families. One of the latter was Maria Yeines, Stepan Zavgorodnev's mother. She had been a medical student in Minsk when she gave birth to her son in 1926. He remembered nothing of his birth father, so perhaps Maria had divorced this man when her son was an infant or had never been married. Maria and her son moved to Vitebsk in 1931, and soon thereafter she married Mikhail Zavgorodnev, a student and Red Army veteran.[43]

Marriage likely eased Maria's challenge of raising a child alone. Even so, the family struggled financially because Mikhail brought in only a small student stipend. Some relief came from Maria's job at a kindergarten, which gave her access to rationed consumer goods during the shortages spurred by the collectivization of agriculture (1929–33) and the first Five-Year Plan. In time, young Stepan formed a close bond with his stepfather, who legally adopted the boy. Stepan loved to sit with Mikhail in the evenings and listen to stories about the army. Stepan's family was rounded out by his maternal grandparents, who moved in with them because of an urban housing shortage. His mother's brother, also named Mikhail, lived nearby.[44]

Grandparents like Stepan's provided child care, which was especially helpful when mothers worked outside the home. Mothers went to work when fathers were absent owing to divorce or, during the purges of the late 1930s, to arrest.[45] The early death of the male breadwinner was also not unknown. We have already seen how Sonia Markelis took a factory job after the death of her husband, David. Grandmother Rosenthal moved in to care for ten-year-old Fivel and his older siblings. They lived in three small rooms of a house shared with many others.[46]

Like Fivel Markelis's mother, Elena Choukmazova's mother, Dora Drozdnik, worked outside the home, although in her case doing so was necessary because of her divorce from her first husband, Nikolai Choukmazov. It was unlikely she received any child support.[47] Dora took double shifts at her restaurant job to support Elena and her younger daughter. Dora's second husband, Isaak Heinson, worked in a factory, stabilizing the financial situation of the blended family, which grew with the birth of a son in 1940. Although the family had few luxuries, young Elena recalled going to the Spartacus movie theater on Lenin Street with friends and to the Jewish theater with her parents. But death haunted Elena's family, as it did many others in the city. Her younger sister died in 1939, and her stepfather died in early 1941.[48] Such losses left children with the knowledge that their siblings, peers, and parents were vulnerable to fatal illnesses.

Other Vitebsk Jews remembered family life in the 1930s as good years untroubled by want. Vera German (born 1927) had a carefree life making paper dolls, wearing fancy homemade dresses, and dancing amid the overstuffed furniture in the family's living room. Her family's economic circumstances appear to have been somewhat better than most; her father worked a white-collar job, and they had enough disposable income to frequent Russian-language plays at the

Neboknavernya Theater in Vitebsk.[49] Vera had an older sister and two older brothers. One of her brothers, Motl, was so engaged with the Soviet system that he migrated to the Jewish Autonomous Region of Birobidzhan in the Russian Far East. He must have been an adventurer because contemporary newspaper accounts described Birobidzhan as a "colossal territory" requiring much effort to clear the land.[50] Vera remembered that Motl was drawn to a wilderness with crystal-clear streams. And when he wrote home from Birobidzhan, he put a positive spin on his experiences.[51]

The Soviet experience drew Jewish families as émigrés. Dmitri Khvat (born 1928) was only two when his parents decided to leave Białystok in Poland and settle in Vitebsk to escape the antisemitic state policies that restricted his father's career opportunities. Dmitri's father, Dr. Girsh Khvat, obtained a position at Kalinina Hospital, and his mother, Etna, took care of the apartment on Petrovskaya Street. Despite the Khvat family's relative affluence, they also needed the parcels that Girsh's parents in Białystok sent to alleviate Vitebsk's shortages.[52]

Girsh Khvat immigrated to the Soviet Union from Poland for employment opportunities open to Jews under Bolshevism. Vitebsk native Boris Pipkin took advantage of the advancement possible within the Communist Party. By 1933, he had moved from shoemaking at the Vitebsk shoe factory Red October to administrative work within the regional party administration. His wife was a librarian and cultural worker at the Profintern factory. So dedicated were the Pipkins to Communist ideals that they named their sons Lenin (born 1931) and Marx (born 1934).[53]

The Pipkins sought to join the revolution, one measure of the integration of Jews in Soviet Vitebsk. Yet they followed the pattern of Jews marrying other Jews in Soviet Belarus. About 95 percent of Jewish women registering marriages in the mid-1920s married Jewish men. Even ten years later, 85 to 90 percent married Jews. Jewish men registered even higher percentages: about 98 percent married Jewish women in the mid-1920s, a portion dropping to 88 percent in the mid-1930s.[54] When intermarriage occurred, it was because of love.

Elena Choukmazova's mother, Dora Drozdnik, married an ethnic Russian. If there was anything problematic about her mother marrying a Gentile, Elena never heard about it.[55] Elizaveta Gurevich, born in 1914, did hear strong objections—from her own parents. Upon finishing school, Elizaveta wanted to marry one of her teachers, an ethnic Russian ten years her senior. "My father was a religious man, and he wanted me to marry someone of my own nationality," she recalled, citing her long-held Soviet identity marker (nationality) even after the collapse of that political system. Elizaveta's younger brother pressured their father to approve of the union. Still, she remembered her father's unhappiness by her marriage to a Gentile. "He didn't speak to us for a while."[56]

Far more typical than Elizaveta Gurevich's marriage outside her faith was the secular shift in daily life. The Yevsektsiya, the Jewish section of the Bolshevik Party, had led these changes during the 1920s, dismantling Jewish communal institutions, seizing synagogues and other buildings, and promoting antireligious propaganda. Efforts were made to disparage Rosh Hashanah (Jewish New Year) and Yom Kippur (Day of Atonement) as capitalistic exploitation of the poor and to promote Red Passovers accompanied by a highly modified Haggadah to celebrate Bolshevik liberation.[57] The Yevsektsiya accomplished much before it was disbanded in early 1930. Anti-Judaism campaigns continued, however, principally targeting women because of their traditional role in preserving Jewish customs.[58] *Vitebsker arbet* (Vitebsk Labor), the periodic Yiddish supplement of the periodical *Zarya zapada* (West Dawn), reported on accusations against opportunists, or "speculators," acting in cahoots with Jewish clergy to persuade craftsmen's wives to send their children to a *kheder*. These nefarious characters "catch innocent souls in their nets, especially women."[59] Another case drew a connection between the male gender and good Bolsheviks. A Dr. Sternin was reviled for performing circumcisions on male infants against the wishes of their proletarian fathers. These acts of "religious intoxication," along with antisemitism and pro-Jewish chauvinism, interfered with a worker's "proletarian unity, his international consciousness, and the peace of his family."[60]

Such rhetoric added to the pressures on women. Not only were they expected to be wife, mother, and possibly the family's wage earner, but they also faced potential allegations of political unreliability. Despite the party's efforts, some women maintained their religious practices in their families. Dora Drozdnik made matzah, challah, and other traditional foods. "At Passover everything was as it had to be," remembered Elena Choukmazova of her mother's dedication.[61] Vera German's mother kept kosher whenever possible and set the table for Shabbes.[62] Mothers working in factories or offices often were too busy to uphold Jewish traditions or pass them on to their children. Sometimes grandparents did so instead. Fivel Markelis learned about Judaism from his grandmother Rosenthal. He remembered that she took him to "a kind of a house . . . a prayer house."[63] She had few such institutions to choose from. Of the more than fifty synagogues and prayer houses in Vitebsk before the revolution, only nine functioned by the end of 1936.[64] Grandmother Rosenthal also gathered with other women to bake matzah.[65]

Some Jewish families, either enmeshed in revolutionary ideals or simply secular in their attitudes, were not observant. Marx Pipkin noted in the memoir written when he, ironically, became head of the Vitebsk Jewish community in the 1990s that his Bolshevik parents followed no traditions. Neither did Lev Fleish's family or any other Jewish family that Lev knew. Moreover, Judaism and Jewish traditions became clandestine or even criminal in his memories, although strictly speaking this was not so. "You know, in my Vitebsk days we didn't celebrate any holidays," he said, but "older people celebrated them somehow illegally." Lev said his family wasn't observant "because it [such religious practice] was outlawed" and also because of the expense. "It was necessary to choose special foodstuff, special meat," he remembered. But Lev was circumcised, a curious inconsistency, whereas his brother, born a few years after Lev, was not. His explanation? "The times were different."[66]

A marker of the Communist Party's progress in dismantling Jewish religious identity was the range of beliefs and attitudes that might exist within one family. Stepan Zavgorodnev's grandparents were observant, but his parents were not, and his uncle Mikhail was a committed Communist. Stepan saw remnants of religious traditions around him, such as Jews who went to work on Shabbes or built sukkah huts in the courtyard.[67] But such traditions weren't part of his life. Other memories of Jewish holidays illustrate a sense of distance as well. Vera German vaguely remembered Passover as the holiday when the family "sat down at the table, if it was the holiday when you were not allowed to eat, for instance, something like butter, or something else."[68] And in answer to a question about her family's observance of Friday evening, the start of Shabbes, she said, "Yes, we did something, but I don't remember what."[69] Fivel Markelis best remembered Passover as a time when he pulled a prank on his grandmother, stealing her matzah.[70]

Language and Education

To many among the first generation of Soviet Jews, identity meant nationality, not religion. Dmitri Khvat knew only a little of what it meant to be a Jew after he asked his mother about the different kinds of cemeteries he saw. Prior to this, his parents had not talked to him or his younger sister about the differences between Jews and Gentiles. "How do you know what kind of cemetery—Jewish or Russian?"[71]

The incident highlights the questions ethnic divisions posed for Jewish children within the revolutionary environment of the Soviet city. What did it mean to be a Jew? How was it different from other ethnic identities? The education system in Soviet Belarus sought to provide some answers because it tried to compartmentalize children by nationality. "Every child with a school in his mother tongue" was the scholastic policy in the BSSR.[72] This meant schools taught in Belarusian, Russian, Yiddish, and Polish, the four official languages of the republic, along with a few in Latvian.[73] Such an approach fell in line with the overarching principles of Soviet nationalities policies of the 1920s and early 1930s. Centered on the concept of *korenizatsiia*, "putting down roots," these policies sought to advance the cultures and interests of traditionally marginalized nationalities, including Jews.[74] The concept had limits, however. "Socialist according to content and nationalist according to form" was the oft-repeated phrase of the day. Content was polemical in nature, with national character used as window dressing. Ethnic identity as manifested in language, literature, and history was viewed through the lens of class struggle.

Although the republic built a multilingual education system in its early years, Belarusian dominated. Despite its unpopularity in urban areas, the language played a crucial role in shaping the identity of the young Soviet republic's life.[75] The Belarusization of the republic's largely Russian-speaking cities focused on the education system in addition to newspapers and official notices. The republic's Yiddish-language newspaper, *Oktyabr* (October), reported in mid-1935 that the BSSR had 891,986 students attending 7,020 schools, with the overwhelming majority of pupils (90.2 percent) enrolled in Belarusian-language schools. Only 221 Yiddish-language schools, 180 Russian-language schools, and 135 Polish-language schools operated.[76] Another contemporary news story acknowledged a slightly different total of 216 Yiddish-language schools in Soviet Belarus, with 32,738 students: 90 four-year elementary schools (4,413 students), 107 seven-year ("not-full") middle schools (23,126 students), and 10 ten-year ("full") high schools (5,099 students).[77]

Jews found these statistics verifying the official campaign of Belarusization in their republic's Yiddish newspaper. Yet factors other than pressure from Commissariat of Enlightenment officials in Minsk suppressed enrollment in the Yiddish schools. Many Jewish parents, particularly in urban areas, failed to be swayed by the promise of Yiddish-language education. Propaganda tried to sell the public on the advances and advantages of the republic's multilingual system, but Russian and Belarusian education was the path to advancement.[78] The literary scholar Elias Schulman noted such attitudes during a visit to family in Slutsk in the BSSR in 1936. His uncles and cousins explained to Schulman, "If we speak to them in Yiddish, the children will be sent, by local school authorities, to Yiddish-language schools, but if we talk to them in Russian, they can claim that their native language is Russian and they can enter a Russian-language school. There is more *takhles* [results] in a Russian than a Yiddish school, and it is more practical."[79] Knowing Russian brought results, Elias Schulman's relations recognized. Furthermore, many Jewish parents believed that Yiddish-language schools were inferior to their Russian- and Belarusian-language counterparts, particularly in mathematics and the sciences.[80]

These trends followed the general decline in Yiddish as the declared native tongue among Belarusian Jews. In Vitebsk, 84.1 percent of Jews in that city cited Yiddish as the language they used on the Soviet census of 1926; by 1939, that figure had dropped to 51 percent.[81] This drop translated into reduced enrollments in Yiddish-language schools, more so in larger urban areas. Back in 1927, only 36.1 percent of Jewish children in Vitebsk attended Yiddish-language schools; the remainder attended Belarusian- or Russian-language schools. Attendance figures were higher (79.3 percent) in the surrounding shtetlekh (plural of *shtetl*), where there were fewer options as well as greater reception among parents to Yiddish education.[82]

After a period of experimentation in the 1920s, Soviet teaching practices grew increasingly rigid.[83] Learning was increasingly done by rote instead of by analysis and synthesis. Teachers focused on what, who, and how, but very little on why. There were few occasions for independent thought, at least not where it would improve a student's grade. With classroom time rigidly controlled, deviations to explore issues in depth were not possible. Moreover, standardized examinations introduced in 1935 meant a significant part of the school year was devoted solely to exam preparation.[84]

Dmitri Khvat attended the Russian-language School Number 27, where the director was Jewish. This use of Russian at school extended into his home life because Girsh and Etna Khvat encouraged their children to speak Russian, not Yiddish.[85] Stepan Zavgorodnev was about two years ahead of Dmitri at School Number 27. Stepan remembered he was devoted to mathematics but couldn't find Africa on a map.[86] Elizaveta Gurevich, a half-generation older than Dmitri and Stepan, went to a co-ed Russian-language school attended by many nationalities.[87] And some Jewish families in Vitebsk, such as Vera German's, had long acculturated by speaking Russian at home.[88]

Jewish children were unlikely to hear anything about their heritage in a Belarusian- or Russian-language school, but students at Yiddish schools fared no better. Perhaps out of loyalty to the party and its policies, Vera's parents initially sent her to a Yiddish-language school, although it did little to shape her Jewish identity. She vaguely remembered decades later learning about Rosh Hashanah in school.[89] Fivel Markelis recalled studying mathematics, geography, and history but nothing at all about Jewish holidays and history.[90] Teachers in smaller shtetlekh could discuss Jewish holidays with greater freedom because they were subject to less scrutiny by education officials.[91]

Yet some educators openly lamented this state of affairs. Kusiel Beravich Hadashevich taught history at the Vitebsk Jewish Pedagogical Tekhnikum, the teacher-training institute that brought Hirsh Reles to Vitebsk. Hadashevich wrote in *Oktyabr* about the "true empty space" left by the lack of Jewish history in elementary schools because there were "no programs, no textbooks" on this subject.[92] Indeed, Jewish history courses were found only within institutes of higher education.[93] Whether at the primary-school or university level, Jewish historical narratives of the era yielded to Marxist ideology. One text interpreted events leading to the Great Revolt in 66 CE as owing to class conflicts between "the oppressed and doomed [Jewish] masses against their own [Jewish] exploiters and bloodsuckers."[94]

Vitebsk Jewish Pedagogical Tekhnikum

Hirsh Reles studied for a year at the Vitebsk Jewish Pedagogical Tekhnikum before transferring to the Film Technical School across town, enrolling in the Scenario Department.[95] Perhaps he grew impatient and wanted a faster path to a writing career. Whether because of his own counsel or receiving, once again, practical advice from his father, this diversion lasted only a semester before he reapplied to the Pedagogical Tekhnikum in September 1933.[96] Far from aimless, Hirsh's actions demonstrate his eagerness to find a place in the Soviet world.

Many educational institutions in Vitebsk fostered the hopes of resolute young people, drawing enrollees from the smaller cities and shtetlekh of eastern Belarus. The Vitebsk Jewish Pedagogical

7. Building that formerly housed the Vitebsk Jewish Pedagogical Tekhnikum, originally constructed as a Talmud Torah school on the eve of World War I. At the time this photograph was taken (2008), the Lyalka puppet theater occupied the structure. Photograph by the author.

Tekhnikum had been founded in 1921 in tandem with a sister institution in Minsk.[97] It was one of a network of technical schools that bridged the gap in the Soviet education system between the seven-year primary school and university. Repeating the practice at other Soviet institutions, the school carried the dedication name of a revolutionary hero, Esther Frumkina. She had advocated Jewish cultural projects from her leadership position in the Yevsektsiya.[98] A former Talmud Torah school building at Pushkinskaya-Naberezhnaya 4 near Vitebsk's center served as the Vitebsk Jewish Pedagogical Tekhnikum's home (figure 7). Two dormitories (located at Kalinina Street 20 and Frunze Street 46) housed students who could not find lodging or did not have family in the city. The *tekhnikum* also supplied a small living stipend.

Surviving enrollment records for the 1935–36 academic year, a few years after Hirsh Reles's term as a student, list 127 new students, the majority (81 percent) from tradesman, worker, or peasant families.

Only 19 percent grew up in households of white-collar employees.[99] Most new students (70 to 80 percent) were young women. Enrollees had finished their studies at a seven-year school, and their minimum age was fifteen. Many were at least eighteen. At thirty-seven years old, Polish-born Ginda Simkhanavna Tsukerman was an exception. She was also a full Communist Party member, an unusual rank when most students were still joining the party's youth section, the Komsomol.[100]

Activism of the student body went hand in hand with professional training at the *tekhnikum*. Manya Moishevna Izrail had been born in 1910 in Warsaw, the daughter of a stocking maker. Manya had worked at the Banner of Industrialization, where she joined the factory's party-branch secretariat. Her engagement with socialism continued at the *tekhnikum*, where she joined the culture commissariat and student dormitory party cell and became a member of the Mezhdunarodnaia organizatsiia pomoshchi revoliutsioneram (International Aid Society for Revolutionary Fighters).[101] Her contemporary Monya Glinik was an orphan from Slutsk. He had risen through the ranks of the Pioneers and the Komsomol, the party's youth organizations, before pursuing teacher training. In addition to his activities in the Tekhnikum Komsomol, Monya edited the institution's wall newspaper.[102]

Unlike some students, few *tekhnikum* instructors were party members. The teaching staff at Vitebsk Jewish Pedagogical Tekhnikum numbered ten full-time instructors in the early 1930s, with several adjunct instructors shared with other educational institutions in the city. Full-time instructor Kusiel Beravich Hadashevich taught history and party history. Hirsh Reles remembered him as being very knowledgeable about Jewish history.[103] Most instructors were old enough to have had some teaching experience before the revolution. The oldest, Hirsh Beker, had taught geography since 1898. The youngest instructor was Matsvin Efimavich Khanin (born 1906). An "excellent speaker and lecturer," as Hirsh Reles remembered him,[104] Khanin, a teacher of Yiddish and Russian, characterized the younger generation of Soviet Jews because of the social distance he had traversed—from rural peasant to urban language instructor.[105] Although most instructors were

Jews, an exception was Iosif Gavrilavich Lades, a Belarusian who taught Slavic languages and literature.

Director Feskin (first name not known), who had arrived at the *tekhnikum* in 1930, was "liberal, tolerant, softhearted," characteristics deemed inadequate for the era. Teachers were increasingly expected to be agents of social surveillance for proper Bolshevik attitudes among their students.[106] Feskin was replaced by Zalman Moishevich Babitski in March 1933.[107] Soon thereafter Babitski demonstrated his commitment to imparting polemical and political education among his students at the *tekhnikum*, declaring as much in an editorial in *Vitsebski praletarii*.[108]

Babitski sought to instill order and discipline in the *tekhnikum*, issuing a stream of internal orders and changes. For example, a new bell system regulated class time: a first bell called tardy students to their places, and a second two minutes later signaled teachers to lock the classroom doors.[109] Such regulation, a feature of regimented Soviet life, extended to the teaching staff as well. Vitenson, instructor of mathematics, received a reprimand for "changes in the hourly divisions," which apparently brought "disorder" to the teaching schedule.[110] Regimentation extended to the students' bodies as well. Backed by regulations from education officials in the Commissariat of Enlightenment in Minsk, Babitski imposed heightened standards of cleanliness in the student dormitories.[111] All students were also required to bathe three times a month, with two students designated to monitor this directive.[112] Furthermore, Babitski set bedtime at 9:00 p.m.[113]

Babitski and the Vitebsk Jewish Pedagogical Tekhnikum commanded students' bodies in other ways. Gymnastics equipment offered opportunities to attain physical fitness.[114] Military training extended such activities. Civil defense activities bolstered students' understanding, in the director's words, of the "seriousness of the international position of the USSR."[115] Young women received some instruction, but young men took part in mock military maneuvers in September 1936. The school administration subsequently commended these youths for service that expressed "love of our valiant Red Army," which "guards the border of our great, great native land."[116]

Not all students complied with the new standards. Some marked the student club walls with graffiti. "I warn all students that such a situation is not normal," chided Babitski in an internal reprimand, declaring that offenders "need to learn some manners."[117] Others were more formal and direct in their objections. Moishe Slivko, perhaps emboldened by his age (thirty years), reminded the director, party, and government in a letter published in *Vitsebski praletarii* that the most important task of the *tekhnikum* was the preparation of qualified teachers, not the preparation of cadres to build socialism.[118]

Soviet Yiddish Literati in Minsk

Hirsh Reles wrote little about his time at the Vitebsk Jewish Pedagogical Tekhnikum, yet its influence was apparent in his immediate and long-term development as a writer and teacher. After he finished his course of study in Vitebsk in September 1934, he was offered a job teaching in a Yiddish-language school in Yanovichi, but he decided to pursue further pedagogical studies in Minsk.[119] His ambitions also took him to the pages of *Shtern* (Star), the premiere Yiddish-language literary journal in Soviet Belarus. Having already published in *Vitsebski praletarii* and other venues, Reles confidently submitted several poems to *Shtern*. When he received no reply, he paid a visit to the paper's editorial offices in Minsk. Assistant editor Zelik Akselrod met with the young writer, who read his poems while chief editor Izi Kharik listened from his office. Liking what he heard, Kharik accepted three of the four works for publication.[120]

Thus began Reles's mentorship under Izi Kharik, whom Reles later referred to as "the spiritual father of Soviet Jewish writers in Belarus."[121] Kharik spoke to the deputy commissar of enlightenment on Reles's behalf to release him from his teaching commitment in Yanovichi.[122] Also with Kharik's assistance, Reles was accepted into the Yiddish Literature Department of the Minsk Pedagogical Institute. By the 1930s, Minsk had become one of the Soviet Jewish cultural centers. The state publishing house issued more than twenty books annually in Yiddish, and Yiddish theater and higher education thrived.[123] Reles later remembered that time as "a glittering epoch" of Soviet Jewish intellectuals.[124]

Izi Kharik led the literary wing of this movement in the BSSR. Born in 1896, Kharik had gained fame in the 1920s with his verses depicting the revolution's impact on Belarusian Jews. Children in schools memorized whole sections of his poems, such as "Minsker blotes" (Minsk Mud, 1924) and "Broyt" (Bread, 1925). His thick mane of curly hair and pince-nez glasses on a gentle face became synonymous with the image of a poet, and his portrait adorned the walls of classrooms in the Yiddish schools.[125] As a well-known cultural figure, Kharik could cause a crowd to form when he was present in a Jewish milieu. Hirsh Reles witnessed one of these appearances when the poet visited Chashniki in 1929. A large group gathered outside a house where Kharik was meeting with a local party executive committee member named Levin. As the excited throng peered through the windows, Levin's wife came outside and scolded them: "Why are you here? It's an embarrassment. You'll give the impression that Chashniki is a shtetl of crazy people!"[126]

The historian David Shneer has assessed Kharik as "one of the most powerful Yiddish writers in the Soviet Union,"[127] a position substantiated through translation of his works into Belarusian in his native Soviet republic. He joined the Communist Party in 1930 to consolidate his standing in the Soviet cultural hierarchy and later accepted an appointment to the Belarusian Central Committee. In the modern age of Soviet mass media, Kharik made radio appearances to read and discuss his work.[128] Yet he held misgivings about the Soviet Yiddish experiment and confided them to a limited circle of colleagues. Some Jewish writers had abandoned their native language for Russian or Belarusian in hopes of reaching wider audiences. Kharik wished to connect to Jewish life beyond the Soviet frontier, despite the suspicions such actions might raise within the party. The intrigues and denunciations in Soviet cultural life added to his apprehensions.[129] Nevertheless, Kharik was tied to Belarus. In what turned out to be his last major published work, *Af a fremder khasene* (A Stranger at the Wedding,

1936), he reaffirmed his love for his homeland with the opening line: "Ikh ken dikh, Vaysrusland, azoy vi ikh ken mayne eygene finger" (I know you, Belarus, as I know my own hand).[130]

Kharik was generous in both his literary and his financial support of younger colleagues, and *Shtern* became the publishing venue for a new generation of Yiddish writers.[131] While Kharik guided young writers from his office at *Shtern*, the other giant of Soviet Yiddish literature in Minsk, Moishe Kulbak, developed literary talents with a salon in his apartment.[132] Kulbak's acerbic personality couldn't have contrasted more with Kharik's geniality, though the two writers were on very good terms. Born in the Belarusian shtetl Smorgon in 1897, Kulbak initially found literary success outside of the region as he drifted from Kovno to Vilna in Lithuania, then to Minsk and Berlin. He returned to Minsk in 1928, where the Soviet literary scene offered opportunities to Yiddish writers. Most of his close relatives had already settled in the Belarusian capital.[133]

Kulbak initially flourished in the Soviet regime, teaching at the Belarusian Academy of Sciences and contributing to *Shtern*. His literary output included the verse cycle *Disner Tshayld-Harold* (Child Harold from Disna, 1933) and the novel *Zelmenyaner* (book 1, 1931; book 2, 1935). The latter two-volume work, Kulbak's best known, describes how two generations of the Zelman family contended with Bolshevism. Deviating from the emerging forms of socialist realism, the youngest generation of Zelmans are less than heroic in stature, while their elders retain a measure of dignity despite their idiosyncratic nature. Kulbak used a similar approach in his penultimate work, the stage drama *Boytre* (1936). His title character, a Jewish highwayman modeled on a Belarusian Jewish folk tale, is less sympathetic than the older *kehilah* leaders with whom he comes into conflict.

Kulbak understood the value of cultural continuity; many younger Jewish writers had abandoned the language of their heritage in return for publishing opportunities in Slavic languages with larger audiences. Among the leading younger writers who continued to write in Yiddish was Zelik Akselrod, born in Molodechno in 1904. He remained on the fringe of Soviet Yiddish culture until his style conformed to socialist realism, and he received a seat on the *Shtern* editorial board as a reward.[134] He subsequently taught young writers such as Hirsh Reles at the Minsk Pedagogical Institute.[135] Another prominent young writer, Aron Yudelson, jumped into Bolshevik life with both feet. Born in Riga in 1907 and raised according to a traditional Jewish education, Yudelson became disillusioned with the capitalist world during his subsequent public-school years. He crossed illegally into the Soviet Union from Latvia in 1928 and by 1934 had attained Communist Party membership and an editor position at *Oktyabr*.[136] Reles remembered Yudelson as "young, energetic, with body and soul given over to the new Soviet power."[137]

The younger men and (few) women surrounding Hirsh Reles, such as Ruve Reyzin, Leib Talalay, Mote Dekhtiar, Lipe Heler, Pinie Plotkin, Rokhl Boimvol, and Ziame Telesin, were equally eager about the Soviet future.[138] Yet, as Reles later admitted, their fervor for Bolshevism often compromised their work "with fanatic enthusiasm, appalling sycophancy, and hypocritical literary conglomerations."[139] One aspiring writer peripherally in Reles's circle was Henekh Shvedik, a student of Moishe Kulbak.[140] Shvedik maintained another identity: informant for the NKVD.[141] Although the extent of Shvedik's covert efforts is unclear, this connection illustrates the hazards that lay within Reles's new collegial environment. It is unclear if Reles ever knew of Shvedik's role as an informant or if he simply chose not to acknowledge it in his memoirs.

Reles had long understood that aspects of his heritage required concealment under Bolshevism, such as his mother's family's wealth and his father's prewar interests in Zionism.[142] Another aspect of his father's past nearly became Reles's undoing. When Hirsh was a student at the Minsk Pedagogical Institute, an informant in Chashniki wrote to the institute's administration about Leib Reles's former profession as a *melamed*, teacher. "Why did you hide your origins?" asked a school official. Hirsh replied that his father's teaching activities were long over and that he had since worked solely at menial jobs. Once again, Izi Kharik interceded with authorities to call off the investigation, and the young writer was allowed to finish the academic year at the institute. Ironically, it was Henekh Shvedik who encouraged Reles to appeal to Kharik for help on the matter.[143]

Unlike some of the younger writers in Minsk, Reles never sought party membership and put off joining the Red Army—both of which were clear markers of allegiance to the Soviet Union. He was quick, however, to leave his imprint on the cultural scene. Fellow writer Lipe Heler recalled a literary evening in April 1935 when Reles read his "intimate lyric verses about love and friendship and about his home town: Chashniki."[144] His first poem to be published in *Shtern* appeared a few months later, a moment Reles recalled as the happiest time in his life.[145] "Maydl komiugistke" (Komsomol Maiden) tells of an attack by White Guards—compared in the poem to Cossacks—and the revenge exacted by a band of Bolshevik lads.[146] "Afn tish a bintl blumen" (On a Table a Bunch of Flowers),[147] a sentimental daydream about a lost love, appeared a few months later. Upon Kharik and Akselrod's recommendation, Reles was accepted into the Belarusian Writers' Union in 1936, joining some fifty authors in the Jewish Section.[148]

The Great Terror and Yiddish Culture in Soviet Belarus

Vulnerability—the obverse of fame, power, and influence—was perhaps unavoidable for the prominent living under Stalin. It extended to Sergei Kirov, Communist Party leader in Leningrad, assassinated on 1 December 1934 by a young disgruntled former party member. His murder occurred amid alleged threats of external aggression from the east (Imperial Japan) and the west (Nazi Germany and Poland) as well as amid internal fears of sabotage, party corruption, and foreign agents. And it amplified these anxieties, providing the trigger for waves of arrests and show trials of Stalin's political adversaries and their associates. The arrests escalated dramatically in late 1936, devouring both the prominent and the obscure across a broad spectrum of Soviet society. Over the next two years, the party's agents in the NKVD pursued Red Army officers, government bureaucrats, factory managers, and ordinary citizens, until finally the terror consumed many of the very officials who had set it all in motion.

Scholarly understanding of what happened in the Soviet Union from 1934 to 1939 has emerged over decades, along with significant debate over its structure and scope. This debate extends even to the name given to this period. The purges of 1937–38 are referred to as the Yezhovshchina in Russian historiography, referencing NKVD chief Nikolai Ivanovich Yezhov. In western historiography, Robert Conquest dubbed it the "Great Terror" in his monograph of the same name published in 1968. Conquest interpreted events as largely directed by Stalin from the top down within a totalitarian system.[149] In a study published in 1985, J. Arch Getty revealed the participation of local leaders working in tandem with the center in Moscow and called the purges the "Great Purges."[150] Yet such comprehensive explanations largely addressed the suppression of party representatives and military leaders known to historians before the 1990s. The discovery of the NKVD orders for "mass operations" in archives of the former Soviet Union in 1992 revealed the greater complexity of the purges. Authorized by Politburo resolutions, the mass operations were conceived to eliminate perceived anti-Soviet and counterrevolutionary elements. These elements included former "kulaks," members of opposition political parties, Imperial Russian bureaucrats, religious leaders, speculators, and other "social outcasts."[151] An additional and significant component of the mass operations was the "national operations," which sought to root out foreign spies among the national minorities in the borderland regions. The diverse nature of the mass operations has prompted the historian James Harris to refer to the era as the "Great Fear."[152] The present study simply uses the expression "the Great Terror," although it does not seek to address the overriding forces behind the purges. The Great Terror touched the lives of most ordinary people in one way or another. Nomenclature aside, it was under the national operations in Belarus that Yiddish cultural leaders were purged, concurrent with the closure of Yiddish-language institutions in the Soviet republic.

The hunt for enemies unfolded at the periphery as well as at the centers of power. Those hunts conducted in 1935 by the Belarusian Commissariat of Enlightenment in Minsk to look for "Trotskyist–Zinovievist counterrevolutionary activities" worked their way into institutions such as the Vitebsk Jewish Pedagogical Tekhnikum.[153] One internal order from the institution reported how an instructor named Khanin was singled out for suspected anti-Soviet behavior.[154] Semyon Gendelman, a student from Ukraine with a good record of Komsomol activity prior to entering the *tekhnikum*, committed the error of voicing support for the outcast instructor.[155] He was expelled for this misstep on 29 January 1935.[156] Another *tekhnikum* student, T. Byaznosik, engaged in an act of youthful mischief by swinging his fist and cursing a portrait of Karl Marx, but it was interpreted as counterrevolutionary activity. Byaznosik compounded his troubles by saying within earshot of an informant on the anniversary of Lenin's death, "If more leaders died, we'd get more days off."[157] Byaznosik was expelled the same day as Gendelman.[158]

Gendelman and Byaznosik had the good fortune of receiving rehabilitation within a few months, although they likely remained under scrutiny. During a review of his case six weeks after his expulsion, Gendelman admitted he made a mistake in defending instructor Khanin. Given a severe reprimand, he was restored to the student roster.[159] Gendelman's rehabilitation was so complete that he participated in Vitebsk's May Day demonstrations in 1935.[160] His case remained within the *tekhnikum* administration, which may explain its quick resolution. Byaznosik's actions, however, resulted in a paper trail that led to Minsk. The Commissariat of Enlightenment investigated and subsequently labeled his actions a "manifestation of class hatred."[161] Yet the investigation also revealed certain mitigating circumstances. Not only did Byaznosik confess his crimes, but officials also discovered that the youth lived in Vitebsk with a grandfather because his father worked in the Soviet industrial city of Magnitogorsk and his mother was an invalid in Ukraine. Living with an older and therefore reactionary relative had corrupted the youth's attitudes, the investigation concluded. Byaznosik's transgressions were forgiven, and he was readmitted to the *tekhnikum* in August 1935.[162]

Hirsh Reles's new literary mentors in Minsk also fell under scrutiny. Khatskl Dunets, editor of the Minsk newspaper *Oktyabr*, was one of the first to be targeted among the Belarusian Jewish intellectuals.

In 1935, he faced expulsion from the Communist Party and the Belarusian Writers' Union based on accusations of "counterrevolutionary activity." Adding to his disgrace was Izi Kharik's public denunciation of him at a Writers' Union meeting.[163] Dunets was arrested, tried, and in 1936 sentenced to a gulag camp. It was then Kharik's, Kulbak's, and Yudelson's turn. During the summer of 1937, the NKVD repeatedly called in Kharik for questioning.[164] Kulbak had faced severe criticism the previous year for his play *Boytre*, which was found to be a "hyperbolic, grotesque depiction of the past, as well as [to place] form over content."[165] Although such disapproval highlighted Kulbak's failure to conform with socialist realism, it hardly forecast his ultimate fate. Adding to his troubles, however, was his last major work, the drama *Benyomin Magidov*. A planned performance in Birobidzhan was cancelled after it was banned.[166] Aron Yudelson also faced difficulties. After losing his radio committee appointment, his writings were banned.[167]

Kulbak's and Yudelson's arrests followed on 11 September 1937. The two writers were picked up at their apartments in Minsk. The NKVD found Kharik at a rest home in Pukhavichi and transported him back to Minsk in one of their "black raven" vans. The three Yiddish writers joined thousands of other victims facing weeks of interrogation designed to extract confessions, even if false, and to name accomplices. Belarusian poet Stanislav Shushkevich, who survived the Great Terror, was in a cell adjacent to Kharik. He heard NKVD torturers beating the Yiddish writer's head against the cell wall in an effort to get him to confess his crimes. Kharik was heard to scream "Why?!" in both Russian and Yiddish: "Za shto?!" "Far vos?!"[168]

Kharik, Kulbak, and Yudelson were tried before a troika (three-judge) court on 28 October 1937, where each was adjudicated and condemned in fifteen minutes. Dunets, brought back from a gulag camp to be tried a second time, was sentenced to death on the same day as the others. All four were executed that night in the Minsk prison Amerikanke.[169] Their bodies were probably dumped in mass graves in the Kurapaty forest on the northeast edge of Minsk.[170] Sixty-six other men and women, including several Belarusian and Polish writers and cultural leaders, were executed on the same night, 28–29 October 1937, the Belarusian "night of the murdered poets."[171]

The wives and children of Kharik, Kulbak, and Yudelson also faced punitive measures despite Stalin's much repeated pronouncement that "a son does not answer for his father." In practice, retributive punishment of family members was common during the Great Terror.[172] Dina Kharik, Zelda Kulbak, and Basia Shur, Yudelson's wife, were arrested on 5 November 1937. The three women were tried on the same day as well, 28 November 1937, and convicted on the charge of being a "family member of a traitor and enemy of the people." Each received sentences of eight years confinement in the gulag system.[173] Their children were sent to NKVD-operated orphanages.[174]

Jews and the Polish Operation

"Far vos?!" (Why?) Kharik was heard to scream in his cell. Why, indeed? Kharik and his colleagues represented the apogee of Soviet Yiddish culture in the BSSR. Their elimination, although appearing to be an attack on the status of Jews, was principally collateral damage in the repression of ethnic Poles. The latter were targeted in the national operations, along with Latvians, Estonians, Germans, Finns, Rumanians, and other ethnic groups with potential cross-border connections.[175] Soviet Jews, however, were not explicitly identified among these groups.

Jews could have posed the same perceived risk for Soviet authorities as other nationalities. Despite the absence of a Jewish national state, they shared transnational characteristics with other borderland ethnic groups. Soviet authorities avoided naming Jews in their decrees because this might appear to be antisemitic. Stalin, for all his personal feelings against Jews, feared how the appearance of antisemitism would play abroad, particularly in Nazi Germany. Antisemitism remained a punishable "anti-Soviet" offense during the Great Terror. In addition, antisemitism appeared among the list of charges against suspect individuals, even when such allegations were implausible.[176]

Ethnic Poles were another matter. They were considered the greatest threat along the western border. Soviet paranoia over an independent and capitalist Poland was triggered by the Polish–Soviet War of 1919–21 and continued long afterward. During the late 1920s, the Polish state engaged in limited acts of espionage with the goal to undermine Soviet rule in Ukraine. By the start of the 1930s, however, the Piłsudski government in Warsaw curtailed such operations in the face of Poland's growing economic crisis. The Poles even signed a nonaggression pact with the Soviet Union in 1932. Yet when the lethal famine struck Ukraine in 1932 and 1933, Stalin wanted a political explanation—no matter that it was his own policies, implemented by thousands of party officials, that provoked the crisis and the associated mass starvation of Ukrainian peasants. Vsevolod Balyts'kyi, a secret-police chief sent to the stricken Soviet republic, served up a response suitable for Stalin's preconceptions: the Polska Organizacja Wojskowa (Polish Military Organization, known in Russian by the initials POV) was responsible for sabotage in preparation for an invasion from the west. It mattered not that the POV, which existed from 1914 to 1921, had long been dormant.[177]

Such libels provided the justification for the marginalization of the Polish minority along the western Soviet borderlands. Beginning in 1933, Polish-language newspapers disappeared, and Polish-language schools closed. Persecution escalated in 1935 when thousands of Poles were deported to Kazakhstan.[178] Anti-Polish persecution reached its climax in mid-1937 with NKVD Order Number 00485, which called for the identification and liquidation of Polish-directed intelligence, sabotage, and terrorist activities. Specific categories of the NKVD order included "anti-Soviet and nationalistic" ethnic Poles, former residents of Poland, former members of Polish political parties, and all Soviet citizens who had had some sort of contact with Polish government representatives in the Soviet Union.[179]

A key aspect of the national operations, however, was simple guilt by association, sweeping up those with ties, real or imagined, to suspect ethnic groups. Nationality alone was not a requirement. Ethnic Poles throughout Belarusian society—from the editorial staff of the Polish-language newspaper *Orka*[180] to ordinary farmers, workers, or railway men[181]—were included in the decree, NKVD chief Nikolai

Yezhov confirmed in a letter that accompanied the order that "'defectors' from Poland, regardless of when they entered Soviet territory," were suspects as well.[182] Indeed, statistics reveal the broad nature of the NKVD's Polish operation in Belarus. By December 1938, as the purges drew to a close, 21,407 people had been arrested: 9,196 Poles, 10,120 Belarusians, 1,059 Jews, 383 Russians, 181 Ukrainians, 105 Germans, 122 Latvians, 133 Lithuanians, and 108 persons of other nationalities. More than two-thirds of those arrested were executed; most of the rest were sentenced to gulag camps.[183]

Kulbak and Yudelson were émigrés who had spent time in Poland, so they readily fit the profile of the NKVD dragnet. Kharik did not fit the criteria for the Polish operation; unlike Kulbak and Yudelson, he was not an émigré and did not have a prior literary career in the "capitalist" West. So the troika instead accused Kharik of being a member of a terrorist group preparing to assassinate Red Army marshal Kliment Voroshilov and USSR Supreme Soviet chairman Mikhail Ivanovich Kalinin and of being a German spy.[184] The terrorist group, as explained in the troika's judgment of Kharik, was a counterrevolutionary organization purported to be led by Stalin's former rivals Leon Trotsky and Grigory Zinoviev.[185] The specific charges against Yudelson included membership in an unspecified subversive Trotskyite organization and participation in a terrorist group.[186] Kulbak was charged with membership in a Trotskyite organization in addition to Polish espionage.[187] Using another chimera, the NKVD tied Trotskyite–Zinovievite conspiracies to both Polish and German intelligence services.

In the months following these writers' trials, the purge of the Jewish intelligentsia in Minsk rolled on. Four editors at *Oktyabr* were arrested, tried, and executed.[188] Yiddish literary critic and linguist Moishe Litvakov was executed in Minsk at the end of 1937.[189] Berka Shloymevich Okun, former director of the Minsk Jewish Pedagogical Institute, met the same fate on 29 June 1938.[190] This purge of the Yiddish community in Belarus was largely a regional phenomenon, barely registering outside the Soviet Union at all. Prominent Yiddish writers in Moscow and Kharkov (Ukraine) continued to receive official support. Literary specialists in the West noticed Kharik's and Kulbak's disappearance but heard only rumors of what had happened to them.[191] One historian writing in the 1960s claimed that "the cultural leadership of Soviet Jewry . . . had largely been unaffected by the 1936–38 purge."[192]

If the Yiddish cultural purge in Belarus holds a place in the development of Soviet antisemitism, it also appears to have set a precedent for the marginalization of Jews elsewhere because of their identity. Subsequent events reveal as much: the wartime purge of Jews from Soviet cultural and educational institutions; the murder of Solomon Mikhoels and the dissolution of the Jewish Anti-Fascist Committee in 1948; the trial and execution of Jewish intellectuals in 1952 (known commonly as the "Night of the Murdered Poets" because of the killings of prominent Yiddish writers based in Moscow); and the "Doctors' Plot" just months before Stalin's death.

Charges of Polish or Trotskyite conspiracy could not efface the Jewish identity of the purged writers, however, particularly among their readership. Kharik (born 1896), Kulbak (born 1897), and Yudelson (born 1907) were initially educated in *khedarim* (plural for *kheder*) and yeshivas. Kharik and Kulbak, for all their efforts on behalf of the Soviet regime, drew upon character types and traditions from the shtetl and urban Jewish street in their writings. Their removal marked a break with the Jewish past. Younger writers such as Hirsh Reles largely conformed to themes of socialist realism.

Belarusian writers and their works were also eliminated in the Great Terror, but they were largely younger or lesser-known figures. Yakub Kolas (1882–1956) and Yanka Kupala (1882–1942), the two most popular Belarusian writers, faced investigation and harassment but survived.[193] The suppression of Yiddish in Belarus is perhaps best viewed in the context of national minorities policies in the western borderlands. Polish, German, and Latvian cultures were gone. The historian Tatiana Protko observes that the NKVD in Belarus labored to eliminate "'the problem' of national minorities (Jews, Poles, Latvians, Lithuanians, Germans), first by the destruction of their cultural organizations, and then by their physical destruction, carrying out 'Polish,' 'Latvian,' 'German' operations."[194] The promotion of national cultures, *korenizatsiia*, in retreat for many years, was abandoned after the Great Terror. Belarusian and Russian dominated the BSSR. Yiddish ran a distant third by comparison.

Terror in Vitebsk

Waves of arrests swept across the Soviet Union. In Vitebsk, one list records that more than 3,000 political arrests occurred from the late 1920s through the early 1950s, and 1,355 of these detainees were executed.[195] The greatest concentration of victims came during the Great Terror of 1937 and 1938.[196] Foreign contacts alone could trigger an investigation. Fivel Markelis's grandmother Rosenthal received money and parcels from a brother in America. When she took some of the money to buy flour, a neighbor in their communal dwelling denounced her. The police came and confiscated not only the flour but also some of the family's valuables, including the kitchenware. No one was arrested, however. Later, when Fivel's grandmother came across one of her favorite cooking pots in a shop, she paid to get it back.[197]

Fivel's family's relatively benign experience contrasts with that of Stepan Zavgorodnev and his relatives. Stepan's maternal uncle, Mikhail Yeines, "loved all things political." Stepan remembered his uncle and stepfather (also named Mikhail) in heated discussions while out walking. But "their attitude was pretty loyal," Stepan recollected. His uncle's argumentative nature did not go unnoticed, however. When the NKVD arrests began, usually at night, first one neighbor disappeared, then another. "A car comes," Stepan recalled, "and everyone was listening attentively and wondering whether or not it would come for us." The Zavgorodnev family tried to hide out in Konstantinovka (Donetsk Oblast, Ukraine). NVKD agents found them in Ukraine, and a search of his uncle's books revealed two or three that provoked his arrest. As Uncle Mikhail was taken away, one agent turned to the rest of the family and asked harshly, "'And who are you?' 'We're just visiting,' one of the adults replied. 'You must leave in twenty-four hours,' the agent declared. I remember my grandmother escorted us," Stepan related. "We were sitting in a train station. And she was whispering and praying all the time. We left. We were okay."[198]

Dmitri Khvat, Stepan's younger classmate at his Vitebsk Russian-language school, also felt the impact of the Great Terror. Not only did his grandparents live in Poland, but the Khvats were also recent immigrants. These circumstances alone could have condemned Dmitri's father, Girsh Khvat, to arrest and execution. Yet the Khvat family survived. The NKVD instead struck against one of Girsh Khvat's Kalinina Hospital colleagues. Dr. Viktar Stanislavavich Stalevsky was a Polish Gentile educated in Paris.[199] He was arrested on 18 December 1937 as a suspected Polish agent and executed in Minsk the following March. His family suffered as well. Dr. Stalevsky's sisters, Elena and Maria, and brothers, Genrikh and Lev, were arrested, also for suspected espionage activity. Elena and Genrikh were sent to a gulag camp for ten years. Maria and Lev were executed about the same time as their brother. Dr. Stalevsky's wife, also named Elena, received a sentence of five years internal exile.[200]

Targets of the purges included faculty and former students of the Vitebsk Jewish Pedagogical Tekhnikum. Iosif Gavrilavich Lades, a Belarusian national who taught Russian and Belarusian language, was arrested on 1 November 1937 and charged with spying for the Polish government.[201] He was executed in Vitebsk on 29 December 1937.[202] Polish-born Ginda Simkhanavna Tsukerman, party leader during her studies at the *tekhnikum*, taught in Vitebsk after her graduation in 1935. Her husband, Fishl Shloymevich Tsukerman, born in Poland and employed at the newspaper *Vitsebski praletarii*, was arrested on 24 August 1937, followed by Ginda on 17 September 1937. Both were tried and condemned on 22 October, accused on counterrevolutionary activity. They were also executed on the same day: 4 November 1937.[203] It is possible that when one came under investigation, both fell victim simply because they were married.

Some party functionaries such as the Tsukermans were a prime target for arrest. Others managed to elude the purges, such as Boris Pipkin and his wife. Boris dropped out of sight, leaving his local party post in 1937 and returning to the assembly line of a Vitebsk shoe factory. But even there the atmosphere was tense. "In the morning, when workers arrived and sat themselves down along the conveyor," his son

Marx later related of his father's experience, "they silently looked to one side and the other to see who was missing."[204]

Yiddish Culture in Retreat

Concurrent with the purge of the leading Jewish writers in Minsk, Yiddish-language education experienced a precipitous decline. Small measures signaled the change. In January 1937, the name "Frumkina" was removed from the Vitebsk Jewish Pedagogical Tekhnikum when the revolutionary Esther Frumkina fell from favor.[205] No other Bolshevik was subsequently named as symbolic patron. In March, the *tekhnikum* itself was scheduled to be closed with the end of the academic year.[206] The remaining students were transferred to the Minsk Jewish Pedagogical Tekhnikum. Although surviving documents do not mention how the Vitebsk Tekhnikum staff justified these actions to their students or themselves, the closure occurred in the context of pressures from above and the loss of popular support from below.

Centralization of Yiddish education, such as the merging of the *tekhnikums*, fell in line with party directives to improve political surveillance. These directives followed the push some years earlier for greater order and discipline in the Soviet education system, as exemplified by Zalman Babitski's work at the Vitebsk Tekhnikum after his arrival in 1933. Little did he know that his efforts would eventually put him out of a job. On 8 July 1936, the Belarusian Commissariat of Enlightenment ordered the concentration of authority over pedagogical issues in each educational institution.[207] The order came in response to one issued four days earlier by the Central Committee in Moscow, denouncing the exploratory methods still carried out by some educators.[208] Given the drive to centralize control over pedagogy—and, by extension, over ideological education—it seemed unlikely that two Jewish pedagogical institutes could remain.

Tekhnikum graduates were also having greater trouble finding employment.[209] Indeed, demand for their services lessened as year by year enrollments in Yiddish schools declined. Some schools terminated their lower grades.[210] *Tekhnikum* graduates in Vitebsk fortunate enough to receive positions from the penultimate graduating class (1936) found placement in smaller and more obscure towns.[211] Many of these positions were obtained through the intervention of Director Babitski, who had contacted school superintendents across the republic: "The Vitebsk Jewish Pedagogical Tekhnikum urgently asks you about your needs to teach Yiddish literature, language, and history."[212] In mid-1937, the Commissariat of Enlightenment in Minsk wrote to Babitski to ask for a list of top graduates from the *tekhnikum*'s final class.[213] Although the letter does not explicitly mention language skills, Minsk was probably not looking for students who could teach only in Yiddish. Proficiency in Russian and Belarusian had been a requirement since the start of the year.[214] Concurrent statistics from the Minsk Jewish Pedagogical Tekhnikum confirm this development. Only 17 of 135 graduates in the 1937 class received jobs in Yiddish-language schools. The rest went to work in Russian- and Belarusian-language schools.[215]

Decline turned into collapse in 1938. First, the Minsk Jewish Pedagogical Tekhnikum was shuttered at the end of the academic year, reopening in September 1938 as a Belarusian-language institution. The Jewish departments of the Gorky Pedagogical Institute and Belarusian State University also folded. With the academic year over and faculties on summer leave, the Central Committee of the Communist Party of Belarus issued a resolution on 3 July 1938 changing the instruction language in all Yiddish-language schools to Belarusian. The impetus for closure, so it was claimed, came from "the Jewish population, from parents and pupils in Jewish schools in Belarus."[216] The reorganization was to be completed by 1 September 1938.

A small number of schools retained Yiddish as the primary language of instruction, mainly for practical reasons, but then none remained by January 1940.[217] For most students, however, the language shift occurred over the summer of 1938 as decreed. In Vitebsk, Fivel Markelis attended the Yiddish-language School Number 23, which became a Belarusian-language institution upon his return for the fourth class level in September.[218] Vera German recalled the same experience after her summer vacation.[219] And language changes did not stop there. When students returned in September 1940, classes were taught in Russian, not Belarusian. The latter move fell in line with the increasing Russification of the Soviet Union. With the retreat from *korenizatsiia*, begun in 1933 during the suppression of national minorities, Russian took prominence. This process was still unfolding when Nazi Germany invaded the Soviet Union in 1941.

Some teachers objected to the end of Yiddish education, but their voices carried little weight as they faced a wave of persecutions that restricted their influence. Commissariat officials endorsed the purge of teachers with links outside the Soviet Union, Bundist or Zionist leanings, relatives who had been arrested, or "class enemies" in their family backgrounds.[220] Many teachers simply accepted their new assignments. Rachel Geyduk and Raisa Epstein, both graduates of the Vitebsk Jewish Pedagogical Tekhnikum, taught mathematics and chemistry, respectively, in Gorodok, north of Vitebsk. They taught in Yiddish one academic year and in Belarusian the next in the same school building.[221] Others felt the loss of Yiddish acutely. Matsvin Khanin, the young Yiddish and Russian language and literature teacher at the Vitebsk Jewish Pedagogical Tekhnikum, went to work at the Pedagogical Institute in Mogilev teaching Russian literature. Yet he missed Yiddish, and his former student Hirsh Reles later wrote how during their visits they reminisced about their vanishing culture.[222]

Yiddish authors also feared the gradual loss of their audience, although their entreaties failed to persuade authorities in Minsk.[223] Zelik Akselrod, Eli Kahan, Hirsh Berezkin, and Henekh Shvedik met to lament the liquidation of Yiddish culture. Either Berezkin or Shvedik, both NKVD informants, reported that Akselrod stated:

> The newspaper *Oktyabr* intends to publicize the decision of the Bureau of the CC [Central Committee] to close down Yiddish schools, so I asked them: "How can you publicize a situation in which Jews will not be speaking Yiddish? It would be better if you held a memorial service for yourselves and wrote in the lead article 'Don't read or write Yiddish.'"[224]

Sarcasm probably didn't play well with the NKVD. Akselrod soldiered on, however, filling the vacuum left by the removal of Kharik and Kulbak by fostering younger Yiddish writers in Minsk. Among them was Hirsh Reles. Despite the repressive conditions, Reles was still able to publish Yiddish poems in *Shtern*, which lived on under an editorial board made up of second-rate writers and journalists.[225] "Fun shtetl" (From a Shtetl) was a farewell to his hometown: "I scattered my childhood here on every street, and my youth wore it out."[226] "In lazaret" (In Hospital) narrates the delirium of an injured soldier recalling the sights and smells of battle.[227] These two works framed Reles's life up through the era of the purges: from shtetl to city to survivor of a great battle.

One way Reles endured was to leave Minsk. In late 1937, he took a Yiddish school teaching job in the less conspicuous venue of Slutsk. It was there that he heard about the persecution of his literary heroes and subsequently encountered the librarian destroying their works.[228] When he traveled to Chashniki for a family gathering during this time, his father, Leib, offered him and his siblings more pragmatic advice. "'Don't recklessly denounce others,' my father advised us. 'But if you speak too well [of the wrong people], you may be arrested yourself.'"[229] Reles followed this guidance to be inconspicuous. By early 1939, he had new responsibilities at home: he had married, and his wife, Yekha, soon gave birth to a daughter, Raisel.

Reles continued to participate in Yiddish culture in Soviet Belarus, publishing his first poetry collection, *Onheyb* (Beginning), in 1939.[230] Zelik Akselrod supported his younger colleague by serving as the book's editor.[231] Other developments appear less positive. In a cynical act that Moishe Kulbak might have appreciated were it not seemingly at his expense, the new editors of *Shtern* published the poem "Tshayld-Harold" in the January 1938 issue. This was not Kulbak's work with a similar title, but the original by Byron in a Yiddish translation. Jewish writers maintained their public profile, such as a meeting in August 1938 to discuss "cooperation among Jewish writers of Belarus," as reported in *Oktyabr*. Yet Akselrod, Mote Dekhtiar, Eli Kahan, and others used the opportunity to declare their allegiance to party principles.[232] Many of the same writers contributed to the literary anthology *Ordentregerishe Vaysrusland* (Belarus, the Common Porter, 1939), penning verses and essays rife with sycophantic praise for Stalin and the Soviet regime.[233]

Outside of Belarus, the Soviet Yiddish literary scene was less bleak. Prominent writers Itzik Fefer, Dovid Bergelson, and Peretz Markish continued to publish within the confines of socialist realism. Although the Moscow Yiddish newspaper *Der emes* (The Truth) ceased publication in 1938 after most of its editorial staff were arrested and executed, and many other Yiddish periodicals had been shut down in the years just before the Great Terror, a few remained in circulation until the German invasion in 1941. One laudatory essay written by a Soviet Jew declared: "Soviet Jewish literature in the USSR [is] the most beautiful, the richest with lofty thoughts, the most progressive literature by the Jewish people in the entire world."[234] And some still believed that. What else could they do?

Shaping Identity

In Soviet Vitebsk of the 1930s, a young Jew raised in a religious family did not necessarily observe traditions. He often migrated from shtetl to city, dropped many of the traditions of Jewish life, and went to work in a factory or enrolled in an institution of higher learning. If a child born into a Jewish family learned about Jewish customs, it was principally a matter upheld by her mother or, more likely, a grandparent. A young Soviet Jew frequently kept company with other Jews, but not exclusively. He played with neighbor children, usually aware of each one's nationality. A Jewish child went to a Yiddish-, Russian-, or Belarusian-language school, where she was indoctrinated with Bolshevik ideology. She joined a Belarusian folk dancing troupe. A Jew in the nascent Soviet Union spoke Russian or Yiddish, sometimes both. When he grew up, he married another Jew or a Russian or a Belarusian. When her husband died, a Jewish widow and mother became a worker, if she wasn't already employed outside the home because of economic necessity. And within the Soviet system, a young Jew could advance to the center of cultural life within a few short years. These many facets illuminate the dimensions of

Soviet Jewish identity in Vitebsk—not a single identity, but rather several coterminous identities.

Identities became fluid as the Bolsheviks built a new society. Hirsh Reles reached for the ideals that the Soviet system held out in front of him, a society in which, in his own words, "you could be what you wanted to be, you could realize all your talents."[235] Yet to do so demanded concessions and compromises. Following your dreams meant leaving behind the sheltered life of the traditional Jewish community. The Red city offered opportunity but did not readily accommodate religious or cultural traditions. Jewish children could learn in Yiddish, their "national language," at least until it appeared disadvantageous to do so, and later they couldn't speak it at all, except at home. Elements that had defined Jewish life before the revolution were confined to the home as well, where grandparents recited prayers and prepared for Passover. Language shifts at school pushed young Soviet Jews to learn more than just the everyday speech of their ethnic neighbors. Many acquired detailed knowledge of cultural practices.

The party mingled the construction of socialism with destruction fueled by paranoia. Every Soviet citizen experienced loss during the Great Terror: a family member, a neighbor, a teacher, a competent supervisor or employee, a favorite writer, or an army officer who helped keep the nation secure from attack. Within the compartmentalized world of Soviet nationalities policies, however, where the party and state assigned each ethnic group an official classification and associated culture, all Belarusian Jews, like the remaining Poles, Germans, and Latvians in Belarus, experienced a double blow: a deep devaluation of their culture and the guarantee that future generations would no longer have the option to speak or read their assigned language. The party may have dismantled national cultures, but the NKVD augmented the markers of national identity in the internal passports of Soviet citizens. In April 1938, the NKVD required the specification of the bearer's parents' nationalities as well as the bearer's declared nationality. Although this modification was meant to catch "foreign" nationals such as Poles and Germans,[236] during the German occupation in 1941 it proved to be deadly for children of marriages between Soviet Jews and Gentiles.

Such were the direct actions of the state. Within each individual, the purges fostered a sense of alienation and disassociation at odds with the official rhetoric promoting unity. Jewish children felt this in particular. It must have been disorienting to have Izi Kharik's portrait on the schoolhouse wall one day but not the next. Schoolchildren memorized his Yiddish verses, only to be told one day to forget them. Nor was their national language a haven. When they returned to school in September 1938, their teacher spoke to them in Belarusian.

The sense of disassociation extended beyond the individual life. People became afraid to trust one another, which fostered social alienation. As Sarah Davies has noted, the purge years led to "a strong sense of social cleavage, of 'us' and 'them.'"[237] Another historian of the period, Wendy Z. Goldman, has noted that "the terror did not unify people in common suffering."[238] On the contrary, the fragmentation of the social order did not dissipate with the conclusion of the purges. Friend had abandoned friend. Families blacked out the faces on photographs of executed or imprisoned loved ones. Even someone as genial as Izi Kharik participated in the denunciation of his friend Dunets. Stepan Zavgorodnev's family was quick to separate themselves from his uncle Mikhail when the latter was arrested. "And who are you?" asked the NKVD officer. In his account of the arrest decades after the fact, Stepan omitted the responder's name, possibly out of shame. "We're just visiting," the responding adult replied.[239] Hirsh Reles and his colleagues were afraid to visit the denounced writers Khatskl Dunets and Aron Yudelson and even to converse with them in the street.[240] Reles's lack of connection is palpable in his memoirs written during the 1990s: he never really discusses his personal responses to the arrest of his mentor Izi Kharik or the others.

Another consequence of the purges, one that had profound effects on the future lives of Soviet Jews, was the resurgence in antisemitism. The purge of Zinoviev and others raised hopes among secret antisemites that future Soviet policies would target Jews specifically.[241] The closure of Yiddish-language institutions in Belarus and the affiliated suppression of leading Jewish cultural figures promoted such expectations. An informant's report in 1939 told party authorities in Minsk about antisemitic graffiti in Kolyshki, a town southeast of Vitebsk near the Russian border, the gist of which was that the party would soon enact restrictive measures toward Jews similar to those in Germany.[242] The purges were soon followed by the rapprochement between the Soviet Union and Nazi Germany, and a near total news blackout of German antisemitic policies was in place by mid-1939.[243] Although no overt antisemitic policies materialized from Moscow or Minsk, trends seemed to indicate they were coming.

The era promoted an alertness among young Jews to respond to fluid situations, skills that aided their survival years later during war and genocide. They demonstrated as much as the Great Terror drew to a close. Hirsh Reles continued to write and teach school, and he married and had a child. Stepan Zavgorodnev accommodated the terrible tragedy and social stigma of a family member ripped away. He never commented on whether the experience drew his family together or damaged relationships or whether they were able to help him, an eleven-year-old child, cope.[244] Dmitri Khvat's family survived the purges, although his father's close colleague was arrested along with his entire family. Young Dmitri may not have experienced this loss directly, but he observed how his parents dealt with it. Fivel Markelis remembered the police raid on his home and the confiscation of his grandmother's cooking pots, incorporating the experience and his family's responses into his social vocabulary. Such actions display essential accommodation and endurance skills essential in the year to come.

Beyond the Soviet Frontier

Although polemic fogged domestic news, the Soviet Yiddish press delivered international updates straight from Reuters and other wire services, albeit chosen with leftist editorial selectivity. Many stories focused on the chaos of the West's economic depression, but others underscored war and conflict. Spain erupted in civil war;[245] France prepared its population for fighting on the home front;[246] and Poland endangered Soviet security with self-defense measures.[247] Palestine, the goal of Zionists, was the scene of periodic violence among the English, Arab tribes, and Jewish settlers.[248] Germany appeared headed for proletarian revolution with the collapse of the capitalist order in 1931 and 1932, but events there took a different turn when "the bloody Hitler" was appointed chancellor on 30 January 1933.[249]

Vitsebski praletarii published political cartoons of Hitler as a grotesque dwarf, the ugly hatchet man of capitalism.[250] Print stories presented the first year of Nazi rule as a conflict between Nazism and communism.[251] The Yiddish press highlighted the assault on German Jews. *Oktyabr* informed its readers of the boycott of Jewish shops on 1 April 1933.[252] Nazi antisemitism escalated in the summer of 1935 with pogroms in Berlin, Augsburg, and Breslau,[253] followed by arrests of individual Jews suspected of miscegenation with "Aryan" women.[254] The Nazis' codified their racism and biological determinism in the Nuremberg Laws of September 1935, banning marriage and physical contact between Jews and "Aryans."[255] German Jews also lost their status as equal citizens, becoming "subjects of the Reich."

These events, however, were far away in the capitalist West. Some Jews in the Soviet Union knew of Hitler's rearmament from stories carried in *Oktyabr* and *Der emes*. A young Belarusian teacher remembered after the war that he knew about German militarization from Jewish contacts who tracked such reports.[256] But nothing pointed toward such an absurd notion as a German invasion. As the purges unfolded in the Soviet Union, Germany revealed its expansionist agenda. Hitler made a mockery of Austrian and Czechoslovakian sovereignty in 1938 under the guise of German brotherhood and regional security. And within the greater Reich, antisemitic agitation escalated into mass violence.

On 11 November 1938, *Oktyabr* printed a photo of the Soviet leadership atop Lenin's tomb reviewing the parade commemorating the October Revolution. Immediately below the photo ran a startling news item: "Jewish Pogroms in Germany."[257] The assassination of Secretary Ernst vom Rath of the German embassy in Paris served as a pretext for the acute intensification of German terror against Jews, the article reported. The scope of violence on this night, later known to history as "Kristallnacht," was unprecedented: Jews beaten in their homes and in the streets as well as extensive damage to Jewish-owned property.[258] During the following days, further news reports discussed specific attacks against Jews in Berlin, Frankfurt, Vienna, and other cities.[259] Accounts published in Paris and London told of mass arrests of Jewish men.[260] A Swiss news report ascribed the organizing role to the German government, contradicting the Nazi leadership's assertions that the violence was merely a popular uprising.[261]

Despite their frequency, the reports had little impact on Jewish readers in Belarus. Not only was the Third Reich a remote land, but the Soviet frontier was also well guarded—or so the same newspapers asserted. Then, too, newspaper circulation was limited.[262] Copies passed from hand to hand only went so far. Nor was news by radio universally available, except through loudspeakers mounted in the street. Vera German's and Dmitri Khvat's families had radios, although Dmitri's did only because a family friend gave it to them when her husband was arrested. He remembered it was forbidden to listen to foreign radio broadcasts.[263] None of the young people discussed in this chapter remembered any special concern within their families about Hitler, either because parents kept such information from children or because their focus on work and everyday needs left little room in their lives for awareness of such matters.

Soon, however, the Soviet Union initiated a stunning course change in international relations that brought the Reich much closer. Stalin felt increasing unease over the situation in Europe in late 1938 and early 1939. Britain paid for appeasement with Czech territory, the Nationalists won the civil war in Spain, and the unpredictability of French governments, which came and went with the seasons, undermined the Soviet Union's mutual-assistance treaty with that nation. After the dismissal of the Jewish-born Maksim Litvinov as commissar of foreign affairs in May 1939, his replacement, Vyacheslav Molotov, signaled Berlin that the Soviet Union might be willing to engage in talks for a nonaggression treaty. Armed conflict between Nazism and Bolshevism appeared inevitable, but neither party was ready for that fight. British and French negotiators botched their attempt to forestall the Nazi–Soviet pact announced to the world on 24 August 1939. Stalin enumerated the benefits of the ten-year agreement to the Politburo on 19 August. "The first advantage we will gain will be the destruction of Poland right up to the gates of Warsaw," he declared, beguiling his audience even further by adding, "Germany is giving us complete freedom of action in the Baltic states." We can measure his gamble by a prediction he made about the outcome of the expected conflict between Nazi Germany and France and Britain. "In the event of [Germany's] defeat, the Sovietization of Germany will inevitably follow."[264]

After Germany invaded Poland on 1 September 1939, the Soviet Union waited for its opportunity to occupy eastern Poland. When the opening came on 17 September, Molotov's radio announcement justified the incursion as the "liberation" of "western Belarus" and "western Ukraine."[265] Although Red Army forces entered the region intent on reuniting kindred Slavs, they also encountered Jews separated from their Soviet coreligionists for some twenty years under Polish rule.

2

Responses to Exclusion and Violence

Grodno, 1933 to 1939

On the evening of 7 June 1935, fourteen-year-old Lev Zhubov met with friends in Miejski Park in Grodno, Poland. Sundown marked the end of the first day of the Jewish holiday of Shavuot, the day God gave the Torah to Moses and the Israelites at Mount Sinai. Their conversation, which he later documented in an autobiographical essay for the YIVO Institute in Vilna, focused on the future. Lev recalled, "We talked about Eretz Yisrael [Palestine] and Birobidzhan." Their discussion was interrupted by noises coming from outside the park. Shouts of "Żydzi" (Jews) pierced by breaking glass meant only one thing—a pogrom. The group tried to flee, but they were met at the entrance by "shkotsim mit shtekns" (Gentile boys with sticks). Lev was caught and severely beaten. When he regained consciousness, some bystanders took him into a movie theater turned triage center. His wounds temporarily mended, he made his way home. Glass covered the street.[1]

By the next morning, rioters had killed two Jews, wounded forty, and vandalized Jewish property across the city. The pogrom underscored the bleak situation that young Jews such as Lev Zhubov faced in the Second Polish Republic. Whereas the Soviet Union supported its youth regardless of "nationality," the Polish government adopted discriminatory policies against its minorities. These policies in turn inspired the initiators of interethnic violence, such as the pogromists in Grodno. Other restrictions blocked access to higher education, worsening the already poor economic prospects of Jewish youth. Their community leaders offered few practical solutions.

These frustrations underlay the evening conversation between Lev Zhubov and his friends. Was a Jewish homeland carved out of British Mandate Palestine the answer to their problems? Or was the Soviet Union showing the way forward by establishing the Jewish Autonomous Region? Poland was not the answer; the attack made that clear.

Central to such discussions were the social ties that made them possible. Some young Jews joined youth organizations with Zionist or socialist platforms. Lev Zhubov, for example, belonged to Tsukunft (Future), the youth section of the socialist Bund (Algemeyner yidisher arbeter bund in Poyln [General Union of Jewish Workers in Poland]). Other young people floated between formal group settings and established connections among their own peers. In each of these cases, young Jews marginalized by the state, attacked by antisemitic neighbors, and abandoned by overtaxed community leaders built networks to shape their own futures. In contrast to the Soviet system, where nationalities policies had the effect of disassociating young Jews from their heritage, the networks across the border in Poland reinforced connections to their Jewish identity.

A Multiethnic City

Grodno's ethnic mix of Poles, Jews, Belarusians, Lithuanians, and Germans stemmed from its position as a historic borderland settlement dating back nearly a millennium. After the turmoil of World War I, the Russian Revolution, and the Polish–Soviet War of 1919–21, the population stood at around 50,000, half as large as Vitebsk. Grodno had a far higher percentage of Jews, although this proportion fell during the interwar period—from 53.9 percent in 1921 to 42.6 percent in 1931.[2] The decline was owing to Jewish emigration as well as to the influx of Poles to the city; the latter numbered 34.7 percent in 1921 and increased to 43.4 percent ten years later.[3] The other ethnic groups mentioned earlier composed the remainder of Grodno's urban population. Much of the surrounding agricultural and forest land was inhabited by Belarusian or Polish peasants as well as by Polish World War I veterans given land as settler farmers.

Young Jews grew up aware of the connections among language, ethnicity, and power. Zelda Grodzienska, born in 1922, noted in an interview in 1994, "[Grodno] was changing hands whenever there was some military [conflict] with Russia."[4] These border shifts influenced the predominant language in the city, irrespective of ethnic identities. Zelda's older siblings, born before World War I, when Grodno lay on the western rim of Imperial Russia, spoke Russian, not the Polish that Zelda learned in public school. Yiddish was their family's language at home.

Unlike Vitebsk, Grodno lay in a combat zone during World War I. The German army advanced on the city in September 1915. Iosif Zbar, born in 1906, remembered, "When we learned that the Russians had to retreat, we barricaded the front door and the gate." Iosif's family feared Russian soldiers would carry out a pogrom, so the Germans' arrival brought much relief to the city's Jews. "It turned out that Germans themselves became the initiators of the creation of the Jewish community," Iosif recollected, because German occupying forces permitted a Jewish *kehilah* to take care of community needs.[5]

For more than two years after the armistice in November 1918 and the subsequent German withdrawal in eastern Europe, Grodno passed back and forth between Polish and Soviet military rule. Polish officers permitted anti-Jewish attacks, whereas Soviet commissars confiscated the property of merchants and the wealthy. Iosif Zbar remembered that "Jews felt free and easy" under the Bolsheviks, "but not rich Jews, of course."[6] Grodno suffered heavier damage during the Polish–Soviet War than during World War I. One eyewitness wrote later of his recollections of the Polish reconquest of the city in September 1920, when he was a child. "We all sat shivering. Guns cracked. Artillery thundered. Bombs crashed."[7] Another youth named Hanan, born in 1916, recalled that Grodno's suburbs caught fire during the battle. His uncle was seriously injured in fighting the flames surrounding the family home and died soon thereafter.[8]

After the Polish victory and consolidation of order, the city became a haven compared to the upheavals of the nascent Soviet system.

Refugees from the revolution and civil war in Russia settled in Grodno, such as a boy here called "Yankl." (His autobiographical essay written in 1934 for YIVO is unsigned.) Yankl's family came to Grodno from Russia in 1921 when he was a small child. He remembered little of the place he knew only as "Russia," nor did he know why his family left there.[9] The prominent settled in Grodno as well. Like Yankl's family, Imperial Russian army medical officer Chaim Blumstein fled from the violence of the Russian Civil War with his wife, Estera, and settled in Grodno in 1921.[10]

The Polish–Soviet War gave Poland control of a wide swath of territory east of the Curzon Line, the British Foreign Office's proposal in 1919 for the eastern Polish border, noted in figure 8. This territory came to be known as the Kresy Wschodnie, a centuries-old Polish name for the eastern borderlands. Grodno, formerly on the western edge of Imperial Russia, lay at the heart of the multiethnic Kresy.[11] Yet Grodno remained a border city, with international trade as the foundation of its economy. Timber and grain (the region's primary commodities) flowed out, while manufactured goods flowed in (Grodno had very little industry). The Soviet border, more than 200 kilometers to the east, cut off Russian markets, but Lithuania was only a dozen kilometers to the north, and Germany (East Prussia) less than 30 kilometers to the northwest. The city was an important railway junction as well, with the Polish cities of Warsaw and Białystok to the southwest and Wilno (Vilna) to the northeast.

Many of the parents of Grodno's interwar generation owned or worked in small businesses, serving as timber and coal dealers, tradesmen (tailors, shoemakers, and the like), shopkeepers, and professionals. The economic depression of the 1930s harmed everyone and put many out of business entirely. Increased competition from government-backed Polish-owned enterprises worsened the situation. The percentage of Grodno's shops owned by Jews dropped from 84.3 percent in 1932 to 71.1 percent in 1937, even though the overall number of shops increased from 694 to 710.[12] Competition from Gentiles was greater in other Kresy communities. In Jedwabne,[13] 100 kilometers west of Grodno, only 3 of 25 shops owned by Jews closed between

8. Map of the Second Polish Republic after the Polish–Soviet War of 1919–21 fixed the eastern border considerably farther east than the Curzon Line of 1919.

1932 and 1937, but the number of Gentile-owned business increased from 4 to 28.[14] As Menachem Linder noted in the economic study from which these figures are drawn, the numbers don't tell the whole story because the psychological pressure from competition with Poles accelerated the economic decline of Jewish merchants.[15]

The demographic composition of Grodno meant that commerce was a significant meeting point for Jews and Gentiles, a circumstance well remembered by shop owners' children decades later. Sima Kapulska, born in 1919, recalled that many of her mother's customers were Polish officers' wives.[16] Elka Fomin's father, Berl, did tailoring work for a largely Polish clientele. Yet Elka, born in 1928, also remarked that her family had little else to do with Poles.[17] Leib Bialo, born in

1923, remembered Polish customers of his parents' granary and general store who had been Marshal Jósef Piłsudski's Polish volunteer soldiers and were "like gentlemen farmers . . . and they were gentlemen till the end."[18] Customer relations were not always cordial. Lev Zhubov, born in 1921, had a brief, unhappy period of employment for a local grain merchant. On one occasion, a Belarusian peasant grew angry and smacked the youth with a whip for his perceived insolence, although the violence also had to do with Lev's inability to adequately speak the peasant's native language.[19]

Young Jews also encountered boycotts and picketing of Jews' shops organized by nationalist political groups and reactionary social committees,[20] such as Grodno's local Anti-Communist Committee. Ann Lewin, born in 1924, remembered boycotts of Jewish wagon drivers and picketing of shops.[21] Leib Bialo recalled Gentiles wearing armbands that read "Nie kupuj od Żydów" (Don't buy from Jews).[22] Such acts targeted their parents' livelihood, but Jewish children endured other assaults firsthand. Sixty years after the fact, elderly Jews recalled particular insults by Gentile children. Jewish schools were open on Sundays, not Saturdays, like Polish schools, and Vichna Sidranska remembers Gentile children throwing stones at her one Sunday. The experience left little Vichna insecure and confused because she regularly played with some very nice Polish neighbor kids.[23] Fenia Muller, born in 1922, remembered an incident on a Palm Sunday when a group of Polish boys slapped her and her friends with palm fronds as the latter passed on the way to school.[24] Other insults referenced specific antisemitic myths. Rivke Altshuler, born in 1926, recalled hearing the libel that Jews poisoned wells.[25] Leib Bialo recalled, "Sometimes you hear from [a Gentile] that we killed Jesus, you know, that kind of thing."[26]

Newspaper stories reported how some confrontations led to violence, such as an assault by Heronim Patignovski on Yakov Taub in November 1933.[27] Such attacks instilled a fear of Gentiles. Yehuda Rabinovich, born in 1922, recalled his trepidations about walking in some neighborhoods, even though he described himself as "assimilated" in appearance.[28] Gedaliah (Daniel) Klovsky, born in 1928, recollected that "we, the Jewish children, used to walk only in groups" to avoid encounters with Gentile ruffians. Intergenerational contacts reinforced these fears; Daniel's grandfather, for example, told him about the pogroms he had witnessed in Ukraine during his youth.[29]

Not all young Jews grew up with wholly negative impressions of Gentiles. Mina Muller, born in 1927, contradicted her older sister Fenia, insisting in an interview in 1996 that Jews and Gentiles had "a wonderful relationship" before the war. A Polish officer lived harmoniously with the Muller household in a rented room, and Mina had several close friends who were Poles.[30] Bronia Winicka, born in 1924, attended a Polish-language school and had many Polish friends.[31]

Within this sometimes contentious and sometimes harmonious environment, Jews and Gentiles lived side by side across Grodno. Only the *shulhoyf* (synagogue courtyard), the neighborhood around the Great Synagogue, and Slobodka District, which lay across the railroad tracks from the city center, were primarily Jewish. Other neighborhoods were ethnically mixed, sometimes in the same building. "The front of the streets was always owned by Jews, in the back, or higher up, there [were Gentiles]," Leib Bialo said about the spatial intimacy—and his perceptions of class distinctions—in the city.[32]

Jewish Community Life

Young Jews of Grodno grew up in an environment far more tangibly Jewish than their counterparts in Soviet Vitebsk (figure 9). The Great Synagogue, built circa 1700 and rebuilt in 1900 following a fire that swept through the city center, dominated the western edge of central Grodno (figure 10), while a nearly 300-year-old wooden synagogue lay perched on the bluff across the river Niemen. Forty-one other synagogues and prayer houses also functioned during the 1930s (table 1).[33] A ritual bath house, kosher butcher shops, and extensive educational and social welfare institutions met Jewish communal needs.

The *kehilah*, dominated by local elites, administered and coordinated the community's functions. Funding came from taxes imposed primarily (but not exclusively) upon affluent Jewish families, with additional funding from Polish government subsidies and overseas organizations, such as the New York–based Fareynigtn Grodner hilfs

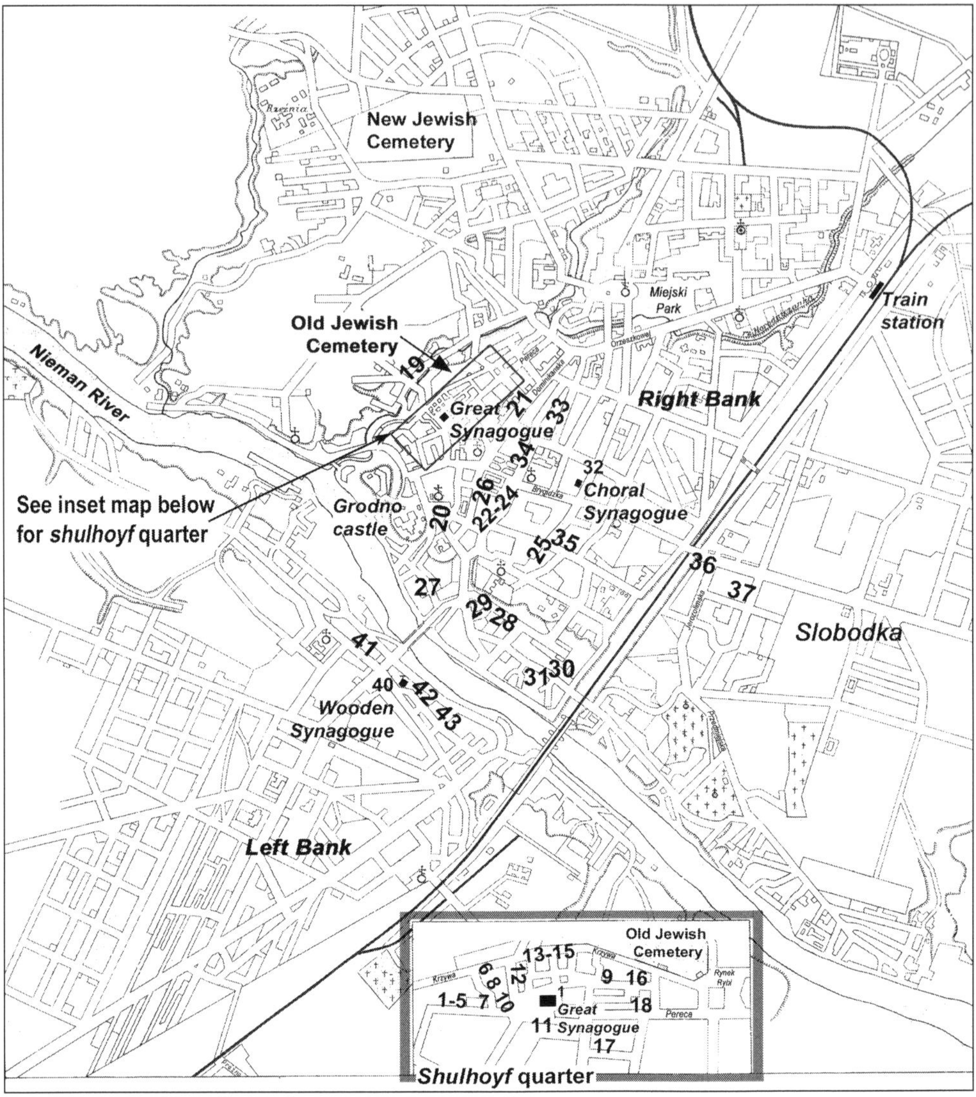

9. Map of Grodno, based on a historical map dated 1935. Numbered on the map are the forty-three synagogues and prayer houses dispersed throughout the multiethnic city (see table 1). The Jewish neighborhood known as the *shulhoyf* (synagogue courtyard) sited adjacent to the Great Synagogue formed part of the old city center. Dividing the city is the railroad line connecting Grodno to Białystok to the southwest and Vilna to the northeast. More affluent residents lived in the old city center or on its northern edge, whereas lower-income families lived across the railroad tracks in the Slobodka District or across the river on the left bank.

10. The Great Synagogue in Grodno, 2007, before the restoration of its facade. Seized by the Soviet government after the war, the synagogue was returned to the Grodno Jewish community in the early 1990s. Photograph by the author.

komitet (United Grodner Relief Committee). Other *landsmanshaftn* (immigrant aid) societies and individuals in Boston, Chicago, Detroit, Los Angeles, and Altoona, Pennsylvania, contributed as well.[34] The largest proportion of outside funding came from the American Jewish Joint Distribution Committee (JDC) and the London-based Federation of Jewish Relief Organizations.[35] Donors' earmarks and the *kehilah*'s own allocations reveal that about one-third of the external support went to the "Matzah Committee" to aid proper Passover observance. One-quarter to one-third of the funds passed to the local branch of the Towarzystwo Ochrony Zdrowia Ludności Żydowskej (TOZ, Society for Safeguarding the Health of the Jewish Population),[36] the orphanage,[37] schools, and like institutions that benefitted Grodno's Jewish children. The remainder supported the emergency-loan society, the Jewish hospital, the old-age home, the public kitchen, and other smaller societies. Such organizations reinforced community

Table 1
List of Synagogues and Jewish Houses of Prayer in Grodno, Mid-1930s*

1	Great Synagogue	16	Shomer Emunim	31	Weisbrem
2	Chevra Shas	17	Tailors’	32	Orach Chaim Choral Synagogue
3	Kirshner	18	Chayai Odom Hagodol		
4	Halvoyaz Hamei	19	Shulchan Aruch	33	Frumkin
5	Bais Hamedresh Hagadol	20	Leib-Arie	34	Kurlandzki
6	Klojz	21	Zakheim	35	Kulbacki
7	Chevra Mishnayot	22	Bregman	36	Slobodka
8	Chevra Thilim	23	Baalei-Agołot	37	Prudowski
9	Chevra Medrash	24	Rabonis	38	Grandzicki
10	Hasidim	25	Mordchelewicz	39	Hirshorn
11	Waserfirer	26	Glezer	40	Synagoga Wielka Wooden Synagogue
12	Kacowim	27	Eyn-Jakob		
13	Chayai Odom Hachodosh	28	Magid Mishne	41	Kneses Israel
14	Poale Zedek	29	Kaleckiego	42	Hayoshon-Hachodesh
15	Ałszych	30	Rabbi Eliyahu	43	Chayei-Odom

* Based on “Wykaz—Bóżnic na terenie Gminy Wyznaniowej Żydowskiej w Grodnie” [List—Synagogues within the Jewish Religious Community in Grodno], GERO, f. 56, op. 1, d. 82, l. 345 and 345 ob., GAGO (see abbreviations on p. 277).

identity in Grodno and stand in contrast to the Soviet Union’s state-sponsored institutions.

The economic depression hit the *kehilah* hard. Deep cuts in government subsidies for education and social welfare during the late 1930s added to their burdens. *Kehilah* priorities largely favored the sacred over the secular and the traditional over the institutional in shaping the future of Jewish youth. A *kehilah* special commission meeting in January 1933 cut the salaries of lower-paid administrative and maintenance staff as much as 50 percent; significantly, higher-paid rabbis and ritual slaughterers received cuts of only 20 to 30 percent.[38] Four years later, when the government slashed funding for Jewish schools by 50 percent, the *kehilah* cancelled the minimal financial support provided for sport clubs and Zionist organizations rather than raise tuition.[39] In the local *kehilah* elections in 1936, funding for youth- and child-oriented institutions and programs lay at the core of the campaign by the socialist Bund.[40] The Bund's full slate of candidates won a number of seats that year in Grodno, but they were still outnumbered more than two to one by a conservative coalition of religious Zionists.[41]

The *kehilah* did the best it could with limited resources. Abram Trop-Krinski, board chairman during most of the 1930s, exemplified its honorable aims. He practiced charity in his own profession as a pharmacist by providing medicine gratis when clients (Jews and Gentiles alike) could not afford to pay.[42] In determining priorities, the *kehilah* had to balance traditional religious institutions with schools and organizations. Although schools held their place, many groups that benefitted young people lost ground. The Jewish community leadership's decisions to cut the latter placed a wedge between them and the youth they claimed to represent.

Jewish Family and Religious Life

Bolshevik ideals infused the environment of Soviet Vitebsk. Industrial expansion prompted migration from shtetl to city. By comparison, Grodno stagnated, fostering a sense of continuity with prewar religious practice and stability in family life. Some families grew large in the gradual recovery after World War I. Josef and Sonia Muller had five children, including daughters Fenia and Mina.[43] Zelda Grodzienska was the youngest of seven children.[44] Berl and Golda Fomin had ten living children; three others had died in infancy.[45] Such large households often required two incomes. Zelda's parents worked together in their own tailoring business. Besides Berl Fomin's income from tailoring, Golda worked in Grodno's tobacco factory or carried baskets of fruit produce to market. Their older children cared for the younger ones.

The Fomin family lived in a small house without running water or electricity in the *shulhoyf* quarter; at least a couple children slept in each bed.[46] Their neighbors included Lev Zhubov's family, which numbered five boys and three girls. "The sun seldom shone in our tiny slanted house, just like all rooms on our street," young Zhubov wrote in his YIVO autobiography: "No garden surrounded our house, and grass barely sprouted from the earth in summer."[47]

The worldwide financial collapse worsened the already insecure economic environment in the Kresy. Abram Kremer had a shop selling stationary that went out of business. But he continued to work with paper—hanging it in other people's homes. Wallpapering and painting work was seasonal, however, and at times insufficient to support his family of seven. The family had to move from a two-bedroom apartment on the edges of the Slobodka District to a smaller one in the even poorer neighborhood across the Niemen. Abram's wife, Ida, did not want people outside the family to know how little food they had. Their eldest son, Moishe, born in 1918, remembered "going to school hungry and coming back to nothing." Yet even in hard times, Ida labored to prepare a proper Shabbes meal. Moishe appreciated his mother for how hard she struggled, facing adversity with a proud face.[48]

As in Vitebsk, extended families shared homes. Whereas the housing shortage made such sharing increasingly necessary in the Soviet city, families in Grodno continued to do so because it was customary. Sidney Sisun, born in 1924, grew up in a five-apartment residence, each housing an uncle or aunt.[49] Vichna Sidranska, born in 1927, also lived in a five-apartment house, owned by her maternal grandmother.[50] Feliks Zandman, also born in 1927, was raised in a building at 28 Brygidzka Street near the city center, which housed his mother's extended family on the upper floors. Feliks's maternal grandfather, Nahum Freydowicz, operated his building-supply company on the ground floor.[51] Ephraim and Anya Ilin and their daughter Bella (born in January 1937) shared a house of two floors with Anya's sister and her family upstairs.[52]

We have seen that in Vitebsk the early death of fathers pushed mothers into the workforce. The same was true in Grodno. Sima Kapulska's father died when she was only eight months old, and her mother, Rokhl, labored to hold her family together by engaging them all in a dressmaking business. "Never will I give my children to an orphanage," Sima remembered her mother saying.[53] Yehuda Rabinovich's mother also supported her three children by dressmaking, but not because of death; her ex-husband never gave her child support.[54] Circumstances forced other mothers to leave their children in the Jewish Orphan Asylum. "Hanan L." wrote in his YIVO autobiography how his mother placed him in the orphanage in 1921 after the death of his father and uncle. "On a cold winter evening . . . she told me that I would not live in our pitiable little room, but in a great house," he wrote. After meeting the chief nurse at the orphanage, Hanan's mother kissed him good-bye and disappeared.[55] She seems to have had only intermittent contact with him thereafter, but the boy thrived at the children's home, making friends and receiving a good education.

Circumstances also forced fathers to give up children after their mother's death. Yankl's mother died soon after the family settled in Grodno, and his father could not cope with raising the five-year-old boy and an even younger daughter. Although the children lived in the Jewish Orphan Asylum, their father took them to local orchards and parks on Sundays. Yankl remained there until 1934, when he turned eighteen and entered the locksmith trade. He commented in his YIVO autobiographical essay that his father's visits had "such a great significance for my subsequent development and future."[56]

No matter the upheavals, religious life remained a constant in Grodno. Most families observant to a greater or lesser degree belonged to a synagogue close to home or to a congregation composed of particular tradesmen. Religious life and family life were more closely intertwined in Grodno than in Vitebsk. Leib Reizer, born in 1910, recollected in a memoir the preparations for Shabbes: pump a jug of water, polish his father's shoes, wrap up the *cholent* to take to the baker, and set out the candles.[57] Dressed for *shul* (synagogue), the family would walk over the cobblestone pavements to the butchers' synagogue Zivhei Tsedek, seeing candles lit for Shabbes in other homes they passed.[58] Gender and generational differences also delineated religious observance. Chasia Bielicka's father attended synagogue on Friday evening, and her mother blessed the candles at home.[59] Bella

Ilin, born 1937, retained dim childhood memories of her paternal grandfather Zachariah as "a sort of traditional Jewish man with a beard." She would watch him pray with tefillin. Younger generations dropped some of these practices. Bella's father, Ephraim, for example, observed the holidays but did not engage in daily prayers.[60]

Education and Employment

After World War I, Jewish elementary education in both Vitebsk and Grodno moved beyond traditional *khedarim*. Although Marxism and Bolshevism shaped the ideological core of Soviet pedagogy, a spectrum of socialist and Zionist ideologies formed the foundation of Poland's private Jewish schools.[61] About 80 percent of young Jews across Poland attended state-run, Polish-language public schools.[62] The figure for Grodno appears to be smaller, with perhaps 50 percent enrolled.[63] Jewish elementary schools (first through sixth or seventh class levels) supported Jewish identity, although the instruction language (Yiddish, Hebrew, or Polish) sometimes varied from course to course.[64] State certification required Polish in the gymnasium (academic high school, composed of class levels 7 through 10) and lyceum (levels 11 and 12). Less than half of the Jewish children in Grodno went beyond elementary school, either because parents could not afford their children's tuition or because additional labor income from the children was necessary to support the family. Elka Fomin's siblings, for example, worked instead of continuing school.[65]

Private Jewish elementary schools in Grodno shaped key linguistic, political, and social identities among their students. The Yavneh school, which Leib Bialo, his sister Miriam, and brother Shloyme, attended,[66] was part of an education network established by the Orthodox Zionist Mizrahi organization. Yavneh taught lessons in Polish to receive government certification but also offered students Hebrew-language instruction. Other schools maintained secular approaches to Jewish identity. Yehuda Rabinovich attended the socialist-leaning Tsentrale yidishe shul-organizatsie (Central Jewish School Organization) school, where classes were taught in Yiddish.[67]

Despite the emphasis on Hebrew and Yiddish, private and public schools also served as instruments of language assimilation as students were increasingly taught in Polish. Lev Zhubov wrote about an unwelcome encounter with Polish at the Talmud Torah, when his mathematics teacher switched instruction to that language and even reprimanded students who responded in Yiddish to questions posed in Polish. Yet this approach forced Zhubov to practice Polish and eventually learn it.[68] Given such trends, some parents felt the need to reinforce Jewish language identity. Zelda Grodzienska's parents made sure she learned Yiddish and Hebrew because she learned Polish at her public school.[69]

The most popular Jewish schools were the Tarbut and Talmud Torah. Tarbut, which one in three Jewish children in Grodno attended in 1927, operated two kindergartens, an elementary school, a gymnasium, and a teacher's seminary, all with Hebrew as their primary instruction language.[70] In his memoirs, Feliks Zandman called the Tarbut "a place for intellect and rigor."[71] Tarbut educators based lesson plans on children's developmental growth, with hands-on experimentation, physical activities, and excursions to supplement classroom teaching.[72] Like the Yiddish education system across the border in the Soviet Union, Jewish schools in Grodno served a larger ideological goal. Tarbut instilled Zionist ideals for founding a Jewish state. Hanan studied at the Tarbut school after attending the Talmud Torah. Besides a new language, this school meant new friends, new teachers, and a new ideology. He became, in his own words, "a dedicated Zionist and patriot for the fatherland."[73]

Tarbut charged a high tuition that many families could ill afford. The Talmud Torah, located at the north end of the *shulhoyf* quarter, provided an elementary-school education to students from the opposite end of the economic spectrum. Unlike some schools, Talmud Torah engaged teachers with diverse political beliefs, from Polish-speaking "assimilationists" to Bundists and Zionists.[74] Except for the Polish language and literature courses and courses such as geography and mathematics, most classes were in Yiddish. Sidney Sisun also remembered a Hebrew-language curriculum of Jewish history, Khumesh, and Tanakh.[75]

Many former Talmud Torah students recalled an education infused with imagination and exploration, in contrast to the rigors of Tarbut. Sima Kapulska took part in a school play in which she wore a feathered Indian headdress.[76] Some teachers made lasting impressions on their students. Lev Zhubov praised Fraylin (Miss) Zaks because she was "interested in the child's life in the home."[77] Moishe Kremer, speaking some six decades later, used nearly the same words to describe his Talmud Torah instructors: "They took an interest in every child's life."[78] In Zhubov's view, Miss Zaks sought to understand her students by asking them to write about their joys, sorrows, and perceptions of injustice. The boy dubbed "Yankl" here, a few years older than Zhubov, also spoke highly of Miss Zaks. He wrote that another teacher, a Mr. Abramski, alternated Hebrew prayer lessons with an activity much more interesting to his students. He did not simply read the newspaper or scary folk tales aloud but performed them.[79]

Lev Zhubov attended the Talmud Torah because his mother, barely literate, sought the best education for her sons that she could afford. She even cleaned chickens to pay the tuition.[80] Some parents may not have been motivated by the promise of future opportunities. Concerned for their children's safety, parents chose private Jewish school to protect them from possible harassment by Gentiles. Newspaper accounts, contemporary youth autobiographies, and Holocaust survivor testimonies (even those written by individuals who were mere children in the 1930s) reflect the "us and them" society in Grodno, providing support for this contention. But economic reversals forced parents to move their children to public, state-run schools, which were perceived as a social step downward. Fenia, Bluma, and Mina Muller stopped attending the Tarbut school—which Fenia described much later as "for the upper-class Jewish children"[81]—after their father's wood and coal business encountered problems. Such decisions were determined by gender as well as by economics. The Muller girls attended a public school, while their brothers Velvl and Dovid continued to go to Tarbut.[82] Chasia Bielicka, born 1921, was also removed from Tarbut owing to her family's financial difficulties, but her brother Avramele was not.[83]

In interviews recorded in the 1990s, neither Mina nor Fenia Muller discussed public-school life, perhaps because it marked a transition from their Jewish world to one dominated by Gentiles. The linguist and YIVO research director Max Weinreich wrote about this experience in *Der veg tsu undzer yugnt* (The Way to Our Youth, 1935), his study of submissions from the YIVO youth essay contests in 1932 and 1934. Weinreich observed that upon entering public school, "the Jewish child discovers that which they [*sic*] previously knew only quite vaguely: that the larger community is in . . . conflict with their community."[84] Alexandre Blumstein, born in 1930 to Dr. Chaim and Estera Blumstein, trotted off enthusiastically in a white shirt and red tie for his first day at the Eliza Orzeszkowa School.[85] He learned a new word during recess that day. "What is a 'kike'?" little Alexandre, the only Jew in a class of twenty-five, asked his parents upon his return home.[86]

Many public-school alumni in Grodno studied primarily with other Jews. Vichna Sidranska even learned Jewish history and Hebrew prayers at her public school.[87] And young Jews who went to school mostly with Gentiles did not necessarily experience a complete detachment from their heritage. After attending a Polish-language public school, Ann Lewin entered an unnamed "selective" gymnasium because her father, a local wood and coal supplier, could afford the tuition. One of only five Jewish girls in her class, she received religious instruction from a rabbi. During morning Christian prayers, however, Ann and her Jewish classmates had to stand and listen.[88] Alexandre Blumstein had a similar experience in school, which he described as a "daily reminder that I was different than others."[89]

The generation that went to school during the interwar period in Poland had greater educational opportunities than their parents, inspiring young people's desire to overcome problems in the world around them.[90] This was unfortunate because young Jews of eastern Polish cities such as Grodno faced limited economic opportunities no matter their primary-school education. A young woman named Hannah told as much in a handwritten article for her Zionist youth-group newspaper. "When I was small, I thought that as soon as I had finished high school, I would be able to do everything and that nobody could forbid me anything." But as graduation approached, she realized that such notions were foolish. Young law and engineering graduates could not find work because they were Jews, and medical students worked in shops owned by their parents.[91]

Whereas the Soviet system offered young Jews many opportunities for education and employment, their counterparts in Polish Grodno were not so fortunate. The path to secondary-school education, for example, was often restricted. Chasia Bielicka remembered that an informal *numerus clauses* limiting Jewish enrollment was practiced in some Grodno gymnasia.[92] With few institutions of higher education in the region, a university degree necessitated relocating to Warsaw or Vilna, although the establishment of "ghetto benches" in 1937 to segregate Jewish students made studying abroad preferable to those who could afford it. Some had done so before the imposition of restrictions in the 1930s. Aaron Zandman, Feliks's father, had gone to Vienna to earn a PhD in chemistry in the early 1920s. Yet few with an advanced degree, like Dr. Zandman, found appropriate employment back home.[93] Not everyone despaired for the future. Alexandre Blumstein's parents sent him to a well-regarded private Polish-language elementary school as the first step to a state gymnasium and, they hoped, a Polish university.[94] Leib Bialo's older sister Miriam was sent to study in Vilna. "She had the brains for it," he recalled. Such cases were rare. Leib and his brother Shloyme finished only six years of school before they went to work in the family business.[95]

After elementary education, many Jewish youth entered a vocational or technical school rather than a gymnasium. With high unemployment, practical education would augment their chances upon graduation. Skills in a trade were also portable; young people could take them abroad should they emigrate. The local JDC-subsidized ORT trade school (Obshchestvo remeslennago i zemledelecheskago truda sredi Yeveev v Rossii; Society for Handicraft and Agricultural Work among the Jews of Russia) provided mathematics and practical mechanics courses in addition to vocational training set up along gender lines.[96] Young women learned seamstress work, and young men trained to be locksmiths and furniture makers.[97] Tarbut ran a smaller program to teach typesetting and printing.[98] Yehuda Rabinovich learned to be a fitter and lathe worker. Graduating from the craftsmen school in June 1939,[99] he subsequently got a job several hundred kilometers from Grodno.[100] Fenia Muller studied bookkeeping with the intention to work in an office.[101] Sidney Sisun trained as a tailor's apprentice because his mother did not want him to be a kosher butcher like his father.[102] But when these people sought to enter a trade in Grodno, the preferential hiring practices of both Jewish and Polish entrepreneurs meant they competed primarily with fellow Jews. In 1938, for example, 322 of the 364 tailors in the city were Jews, as were most of the cobblers, metal workers, and carpenters.[103] Government-subsidized Polish-owned shops worsened the situation. As Moishe Kremer recalled, "We were pushed in a corner; we didn't have what to look forward to."[104]

Emigration

The politically oppressive and economically limited environment within Poland prompted some Jews to consider emigration. For most, their goal was to reach Palestine, the United States, or South America. Immigration quotas in these receiving countries kept many from pursuing this option, however. Although many of Moishe Kremer's cousins had escaped to Argentina and America during the 1930s, this opportunity eluded his financially strained immediate family. "Everybody was looking for a way to get out," he remembered, "but the problem was money, and the problem was visas."[105] Kremer was right. Even with the will and money to emigrate, international politics prevented Jews from entering another country.

Just as governments in the Americas limited immigration, so too did British officials in the mandate territory of Palestine. From a peak of 30,593 Jewish emigrants from Poland to Palestine in 1935, the total dropped by more than half the next year and fell below 4,500 in succeeding years through 1939.[106] British intransigence was one issue; tensions in Palestine another. Sporadic news stories in 1933 reported on Jewish settlers' fears of Arab uprisings.[107] Their trepidations materialized a few years later with the revolt of 1936. "We fretted over every report from Palestine about the 'disturbances,'" Chasia Bielicka recalled of her Hashomer Hatzair (Young Guard) group's concerns.[108] Nevertheless, not all Grodno Jews extolled the virtues of Palestine. "Barren desert broken by malarial swamps, impoverished villages, and struggling farm communities" was the attitude that Feliks Zandman recalled hearing from some.[109] All the same, many Zionists were swept up by the exciting prospects of a Jewish state.

Some of those who had the opportunity to emigrate chose not to do so. The Mullers had relatives in America who would have aided with immigration documents. Josef Muller decided to stay, however. "We didn't think of the consequences," recalled his daughter Mina.[110] The Bialos actually had visas in hand in late 1938, but Samuel Bialo, who had two sisters in the United States, did not want to go. After all, the elder Bialo told his son Leo, hadn't Jews survived the pogroms, wars, and revolutions of the previous fifty years?[111]

The growing threat of German aggression prompted relatively few to accelerate their emigration plans. Grodno newspapers, supplemented by the Warsaw press, kept readers informed about Nazi persecution of German Jews. As in the Soviet Yiddish press, the events of Kristallnacht in November 1938 took prominence in papers such as the *Grodner lebn* (Grodno Life).[112] Yet competing for space in such papers was news of the indecision emanating from the British government's Woodhead Commission. Charged with finding a solution to the partition of Palestine, commission members threw up their hands in the effort to reconcile Jewish and Arab interests.[113] The attention paid to both issues reveals the deep concerns Jews held about circumstances outside Polish borders shaping their destiny. Some witnesses remember well their awareness of the dangers posed by Nazi Germany. "I was very much interested in politics, international politics," Moishe Kremer recalled, "and I read the paper every day, starting, I think, when I was seven or eight years old."[114] Fenia Muller recalled how she was told that the Nazis "were very bad with the Jews."[115] She also knew about the plight of German Jews seeking to emigrate.

Few considered immigration to the Soviet Union. Most Jews in Poland understood that the Soviet border was effectively closed to them during the 1930s because they were no longer able to visit relatives who lived there.[116] Yet some active Communists tried. *Grodner moment* (Grodno Moment) reported in 1933 on five Jewish and two Gentile craftsmen who traveled to the Soviet Union in search of work.[117] Their fate is unknown, but as we have seen, anyone of Polish origin was suspect in the eyes of the Soviets.

Youth Groups and Social Engagement

Whether Bundist or Zionist, political or religious, or simply focused on a particular pursuit such as athletics, youth groups gave young Jews in Poland relief from the pressures of daily life. Those groups with a strong ideological focus offered a path forward from the bleak economic and political outlook in Grodno in the 1930s. Most organizations emulated a parent organization, although others were not affiliated with a political party. According to the historian Yisrael Gutman, "political parties and public figures"—that is, the adult world—did not hold "these young people in high regard" and had no "use for them whatsoever" during the interwar period.[118] These circumstances freed youth groups from adult scrutiny, permitting them greater freedom to pursue their own interests and activities.

Hashomer Hatzair, which counted about 500 Grodno members ages twelve to twenty in 1939,[119] trained its youth for *hakhshore*, agricultural work in preparation for immigration to Palestine. Hehalutz (Pioneer) had similar goals. Bnei Akiva (Children of Akiva) fused religious study with socialist dreams of a Jewish state. Betar, founded by right-wing Revisionist Zionist leader Vladimir (Za'ev) Jabotinsky in 1923, engaged in paramilitary training for Jewish defense.[120] Sport clubs, to strengthen the minds and bodies of Jewish youth, operated as adjuncts: Shomeriyah of Hashomer Hatzair, Maccabi of Agudath, and Morgenshtern of the Bund.[121]

Despite the groups' ideological foundations, young people joined particular groups for personal reasons.[122] One example is Batya (we don't know her last name), a girl who joined an organization to assuage her teen angst. In a diary entry that she later transcribed for the group's newspaper, Batya confided, "I want to live for something, for somebody. I want to feel that I am needed." Her life changed after attending a meeting of Bnei Akiva, a religious Zionist youth organization. "A week ago I joined an organization. Different people come here, people I don't know, who talk about a homeland for Jews." Batya responded as much to the immediacy of interaction with her peers as to the long-term hope for a Jewish homeland. "I am surrounded by people who understand me. I am no longer alone."[123]

Purpose for Batya meant social engagement and comradeship. Some looked around for the right fit. Feliks Zandman initially wanted to join Betar because he liked its uniforms. Far from a trivial motive, this preference revealed his desire to fit visually into a strong Jewish vanguard. Yet he didn't join Betar because his father, Aaron, a Zionist socialist, objected to the group's unilateral approach to the formation of a Jewish state. What of the rights of the Arabs in Palestine? the elder Zandman questioned. So Feliks continued his search. He tried Hashomer Hatzair, but he rejected the group leaders' attempts to give him a new Hebrew name. "The guy didn't like my name," Zandman later wrote, "so he tried to get rid of it, my perfectly good Hebrew name, Shrage Feliks. Shmuck, I thought."[124] Like Batya, he found a happy compromise in Akiva.

In remembering their affiliations sixty years later, other witnesses speak of a group's politics tempered by their personal feelings. Leib Bialo was drawn to Betar's promise of empowerment. "We had meetings; we played soldiers," Leib recalled. "The organization [wanted] to take Israel by force."[125] Fenia and Mina Muller sought the promise offered by Hashomer Hatzair because it trained members for aliyah, immigration to Palestine.[126] Bronia Winicka joined the more egalitarian Hehalutz, finding it to be less "exclusive" than some other Zionist organizations "for the rich."[127]

Some young people sought engagement with the surrounding community. Lev Zhubov joined his third-level classmates in the Bund's organization for children, Sotsialistisher kinder-farband (SKIF), and later he moved on to the same party's league Tsukunft for adolescents.

Yet he had a greater affinity with an afternoon reading club arranged by his Talmud Torah teacher, Miss Zaks. This led to a unique form of group engagement. On one occasion, she invited a representative from YIVO to discuss the institute's activities to encourage young people to become a *zamler* (collector) of social history. His appetite whetted, Zhubov volunteered to transcribe stories he heard older Jews tell around the *shulhoyf* and to form a *zamler* group in school.[128] Such undertakings enhanced his literary gifts, apparent in his entry to the YIVO essay contest.

The personal on occasion overtook the political even in the most ideologically driven youth. Hanan joined Hashomer Hatzair in the early 1930s, but he came to the conclusion that the group was out of step with the economic troubles of the times. "The illusions and fantasies in which they wrap themselves," wrote Hanan in his YIVO essay, "while here I see thousands of miserable unemployed on every stoop." Yet he stayed because of the affection he felt for a young woman in the group. "I often blushed. She used to throw a glance at me, as [if] she understood that I was powerless." He abandoned Hashomer for a socialist organization when the girl emigrated from Poland.[129]

These examples demonstrate the role of social connections in fostering group development. Batya found a friendly crowd. Feliks fled a group whose leader he detested. Leib Bialo felt empowered. The Muller girls, lacking the Tarbut education given to their brothers, looked out for their futures. Lev Zhubov discovered his neighbors' stories and shared them with other *zamlers*. Hanan found love.

In their search for welcoming peers, many young people drifted from one group to another. "One comes to [a youth group] as to a station, as one waits for a train with suitcase in hand," Max Weinreich quoted one youth who left the Bund for a Zionist group.[130] The ideological leap from Bundism to Zionism was like the choice of taking one train or another. Although for most rank-and-file members ideology mattered less than personal satisfaction, each group's leaders held ideology paramount. They understood the importance of building and maintaining the group's numbers. To do so, they and group organizers stole members from their rivals. In an anonymous letter from

1938 to the editor of the Bund's paper *Grodner shtime* (Grodno Voice), a former Frayhayt member complained that Hehalutz leaders not only pilfered members from his group but disparaged the socialist ideology of Poalei Tsiyon (Workers of Zion).[131] Conflict also served a social function to engage and bond members. Chasia Bielicka reported an ongoing feud between Betar and Hashomer Hatzair, beginning with the former stealing the Hashomer flag from camp and culminating with Betar members ransacking their rival's meeting rooms.[132]

Youth groups, regardless of ideology or rivalries, shared many activities in common, including after-school and evening pursuits in the city and camping in Grodno's surrounding forests. Team sports such as soccer, basketball, and volleyball built ties of interdependence as young people gathered and competed. For those who could afford the time and expense, recreation was becoming a value of everyday life. Jewish youth organizations contributed to this trend, carving out social space in and around Grodno, apart from Polish authorities or even their own parents.

Many adult and youth groups in Grodno shared the Zionist House (sometimes called the Movement House) at Witoldowa 44, its large meeting room lined with dark drapes and pictures of famous Zionists. The building became a special gathering point for young Jews engaged with Zionism.[133] Mina Muller described the Zionist House as "a beautiful place that we used to gather [for Hashomer meetings] in the evening . . . dancing and singing and celebrating each holiday."[134] The forests and countryside surrounding Grodno offered a further degree of isolation from the problems of daily life. In their YIVO essays, Hanan and Yankl reported on attending camps for orphan children in the nearby spa town Druskeniki, where they made new friends, heard educational lectures, and spent song-filled evenings by the campfire.[135]

Ideology structured Jewish youth groups, while personal feelings motivated individuals to maintain their connections to these organizations. When we examine the activity of young Jews entrapped during the Holocaust, a key point that emerges among Polish Jews is a culture of interdependence. Group divisions remained significant, obstructing cooperation across ideological divides. The essential point, however, is that adolescents learned to look to each other for support, a pattern they followed in the coming years.

Grodno Pogrom

The violence of the Grodno pogrom in June 1935 added urgency to youth-movement activities. "People started to get more organized," recalled Moishe Kremer.[136] Some joined sports organizations for improved physical fitness. Plans for emigration took on added urgency. "The ones who could afford started seriously to prepare themselves to emigrate," Moishe also remembered, and to head "either to [Palestine] or to Latin American countries . . . or to the United States."[137]

The pogrom added terror to the atmosphere of exclusion and hopelessness experienced by Grodno's Jewish community. Many secondary sources provide fragmentary data on the timeline of events. Grodno's Polish-language newspaper *Kurier Grodzieński* (Grodno Courier) delineated the sequence of stages even as its editors downplayed the pogrom's scope. Local Yiddish newspapers from June 1935 appear not to have survived, but a full-page overview was published in the American newspaper *Forverts* (Forward, New York). Numerous eyewitnesses also provide their viewpoints on the nighttime attack, with most recounting their experiences decades later.[138] The initial trigger for the pogrom was a knife fight, reported in *Kurier Grodzieński* for Thursday, 6 June 1935:

> Last night at 1:00, a bloody row took place on Brygidzka Street. Twenty-two-year-old Władysław Kuszcz of Brygidzka Street 10 and two persons of Jewish faith with names still not identified started to quarrel over a personal matter. At some point, one of them stabbed Kuszcz in the back with a knife. They then escaped. Kuszcz, in very severe condition, was brought to hospital, where he died after a few hours of suffering.[139]

This initial attack occurred after a less-violent encounter between Poles and Jews the evening before, when a young Jewish man danced with a Gentile woman at a Jewish-owned dance hall or dancing school.[140] Whether this was the cause of the fight on Brygidzka Street is unclear, but words escalated to a fistfight outside the same dance hall. One Jewish youth, Meilach Kantorowski, pulled a knife and stabbed Władysław Kuszcz, a young Polish navy veteran. Police soon identified and arrested the knife-wielding youth along with an accomplice, Shmuel Shneider.[141]

This incident transpired at a particularly sensitive moment when antisemites felt less restrained. Less than three weeks earlier, on 12 May 1935, the nation's de facto dictator, Marshal Piłsudski, had died. Grodno Jews spoke decades later of Piłsudski with affection. "Poles thought that he was our grandfather," recalled Mina Muller.[142] The marshal had kept in check the most extreme antisemites among the Polish political elites. With his death, Polish nationalists sought to escalate anti-Jewish rhetoric and action.[143] The antisemitic Endecja (National Democracy) Party, for example, began to advocate violence to spur Jewish emigration.[144] Another faction was the Camp of National Unity, known better by the acronym OZON for its Polish name Obóz Zjednoczenia Narodowego. OZON sought to capitalize on antisemitic attitudes and policies emergent in Polish politics.

These developments among political elites unfolded over time. OZON did not form until 1937. The events in Grodno were guided by people from the opposite end of the social spectrum. They also marked the first large-scale pogrom against Jews in the country in many years. Tensions escalated suddenly at Kuszcz's funeral on Friday, 7 June. A representative of the county governor, quoted in *Kurier Grodzieński*, commented that many local residents were in attendance.[145] *Forverts* (New York) later put the figure at 1,000, some of them described as petty criminals.[146] The county governor's representative echoed this assessment when he referred to the participants in the violence as "groups of social scum."[147] *Forverts* also reported that many other people from outside Grodno were present at the cemetery east of the city, possibly Polish settler farmers or Belarusian peasants. City authorities were certainly aware of the dangerous atmosphere because the police posted eleven uniformed and undercover officers among the mourners.[148]

Calls for revenge swelled throughout that Friday afternoon as pogromists prepared. Minor scuffles occurred throughout the city. One Jew, twenty-nine-year-old Hirsh Atlas, was pricked in the back with a knife on Brygidzka Street, not far from the site of the original attack.[149] Sundown brought the Jewish holiday of Shavuot. Many Jews were at home preparing for Shabbes, while others were still out shopping for the holiday or enjoying the late spring evening.

Around 7:30 p.m., with twilight two hours away, a gang numbering at least 100 stormed out of the Christian cemetery on Przedmiejska Street and headed up Jerozolimska Street. They fanned westward across central Grodno, attacking Jews in the streets, breaking into Jewish shops and stealing merchandise, and smashing the windows of Jews' homes.[150] Moishe Kremer recalled that the rioters had a ready supply of cobblestones from sewer work in the city center.[151] The mob, mostly adult males, expanded in composition to include young people and women. *Forverts* reported that youths and prostitutes in addition to the core group of criminal thugs and right-wing nationalists joined the rolling mêlée.[152]

Many accounts assert that police were nowhere to be found, and military men from the town's garrison refused to intervene. When the *kehilah* chairman, Abram Trop-Krinski, telephoned the county governor pleading for action to quell the growing unrest, the latter shrieked, "You presume to meddle in my affairs!"[153] Daniel Klovsky, however, specifically remembered that police protected property in the city center belonging to wealthier Jews.[154] Only much later, after two in the morning, did police reappear in force.[155]

Not all Poles in Grodno turned to violence against their Jewish neighbors. According to Leib Bialo, participants included "the ones who had a grudge, the ones who didn't like us."[156] Many later reported rescue and protection by their Gentile neighbors. As the pogrom began, Daniel Klovsky's father, David, sought assistance from a Polish coach driver, who took Daniel safely home.[157] Fenia and Mina Muller recalled that many of their father's employees lived nearby and guarded their house.[158] Polish neighbors also protected Ann Lewin's family.[159]

11. Storefront window shattered in the Grodno pogrom, June 1935. Photographer unknown. Photograph used by permission of the American Jewish Joint Distribution Committee Archives, New York, reference number NY_01839.

Forverts reported that the Kantor family received refuge from a Polish officer next door while "hooligans" vandalized their rooms.[160]

Broken glass was a common spectacle, such as the shattered storefront shown in figure 11. In her diary, Batya obsessed about "glass, glass, glass everywhere," in and around Jewish-owned homes, while the "wind blew through empty window frames." She also reported the spreading sense of trauma communicated by telephone. "It's bad over here, it's bad everywhere," was one neighbor's message.[161] Even sixty years later, Fenia Muller remembered the experience as both immediate and fragmentary as attackers came in waves for hours and hours.[162] The fear lasted into the night. Batya, her frequent melodramatics not out of place here, wrote in her diary, "Not one Jew out of 20,000 is sleeping."[163]

With little visible police protection, Jews defended themselves as best they could. Workers were among the first to respond. Lev Zhubov reported that the attackers spared only the *shulhoyf* quarter, where many burly Jewish manual laborers and blacksmiths stood outside their homes as a deterrent.[164] A hastily arranged meeting in Zionist House in the city center organized a defense force.[165] One group of youths was given the job of making street-by-street observations and relaying information back by telephone or runner. Communist Party members, their organization officially banned in Poland, reportedly mobilized 200 people to patrol the streets.[166] Although some urban Communists were Jews, many Gentiles may have aided in this response because 90 percent of party membership in the city's outlying regions were composed of Belarusians and Poles.[167] Members of some of Grodno's Jewish youth organizations were not in the city at the time. The Maccabi sports club was in Białystok for a match, and other groups were encamped in the forests surrounding Grodno.[168]

Most reports listed at least forty persons injured during the pogrom.[169] *Forverts* reported that two Jews, Gedaliah Becher and Israel Berezowski, had died by the end of June.[170] A third unnamed Jew was killed on the street seventeen days after the pogrom.[171] *Kurier Grodzieński* reported that the damage to 280 shopkeepers' and homeowners' property amounted to 1,000 zlotys or more in many individual cases.[172] Much later the county distributed a meager 1,000 zlotys to be divided among all injured parties.[173]

Some personal losses resonated long after the violence. Shlomo Pozniak and his family faced eviction from their apartment when he couldn't afford to pay his hospital bill. Leib Buchinski was sent to Warsaw for treatment but lost his hand anyway.[174] Leib Shapiro was also hospitalized in Warsaw. He was unable to work for a year, so his wife sought assistance from Mrs. Lipke Lipof, a relative in America who served on the board of United Grodner Relief. Mrs. Lipof sent $10 to Leib Shapiro on at least two occasions, May 1936 and February 1937, via the relief organization.[175] By April 1938, however, Leib Shapiro had died.[176]

Trauma marked young and old. Immediately after the pogrom, Lev Zhubov wrote that "Jews were afraid to go outside."[177] The fourteen-year-old son of the Kantor family suffered a nervous collapse after the vandalism to their home.[178] Mina Muller faced the realization that "I'm different than anyone else."[179] Sima Kapulska, sixteen years old in 1935, remembered that the pogrom was the first time she shook and trembled with fear.[180]

Shaping Identity

Compared to their coreligionists in Soviet Vitebsk, the Jews of Polish Grodno were far less integrated into the local social and political environment. Although they shared the Yiddish language with many Vitebsk Jews, and many in Grodno often spoke Polish as well, they seldom replaced the former with the latter, as Vitebsk Jews replaced Yiddish with Russian and Belarusian under Soviet nationalities policies. Grodno Jews also learned Hebrew in the synagogue, at school, or with a youth group. Judaism meant different things to grandparents, parents, and children, but religious observance nevertheless remained strong among all. Intermarriage with Gentiles occurred much less frequently than in Soviet Vitebsk. Jewish children might play with Gentiles, but such contacts diminished if children attended the privately run Jewish schools that most parents preferred or if they enrolled in a public school designated for Jews. During their adolescent years, their connections with Gentiles grew more distant as each group engaged in ethnically separate youth activities. Oppressive state policies and violence by local troublemakers tested relations with Gentiles.

Jewish youth in Vitebsk received considerable exposure to Belarusian and Russian cultural identities, and they incorporated them accordingly into their own. A Jew's place in Grodno did not allow for the same social intimacy. Children and young adults learned the Polish language and Polish history in school, but their sense of Polish citizenship was ill developed. During the 1930s, nationalist political parties excluded Jews from the domestic community and sought to make the exclusion legal. Then, too, Polish identity was fused with religion because to be Polish was synonymous with being Roman Catholic. "A Jew could not say the words 'I am a Pole' because that would be the same thing as saying 'I am a Catholic,'" Feliks Zandman recalled decades later.[181] Yet some Jews extolled Polish patriotism. Chaim Blumstein, born 1886, chose Poland over revolutionary Ukraine, believing that the reborn democratic state would be a haven for Jews. He became a prominent *kehilah* council member and physician in Grodno, and he operated a spa hotel in the resort area of Druskeniki, 30 kilometers from Grodno on the Lithuanian border. But his nationalism could not weather oppression and violence. "It took a lot to convert father from a Polish patriot to a Zionist," Alexandre Blumstein wrote decades later, "but in the end he could no longer swallow the sordid antisemitism of this new country in which Jews were blamed for every misdeed under the sun." By the late 1930s, the elder Blumstein wanted nothing more than to go to Palestine.[182] Children growing up in the 1920s and 1930s felt just as uncomfortable in the Polish state. When Hanan wrote about becoming "a dedicated Zionist and patriot for the fatherland" (that is, before he became a dedicated socialist), of which fatherland was he speaking: Poland or Palestine?

Violence and prejudice also shaped young people's lives. Following the Grodno pogrom, anti-Jewish violence swept through other Polish towns during 1936 and 1937.[183] It recurred in Grodno well. The TOZ office was bombed in late 1936.[184] The attack occurred in a climate of escalating anti-Jewish postures by the state and nationalist political parties, including increased economic marginalization of Poland's Jews and a ban on kosher slaughtering.[185] The latter was first proposed in the Polish parliament, the Sejm, at the end of 1936, ostensibly to prevent animal cruelty but really in an effort to push Jews out of the cattle trade. The ban interrupted the supply of kosher meat until amended in January 1937 to permit the practice wherever Jews composed at least 3 percent of the population.[186]

Perspectives and relationships shifted again in late 1938 and 1939 as tensions increased in Europe. Yisrael Gutman notes the "movement toward reconciliation between Poles and Jews as they perceived the common enemy."[187] A series of stories ran in the Grodno press highlighting the role of Jews in Poland's independence and national defense.[188] The summer of 1939 brought reports of the Grodno Jewish community's contributions to the nationwide subscription drive for airplanes and air defense,[189] and the *kehilah* stepped in when subscriptions fell 20,000 zlotys short.[190] "We all are loyal Polish citizens, and we all need to carry the burden of protecting the state," remarked Bundist board member Benjamin Yelin.[191] One measure of the extraordinary situation in August 1939 is that the Bundists argued for patriotism, whereas religious conservatives on the council resented channeling money away from the needy.[192] Jewish youth also gave to military funding drives, with nearly 2,800 zlotys collected at public schools and more than 3,100 zlotys at private schools and vocational institutes.[193] Young men such as Leib Bialo contributed in another way, watching for German reconnaissance planes and spies along the Polish–East Prussian border.[194]

The tensions young Jews lived with were accentuated by a Jewish community fractured by deep ideological divisions. In Feliks Zandman's family, his father was a left-wing Zionist, one uncle was an apolitical Zionist, and another uncle a Bundist who organized against Grandfather Freydowicz's building-supply company.[195] Young Jews not only had to navigate the Polish system but also had to choose among the myriad Jewish political and social movements established in response to that system. At least they had choices, though, unlike young people in Soviet Vitebsk, who had only Communist Party organizations, the Pioneers, and the Komsomol. Members of Jewish youth groups looked beyond the Polish political and social order as well as beyond the limitations of the Jewish oligarchy to find their own solutions. Hashomer Hatzair, Betar, Akiva, and other groups reinforced Jewish identity, certainly not the intent of Soviet organizations.

The spectrum of youth groups in Grodno, from Zionist to socialist, instilled characteristics of collective identity, interdependence, and group agency that surpassed the best efforts of the Pioneers and the Komsomol. Yisrael Gutman has made the keen observation that Polish Jews shared "an agitated state of mind, a dissatisfaction or even rejection of existing realities, a striving for change and innovation, and the desire to break the rules of the game."[196] Rebellion, although often subtle, supplemented these qualities. Witnesses rarely speak of discord with parents or authority figures, but it is unlikely that such negative issues would arise in recollections that usually discuss close relationships with other Jews in a positive light. The historian Avraham Barkai has noted such responses among the German Jewish youth after the first few years of Nazi rule. "Young people were disillusioned with their parents' generation: they [their parents] had not foreseen the hopeless situation and now they could find no way out."[197] The young Jews of Germany faced more visible and sustained persecution. Their counterparts in Poland, however, may not have wanted consciously to lay blame on their elders.

Young Polish Jews voiced their frustrations through their actions. As the historian Yehuda Bauer has noted, group activity offered a collective form of revolt. Not only did it provide an escape from the adult world, but certain groups such as the socialist Hashomer Hatzair also attracted middle- and upper-class youths rebelling against their parents.[198] Young people sought their own solutions because their parents or the Jewish community at large offered little guidance. "It is no accident that youngsters joining these movements referred to them as their 'new home,'" writes the historian Ezra Mendelsohn.[199] Youth movements established a framework for new communities.

Last Summer before the War

When the summer of 1939 arrived in Grodno, nobody knew, despite portents rippling through the press, that war, occupation, and revolution would soon revisit the city. In mid-June, TOZ opened its camp for 192 children, 20 more than the previous year.[200] The military orchestra played a concert in Grodno's city garden every Wednesday evening from 6:00 to 8:00.[201] Youth-group activities continued as usual. Chasia Bielicka traveled to the Carpathian Mountains for a youth conference, while most of her fellow Hashomer Hatzair members headed to a training farm near Slonim.[202]

That summer also brought personal losses. Chasia's maternal grandmother, a woman from another age who clung to Yiddish superstitions about black cats and empty buckets, passed away.[203] Zelda Grodzienska's father died, too.[204] Bella Ilin, only two-and-a-half years old, experienced her own tragedy. As she and her older cousin and playmate Izia wandered away from her parents' home, her little white dog followed behind and was run over by a horse cart. "I remember being very distressed," she recalled decades later, "and the dog was buried in our garden under a tree."[205]

As young people proceeded with their summer activities and experienced patterns of loss normal for people their age, far greater dangers lurked in the world outside Grodno. As a poem published in the *Grodner moment* to mark the season's start illustrates, however, young Jews were well aware of the larger threats present in the world:

> I think not of humanity,
> Culture, civilization,
> That we boycott—
> Mass emigration
> That we decree,
> Speeches and orations,
> Aryan paragraph,
> Endecja . . . *Dva groshes* . . . [206]

"Boycott . . . emigration . . . Aryan paragraph" were inescapable elements of the times, as were the antisemitic Endecja Party and the reactionary scandal sheet *Dva groshes* (Two Cents). The refugee situation was also on the minds of Grodno's Jews. The poem's subsequent lines, "And ships with Jews / That ramble on the seas," reference the recently concluded plight of German Jewish refugees aboard the *St. Louis*. No nation would take them ("And countries have all together agreed / To choke and oppress Jews") until Britain, France, and the Netherlands finally relented. Hitler's speeches, filled with "war provocations," only make the author laugh at the world and its alleged "culture, civilization."[207] To the author of the ode to summer, this season was supposed to be devoted to life on the river Niemen and the beaches along its shores, to the forests and *dachas* surrounding Grodno. Family and friends were to gather and gossip, and somber thoughts were forbidden. Serious matters had no place on a summer evening.

3

Red Revolution in Grodno

September 1939 to June 1941

"Dark clouds hover over the beautiful world, the modern educated world, and if they could speak would say nothing good awaits humanity." Sixteen-year-old Sarah Fishkin made this observation in her diary on 29 August 1939 as Germany threatened to invade her country. Sarah lived in Rubiezewicze, a shtetl 200 kilometers due east of Grodno on the Polish side of the border with the Soviet Union. The start of war three days later deepened her unease. Rosh Hashanah arrived on the evening of 13 September, instilling some sense of hope. Sarah, well aware of the threat that Nazi Germany posed for Poland's Jews, wished that "good will mark the new year." Her hopes were actualized by an unlikely source on the morning of 17 September 1939. Rubiezewicze's inhabitants were among the first to hear the noise and feel the ground shake as Red Army trucks and tanks poured across the Polish–Soviet border a mere three kilometers away. Sarah wrote in response, "Now we anticipate that the terrible, tortured times for the Jews will end and better times will come."[1]

Sarah was hardly an enthusiast for Bolshevism. Before the war, she had been a member of Banot Agudat Israel (Daughters of the Union of Israel), a conservative Zionist organization for young women, and she dreamed of making aliyah to Eretz Israel. Perhaps, like so many Jews in the Kresy, she viewed the Soviets simply as the lesser of two evils. Yet the Bolsheviks tempted Sarah Fishkin and other young Jews with prospects for advancement unavailable in the Polish Republic. This came at the price of the institutions framing their former lives.

Nevertheless, many took advantage of these new opportunities. Sarah, for example, later found work at a small party newspaper while continuing her education.[2]

The young Jews of Grodno, like Sarah Fishkin of Rubiezewicze, were swept up by the promises offered by the Soviets. Many sought to embrace a new political and social reality, although their motives and goals varied. A few truly sought to join the revolution and become Soviet citizens. Others tried to harness the opportunities presented by Soviet life to achieve prewar ideals. Most young Jews were simply dazzled by the prospects before them and followed paths that were not to reach fulfillment by the time the Germans invaded the Soviet Union in June 1941.

War

The German invasion of Poland on 1 September 1939 interrupted late-summer idylls. The day was traditionally the start of the school year, but in the turmoil of mobilization for war most schools remained closed. Many children and young people remained preoccupied with the activities of summer camps, hastily extended because of the disruption to the school calendar. Daniel Klovsky had arrived at a day camp just outside the city on the morning of 1 September 1939 when a counselor gathered the children to tell them war had begun. They ran home without any further instructions.[3] Ann Lewin was near Lunna, 40 kilometers to the southeast, where her brother Nathan was camp director. They, too, headed back to Grodno once the news broke.[4]

German bombs fell on Grodno that first day of the war.[5] Vichna Sidranska, her father already drafted into the Polish army as a medic, heard explosions in the late morning; her mother responded, "Oh my god, it's war!"[6] On Brygidzka Street, where Feliks Zandman lived in the house owned by his mother's parents, residents were injured by flying debris.[7] Moishe Kremer remembered that bombings damaged the two bridges crossing the river Niemen, thus cutting a primary rail and road corridor between Warsaw and Vilna.[8]

Some fled the city for the countryside or to smaller towns. Bookkeeper Hershl Abramovich sent his wife and son some 80 kilometers east to the shtetl Derechin on 4 September; he joined them a week later when it appeared that the Germans might occupy Grodno.[9] The Zandmans and Freydowiczes also fled the city, hiring three taxis to take the extended family to Lida, 90 kilometers to the east.[10] The Mullers piled belongings into a trunk and fled the city. Fenia Muller recalled that they traveled (she did not specify how) to her aunt's shtetl, Kamionka, a distance of 50 kilometers.[11] Grodno Jews traveled as far as Glubokie, 300 kilometers northeast.[12]

In Grodno, periodic German air attacks and flyovers drove the population into hastily improvised shelters. The beginning of Rosh Hashanah on 13 September did little to ease the nerves of the Jewish community as war damage and casualties mounted. Most of Zelda Grodzienska's siblings lost their homes in the bombings, forcing them to return to the primary family dwelling.[13] The Muller family residence was destroyed as well.[14]

Although many later recalled the Luftwaffe's attacks, few mention the Wehrmacht. German troops arrived in Białystok on 16 September 1939 and stayed for nearly a week, killing about 100 Jews during their brief occupation. In Sokolka, halfway between Białystok and Grodno, German troops harassed and robbed Jews at random.[15] The German presence in Grodno appears to have been much smaller. Chasia Bielicka, whose family lived on the northwest suburbs of the city, remembered placards printed in Polish and German imposing an 8:00 p.m. curfew. Two German soldiers even came into Chasia's home, demanding fur coats.[16] Ann Lewin also remembered that the Germans occupied Grodno for a few days in September 1939.[17] Few other survivors mention them, perhaps because, according to Moishe Kremer, German troops remained on the city's outskirts.[18]

Concurrently, Soviet armed forces prepared to occupy the entire Kresy (figure 12). Leah Katzenlenberg later recalled a curious sight in Disna, a shtetl at the far northeastern tip of Poland: a great forest sprouting on the opposite shore of the Dvina River and moving closer each day.[19] Like Burnham Wood in *Macbeth*, this "forest" was actually camouflaged Soviet tanks and trucks preparing to invade. When they advanced on 17 September 1939, Grodno native Yehuda Rabinovich

12. Map of northeastern Poland after Red Army occupation in September 1939. Although "Western Belarus" and "Western Ukraine" were annexed by their respective Soviet republics in November 1939, authorities in Minsk and Kiev maintained an internal border to prevent the free movement of inhabitants and refugees from leaving the newly added regions.

was in the border shtetl Koretz staying with his father to escape German bombs and, like Sarah Fishkin in Rubiezewicze, witnessed the Soviets crossing.[20]

As Red Army forces drove westward, they were greeted by a peculiar mixture of stunned silence and wild cheers. Jews frequently, but not always, welcomed the Russians' arrival with relief. Many thought at least it wasn't the Germans. In Dokshitzy, 200 kilometers to the northeast of Grodno, some Jews met the Soviets with indifference, others with dread. "Anything but the Germans," was how local Josef Shapiro later described the shared resigned attitude.[21] Hershl Abramovich recalled more enthusiastic responses among Jews in Derechin, 100 kilometers southeast of Grodno, where ovations and flowers greeted Soviet troops.[22] Feliks Zandman, still in Lida, noted how Poles reacted with sorrow. "I could see it was a tragedy for them," he wrote in a memoir. "For us [Jews], though, maybe not."[23]

The violence and speed of the German advance traumatized Poles, their national pride further wounded by the catastrophic Soviet incursion from the east. Russia, after all, had been the historical oppressor of Polish independence and identity. The perception that some Jews welcomed Bolshevik rule gave a boost to the libel of "*Żydokomuna*," the allegation of Jewish–Communist collaboration. Such prejudices remained in the memories of Grodno Poles decades later, particularly about the few days between the Red Army's march across the border and their capture of the city four days later. The Red Army reached the city's outskirts on 20 September, giving local Polish army units a chance to mount a defense. With the military and local police thus engaged, unrest broke out on some streets. Jan Siemiński, a Polish Scout who participated in the defense of Grodno, later attributed these actions to Jewish and Belarusian Communists. "The initiators of this rebellion were probably the secret associates of Stalinist NKVD," Siemiński alleged.[24] Another witness remembered attacks on Polish forces on one of the city's main streets, led by "groups almost exclusively composed of local Jews."[25]

Underlying these statements, however, were assumptions that all anti-Polish acts stemmed from Jews. Jewish witnesses, by contrast, remembered those few days as a time when "hooligans" attacked Jews and vandalized their property. In response, Jews and Poles from the suburban glass factory tried to patrol the streets.[26] A second and more violent rush of rioters composed of prisoners freed from Grodno's jail joined members of the Polish nationalist OZON in a pogrom.[27] Dovid Berezovski confided in a letter that these assailants killed twenty-eight Jews.[28] Still others recall cooperation. Daniel Klovsky later heard how Poles and Jews stood side by side to dig trenches.[29]

As Polish rule in Grodno frayed over the course of early to mid-September, extremists at opposite ends of the political spectrum sought to capitalize on events. The Soviet capture of the city on 21 September put a stop to these acts of violence. Many expressed relief at a return to order. Chasia Bielicka recalled that Poles threw flowers as Red Army troops and vehicles wound through Grodno's street.[30] Leib Bialo recalled, "It lifted our spirits, mostly for the Jewish people."[31] Dovid Berezovski remembered that "the enthusiasm for the Soviets is indescribable,"[32] a sentiment that is understandable, given the alternative—living under the Nazis.

Not all was calm, however, as the Red Army's own brand of violence erupted with its arrival. Dozens of captured Polish officers and random others, including several foresters and railway workers, were executed in the Franciscan monastery courtyard.[33] Other executions occurred in the following days on the city's outskirts. Women from the Polish Red Cross and teenage boys—Polish scouts—reportedly numbered among the victims. "Anyone who showed the least bit of resistance was shot," recalled one witness, indicating the motive for the killings.[34] All told, 130 people were shot without trial. Several witnesses recalled collaboration by local Communists in rounding up suspected resisters.[35] And although some of local Communists were Jews, fueling antisemitic myths of *Żydokomuna*, many more of the local Communists were Belarusians or Poles. For most witnesses, however, the collaboration by fellow Poles seldom remained in their memories.

More Soviet forces streamed into the Kresy, which Moscow now designated as the western oblasts Soviet Belarus and Soviet Ukraine. This was not simply an occupation; it was a revolution, intended to transform the social and economic order. The occupiers staged elections for "People's Assemblies" in October 1939, which were given the task to approve the annexation of western Belarus and western Ukraine to their respective Soviet republics. Annexation was accepted by Moscow on 1–2 November 1939. There was no going back. How inhabitants of the former Polish Kresy experienced the things to come depended on whether they were Pole, Belarusian, Ukrainian, or Jew. Their experience also was shaped by age. Many adults had their worlds turned upside down. Young people, by contrast, could be fashioned into tools of the revolution.

The City Takes on a Soviet Face

Party officials and Soviet bureaucrats arrived in the wake of the Red Army. Internal memoranda and decrees, distributed over the coming weeks and months to Communist Party organs in eastern Belarus, outlined the plans of sovietization of this "liberated" territory. Securing lines of communication—telegraph, telephone, radio, and post offices—took precedence on a prioritized list of occupation plans. Warehouses were next. Banks were third. Workers and leftist intelligentsia were to be culled as potential collaborative leaders.[36] More proclamations and orders followed: on interim authorities; on Polish army disarmament and weapon confiscation; on the provisional status of money, trade, and property; and on the formation of peasant and worker committees. Economic structures, in particular those of industries and larger businesses, were nationalized; entrepreneurs' assets were heavily taxed. Existing political and community structures were dissolved, their functions incorporated into Soviet-led institutions. Individual obedience was secured through the careful implementation of reward and punishment, with the latter escalating after the new year in 1940.

After pacifying overt signs of resistance, the Soviet occupiers began their takeover of the economy. The new authorities imposed parity between the ruble and the zloty, and soldiers and political personnel purchased anything from local shops that they could easily ship home. They particularly fancied wristwatches, even bartering with locals to obtain them.[37] The practice had less to do with a methodical plan as it did with the Soviets' hunger for consumer goods. The spending spree continued until most store shelves were empty. Shop owners, initially delighted, soon realized there was little the rubles they had received could buy; taxes took most of this windfall later.

When Hershl Abramovich took his family back to Grodno at the end of September, he noticed the empty stores and the first signs of shortages. "The city already seemed gloomy," he wrote later.[38]

Queuing at shops became common as rationing and the *defitsit*—"shortages" in Russian—spread across the region. Townspeople joined lines even before they knew what might be available. Vichna Sidranska later recalled getting in line after school to help her mother.[39] "Little by little we started to get a taste [that] their [the Soviets'] economy was in a shambles," Moishe Kremer recalled, noting the imbalance as more commodities left the area than came in from Soviet stockpiles.[40] Impoverishment spread when the authorities abandoned the zloty literally overnight. On 1 January 1940, holders of savings accounts in the Polish currency were limited to a maximum 300-ruble payout.

Initial property confiscations included commercial enterprises, factories, bathhouses, hospitals, theaters, cinemas, restaurants, libraries, and schools.[41] The revolution spread from the public world to private lives. Dr. Chaim Blumstein lost his Druskeniki spa hotel.[42] Vichna Sidranska's parents lost their home, although officials permitted the family to rent back a few rooms.[43] Property nationalizations continued well into 1940, with the twin goals of housing new Soviet personnel and dispossessing the middle and upper classes in the Kresy. One Soviet order issued in May that year called for confiscations of homes more than 113 square meters in size (1,200 square feet, equivalent to a four-room apartment).[44]

Military and political staff were billeted in homes as well. A well-mannered political commissar moved in with the Abramoviches.[45] Bella Ilin, not yet three years old when the Red Army arrived, retained a dim memory of a Russian officer staying in her parents' spare room.[46] Two Soviet officers occupied a room in Chasia Bielicka's family home. Her parents were able to use the Russian they learned in their youth, but Chasia and her siblings took to speaking in whispers even though the officers knew no Yiddish.[47]

Soviet personnel seemed to be everywhere, displacing former community elites and their policies. All private philanthropy was halted. Organizations such as the *kehilah* could no longer levy taxes or receive money from abroad, effectively blocking all Jewish community operations. Charitable support from abroad was not possible either. The last remaining Jewish aid agency on Soviet territory, the

JDC's Agro-Joint, had ceased operations in August 1938.[48] Yet the new authorities did not have to act to unseat the Grodno *kehilah*; the Jewish community's representative body dissolved itself soon after the Red Army's arrival.[49] Many of its board members feared arrest. Indeed, former *kehilah* members Noakh Bass, a newspaper publisher, and Leib Shifres, a teacher, were arrested the next year and interrogated.[50]

Whereas the *kehilah* collapsed on its own, the Soviets pressed forward to terminate other components of Jewish communal life. They banned kosher slaughtering and opened to non-Jews the ritual bath and Jewish social welfare institutions for orphans and the aged. Sunday, not Saturday, became the rest day for the work week. The region's new Yiddish-language party newspaper, the *Bialystoker shtern* (Białystok Star), carried antireligious articles similar to those presented in Vitebsk a decade earlier.

Despite these disruptions, religious worship continued and initially appeared to thrive. Synagogue and church attendance were the only public gatherings the Soviets permitted locals to hold; all other groups were banned. Heavy taxes soon bankrupted many congregations, however, and in time many of the synagogues and prayer houses were appropriated for warehouses and workshops.[51] The somber mood tempered spiritual life. Vichna Sidranska recalled that "there was not that joyous feeling anymore; the holidays were not observed as much."[52] Chasia Bielicka recalled that her father put on tefillin every day, as he did before the war, but she could not remember any family holiday celebration during this period of Soviet rule.[53]

Soviet policies toward Jews were a double-edged sword. As discussed later, Jews were given positions of authority previously unavailable to them under Polish rule. Elections to the Belarusian Supreme Soviet in March 1940 gave the illusion of fair representation across ethnicities. Some 7.7 percent of the delegates were Jews, although the region had a Jewish population of around 10 percent.[54] Expressions of antisemitism present during those years came to be designated "anti-Soviet." Yet unsanctioned expressions of Jewish identity also were branded subversive. This extended to Jewish politics, and the adult leaders of the Bund and various Zionist parties burned their archives and fled or went into hiding.[55] Not even potential allies were safe. Chasia Bielicka reported that most members of the local Communist Party were arrested and accused of Trotskyite sympathies.[56]

Refugees from German-Occupied Poland

The Bolsheviks were not the only new presence in the newly annexed territories. Hundreds of thousands of refugees, mostly Jews, fled western Poland in fear of the anticipated brutality under German occupation. Refugees from Nazi Germany were discussed in the pages of Grodno's Yiddish press as early as 1937, but they seldom physically reached the eastern Polish city. The Grodno Jewish community had responded to each call to action, typically with money and blankets, but little else. Even the forced expulsion of some 12,000 Polish Jews in late October 1938 had little direct effect on Grodno because western Polish borderland cities such as Bielitz, Kattowitz, and Kraków disproportionately absorbed the burden. A mere dozen Jewish refugees had made their way to Grodno by the summer of 1939.[57]

Refugees fleeing east to escape German bombs or Nazi brutality journeyed by train, by car or truck, and on foot. The Red Army's presence in eastern Poland took them by surprise as much as anyone else. Warsaw native Lucien Feigenbaum remembered how on his trek he did not go to Russia—"Russia came to me."[58] The collapse of Polish resistance accelerated the flight of people fearful of German rule from October through December 1939. Twenty-five-year-old Rozalia Hollander fled Warsaw with her new husband, Leopold (they had married on 14 July 1939).[59] Joseph Ceder, born in 1926, fled Łódź with his parents.[60] Some, however, ran as much toward the Soviets as away from the Germans. Twenty-year-old Dora Huze, raised by Orthodox parents but enamored of communism, followed a brother who had already left Łódź for Soviet-occupied Poland.[61] Liliana Goldsopl, born in 1923, left Warsaw with her aunt Guta after relatives wrote from Grodno extolling the opportunities available there under Soviet rule.[62]

Those who fled by train on the Warsaw-to-Vilna railroad line passed through the small depot town of Małkinia Górna, the last stop on the German side of the new German–Soviet border. Joseph

Ceder recalled the shocking scene there as a "circus, a free circus, with the Germans hitting and beating," while Polish helpers roughly searched baggage for valuables.[63] Several men, perhaps other Polish collaborators, caught hold of Dora Huze upon her arrival at Małkinia and, searching for money and gold, forced her to undress. The men even cut away her clothing with a knife, leaving her nearly naked. The assailants found some money in her girdle and shoved her into a station room holding several other women. Shivering from cold and fear, she managed to flee with the remnants of her clothes and baggage when the German standing guard momentarily stepped away. "I run like mad," she recalled, her use of the present tense revealing the immediacy of this trauma still decades later. She crossed into the no man's land between the Germans and the Soviets, where other refugees helped her put her tattered clothes in order.[64]

Joseph Ceder described this no man's land as "a muddy field" about half a kilometer wide, with "people dying, children being born, [and] screams to high heavens."[65] Some of the people told Dora Huze that they had been there for weeks. "And they didn't want to go back," she recalled. "The Russian soldiers didn't let them pass, and I thought if I haven't been killed by the Germans, I die here." But Dora could speak some Russian. After she spoke to some of the Red Army soldiers, they let her continue to Białystok.[66] Joseph's parents lost him in no man's land, and the boy found his way separately. They reunited by chance on the Białystok train platform and continued on to Grodno the next day.[67]

Others sought to cross the border covertly. Rozalia and Leopold Hollander were rowed across the river Bug in a peasant's small boat.[68] Liliana Goldsopl and her aunt Guta had a similar but more harrowing experience; they were nearly drowned as their boat took on water.[69] Each pair arrived at a different bit of no man's land holding smaller groups of refugees, remaining there until Soviet officials permitted them to proceed to Białystok and beyond.

The Ceder family found shelter in Grodno's Great Synagogue, sharing the chilly vestibule with dozens of other refugees. Hundreds more occupied the rest of the monumental structure. Although many refugees were young and adult men, Joseph also recalled seeing "rich and poor and beggars and representatives of all the classes of people." But they did not feel particularly welcome, at least initially. "The local population—as a rule—they did not receive us well," he later remembered. "They thought of us as being intruders."[70] Perhaps young Joseph was unable to appreciate the impact that thousands of refugees had on a community reeling under rapid sovietization. One estimate declares that about 4,000 refugees attempted to settle in the city,[71] although many thousands more passed through during the first six months of Soviet rule. Besides providing housing in the community's synagogues, local Jews set up soup kitchens and gathered bedding from their own homes. The Soviets implemented their own relief efforts,[72] in part because procedures for medical treatment and dormitory assignments permitted political screening of the refugees.[73]

Many Grodno families accepted a refugee or two into their own homes. Zelda Grodzienska's family accepted a boy from Łódź, giving her recently widowed mother someone to fuss over.[74] Chasia Bielicka's parents allowed several young Jews to sleep temporarily on their living room or kitchen floor before they found permanent living arrangements or moved on farther east.[75] Rozalia and Leopold Hollander found a friendly reception with a cousin, who had already made room for two Soviet officers.[76] Liliana Goldsopl and her aunt Guta received aid from the uncle and aunt who had urged them to come to Grodno.[77] Alexandre Blumstein's parents took in a niece from Warsaw, followed by her fiancé three weeks later. Before the war, the couple would have been married by a rabbi, but under the circumstances a Soviet civil ceremony provided the only legal means.[78]

After a while, some local people treated the refugees better, Joseph Ceder observed, despite the obvious shortages in Grodno. "We were asked to come in to spend a Shabbat" is how he remembered it. "We were fed and were given stuff to take home." ("Home," apparently, was still the synagogue vestibule.) Such contacts also raised awareness of cultural differences between central and western Polish Jews and their coreligionists in the Kresy. "A Shabbat over [in Grodno] was more of a Shabbat," Joseph noted, his point of reference being religious life in comparatively more cosmopolitan Łódź.[79] Dora Huze also found Grodno Jews to be more devout, a conclusion she drew from the many small synagogues and houses of prayer spread across the city instead of the fewer but much larger structures in Łódź.[80]

Although Soviet media remained mute on conditions in German-occupied Poland (Nazi Germany, after all, was an ally at this time), Jewish refugees relayed their experiences, sometimes to disbelieving listeners. Chasia Bielicka recalled that "every refugee opened our eyes to the terror" across the new border.[81] Feliks Zandman later wrote about the Glass family, who arrived on their doorstep one day from German-held territory, telling about violent threats against Jews.[82] Rumors continued to fly among the dispossessed refugee community encamped in Grodno. "News from 'the other side'—from Warsaw—not happy news . . . atrocity, violence against Jews" was the disturbing topic writer and refugee Avraham Zak discussed with his fellow refugees as their time in Grodno stretched from weeks to months.[83]

It seems, however, that these reports left little impression on Grodno natives. Older Jews may have been too busy trying to navigate the new Soviet system to pay much attention to such "gossip," seemingly from another world. Hadn't the Germans been good masters during the previous war? Why should they be different now? Except for Chasia and Feliks, most young people, too, seem to have ignored these accounts. Many were too deeply engaged in the new lives and new opportunities offered by the Soviets, especially through their education system.

Opportunities at School

The restructuring of the city's school system, which extended to many extracurricular activities, had a more direct impact on young people's daily lives than did the shortage of goods or the influx of refugees. Moishe Kremer later recalled that "at the beginning it was very exciting," adding that there was a festive atmosphere during the first weeks. "They came and pulled up trucks with projectors and movies," he continued. "Naturally Russian movies, patriotic movies about the great life in Russia."[84] Concurrently with these activities, Zionist and Bundist youth groups entered a phase of clandestine activity that would prove crucial to their members' subsequent fates.

Before the war, many poorer Jewish and Polish families in Grodno could not afford to educate their children beyond elementary school. Soviet authorities opened schools within a few weeks of their arrival, with the immediate goal of extending the education of Grodno's working-class children. In the first six months of Soviet rule, the new authorities succeeded in increasing the number of students in Grodno from 10,352 to 11,669, with many of the additional students in the secondary (high) schools.[85] And new venues opened for postsecondary education. Party officials in Grodno boasted a year after annexation that they had organized a pedagogical college, trade and technical schools, and a music academy.[86] Besides limitations by social class, Soviet officials also criticized gender bias in prewar gymnasia and lyceums, which had limited girls to a curriculum in homemaking.[87] Prospects expanded for women of all ages. For example, Genia Zandman, Feliks's mother, received training to be a medical assistant.[88]

Indeed, as Chasia Bielicka later recalled, "a frenzy of study broke out," and many Jews, male and female, benefitted from these developments.[89] Chasia had had little hope of receiving a secondary education before the war. In the fall of 1939, she enrolled in People's High School Number 9, formerly the Realni gymnasium.[90] Yehuda Rabinovich, who had returned to Grodno from Koretz in late October, enrolled in a ten-year school, where he received special music education. His studies on the *domra*, a four-string Russian instrument, led him to win a competition in the spring of 1941.[91] New opportunities also opened in other cities and in areas of study typically blocked to Jews under Polish rule. Alexandre Blumstein's older brother, Tolo, attended a medical school in Lviv.[92]

But along with expansion came suppression of previous educational practices. "Will it be permitted to teach in Hebrew?" was the naive question a music teacher who also taught that language asked at the first meeting for Grodno's Jewish and Polish teachers. An official from Minsk named Shapiro responded coldly, "Hebrew is a language of reactionaries, of Zionism, of bourgeois clericalism."[93] Schools such as the Tarbut thus reopened in October 1939 with Yiddish-language lessons.[94] Hebrew books were pulled from library shelves across the city and pulped to make paper, although Tarbut librarian Shmuel Ginzberg secreted the more important texts in his institution's collection and distributed them among the former staff and pupils.[95]

Belarusian, Ukrainian, Russian, Polish, and Yiddish were the official languages of instruction in the newly annexed western oblasts, even though the latter two languages had been phased out within the pre-1939 Soviet border. Local selection depended on the principal nationality of the students and availability of teachers. Yet, as we saw in prewar Soviet Vitebsk, language choice became less a primary goal than a means to an end. The Białystok regional party committee underlined the point by declaring that "instructing children in their own language facilitates and accelerates their communist education."[96] The number of Yiddish schools in Grodno increased initially with the conversion of Polish- and Hebrew-language institutions serving Jewish students. This increase renewed the prospects for Yiddish-language teachers from the eastern oblasts, such as Hirsh Reles, graduate of the Vitebsk Jewish Pedagogical Tekhnikum. He left his Russian-language teaching job in Slutsk and accepted a position in a Yiddish-language school in Novogrudok, 150 kilometers southeast of Grodno. His wife, Yekha, and daughter, Reza, soon joined him.[97] Prospects also improved for Grodno locals. Viennese-trained Aaron Zandman, for example, taught chemistry for the first time and eventually took positions at three separate schools.[98]

Students accustomed to the pedagogical techniques of the Tarbut, Talmud Torah, or the Polish public-school system soon found Soviet methods to be wanting, however, and recognized key deficiencies. Ann Lewin recalled that she learned "a lot of propaganda" about Lenin and Stalin in her new school.[99] Chasia Bielicka found that she and her fellow students "could not accustom ourselves to dogmatism, the prohibition of independent thinking, the dismissal of any interpretation other than the one handed down by authorities."[100]

In addition to inflexible Soviet pedagogy, young people experienced the shifting sands of language politics. The BSSR's continued push of Belarusian culture, even if tempered by a competing drive for Russian dominance, gained ground in the western oblasts. Belarusian education, newspapers, and culture received top priority. In Grodno, for example, party officials maintained the position that Belarusian and Russian children resided there in numbers equal to Polish children and therefore deserved schools in their own language.[101] In reality, school administrators recruited Belarusian children from the countryside, housing them in hastily organized dormitories.[102] As a consequence, schools in Belarusian grew the quickest, with ten schools (elementary, middle, and high schools) serving 5,110 students by March 1940—no small feat, considering that there had been no Belarusian-language schools six months earlier. Yiddish-language education ranked second at that time, with five schools and 2,569 pupils, followed by Russian (three schools, 2,123 enrollments) and Polish (three schools, 1,757 enrollments).[103] The influx of Soviet military and administrative personnel included families, thus bumping up the student population for Russian-language education. By late 1940, 4,378 students were taught in Russian, followed by 2,700 in Belarusian, 1,851 in Polish, and 1,353 in Yiddish.[104]

Although these figures illuminate a decline in Yiddish-language education, Białystok regional party officials continued to voice support for national language schools. In fact, the recently established multilingual education system presented many administrative problems. Teachers from eastern Belarus working in Polish schools possessed no Polish-language skills; a Polish school changed to Belarusian without hiring proper instructors in the latter tongue; and an inadequate supply of textbooks pervaded the entire system.[105] Such logistical issues appear to have influenced school directors to change languages and bring western oblast school policy in line with the rest of the BSSR. How the directors made this switch highlighted a new problem, as revealed by a reprimand of the directors of three Polish-language schools and a Yiddish-language school: they had failed to secure the local parents' consent.[106]

Parents' agreement, however, was derived less through democratic means than by coercion and social pressure. Just as had occurred in eastern Belarus a few years earlier, some parents in Grodno saw the wisdom of switching to Russian.[107] Chasia Bielicka's father, sensing the importance that the language held, began to teach his children Russian not long after the Soviets' arrival.[108] Even so, authorities summoned parents before many Yiddish-language schools reopened for the fall 1940 term to collect their consent for these school changes.[109] Avraham Zak later described how "someone" at such a meeting proposed to change Yiddish-language schools to Russian, and the assembled parents "freely" approved the resolution.[110] As a Yiddish writer, Zak likely disfavored such a move. Even so, open debate was rarely part of the process.

Language changes meant that many Jewish children attended school with Gentiles for the first time. Yet Holocaust survivors from the Kresy seldom recount stories of friendships formed across ethnic lines during this period. Perhaps this has more to do with subsequent events than with actual associations. Relationships could have formed, particularly considering the amount of time that young people spent together during and after school in Soviet-sponsored activities.

Instead of going home to family or to Zionist youth groups after school, as in prewar years, the Jewish students now went to class meetings, field trips, and student theatricals in the Soviet school. And quite often they loved it. Kept busy with engaging programs, they were untroubled by the language changes. "The center of our life and interests had moved from our family circle to school," Daniel Klovsky wrote later.[111] Feliks Zandman concurred. He had sought membership in a number of Zionist youth organizations before the war but had not quite found a home in any of them. Life under the Soviets, however, offered an enrichment of his extracurricular life. "All the things I had been doing before I still did, even more of them, because the Soviets loved to organize youth activities." Feliks played violin in an orchestra, participated in athletic contests, took cross-country skiing lessons, and received some paramilitary training. "Our parents might have been worrying themselves sick about the future," Zandman observed, "but many of the youngsters were having the time of their lives."[112]

The centers of such activity were the Pioneers and the Komsomol, established by the end of 1939 in the western oblasts' schools.[113] By early 1940, directors dedicated special rooms for lectures, discussions, early military instruction, and athletic training,[114] all activities that enhanced the indoctrination and Bolshevization of young people. Unlike the Jews from Vitebsk, who later in life seldom spoke about these groups, many in Grodno remembered their pride in wearing the red tie of the Pioneers. "For some time I didn't take it off, even at home," remembered Daniel Klovsky. His sister Hannah thought that the red tie gave her a status equal to that of her Polish classmates.[115] Like many of her contemporaries, Hannah felt at last to be an equal citizen under Soviet rule.

Not all joined Soviet youth movements, however. Alexandre Blumstein had no interest in the Pioneers, despite pressure from teachers and fellow students.[116] Some of Chasia Bielicka's school friends participated in the Komsomol, but she did not. Noting that members were somehow better off, Chasia later recalled, "Perhaps they had a stronger sense of belonging."[117] As with any youth organization, however, some joined the Pioneers or the Komsomol less from conviction than from convenience.

Prewar youth groups reemerged clandestinely. Many youth-group leaders had responded to the Red Army's arrival by fleeing, like their adult counterparts, to Vilna or elsewhere. The Soviets closed the Zionist Movement House along with all other prewar youth groups. In response, some former members created underground cells with just three or four members to avoid suspicion.[118] Chasia Bielicka and two neighbors met in the family's secluded courtyard days after the Soviet occupation and began passing messages to other members across the city. She recalled that they dreamed and contrived plans to make aliyah to Palestine, but their meetings also alleviated their loneliness after they lost the intimacies of prewar Zionist movements. Underground groups also learned crucial skills, extraordinarily useful later during the German occupation. "We learned to be furtive," Chasia recollected, "to look for ways to throw [the Soviet authorities] off our tracks."[119]

Even if Chasia did not join the Komsomol, her time in Soviet school constituted a pivotal phase of her development. Not only did she complete her formal education, but she also encountered people who profoundly influenced her future: fellow students Lisa Chapnik and Bronia Winicka, who a few years later formed part of her underground cell during the German occupation, as well as school director Valentina Ochanina, a "true communist in heart and soul," who helped her after the war. She also participated in school activities that exposed her to key aspects of the Soviet system. During elections to the Supreme Soviet, Chasia spent all night helping her classmates set up the polling station in the school auditorium. She also aided in the purge of the school library, reading passages or summarizing whole books because the censor did not know Polish.[120]

Preparing a room for an election or assisting an official censor, although small tasks, demonstrate that the Soviets tried to engage every youth in the revolution, just as educational and extracurricular opportunities drew young people into participatory roles. The system intended to remove Jewish-identified movements (the Bund and the various factions of Zionism) and to replace their ideals with the ideologically grounded Soviet curriculum and after-school activities. Some young people appear to have established boundaries, such as Chasia Bielicka, staying out of the Komsomol, but others displayed more ambivalence. Had events traveled a different path, would young Jews have become peaceful Soviet citizens, trading their individual identities for relative conformity?

Such questions must remain open because history soon engulfed the Jews of the Kresy. If we examine the roads that some followed during what became merely a twenty-one month interval, we see a glimpse of what might have happened. One of these roads was a centerpiece of Soviet life: labor.

Opportunities for Work

The Soviets pushed hard to end unemployment in western Belarus and western Ukraine, not only to rebuild the local economy but to engage as many people as possible in the act of revolution. Various decrees nationalized industrial facilities, some of which had been shuttered since the 1920s, and reorganized them into worker trusts.[121] During the first year under Soviet rule, twenty-five large-scale plants were taken over in Grodno alone.[122] The Soviets also planned expansion of cigarette, bicycle, and leather-goods manufacturing.[123] Factories that seldom hired Jews before the war did so under Soviet management, so that Jews and Gentiles worked side by side, just as their children attended the same schools. Simultaneously, former members of the nationalist OZON and the Polish military faced a purge from industrial jobs.[124]

Nationalizations and purges also removed Jews from positions they held previously. Former entrepreneurs, such as Leib Bialo's father, Samuel, became employees of their own dispossessed businesses. Other merchants and business owners were arrested and deported. Their children often faced discrimination. Leib's Soviet passport, which was extended to all persons resident before 2 November 1939,[125] marked his father's status as a merchant under Polish rule. This designation initially prevented Leib from getting work, but later he received a job in the former Bata shoe factory.[126]

Work was necessary for survival. If it offered hope of rehabilitation for children of merchants, it also provided subsistence. "There [was] no such thing as not working—you had to work," Leib reflected decades later, meaning that under the Soviet system, to work meant to receive sufficient rations.[127] Decades after the fact, Zelda Grodzienska agreed that work meant survival. She found a bakery job to support her mother and the family members who sought refuge in their home. "Whatever amount of bread that store got in that day was sold within minutes," she later commented about Soviet shortages. Zelda felt lucky to have her bakery job because she could take home bread for her family before supplies were exhausted.[128] Sima Kapulska had a similar experience acquiring food through her job doling out rations of sugar and other staples at a state shop.[129] But taking home food from a job was dangerous. Elka Fomin's brother Yosl took home some bread rolls from his bakery job but was then arrested and never heard from again because his action constituted theft of state property.[130]

Aware that the mounting social and economic constraints made their situation increasingly perilous, some workers cooperated willingly with the new authorities. Tradesmen, such as shoemakers, tailors, and wagon drivers, took the initiative to establish cooperative associations called *artels*. Their primary motivation, however, was not an overnight conversion to Bolshevism but the need for raw materials.[131] Some found the *artels* and state shops beneficial because they offered a flexibility not possible for sole proprietors. David Klovsky, Daniel's father, ran his own shop before the war, rarely spending time with his family in boom times. But after the Soviet occupation and annexation, the elder Klovsky closed his business and took a job in a tannery workshop. The position offered a regular paycheck and more time with his children.[132]

The all-encompassing administrative apparatus also provided Jews with opportunities previously blocked by Polish authorities. Hershl Abramovich found work as a bookkeeper in the city's cultural department.[133] Dovid Berezovski took a position in the municipal education department and wrote for the *Bialystoker shtern*.[134] But Jews did not receive public positions in numbers consistent with their population ratio. In Białystok, no more than 15 to 20 percent of the municipal employees were Jews by nationality, slightly higher than their proportion within the regional population but much lower than their number among the urban population.[135] Belarusians usually received the best positions. As with the school system, the Soviets felt it was in their interests to support this nationality ahead of all others in the northern Kresy and Ukrainians in the south to justify their "liberation." Yet the presence of any Jews in positions of authority presented an innovation. The Białystok municipal industrial department's deputy chief was a Jew educated in a Moscow technical school; he supervised two other university-educated Jews, who worked as an employee trainer and a secretary, respectively.[136] Feliks Zandman could look up to Jews who had achieved unprecedented rank.[137] The Grodno police precinct, for example, now had a Jewish chief.[138] The town administration in nearby Sokolka included a Jew named Spector.[139]

Refugees, however, had difficulty finding work in the new western oblasts. Authorities preferred that the refugees accept offers for labor in the Soviet interior, perceiving them as suspect and a burden on the local economy. Joseph Ceder's father signed up for a labor assignment in Nizhny Tagil in the Urals in part because he felt insecure remaining so close to German-occupied territory. The family departed Grodno in March 1940.[140] Some of the young people who stayed with Chasia Bielicka's family also accepted work in the Soviet interior.[141] Many soon found the work too strenuous, menial, and low paying, however. Living conditions were terrible. A few returned to Grodno illegally.[142]

Other refugees managed as best they could, at times earning money on the black market.[143] Dora Huze, for example, bought salt in Białystok and brought it back to sell in Grodno. She and her husband later joined with a group of refugees illegally selling merchandise they found hidden in an apartment. Dora later sought a job as a teacher, taking the entrance exams for a teacher-training program. But she declined to accept a Soviet passport, which raised the authorities' suspicions. As we shall see, Dora and her husband were among the majority of refugees the Soviets deported from the western oblasts in 1940, a fate that ironically saved their lives.[144]

The black market thrived among locals as well because ordinary workers' wages in the new Soviet economy kept some residents' standard of living below subsistence level.[145] Others, however, did better than in prewar times.[146] Chasia Bielicka recollected that "simple folk such as laborers and even poor Jews had jobs . . . and were better off than before."[147] Moishe Kremer agreed. "For the average person in the first year [under the Soviets], it was a lot easier to live in Grodno than in the last years of the Polish government."[148]

Responses to the Soviet System

The Soviets tried to seduce young Jews with promises of education and equality. Some yielded easily, whereas others recognized the dangers cloaked by official declarations, and all felt the impact of the revolution. Soviet life shaped Banot Agudat Israel follower Sarah Fishkin in Rubiezewicze, just as it did the young Bundist Yehuda Rabinovich in Grodno. Religious Zionists and secular socialists alike traded in features of their prewar identity for opportunities to work or go to school. The editors of the volume *Lost Jewish Worlds* characterize succinctly the dilemma facing all Jews under communism: "It was an auspicious period for bettering oneself by acquiring an education, a profession, and general culture; but, at the same time, all Jewish aspects of life were expunged."[149] Indeed, Chasia Bielicka echoed the same trade-off in her memoir: "On the one hand, our Jewish and Zionist lives were over. On the other, we received schooling, free education, and equality before the authorities."[150] Compared to the horrors that followed Soviet rule, it was a good life. Again and again, young Jews spoke positively about this interval of Soviet rule. "Generally speaking, while recalling those times, I see a sort of playful kaleidoscope of different events and impressions which were amazing to me," Daniel Klovsky remembered.[151] Sidney Sisun recalled that despite hardships and even his father's arrest, his life under the Soviets was good.[152]

Along with education and employment, equality offered young Jews opportunities not available in the antisemitic climate of Polish rule. Many acknowledged decades later the liberating aspects of the Soviet nationalities policies.[153] However, anti-antisemitic campaigns did little to resolve underlying ethnic tensions, as in prewar Vitebsk. Unlike in Vitebsk, where an entire generation matured under such strictures and perhaps grew to accommodate a degree of interethnic harmony, the sudden imposition of such policies in Grodno antagonized ardent nationalists. Despite apparent ethnic tensions, the Soviets declared that all conflict had been resolved in the newly created oblasts. In January 1941, *Oktyabr* described a new workers' club in the shtetl Indura, not far from Grodno, as a place "where every evening the youth of different nationalities gather together" and hold discussions on "the interethnic way of life" in the Soviet Union.[154]

Beneath the official rhetoric, however, the new ruling authorities used antisemitism as an additional means to undercut Polish attitudes of supremacy. Feliks Zandman recalled how some Poles found it "disconcerting that antisemitism was now outlawed."[155] Actual numbers show that the Soviets' arrival was far from a "Judeo-Bolshevik" assault. Jewish employees in the Białystok municipal workforce, as we have seen, numbered no more than 20 percent. Party personnel identified as Jews appear to number no more than 15 percent, according to several lists of personnel transferred from eastern to western Belarus in 1939 and 1940.[156] Also, given the purge of most Jews from the NKVD's ranks in late 1938 and 1939, the proportion of Jewish security police was probably less than 10 percent.[157] To Poles who had spent twenty years asserting their identity and hegemony, however, seeing even one Jew as a local authority was startling. Even their everyday language faced the impact of the Soviet takeover. Zandman recalled that use of the Polish term Żyd, a homophone for the Russian pejorative *Zhid*, was no longer permitted, which left some without a name for their Jewish neighbors.[158]

Young Jews formed their own opinions of the Soviet system notwithstanding the allure of official promises and hopes for advancement. Chasia Bielicka's Hashomer Hatzair group had studied socialism and communism before the war, feeling that these political movements were akin to their own Zionist ideals. The reality, they discovered, was much different. When some of her comrades traveled into eastern Belarus, Chasia learned that the restrictive environment of the new western oblasts was common to the entire Soviet Union.[159] Jews in Grodno would witness increasing oppression with successive waves of arrests and deportations beginning in early 1940.

Perhaps this was why Chasia claimed later that her ultimate goal was not to stay in the Soviet Union but somehow to leave for Palestine.[160] Others shared this intention. Chaika Grossman of Białystok, who was later active in underground activities with Chasia Bielicka in that city, commented about her friends' intentions to emigrate. "There were those who imagined they could find [a] personal solution in the Soviet regime."[161] For young Jews who dreamed of emigration, the door still remained open a crack. Opportunities for some were never better. The Soviets had turned over Vilna and a swath of territory to Lithuania at the end of October 1939. Rumors spread that from Vilna or Kovno (Kaunas, the Lithuanian capital) it was possible to travel through Soviet Central Asia to Palestine.

Relatively few young Jews sought escape, however. Those who remained didn't need to join the Pioneers or the Komsomol to reap the benefits on offer. When they later told or wrote about the twenty-one months of Soviet life before the German invasion, many recalled positive developments. Compared to the ineffectual responses of their own community leaders or the oppressive Polish order before the war, the new system offered a future. And if most of Chasia and Chaika's contemporaries maintained sixty years later that they had had no intention of remaining under Soviet rule, that they wished to emigrate, perhaps by the time the Germans attacked the Soviet Union, they simply had not yet reached the conclusion that Bolshevism offered a false dawn.

Although much changed in the lives of Grodno's Jewish youth during the Bolshevik revolution of their city, consistency marked their lives as well. Young Jews sustained close bonds with their contemporaries, no matter if the context was a youth group (Soviet or underground), the schoolroom, or a summer camp. Young Jews also continued to seek direction for the future from those same peer groups, not from their elders, who were even more helpless under the Soviets than under the Poles. Ties of kinship remained strong, to be sure, but as Feliks Zandman observed, parents worried about the future. Their children, seemingly empowered by the Soviet system, plunged headlong. Many young Jews in the new western oblasts not only survived the Soviets but initially thrived. This is to their credit, given that the situation was not just fluid but often inscrutable. Avraham Zak, a perceptive observer of attitudes and events during this time in Grodno, sensed that even local authorities knew little of what to expect next.[162]

The Soviets labored to stitch the new western oblasts into the fabric of Bolshevik society. The process was ongoing, and in the summer of 1941 the Jews of Grodno and Vitebsk retained important distinctions of identity. One opinion they shared was their belief in the invincibility of Soviet power.

4

Faith in Soviet Security

January 1940 to June 1941

"The most important thing now is to defend the Soviet Union," declared Ruve Reyzin, one of Hirsh Reles's literary colleagues, in response to the fascist threat that had erupted in Spain in 1936. By 1940, Reyzin had joined the Red Army, and Reles last saw his fellow Yiddish writer in full uniform at a Belarusian Writers' Union reading. "His tunic buckle shone, as did his boots. . . . Ruve endeavored to appear as a genuine officer," Reles later remembered.[1]

Not everybody could enlist in the Red Army, the domain of male youth. Yet Soviet citizens—whether nurtured under the revolution or relative newcomers from the recently annexed western oblasts—trusted that the Soviet Union was a powerful state, ready to resist any challenge. And they believed in a lie. Well documented are the inadequate preparations along the western border, the bad strategic decisions at all levels of military command, and the disregarded warnings of German military preparations that left the eastern nation vulnerable. We too often perceive the Soviet military collapse during the invasion in the summer and autumn of 1941 as simply the movement of a front line across a map. For civilians on the ground, when their trust in the security of their nation abruptly shattered, the horror was tangible.

We have seen how the Soviets lured young Jews in Grodno in the newly annexed western oblasts into the project of the revolution. Broadening our scope, we now examine the beliefs and awareness that young Jews in Vitebsk and in newly sovietized Grodno held about

Soviet power, the strength of the Red Army, and the threat of a German invasion. Mixed information came in the forms of propaganda, media reports, popular entertainment, public meetings, private letters, casual conversations, and wild rumors. Many of these exchanges occurred as Jews from eastern and western Belarus met for the first time in a generation. The mechanisms of official oppression also left their impression on ordinary Soviet citizens. If the Bolshevik state had the power to remove the alleged dangers posed by individuals or whole populations, didn't it have the means to repel any threat?

The Apparatus of Internal Security

Returning home from a theater rehearsal on the damp evening of 9 February 1940, Yiddish writer and Warsaw refugee Avraham Zak passed a line of empty trucks parked outside Grodno prison in the center of town. He hurried away as some Red Army soldiers approached. The next morning Zak discovered that the trucks he saw were the preparations for the first mass deportation. "My nephew came in from the street and said that thousands of people were taken away in the middle of the night," he later wrote.[2]

The city's mood shifted markedly after that. "People in the street bore apprehensive expressions, faces covered by a mask of anxiety," Zak remembered.[3] After the multitude of revolutionary changes in Grodno since the previous September, the arrest and deportation of whole population groups shook popular perceptions of the new regime. Prior to these deportations, the primary targets for arrest had been elites: local government and community leaders, judges, industrialists, estate owners, bankers, prosperous merchants, and Polish and Jewish political party leaders. Residents had asked, "Do I fall within one of these suspect categories?"

Now everyone felt vulnerable. Alexandre Blumstein, for example, recalled decades later the fears of his bourgeois parents, how they "listened carefully to the noises in the street at night."[4] Dr. Chaim Blumstein faced potential scrutiny as a former clinic operator, hotel owner, and prominent local Zionist. He had also complained bitterly about the operation of his former clinic under Soviet management, where he had become just another employee. The Blumsteins knew of others rounded up and deported, but they were passed over.

The deportations followed a pattern: sudden arrest at home, orders to pack belongings needed for a long journey, and rapid delivery of detainees to local railway depots. Those deported between February 1940 and June 1941 fell once again into distinct categories: members (not just leaders) of Polish political parties and the Jewish Bund, families of imprisoned Polish officers, remaining Polish and Jewish ruling elites, and refugees from German-occupied Poland.[5] But the largest single deportee category was the *osadniks*, former soldiers from Marshal Piłsudski's World War I legion who had been pensioned off with Kresy land and lived in government-constructed settlements called *osadas*. The Soviets viewed these agrarian settlers as exploiters who had displaced the rightful claims of Belarusian peasants.

Bodowla, an *osada* 15 kilometers southeast of Grodno, was one of the targets on the night of 9–10 February 1940. Red Army soldiers arrived in trucks and ordered the residents to pack food, clothing, and bedding. Władysław Krupa, a youth at the time, recalled decades later, "When Mother enquired about our destination[,] [the officer] bare-faced lied that we'd be going no further than the [local] center."[6] Their initial destination was the Grodno train depot, where cattle cars awaited to take them to labor camps in Siberia, the destination of Russian political and criminal exiles for more than two centuries. On a single night, 9–10 February 1940, NKVD units arrested more than 44,000 settlers such as the Krupas from 8,653 farms and residences across the former eastern Polish provinces.[7] They joined an estimated 140,000 people overall, mostly Poles, deported from western Belarus and western Ukraine during the February action.[8]

Besides Polish agricultural settlers, the NKVD targeted refugees from German-occupied Poland, suspecting them of harboring capitalist attitudes or acting as German spies. Soviet officials had two primary means to test these newcomers. As early as November 1939, they offered unemployed refugees work in the Soviet Union. Some of the refugees discussed in the previous chapter accepted this deal. But only those with particular skills, such as engineering or accounting, landed positions in Minsk or another urban center. The rest were sent to mines, lumber camps, and *kolkhozy* (collective farms) in northern and central Russia. As noted earlier, refugee workers returned illegally after experiencing deplorable working conditions. Back in their home towns, they were fair game for arrest.

The Soviet internal passport proved another instrument to assess the potential allegiance of native inhabitants as well as of refugees. Moscow had issued a decree on 29 November 1939 formally extending citizenship to former Polish citizens resident on the dates of territorial annexation—1 November for western Ukraine and 2 November for western Belarus. Officials began to call in Polish identification papers in early 1940. To decline meant unemployment and eviction.[9] Applicants for new Soviet passports filled out questionnaires. Asked about their father's profession, family connections to the White Russian army, and relatives outside Soviet territory, they revealed just the sort of information necessary to ferret out "class enemies."[10]

Upon issuance, not all residents' passports looked the same. As former business owners, Feliks Zandman's maternal grandparents received passports with a clause marking them as unreliable elements. "Oh, you have a passport like that?" a Red Army soldier replied when asked about this notation. "That means Siberia."[11] Fearing deportation, the Freydowicz grandparents fled to the smaller town of Slonim. Two of Feliks's uncles also fled Grodno for the same reason. The Soviet system was inconsistent, however: his father, Aaron, and Uncle Sender had worked in the family business yet were not assigned the compromising clause.[12]

The passport posed a particular dilemma for refugees. After sealing the border with German-occupied western Poland in February 1940, the Soviets extended citizenship to refugees on their territory. But unlike longtime Kresy residents, refugees were not compelled to surrender their Polish identification papers. Some took the passport with a little encouragement. Liliana Goldsopl and her aunt Guta, refugees from Warsaw, were persuaded by relatives who supported the Soviet system. "And all of a sudden at the age of sixteen," she recalled decades later, "I was a Soviet citizen."[13]

Many other refugees declined. They thought, Wasn't their stay under Soviet rule only temporary?[14] Yet to refuse or even to hesitate to accept a Soviet passport exposed them to arrest and deportation. Nothing appeared more suspect to the Bolsheviks than rootless persons with no desire to join the revolution. The first wave of deportations in February forced many refugees to make up their minds. Some panicked and considered a return to German-occupied Poland. "Go back! Go back to Warsaw—before it's too late!" was a frenzied response Avraham Zak recalled hearing.[15]

Aware that some refugees wanted to return to Polish territory under German occupation, the Soviets posted notices beginning in March 1940 offering repatriation.[16] What better way to uncover potential traitors? Some refugees considered going back to reunite with family members. Joseph Ceder's aunt Shifra, married to his mother's youngest brother, cried constantly about her parents in Łódź. His uncle gave in. "One day, against all advice, they decided to make the trip back," Joseph recalled. "They made the trip back, and [it was] like they fell into water. We never heard from them again."[17] More than 160,000 refugees, including many Jews, signed up to return to German-occupied Poland. German representatives accepted some 66,000 people. Suspicious of the remaining applicants' motives, the NKVD swept up most of them for deportation on the night of 12–13 April 1940.[18]

Among the refugees deported was Max Markiewitz. He had fled Warsaw in October 1939. After a few months, he was eager to fetch his parents. "I felt I wanted to go back," he remembered. "I'll try everything . . . to bring them over." Max initially refused an internal passport and signed up for repatriation instead when notices went up offering this option. This act sealed his fate. The NKVD soon arrested and deported him to Vorkuta, north of the Arctic Circle.[19]

Others tried to sidestep the official repatriation process. Rozalia Hollander wanted to return to Warsaw after receiving a letter in March 1940 reporting that her mother was ill. Her husband, Leopold, warned, "Look, once you go, we will never see each other [again]." He agreed to accompany her after some urging. But their plan to walk across the frozen river Bug was foiled when they found open water instead of ice. After the Hollanders sought refuge nearby in Ciechanowiec, the local authorities summoned them: Did they want a Soviet passport? Rozalia and Leopold vacillated and were soon deported to a labor camp in Siberia.[20] The Hollanders weren't alone. Dora Huze, a refugee turned black-market trader, had found legitimate work as a Grodno schoolteacher. Yet she and her new husband felt no desire to become Soviet citizens. "I was thinking the war would be over soon," Dora recalled in an interview in 1997. "I want to go back to my family, and if I take citizenship, I could never leave Russia." Their destination after arrest was a labor camp in the Arkhangelsk Oblast.[21]

The magnitude of the deportation operations is difficult to quantify accurately. One Soviet source declared that 387,932 Polish citizens were removed from the western borderlands between September 1939 and June 1941. The historian Jan Gross has noted that this figure is likely far too low.[22] Upward of 300,000 refugees crossed from German-occupied Poland,[23] and with some exceptions the term *refugee* became synonymous with *deportee*, so the official number 387,932 appears a deliberate underestimate. Another total prepared in 1945 by the Polish army in the Middle East places the number of deportees at 990,000,[24] suggesting that the Soviets deported nearly 10 percent of the Kresy population.

The expulsions doubtless made an impression on the remaining inhabitants. We saw in the previous chapter how Grodno's Jews viewed refugees as a novelty or a nuisance; as a source of rumors about Nazi atrocity, usually doubted; and as a distraction from the challenges of the new Soviet system. Refugees' deportation added a new dimension: terror. Whereas adults passed through a range of responses, from annoyance to fear, young people were perhaps too self-absorbed with extracurricular activities. Vichna Sidranska, for instance, remembered the refugees but little about what happened to them. "The Russians did not allow too many refugees in the city," she recalled decades later, "and they would round them up and ship them out constantly." And where did they go? Her vague memory reveals detachment. "I imagine it was Siberia. I didn't know at the time."[25]

Refugees represented only one segment of the deportees. Young people's recollections of local elites sent to the Soviet interior emerge as class distinctions. Ann Lewin, daughter of a local wood-fuel supplier, remembered the deportees as "the bourgeois, the very rich people from big businesses or whatever"[26]—that is, not someone of her father's status. Liliana Goldsopl, a refugee, took a broader view. She remembered that the deportees included those the Soviets "considered rich—and for them rich was some poor Jew who had a little store and was very, very poor because there were a lot of poor Jews in Grodno."[27] Liliana's pragmatic assessment and the relative risk that many faced might further explain her ready acceptance of a Soviet passport.

Although young Jews had little reason to recall the refugees' plight or the deportations, given their own later challenges, they were far from unaffected by these manifestations of Soviet power. Feliks Zandman missed his grandparents and uncles, who were hiding in towns 100 kilometers away.[28] The force of state security invaded their lives in other ways. Chasia Bielicka witnessed the arrest of her brother Avraham under suspicion of Zionist activities. "One evening, there was a knock on the door," she recalled. "Usually this meant strangers, not family members. We stiffened with fear and dread." The young man was released after his interrogators terrified him sufficiently.[29] Soviet power was manifest in the classroom as well. Alexandre Blumstein recalled how his history reader contained blacked-out paragraphs and pasted-over photographs. Soviet textbooks for the new school system were in short supply, requiring the reuse of editions predating the purges of a few years earlier. Alexandre's teacher explained that the redacted portions showed "enemies of the people," yet this explanation only enticed the boy to lift the black paper covering one photograph, revealing the portrait of a dishonored Red Army general.[30]

East Meets West

In addition to the NKVD agents directing mass deportations, commissars and ordinary Soviet citizens poured into western Belarus. Some came to revamp schools. Others looked to reshape the land. In

1941, engineers began an extensive swamp-drainage program of the Pripyat Marshes in the Polesie region south of Grodno, projected for completion in 1947.[31] Well-known cultural leaders arrived to explain to the various ethnic populations how they fit into the Soviet nationalities policy. As part of this process, the cream of Soviet Jewish writers from Moscow and Ukraine declared Białystok, colonized by refugee writers from Warsaw, a new Yiddish literary center.[32]

Many of Minsk's leading Yiddish writers had fallen victim to the purges, but prominent Yiddish writers from Moscow, including Itzik Fefer, Dovid Bergelson, and Peretz Markish, continued to write and publish. Indeed, Bergelson, along with Der Nister and Leb Kvitko, were nominated by the Jewish Writers' Union for the Stalin Prize in 1941.[33] Joining these cultural leaders on "writers' brigades," meant to promote Bolshevik ideals among Jews in the new western oblasts, was the surviving group of Minsk's Yiddish writers, including Zelik Akselrod, Mendl Lifshits, Rokhl Boimvol, and Ruve Reyzin.[34] Hirsh Reles figured into this expansion of Soviet Yiddish culture when he accepted a teaching position in Novogrudok. He combined these duties with an appointment as content director for a local radio station, a politically sensitive position for such a young writer.[35]

The refugee writers who encountered Soviet Yiddish literati heard oft-repeated tales about the good life artists and writers experienced in the Soviet Union, at least within obvious constraints. Warsaw native Sheyne Miriam Broderzon and her husband, poet Moishe Broderzon, heard in Białystok, "You need to conform to the Soviet reality and write in the Soviet spirit."[36] Writer and critic Moishe Grosman heard somewhat less-strict admonitions. "You need to write using your former themes and approaches, only pay attention to the new relations and conditions," Itzik Fefer told a group. "Endeavor to understand the great Soviet reality!" As Grosman sardonically commented on Fefer's advice, "We need only to be honest, loyal, and sincere, taking to heart the ideals of Stalinist truth."[37]

Zelik Akselrod, by comparison, spoke with less ideological rigidity and even associated with Bundist and Zionist refugees. This was no small act because, as noted in chapter 1, Akselrod had been a close associate of purge victim Izi Kharik. "He had a good word for everyone," Broderzon recalled.[38] Akselrod established a local Jewish section of the Belarusian Writers' Union for refugees in Białystok and married a member of this coterie. His bride was Perl Vaysenberg, daughter of the late Polish Yiddish writer Itshe Meyer Vaysenberg (died 1938).

Refugee writers initially published in *Bialystoker shtern*, the Soviet-sponsored Yiddish newspaper launched at the end of 1939. But a purge began with the arrival of the leading writers from Minsk, Moscow, and Kiev. Only those willing to tailor their work along party lines were employable.[39] The paper went on to publish articles urging conformity: all refugees must take Soviet citizenship, avoid engaging in black-market activities, and join productive elements of the Soviet economy.[40] Even with these modifications, official support for *Bialystoker shtern* waned. Its paper allocation was reduced in late 1940, and its publication was cut from seven to three days a week.[41]

Although such encounters between East and West were initially cordial, refugees stumbled when they asked sensitive questions. Moishe Grosman wrote of a meeting in late 1939 with Rokhl Boimvol, Mendl Lifshits, and a third Yiddish poet whose name Grosman did not catch. The conversation turned frosty when Grosman asked about Moishe Kulbak's whereabouts. Not even these prominent Minsk-based Yiddish writers knew for certain where the once prominent Kulbak was—Dead or in a gulag?—but Grosman received a stock answer about anyone who had disappeared during the Great Terror. "Kulbak was an enemy of the people! A traitor!" Lifshits declared. "He got the punishment he deserved—he was removed from society. He sits in prison."[42] The three Soviet writers apparently did not know that Kulbak was already dead, or if they did, they were unwilling to say so.

The era of cultural openness was short-lived in Białystok. By the time of the German invasion in June 1941, *Bialystoker shtern* as well as *Oktyabr* and *Shtern* in Minsk remained in circulation. Yiddish-language education, already eliminated in eastern Belarus years earlier, was quickly shut down in the new western oblasts. Of the writers who sought refuge in Białystok, some, such as Moishe and Sheyne Miriam Broderzon, remained free. A few migrated to Vilna or other

Soviet cities. But the rest, including Moishe Grosman and Avraham Zak, were deported to labor camps.

And while the Moscow- and Kiev-based writers remained free, Minsk's Yiddish writers faced a new purge. In early June 1941, Hirsh Reles returned to Minsk to see Zelik Akselrod. He discovered, however, that his former editor was under arrest. Sheyne Miriam Broderzon reports in her memoir that in Białystok before this date Akselrod had come into conflict with Soviet commissar Hershman (first name not available), the official responsible for keeping the refugee writers in line. Hershman had summoned Akselrod and accused him of Jewish nationalist chauvinism. Akselrod left Białystok without a goodbye to anyone. "People began to talk," Broderzon recalled, "that this generous poet was in a Minsk prison."[43] In fact, Akselrod had been arrested on 30 May 1941, along with two other well-known writers.[44] They were still in prison awaiting trial as the Germans invaded a few weeks later.

West Meets East

The cultural exchanges passing from east to west revealed the general restrictions on intellectual freedom within the Soviet system. Exchanges also occurred from west to east, crossing the internal border dividing the old and new parts of Soviet Belarus, as thousands of Kresy inhabitants and refugees discovered firsthand twenty years of life under Bolshevism. Some of these Polish Jews passed through Vitebsk, and the memories of old and new Soviet citizens afford us an opportunity to compare the two worlds.

According to Soviet census data, 3,820 Polish Jews passed as refugees through the Vitebsk oblast between the end of 1939 and June 1941.[45] Most did so to fulfill education or labor commitments. One of them was Elias Rubinstein, a twenty-two-year-old from Łapy, southwest of Białystok. He had been recruited to study accountancy at the School of Masters of Socialist Labor in Vitebsk, an opportunity that opened doors. Accountants were the white-collar army that greased the wheels of Soviet progress, often by juggling the books. Perhaps Elias expected to be dazzled or disoriented by a city living under socialism because he commented decades later that he found "quite a normal life" in Vitebsk. Elias wrote to his family to reassure them of his safety and happiness. He was learning new skills, and he got along well with his classmates, despite being the only Jew.[46]

Not all who ventured from west to east felt as optimistic. Moishe Grosman didn't even have to leave Białystok to observe signs of a shortage of consumer goods. After his luncheon with the Yiddish writers, he noted that Rokhl Boimvol from Minsk had only thin, patched shoes to wear in the newly fallen snow. Nothing was available in Grodno either because Red Army soldiers had already picked over the shops in the preceding months.[47] Even deportees noticed the lower Soviet standard of living in the older parts of Soviet Belarus. Like Rozalia and Leopold Hollander, refugee Lucien Feigenbaum tried to return to German-occupied Poland but failed when German border guards turned him back over to the Soviets. His first stop upon receiving a three-year prison sentence was not Siberia, but Vitebsk. During his march across the city to his temporary prison, Lucien noted that many of the city's residents wore cheap-looking canvas shoes, while he and many of his fellow detainees still possessed good-quality boots. Food appeared scarce, and even his NKVD warders ate only dry bread and cucumbers. One guard chided the prisoners for their complaints, "What do you imagine? That you will get mashed potatoes and butter?" Lucien thought this odd—the best thing this NKVD man could imagine was mashed potatoes? Life must be hard in the Soviet Union, he remembered thinking.[48]

Besides living standards, Polish Jews noted clear cultural differences between themselves and their Soviet counterparts in Vitebsk. As we have seen, refugees from central Poland found Kresy Jews to be more devout. Soviet Jews, by contrast, in particular those of the younger generation, displayed a degree of spiritual flexibility that amazed Polish Jews. One such observer was seventeen-year-old Alexander Dimant, a refugee from Warsaw. He accepted vocational training as a metalworker in Vitebsk, a city he recalled decades later as populated with "a lot of Jews." When the school's director, a man named Rabkin, invited his Jewish refugee students to a Passover Seder,

Alexander later remembered it as "not [a] hundred percent like in our case."[49] Not only were the physical accoutrements such as kosher foods largely unavailable, but Bolshevik antireligious propaganda had also reshaped the implementation of traditions.

But if Polish Jews were distressed at the physical and spiritual shortcomings of Soviet life, many felt welcome in the new environment. Lucien Feigenbaum recalled that although some Vitebsk residents mocked him and his fellow prisoners as "Polish lords," others tossed biscuits to the obviously starved detainees.[50] Some took refugees into their homes. A refugee family occupied a spare room in Vera German's family home. The mother and father, caring for a daughter and infant son, also received financial support from Vera's parents.[51]

For some, the refugees' arrival reshaped their worldview and personal sense of identity. "Vitebsk started to be crowded with some strange people," Raisa Gendelev remembered decades later, "and when I started to ask my grandparents, they told me [these were] Polish people who are running from Germany." Raisa's parents, Moishe and Lebe, had sent their eight-year-old daughter from Leningrad to spend the summer of 1940 with her paternal grandparents, Berl and Trina, in Vitebsk. Raisa looked forward to playing in her grandparents' garden, visiting with cousins, and swimming in the Dvina. She also spent time with her *frum* (religious) grandfather, who prayed morning and evening; her parents, by contrast, didn't observe the traditions, like many Soviet Jews educated under the Bolsheviks.

Berl Gendelev expanded Raisa's conception of Jewishness in a way that was not possible in her secular home life or Russian-language primary school. "We did recognize ourselves as Jewish people," she remembered of her upbringing. "I knew I was a Jewish girl." The refugees who arrived that summer expanded her awareness in a wholly different way. "Quite a lot of people were speaking differently—speaking Polish," Raisa recalled. Their presence alerted her to Jews living outside the Soviet Union.[52]

Some Jewish refugees faced rejection as former Polish citizens as well as Jews. Ten-year-old Hanna Davidson had fled Warsaw with her parents in late 1939, eventually settling in Orsha, 60 kilometers south of Vitebsk. At her first day in school, students whispered "polachka"—"Polish girl"—and reached out to touch her "foreign" clothing. She also heard antisemitic stereotypes from her classmates, who could not understand why she did not have a big nose, black hair, and thick glasses. "I was constantly asked why I did not fit into these categories," she wrote decades later. "It was decided among my peers that something was wrong with me."[53] Even her two Jewish classmates, born in the Soviet Union, rejected Hanna.

Hanna's experience reveals not only how antisemitism persisted in Soviet society despite the official measures to suppress it but also the gulf that lay between natives of western and eastern Belarus. Some successfully crossed the border and the social divide. Elias was permitted to enter not just the socialist state but also the crucial profession of accountancy. Lucien, raised in upper-middle-class Jewish Warsaw and university educated, came to understand the limitations of the Soviet experiment. Alexander, who grew up in an observant family, encountered Judaic practices shaped by Bolshevism. Vera played with the daughter of the refugee family hosted in the family home.[54] Raisa, raised in an acculturated household, became fascinated by her *frum* grandfather and confused by the dozens of Polish-speaking Jews seeking refuge in Vitebsk. Hanna, one of those Jews who spoke Polish, wanted to be someone she wasn't. She even joined the Pioneers, forcing a smile during the investiture ceremony despite the obvious height difference as she stood next to the other much younger inductees.[55]

War Talk

Soviet Yiddish writers arrived in the annexed oblasts in the wake of the Red Army to herald the false dawn of Bolshevik Jewish culture to Polish Jews. They crossed paths with Polish Jews headed eastward, who encountered the constraints of Soviet life. A new marriage of peoples and territory unfolded in Soviet Belarus and had not yet settled into domestic stability by the spring of 1941. Each migration wave brought refreshed popular rumors and challenged the official narrative surrounding the issue that triggered everything that was happening in the region—the war. Central to these discussions was the status of Nazi Germany. Was it a friend or foe?

Many Soviet citizens felt confused and disturbed by a sudden shift in foreign policy signaled by the Molotov-Ribbentrop Pact of 1939. One witness, an ethnic Belarusian, remembered after the war her shock at hearing news of the alliance with Germany. "It was as if a bomb had exploded," the young woman recalled. "Up to then we had been told that Germany was the worst of all capitalist countries and was the first enemy of the Soviet Union. And now, here we had a pact with that same country."[56] Some eventually accommodated the notion of such an alliance after realizing its strategic significance. "It was simply a temporary thing, that Hitler and Stalin could be friends," a young Belarusian man remembered his reaction. He was drafted a few months later, and Red Army political commissars clarified the state of affairs. "In the army the *politruki* [political commissar] said that we are still enemies of Germany, even if we had a pact."[57] Civilians, however, believed fully in Soviet peace promises. "I had a real faith in the Nazi–Soviet nonaggression pact," a young Belarusian woman recalled later. At the time, however, her father disagreed, sure that war would certainly come. "We often had many arguments on the subject, and I always tried to convince my parents of the correctness of the *Pravda* point of view," she continued, indicating how the Soviet press pushed the peace-and-protection narrative.[58]

But if war came tomorrow, what kind of war would it be? Would the French or the British strike against the Soviet Union, as they had declared war on Nazi Germany? Would the Germans betray the pact and invade? Or would the Soviets attack first? Two official war narratives circulated. Other nations engaged in wars of imperialist aggression. "The capitalist world enters 1941 devastatingly torn by conflicts," *Oktyabr*'s editors pointed out to their readers on New Year's Day, commenting further how "millions of workers of bourgeois countries are ensnared within the second imperialist war." The Soviet Union, however, led liberation campaigns. The same *Oktyabr* editorial celebrated 1940 as the year that "the Baltic lands Estonia, Latvia, and Lithuania established the Soviet order, uniting with the great Soviet Union."[59]

Simultaneously, Bessarabia and Northern Bukovina were wrested from Romania.

Not all Soviet territorial enterprises were peaceful. After the Finns refused Stalin's territorial demands along the Gulf of Finland, the Red Army invaded with an initial force of 450,000 troops on 30 November 1939, triggering the Soviet–Finnish War or Winter War. Through a combination of inadequate equipment (for example, some Soviet troops wore only their summer uniforms) and faulty tactics (Finnish troops moved rapidly on skis, whereas Soviet troops were stuck in their broken-down tanks), a conflict that should have taken a few weeks lasted until March 1940, when the Finns acceded to Stalin's demands only after a massive Soviet troop surge.[60]

Red Army casualties numbered in the hundreds of thousands. Although kept out of the newspapers, this harsh reality was difficult to hide. A soldier stationed in Chernigov in Ukraine saw multitudes of wounded sent there to recover from the Winter War. He was perplexed. Why so many? Why couldn't the Soviets crush the Finns swiftly? "It was ridiculous," he told an interviewer after the war when he had left the Soviet Union. "Finland had only 3 million people. Leningrad itself has 3 million."[61] Many knew someone or someone's son who was engaged in the fighting. Raisa Gendelev's uncle was a soldier during the Winter War. "He brought some photos from the war," she reported decades later, "and it was frightening."[62]

The war also affected domestic life in cities such as Vitebsk. Fivel Markelis, the ruffian turned Belarusian folk dancer introduced in chapter 1, remembered that food shortages accompanied the Winter War. "At 3:00 a.m. my relatives dressed me in all the clothes possible and sent me to stand in line for bread," he recalled. "Closer to the morning I was relieved by my sister or by my brother. By the opening of the shop when the bread was delivered, all my family had stood in the line."[63] Alexander Dimant also witnessed shortages in Vitebsk. "It was the war between Russia and Finland," he recalled. The director of his vocational school helped. "We got permission [from him] to go to the store with the lineup—even the Russian people were angry with us: How come young boys?—so we didn't always use the advantage."[64]

Although the Soviet media concealed the bloodshed in the Winter War, the conflict in the rest of Europe emerged in time with greater clarity. After initial rhetoric that modeled Britain and France as "'plutocratic' aggressors" in the first weeks of the war,[65] such critiques in the press grew more muted by early 1940.[66] The fall of France in June 1940 shifted the tone again, as Britain stood alone against the Germans. Although Vitebsk's Belarusian-language newspaper *Chyrvonaya zvyazda* (Red Star) explained to its readers in August 1940 that the ruling French capitalists were the reason for their nation's defeat,[67] subsequent stories of German military operations displayed, as the historian Timothy Johnston has noted, a "cool objectivity."[68] Yiddish newspapers available in Vitebsk and Grodno carried brief war reports across all fronts. Indeed, war news was printed straight from Allied and German wire services, the latter edited to exclude any triumphant tone.

Such stories appear sympathetic to the British. A series of reports from September 1940 carried in the pages of Vitebsk's Russian-language paper *Vitsebski rabochy* (Vitebsk Worker) observed that the Germans had begun to bomb London, Portsmouth, Lincoln, and other British cities, part of the sustained campaign later known as the Blitz.[69] America eventually came to Britain's defense, if only in terms of war materiel, with the Lend-Lease Act of 1941. *Oktyabr* called that act an example of international cooperation, not collaboration between capitalist exploiters.[70] On Red Army Day in 1941 (23 February), *Oktyabr* printed the usual war news alongside its effusive praise of Soviet armed forces. Germans and the English fought in North Africa, while the British populace struggled on at home. Industries in occupied France collaborated by supplying the Wehrmacht. From the sidelines, America waged a war of words on German aggression. And Japanese expansion continued in China.[71]

Popular interpretations of these sources distorted their impact. After years of imbibing official propaganda, some doubted the sources' veracity. "I did not believe in them," a young Belarusian respondent remembered after the war when asked what newspapers he read back in 1940. His remark addressed domestic news primarily—the glowing accounts of factory production figures and Five-Year Plans. But if those reports held limited authenticity, what inferences could such readers draw from stories about the Germans bombing British cities? The same ethnic Belarusian offered another statement that illuminates how some Soviet citizens processed this news. "But [the newspapers] stimulated me to think; they gave food for thought."[72] Although the official news was considered untrustworthy, consuming it nevertheless fostered the skill of reading between the lines. This ability was common among those raised under Soviet rule, and refugee newcomers and longtime Kresy residents soon learned of its necessity.[73]

Rumor supplemented the official narrative, elaborating interpretations of printed sources.[74] Yet whisperers and listeners seldom comprehended the seriousness of these tales. Speakers and hearers held differing motives as well. Commenting on the successive war rumors in Stalinist society of the 1930s, the historian Sheila Fitzpatrick has noted how conflict with the capitalist world was "feared by many and hoped for by some."[75] Foreign invasion would deliver them from the Bolsheviks.[76] Even the Germans would be kinder masters, or so some believed despite the reports they may have heard. Although Jewish refugees told about their harsh treatment by the Germans, these stories seem to have made no significant impression on a community already coping with the new Soviet system. Alexandre Blumstein heard a great many rumors about an incipient German invasion from his family's neighbor, an officer in the Red Air Force. This expert, however, blamed the French and British for nurturing Hitler as a weapon against Bolshevism.[77] Such fantastical ideas lessened the urgency of any warning.

Reports also spread by letter, although refugees and former Kresy residents were far more likely to communicate this way than longtime Soviet citizens, who not only had fewer international contacts after twenty years under socialism but also knew that maintaining connections with anyone in the West risked an NKVD investigation. The scope of mail service should not be underestimated, however. One collection of postcards sent in 1940 and 1941 by a mother in Grodno to her son in Boston shows that formal mail exchange existed between

Soviet Grodno and the United States. The postcards also establish that the son sent parcels to his mother in return.[78] Some of the mail between German-occupied Poland and the Soviet Union was carried by smugglers. As Rozalia Hollander observed about the letter that prompted her attempted return to Warsaw, "There was no post office, or mail was not coming the normal way, but people used—for money—to smuggle, going backward and forward over the borders."[79] Official mail service also passed between German-held territory and the Soviet Union,[80] although the mail went through the hands of censors in each zone.[81] Many refugees in Grodno later reported corresponding with relatives in Warsaw or Łódź during the pact period.[82] Even when first-hand accounts told of Nazi atrocities, recipients seldom comprehended the scope of the unfolding persecution in German-occupied Poland.

Jews on Soviet territory looking for official news reports about the treatment of their coreligionists in German-occupied Poland ran into a dead end. Stalin wanted neither any reference to Polish identity nor any report that might anger the Germans.[83] As a consequence, the press ran no stories about German-occupation politics in Poland or elsewhere. By 1941, a few stories filtered through about food and consumer-good shortages in occupied France.[84] Readers could hardly be expected to deduce anything about Poland based on such a limited critique.

Warnings of German aggression against the Soviet Union disappeared as well, at least until late 1940. Oblique allusions reemerged thereafter in the pages of *Oktyabr* and other publications. A report on Franklin D. Roosevelt's "Arsenal of Democracy" speech of 29 December 1940 quoted the president's declaration of America's intention to confront Germany: "The United States has no right or reason to encourage talk of peace, until . . . there is a clear intention on the part of the aggressor nations to abandon all thought of dominating or conquering the world."[85] Significantly, the *Oktyabr* editors issued no comments to contradict Roosevelt's accusations.

The German threat reemerged as a theme in popular culture as well, particularly in the newly acquired borderlands. *Alexander Nevsky*, Sergei Eisenstein's film about the invasion and defeat of the Germanic

Livonian Knights in the thirteenth century, was withdrawn from circulation less than a year after its Moscow premiere in 1938 to avoid irritating the Germans. At least one other regional screening was advertised in the Latvian capital of Riga two weeks after the Soviet occupation of the Baltic countries in June 1940.[86] And the film played to a packed house in Grodno sometime during 1940 or early 1941. Avraham Zak, an attendee at the Grodno showing, reported little about his response to the film.[87] Since the actors spoke Russian, perhaps only viewers with a decent command of the language could understand the anti-German references. But even rudimentary knowledge would have permitted an understanding of the frequent references to *nemtsy* (Germans) as aggressors, along with the less-than-subtle visual allusions to Nazi swastikas on the attacking knights' costumes.

Popular estimations had to navigate the twisted paths and mixed messages in circulation. When the narrative of the evils of German fascism ended abruptly with the pact in August 1939, the news rarely illuminated events with consistency or clarity. Rumors supplemented official accounts in Soviet life yet were dependent on the speaker's interpretations. The Germans' treatment of Jews in occupied countries remained solely the domain of gossip, with some tales too strange or horrible to believe.

Unlike the rhetoric shouted in the 1930s, the subtle references to the threat posed by German aggression in the Soviet press while the pact was in force do not seem to have caught most people's attention. Even if they did understand, it appears that adults often shielded their children from these messages. Vera German, fourteen years old in 1941, could remember the dresses she wore in her youth, yet she didn't recall any discussion of the European war in her family's home despite the presence of refugees in the spare room.[88] It seems improbable that her father, a white-collar worker, and her mother, who agreed to take in the refugees, were unaware of the seriousness of events in German-occupied Poland. Vera, they apparently thought, did not need to know what was happening or did not want to alarm her.

Other Vitebsk families could not believe that the Germans posed a threat. Elena Choukmazova (introduced in chapter 1) turned eleven the year of the German invasion. She recalled in an interview in 1998 that her family "didn't feel that there would be a war."[89] To put it another way, the war would not reach them, a belief reflecting a false sense of security that many Soviet citizens felt in 1941. Yet not all children felt so safe. As Raisa Gendelev stated in an interview in March 2000, "At the age of eight, I did recognize that something is not right in the world, and it can be dangerous." The arrival of refugees in Vitebsk during the summer of 1940 triggered this awareness. Unlike Vera's parents, who told her nothing about the war, Raisa's grandfather offered misinformed words of reassurance. "The *daytshn* [Germans] are educated people, are high-cultured people—they will not do anything wrong to us," she recalled her grandfather saying. Yet neighbors asked, What about the refugees? What has changed?[90] Her consciousness was heightened further the following year in her Leningrad school, where she and her classmates took part in air-raid drills and donned gas masks.

Like many of their coreligionists in Vitebsk, young Grodno Jews held few worries about the German threat. "We were educated people, plugged into the world," Chasia Bielicka later recalled, and ironically this attitude contributed to their false sense of security. With no real news available about what was happening across the border, Chasia remembered, "my parents, like the entire world—not only that of the Jewish exiles—lived in ignorance, incomprehension, and cluelessness."[91] Feliks Zandman observed something similar, although he did not realize the folly of his elders' perceptions until after the German invasion. When the refugee Glass family arrived in Grodno in late 1939 or early 1940, they told the Freydowiczes and Zandmans that they were headed to Vilna to get transit visas for Shanghai. Come with us, they implored. Feliks's elders declined. The Red Army would protect them, they declared.[92]

Even people exposed to rumors about the threat of war lacked crucial information about the Germans' treatment of Jews. As 1940 passed into 1941, the Blumsteins heard from the Red Air Force major living next door that war with Germany was inevitable.[93] The report was vague, though, and they wondered, Who would attack first? The

Soviet military, despite struggling to recover from the disasters of the Winter War, already had massed forces on the western border.[94] Belarusians living outside Grodno confirmed to Dr. Blumstein what many already witnessed: Soviet planes passing overhead and tanks rolling through town, all heading west.[95] And what if the Germans invaded? Again, without essential knowledge, some in Grodno considered the potential of German rule tolerable. "Being sent to Siberia or Kazakhstan in cattle trucks seemed equally distasteful as an alternative to Nazi rule," Alexandre Blumstein recalled later.[96]

Joining the Red Army

Grodno and Vitebsk Jews lived under the same political order during the short Molotov-Ribbentrop Pact era, but their intellectual worlds remained far apart. Perhaps the only domain where Bolshevik and former "capitalist" Jews interacted and cooperated was the Red Army. Indeed, Soviet society, Jewish and Gentile, fractured by the purges and mass deportations, focused its expectations and confidence on these mingled ranks. "To defend the fatherland is the sacred duty of every citizen of the USSR," *Oktyabr* reminded its readers on Red Army Day 1941, quoting Article 133 of the Stalin Constitution of 1936.[97] This was not simply rhetoric. Elias Rubinstein recalled decades later the prevailing yet imprecise "spirit that we have to defend the country."[98]

Defense of the state was personified not only by Stalin but by his longtime political ally Marshal Kliment Voroshilov. In the popular film *If There Is War Tomorrow* (Efim Dzigan, 1938), depicting a farcical German invasion, an actor playing Voroshilov calls upon all Soviet peoples to join the Red Army in repelling the assault.[99] The marshal maintained his high profile in the years that followed. *Oktyabr* readers saw large photographs of him on the occasion of his sixtieth birthday, 4 February 1941.[100] "Voroshilov is the first of our friends," affirmed a Russian poem that *Oktyabr* printed just a couple weeks later in Yiddish translation.[101]

Personality cults focused on the Bolshevik leadership, while other narratives promoted the ordinary soldiers of the workers' and peasants' army. Yiddish writers joined in. Zelik Akselrod's poem "Lager"

(Camp, 1939) recounts the observations of an alert night watchman, closing with the lines:

For bold Red Army fighters,
For bravery,
For clearheaded judgment,
For secure borders of our land,
To the last battle,
For life and for death!
We are ready!
We are vigilant![102]

"Bold Red Army fighters" were prepared for battle, Akselrod declared. Moreover, he reminded his readers of the importance of secure borders to safeguard what lay beyond. Hirsh Reles also penned a patriotic ode. "Afn grenets" (On the Border) described a patrol of three Red Army soldiers. To suggest their alertness to possible invaders, each soldier, in turn, chases wisps of snow and errant ravens.[103] Border security appeared again in a verse by Białystok poet Yosif Rubinsteyn for the New Year's Day edition of *Oktyabr*. "I will stand at the border at midnight with gun in hand," promised the closing line.[104]

Yiddish poet Ruve Reyzin may have felt compelled "to defend the Soviet Union" with the outbreak of the Spanish Civil War a continent away, but most young men entered the ranks of the armed forces through the draft. Conscription age in September 1940 was nineteen, and the first draft to occur across "united" Belarus and Ukraine was held then. Red Army recruiting took place on the local level, with district soviets sorting through the political and medical records for each candidate. An estimated 210,000 young men born between 1918 and 1921 were drafted from the new western oblasts alone.[105] Ann Lewin recalled that many Grodno youths were drafted in the early months of 1941, including her brother Arie.[106] Adult men were also conscripted, such as Daniel Klovsky's maternal uncle.[107] Young men who had crossed the border into eastern Belarus also were called up. Elias Rubinstein, a Polish Jew adjusting to life in Soviet Vitebsk, received his papers after finishing his accountancy course.[108]

In such an atmosphere of popular rhetoric and personal connections to the Red Army, many took security for granted. "We didn't feel that we were in jeopardy," recalled Grodno native Zelda Grodzienska. "We never thought that Germany will attack the Russian army, and we felt like—more secure than the rest of Poland."[109] And, indeed, the Soviet media seemed to suggest that "we will protect you." Images of happy, safe children figured prominently in the pages of *Oktyabr* during the first months of 1941. One photo shows Białystok school students sharing a snowball fight with their teacher.[110] In another, toddlers eye the camera as they are photographed in a Gomel crèche.[111] Children in Brit, however, were shown hiding in a trench, looking skyward in fear of German bombs.[112] To drive the point home, *Oktyabr* printed a series of articles on Soviet military forces in February 1941 under the bold headline "For Our Children."[113]

Propaganda offered images and stories of military readiness. A few weeks after France's defeat, *Chyrvonaya zvyazda* printed a line illustration of Stalin commending a young flyer, his bomber and his flight crew in the background and dozens of flying aircraft overhead.[114] The illustration accompanied an article promoting the achievements of the Red Air Force, in particular its supporting role in confronting the Japanese at Khalkhin Gol, in occupying western Belarus and western Ukraine, and in fighting the Finns during the Winter War.[115] *Oktyabr* also extolled domestic military abilities in an article by division commissar F. Voronin: "Combat operations in recent years have clearly demonstrated the armed strength of the Soviets." Moreover, he cited the "liberation march" into western Ukraine and western Belarus as an example of the army's "exceptional combat expertise." Voronin concluded the article by reassuring readers that the Soviet military had responded to the "second imperialistic war" by strengthening its forces.[116]

Most civilians were oblivious to the truth. Volumes have been written on the Soviets' military chaos, tactical blunders, and intelligence breakdowns even before the German invasion in 1941.[117] Territorial expansion was one factor. The acquisition of western Belarus and western Ukraine shifted the border westward by some 300 kilometers.

Construction on new defenses progressed slowly. The acquisition of the Baltic states and Bessarabia in 1940 compounded the issues. In one case, a military order dated 17 May 1941 called for the completion by October of new airfields near the Belarusian towns of Lepel and Drysa.[118] The party tried to speed up the work. An official responded a few days later by ordering improved support for these construction efforts and declaring a new deadline: 1 July 1941.[119]

Such were the details. Systemic problems existed throughout the Soviet armed forces. Some expert observers noticed obvious flaws in the Red Army's preparedness. The entrance of Soviet forces into Poland in September 1939 may have appeared well coordinated compared to the Polish army's chaotic retreat, but their entrance a few weeks later into the Baltic states to set up military bases revealed many shortcomings. Some locals noticed that officers could not read maps. Trucks, tanks, and other mobile equipment broke down even while being driven on good roads.[120] Refugees from German-occupied Poland had witnessed the Wehrmacht's might, and some felt the Russians were no match.[121] The Winter War demonstrated the widespread inadequacies even to Stalin, but the necessary rectifications would take time.

The military command structure also suffered from numerous weaknesses. The Great Terror accounted for most of them. Many top brass rose in the ranks more for political than martial reasons. For example, Marshal Voroshilov's incompetence during the Winter War led to his removal as the people's commissar for defense in May 1940. Yet he retained his other positions and even remained an iconic figure of Soviet military strength. After the German invasion, the marshal was given command of the northwest flank shielding the key city of Leningrad. Voroshilov, the "star" of *If There Is War Tomorrow*, was as incompetent against the Germans as he was against the Finns, thus validating Karl Marx's observation about the historical process, except in reverse: the first time as farce, the second time as tragedy.

The Soviet system set up its citizens to fail. The regime demanded absolute allegiance. Any other response was anti-Soviet. The media issued contradictory accounts of Germany and its policies, hindering the population's judgment. In their ignorance, all Soviet citizens truly were united. Declared protected from invasion, civilians only had to fear the next purge or mass deportation. They were joined with the Red Army, connected to its destiny in ways few understood or realized.

Hirsh Reles was among the millions whose fate was connected to the Red Army and to the civilians it pledged to protect. The shtetl boy turned poet, teacher, and reluctant polemicist joined the Red Army, apparently after many deferments, in early 1941. Reles had just published his second poetry collection, *Lider* (Poems).[122] He departed his teaching job and radio station editorial work and marched away, leaving his wife, Yekha, and daughter, Raisel, in Novogrudok.

Reles, who had no problem discussing the experiences of his literary colleagues in the period before the war, even those who were killed in the purges, omits any mention of these last days of peace in his reminiscences. On Sunday, 22 June 1941, Reles was in Minsk with his division. On 3 July 1941, the Germans entered Novogrudok, trapping his family. Did he blame himself for what happened to them? Is this why, even decades later, he avoided writing about them? Did he, as a Red Army soldier committed to his nation's defense, feel a particular sense of guilt?

Hirsh Reles and millions of other men in the Red Army pledged to defend the motherland. They were a reassuring presence for civilians in cities, villages, and *kolkhozy*. The Red Army soldier was as visible on *ulica* Peretza in Grodno as on *ulitsa* Petrovskaya in Vitebsk. Soviet soldiers stood side by side with leaders such as Marshal Voroshilov and were praised alongside him. In the ode to the revered Red Army commander, poet Sergey Vladimirovich Mikhalkov affirmed the military's readiness:

> And if suddenly there is war and our land faces peril,
> the border guard and secret police, infantry and tank drivers,
> fliers, parachutists, sailors, artillery, and the agile cavalry,
> will not allow harm to us, never, all are prepared for battle.[123]

But it was a lie.

Saturday, 21 June 1941

Raisa Gendelev arose the morning of Saturday, 21 June 1941, at her grandparents' home in Vitebsk. She had recently completed the first grade in Leningrad and had been sent to spend another summer with her father's parents.[124] Lev Fleish, one of the cohort of young Jews raised in the Red city Vitebsk, had just been released from the hospital. He had had a cyst removed from his neck and still needed two or three weeks to recover.[125] For other Vitebsk residents, that Saturday promised to be sunny and warm, perfect for long walks or swimming, an afternoon concert in one of the parks, or maybe a film at the Proletkino.[126]

For some in Grodno, that Saturday was graduation day. Liliana Goldsopl attended the ceremony to receive her high school diploma. Mina Muller attended a dance given to honor the graduates of her seven-year school. Chasia Bielicka looked forward to studies that fall in Leningrad, an opportunity that the director of her Soviet high school had made possible. Personal dramas occupied others. Alexandre Blumstein's mother, Estera, recovered from a breakdown following her husband's affair with a hospital nurse.[127] The rest of the city remained on edge because the Soviets had just unleashed another mass deportation; the first trainload had departed a few days earlier.

What followed the next day quickly became a catastrophe. Witnesses' initial shock at the German invasion was replaced by another, deeper sense of devastation and betrayal as the Soviet armed forces collapsed over the following hours and days and weeks. "Our troops are retreating!" was one of the shouts Grodno carpenter Leib Reizer heard as Red Army vehicles whisked by while the Luftwaffe dropped bombs onto Grodno. "It was a knife into our hearts," he wrote later. "What would become of us? Our mothers, our fathers, our wives and children? Where should we run?"[128]

5

Invasion and Holocaust

June to November 1941

"The war between Germany and Russia began today," wrote Sarah Fishkin in her diary on 22 June 1941. Sarah, the young Zionist from Rubiezewicze, was in another town, Volozhin, about 200 kilometers from the border, when she heard Molotov's midday announcement. Having spent the previous months working for a local Bolshevik newspaper and continuing her education, she was likely as stunned as everyone else by the news. But what lay ahead? Did she understand the pressing danger? Or did she believe Soviet forces would protect her? Her thoughts that day soon turned to family back in Rubiezewicze. "My mother's heart is in turmoil this day when her children are so far away," she imagined.[1]

After a few weeks under German occupation in Volozhin, Sarah rejoined her family in Rubiezewicze. In doing so, she responded to war like so many other young Jews of her generation, choosing to rejoin or remain with their extended families. Only a few appreciated the mortal threat and tried to outrun the German advance. Those trapped in Grodno and Vitebsk responded to invasion, occupation, persecution, and murder in different ways, and very different genocides unfolded in these two cities, marked by isolation and slow starvation in Vitebsk and by systematic exploitation in Grodno. Jews in both communities clung to their family units in the hope that collectively they could weather the storm.

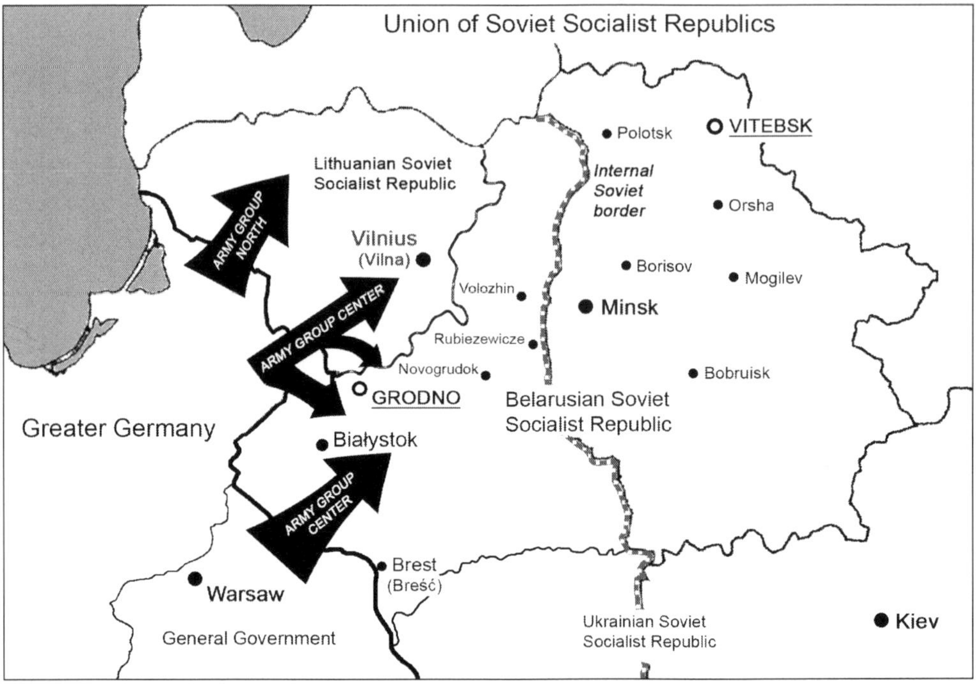

13. Map of the BSSR showing the initial invasion routes of the Wehrmacht's Army Group North and Army Group Center on 22 June 1941. Grodno fell at the end of the first day of the invasion. German forces captured Minsk on 28 June and pushed toward Vitebsk, which fell on 11 July.

Grodno under Attack

Grodno lay in the Białystok region, a piece of territory forming a salient with two exposed flanks fronting East Prussia and the German-occupied General Government, as shown in figure 13. Red Army strategists recognized the region's vulnerability but were still struggling to respond when the Germans attacked on Sunday, 22 June 1941.[2] Dawn arrived that summer morning to find much of the fortified infrastructure half-finished.[3] In one of those defensive positions, the former Imperial Russian fortress at Osowiec, 70 kilometers west of Grodno, twenty-eight-year-old Jewish Red Army junior officer Boris Grayneman heard the sound of explosions soon after he awoke at 4:00 a.m. The first German planes dropped their bombs on the adjacent airfield, followed by five more waves in the space of an hour. German fighters strafed Grayneman and other soldiers as they hastily loaded trucks with food and supplies. "Why aren't any of them [the planes] ours?" he wondered at the time, as the complete lack of a Soviet response added to his shock over what was happening.[4]

"Where are our fighters?" cried the wife of a Red Air Force officer, echoing Grayneman's astonishment, as German planes roared over Grodno that morning.[5] Distant artillery and bombing had interrupted the predawn quiet hours earlier. Mina Muller had returned home late from her school's graduation dance and had been asleep only a short while when tremors shook the house. The thuds soon awakened the whole family.[6] When the muffled booms roused Alexandre Blumstein, he pulled the blanket over his head to continue dreaming. From the bedroom next to Alexandre's, he heard his father tell his mother, "It could be war."[7] Members of other families consulted each other about the meaning of the thunder. Daniel Klovsky recalled decades later that his grandfather David ran into the yard in his underwear and scanned the heavens. The twelve-year-old Daniel, too, wondered how such sounds came from a clear sky.[8] Chasia Bielicka remembered that her family thought it was a Polish pogrom, not a German invasion.[9]

Families congregated instinctively at a common location as the noise and shaking increased. Chasia Bielicka's aunts, uncles, and cousins gathered at her parents' home.[10] If families were not already gathered at home, they sought each other out. Elka Fomin left her summer camp and joined other children making their way into Grodno to find their parents.[11] While the invasion brought some families together, it separated others. Moishe Kremer wanted to be with his wife, Tsipora, and new baby daughter, Ita, but he remained at his post in the local power station.[12] Ann Lewin's older brother Nathan left the house to find out what was happening; she never saw him again.[13] Warsaw refugees Liliana Goldsopl and her aunt Guta were alone on 22 June because her other relatives were away in Minsk with a Yiddish theater troupe. Liliana had witnessed the fall of Warsaw in September 1939, and this new invasion revived a deep sense of helplessness. "Wherever I go, the Germans go after *me*," Liliana remembered thinking.[14]

The bombardment and resulting fires forced most to take shelter. Vichna Sidranska's family crowded into a garden cellar. "We were really afraid," she recalled.[15] Mina Muller's family emerged from a shelter during a lull, only to find another raid commencing. Because it was too far to go back to the shelter, they hid in the old Jewish cemetery.[16] Wood-frame houses were particularly vulnerable to the German bombs, and many burst into fire. Much of the low-income neighborhood across the Niemen went up in flames, including the nearly 300-year-old wooden synagogue perched above the river.[17] Half the city's residents lost their homes in the bombardment.[18]

Whereas some took cover in response to the intense bombardment, others tried to flee. The short distance to the nearest German border (only 30 kilometers) necessitated haste. The Red Army led the way out of town. Leib Bialo told an interviewer decades later, "There was a lot of fighting—but it was a one-sided fight." Red Army soldiers hurried away so quickly, he recalled, they abandoned artillery in the street.[19] Alexandre Blumstein recalled Soviet military, party officials, and other recent arrivals hastily preparing to leave as the first German planes flew overhead; by midday, they were gone.[20] "The Russians ran, as they say, 'without pants,'" Sima Kapulska joked later. "Believe me, they ran without pants."[21]

The roads leading out of Grodno became choked with civilians alongside Red Army soldiers. Many had no notion of trying to outrun the invaders and merely wanted to escape the bombing; most returned after a few hours.[22] Chasia Bielicka heard from friends that few made it very far before German planes strafed them.[23] From his outpost due west of Grodno, Red Army officer Boris Grayneman joined soldiers and noncombatants in flight. He recalled after the war, "All traveled to the east, step by step and kilometer by kilometer, farther and farther from that dark cloud rising in the west."[24]

The train station became a gathering point for others seeking to leave the city. Daniel Klovsky's uncle Izik left for the station and never returned; he was killed either during the bombardment or on a refugee train heading east.[25] Some of the prospective refugees sought to flee as family units. The train was no safer than going on foot because the Germans attacked trains as well as refugee columns. The Mullers made it onto a train in Grodno, but Josef Muller ran home to collect more belongings. Most of the family jumped off when he didn't return in time for departure. One of his sons, Dovid, stayed on the train with his fiancée; the family never saw the couple again.[26]

Others panicked. In his postwar memoir, Leib Reizer later described his hysteria during the first hours of the German bombardment. "I grabbed two loaves of bread from a bakery," he recalled. "For a while I ran around with them in my hands and then I threw them away." He returned home and stretched a hammock between two trees. He lay there for some time, staring at the sky, counting the airplanes. Reizer's behavior underscores his strange flight from Grodno later that morning. Rather than remain in a cellar with his wife, Frumke, and daughter, Bashele, he ran out into the courtyard and shouted, "I have to run away." And so he did. Despite his wife's pleas and daughter's cries, Reizer fled the city, telling his family as well as himself that it was only for a couple of days.[27] His journey, however, took him farther and farther from Grodno; he did not return for nearly three months.

Relatively few were successful in their flight, although those moving on their own without the encumbrances of families stood the best chance. After receiving his father's blessing, twenty-one-year-old Shlomo Bromberg fled east on bicycle; some weeks later he escaped from Mogilev by joining the Red Army.[28] Although many felt betrayed by the Soviet military collapse, a few tried to justify the unfolding disaster. Leib Reizer tells in his postwar memoir that the group he fell into outside Grodno came up with the notion that the old Polish–Soviet border would mean safety and security. "We assumed the Soviet Union would, in all likelihood, fiercely defend its legitimate old frontiers," he recalled thinking. This illusion prompted them to continue their trek.[29]

They had to move quickly because units of the Wehrmacht's Army Group Center reached Grodno's outskirts by nightfall on 22

June. The few pockets of resistance from remaining Red Army units were quelled the following afternoon. Most Jews did not know what to expect. Alexandre Blumstein recalled that initially he didn't fear the Germans; the city's Poles were another matter. "Now that the Russians had fled we feared that the Poles, with the blessings of the Germans, would take a bloody toll on Jewish lives," he remembered. His father thought otherwise. "The Germans will not let this happen," his father remarked, explaining that uncontrolled violence on the army's rear flank was not in the Germans' best interests.[30]

Dr. Blumstein appears to have been correct with respect to Grodno, even though local participation in massacres of Jews did emerge as a particular feature of the first weeks of German occupation. The murder of the Jedwabne Jews by their fellow townsfolk, made infamous by the historian Jan T. Gross in *Neighbors: The Destruction of the Jewish Community in Jedwabne, Poland*, was just one of many anti-Jewish pogroms large and small that occurred in the Brest, Białystok, and Vilna regions in the wake of the German invasion.[31] Yet the Germans determined that because of Grodno's bridges over the Nieman River and its railway junction, the city held strategic importance for supplying the rapidly advancing Wehrmacht.[32] They could not afford disorder at this key connection point.

War Descends upon Vitebsk

Grodno fell on the first day of the invasion. Vitebsk lay 600 kilometers to the east, permitting its civilians more time to flee the oncoming Germans. Successful escape depended on prompt action because the city lay along a significant invasion route, on one flank of the Smolensk Upland, a natural land bridge unimpeded by rivers or swamps. Napoleon used this route in his march toward Moscow in 1812, and the Wehrmacht's Army Group Center followed it in 1941. Four days into the invasion, Soviet forces designated Vitebsk as a key defensive point on a front connecting Polotsk, Orsha, and Mogilev.[33] The Germans needed to capture these cities to move forward to Moscow, and their efforts intensified after the fall of Minsk on 28 June.

On the morning of 22 June, Vitebsk residents such as Grigorii Lesin were awakened not by bombs but by shouting in the streets. Lesin, a twenty-year-old student at the Vitebsk Medical Institute, dressed hastily to discover what was happening, but in the meantime it had grown quiet. "There was an eerie silence," he recalled decades later. "Here and there a little crowd whispered, and some said that the Germans had already bombed Minsk, Kiev, Moscow." He turned on the radio to discover if the rumors were true but heard only a program of upbeat marching band music followed by silence. Finally, Foreign Minister Molotov's speech at noon confirmed the situation.[34] Nineteen-year-old Lev Fleish was at home recovering from minor surgery when he heard Molotov's announcement of the German invasion. "Of course, the people became panic-stricken," he remembered decades later.[35]

General mobilization in eastern Belarus began that very day as reservists and volunteers reported to recruiting stations. "The town became an army camp," Lev Fleish recalled.[36] For Vitebsk residents, it was a period of turmoil. Nine-year-old Raisa Gendelev, spending another summer with her grandparents, recalled Red Army soldiers were everywhere and everyone talked about the war.[37] The Communist Party soon organized civilian labor in the effort to defend the city. Some dug antitank ditches on the city outskirts: the Ulanovskii hills to the north, Ilovsky ravine to the east, the aerodrome to the south, and the Yuriev Gorka neighborhood west of the train station.[38] Grigorii Lesin and his fellow Komsomol members received the assignment to guard an airfield.[39]

Increased German air attacks a few days into the invasion motivated some to evacuate. The train station quickly became the nexus of evacuation activity despite periodic bombardment. Vitebsk was a reception point for those passing through from western Belarus and the Baltic countries. Many refugees fortunate enough to find space on trains were the wives and children of Red Army officers and party officials. "Almost all of them were scantily clad with no household belongings," Grigorii Lesin remembered decades later.[40]

Their haphazard appearance reflected the lack of concrete plans to evacuate the populace. Stalin had stubbornly ignored warnings of a German invasion, holding that making plans for retreat was unnecessary. Faced with the realities of invasion, regional authorities rapidly prepared for the withdrawal of interests important to the state: industrial production, food supplies, and valued workers.[41] Inhabitants in cities such as Vitebsk were baffled when the evacuation began. Why abandon the city when the might of the Red Army will protect us? many still thought. And why do the authorities flee when we are told to remain calm?[42] Indeed, measures to relocate the city's industries provoked fear among residents.[43]

Although many workers in crucial industries received precedence in the evacuation, anyone with party or military connections had a better chance to jump on a train or truck.[44] For others, the decision to stay or go was often made as a family. Vera German's family fled together, if somewhat belatedly.[45] Fivel Markelis's brother worked at the train station and could have helped his family leave. They did not, deceived by the same misapplied knowledge that imperiled so many Jews in German-occupied eastern Europe. Fivel's grandmother Rosental talked of the Germans of World War I and dismissed more recent reports of the persecution of Jews. "She said that [Kaiser] Wilhelm had left Jews alone," he remembered. "She didn't believe the rumors, saying that everything was a kind of propaganda and the people lied."[46]

Similar delusions hindered the departure of Raisa Gendelev and her grandparents. As more of the Gendelevs' neighbors discussed fleeing Vitebsk, Berl Gendelev responded, "The *daytshn* [Germans] are educated people; they are highly cultured people. They [will] not do anything wrong to us." He changed his mind when reminded of the accounts that Jewish refugees brought from German-occupied Poland. Grandfather Berl and Grandmother Trina, their two adult daughters, and granddaughter, Raisa, headed east on foot, taking their cow in tow. Their goal was Usviaty, the Gendelevs' former shtetl 70 kilometers to the northeast, hoping to hide until things quieted down.[47]

The Gendelevs reached Usviaty, yet it was no refuge. The Germans arrived in the shtetl a few days later and in time confined them in a small ghetto with several hundred other Jews. Some who traveled by foot abandoned their trek and returned to Vitebsk, just as some Grodno refugees went back to their city. Lev Fleish and his parents left Vitebsk on foot when they were unable to get onto a train. The family became separated about 50 kilometers to the east, where all but Lev managed to hop aboard a truck. Lev and a group of other refugees continuing on foot were overtaken by German tanks just a half-hour later; they decided to return to Vitebsk.[48] Vera German's family, too, was separated, but even before their flight. Her first memories of war in June 1941—her mother, Leya, crying as she hurriedly packed food and clothing to flee—remained clear decades later, but she remembered little else of that confusing time. Her father, Meier, had tried to enlist but was rejected because of his age. He was deployed to a labor battalion instead. Vera, her mother, brother, and older sister fled on their own.[49]

As with those fleeing from Grodno, people from Vitebsk traveling alone had better luck. Grigorii Lesin fled Vitebsk in the first week of July, tailing Red Air Force pilots and ground crew as they fled east. After several near encounters with the Germans, he managed to find his way to Red Army forces in Smolensk and signed up as a medic to evacuate wounded soldiers to Moscow.[50] Others who made it to Smolensk, however, were just as unfortunate as the Gendelevs in Usviaty. The Germans took the city on 16 July, trapping those who thought it offered a refuge.

Despite the risks of capture by the Germans, refugees who ran away from Vitebsk were spared the horrors that unfolded in the city. Most residents who stayed behind hid in cemeteries or cellars. Fivel Markelis, fourteen years old in 1941, recalled how his family took shelter in a ravine. "The whole town was on fire," he reported. "We were sitting in a ravine, and we didn't see the sky. We could see nothing but tongues of flame." Fivel's older sister Chaya was killed when a wall collapsed during an air raid. She had been searching for milk to feed their aunt's baby. "I found her," he recalled with emotion. "I recognized her by her pink dress. Her head was smashed in."[51]

By 10 July, widespread fires in Vitebsk drove more refugees onto roads already choked with Red Army forces in full retreat. The city's remaining population consisted disproportionately of women, children, and the elderly because most adult men had enlisted and evacuated with the Red Army.[52] As a result of the exodus, Vitebsk's Jewish populace decreased from the 1939 census count of 37,095 (22.2 percent of the total population) to perhaps less than half this figure.[53] The fighting stopped on 11 July as Wehrmacht forces took firm control of the city. But the killing had only begun.

Vitebsk Jews under German Military Administration

Vitebsk and much of eastern Belarus fell within a swath of territory under the German military administration of the Army Group Center, shown in figure 14. Until liberation in mid-1944, the city remained under German military control and was administered with the assistance of a collaborationist municipal government. The rest of the occupied Soviet republic was divided into two administrative units. Central Belarus was designated Generalbezirk Weißruthenien (General District Belarus), which along with the Baltic states composed the Reichskommissariat Ostland. The Białystok District of western Belarus, including Grodno and its environs, was annexed by the Reich as an adjunct to East Prussia.

Three weeks of bombardment of Vitebsk left much of the population without access to food, water, or shelter. The arrival of the Germans did little to improve the situation. In line with the Germans' Hungerplan policy to selectively starve the conquered populations, the invaders had little motivation in the first weeks to reactivate the local markets other than to fulfill their own needs. Urban residents, particularly in cities with Slavic populations such as Vitebsk, were targeted for intentional starvation.[54] Civilians were forced to smuggle in food from the countryside and, in a pathetic display of desperation, to beg for scraps from the transports of German wounded that passed through the railroad yard.[55] Soviet prisoners of war (POWs) held in camps on the city's outskirts faced even more dismal prospects.

Nazi policy shaped military practice with respect to the local populations, but so did conditions at the front and in the rear. Army

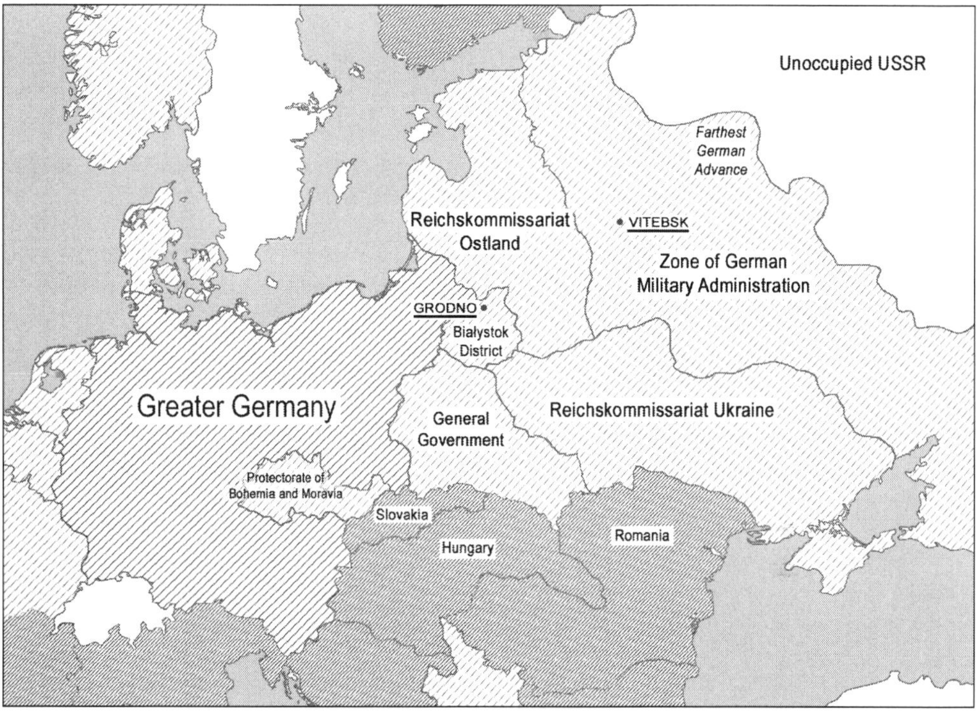

14. Map highlighting the extent of German occupation in eastern Europe, with Axis countries in southern and southeastern Europe, 1941–42. Grodno fell within the Bezirk Bialystok (Białystok District), a region formally annexed to the Reich but isolated by a police border to prevent free movement of its non-"Aryan" inhabitants. Polish collaborators governed in many towns and cities in the Białystok District, including Grodno. Vitebsk lay in the zone of German military administration with a municipal government staffed by Belarusian collaborators.

Group Center confronted a tenuous military position after the fall of Vitebsk and Smolensk. Hurtling through Soviet defenses across Belarus, the Germans' march came to a comparative standstill in mid-July. They took Mogilev (26 July 1941), but the Red Army mounted a fierce defense of the Smolensk Upland to the east, which stalled German forces from advancing toward Moscow, in large part because Hitler diverted forces to Ukraine to undermine Soviet industrial capacity.

Army Group Center lacked the resources to resume its march on the Soviet capital until early October.

Vitebsk lay less than 100 kilometers behind the front lines. The Wehrmacht established a Feldkommandantur (city Military Administration Office) and an Ortskommandantur (regional Military Administration Office) in Vitebsk to secure the army's rear. Civilian matters were delegated to German-appointed municipal and local governments. In Vitebsk, the Wehrmacht appointed Vsevolod Filaretovich Rod'ko as *Bürgermeister*[56] and Lev Georgievich Brandt as his deputy.[57] Both were unassociated with Bolshevism. Rod'ko was an ethnic Belarusian from Poland, and Brandt had been repressed by the Soviets as a "class enemy." Serving under Rod'ko and Brandt was the Vitebskaya gorodskaya uprava (Vitebsk City Council), which in time established departments to manage city services.

Although the collaborationist government in Vitebsk formed a police force, the German military administration addressed security matters, including the perceived threat presented by Jews. Prior to invading the Soviet Union, the Wehrmacht had developed experience initiating anti-Jewish policies, including setting up ghettos in Serbia during the invasion of Yugoslavia in April 1941.[58] Military communiqués from Belarus declared the danger that Jews posed for the military, such as this report from October 1941:

> There is probably no German soldier who doubts that the Jews would have destroyed all Germans in the event of a successful invasion by the Bolsheviks. If a unit on patrol shoots seven Jews, it is incomprehensible why they should be asked to justify its actions. When sabotage has occurred in a village and all Jews are annihilated, you can be certain that [the patrol] has destroyed the perpetrators, or at least the instigator.[59]

German soldiers, the report surmised, recognized the peril presented by Jews and carried no blame if they shot them.

Such attitudes are reflected in German military policies toward Belarusian Jews. Rear-echelon commander General Max von Schenckendorff of Army Group Center took the first step in an order issued

13 July 1941, two days after the fall of Vitebsk. Concerned that homeless Jews posed a security risk for the Wehrmacht, Schenckendorff included the directive: "Jews are to be concentrated in a closed community in buildings occupied exclusively by Jews."[60]

Schenckendorff also ordered the formation of a Judenrat (Jewish Council) in all towns and cities under his jurisdiction.[61] The Vitebsk Ortskommandantur issued an order to form a Jewish Council less than a week after the city was occupied. Given that traditional Jewish community structures had not existed in the Soviet Union for nearly a generation, the Germans turned to members of the professions to staff the councils. In Vitebsk, the Judenrat consisted of a director of a children's art school, a bookkeeper, two schoolteachers, and six others. Two of the ten were women.[62] The Vitebsk Judenrat remained largely in the background, helpless to respond to German persecutions in the following months.

With the cooperation of the Judenrat, the Vitebsk Feldkommandantur and Ortskommandantur posted notices on 17 July to decree that everyone with Jewish "blood," including "half-Jews" and "quarter-Jews," had to register for a census at the former Suvorovskaya Street synagogue by no later than 6:00 p.m. on 20 July 1941. Jews failing to comply would be shot.[63] Aiding the registration process were Soviet internal passports, which noted only the bearer's nationality (*evrei*, Jew) as well as that of the bearer's parents.[64] Such criteria branded as Jewish anyone with one Jewish parent and potentially some with one Jewish grandparent.

The military administration's rationale for targeting so-called half-Jews and even one-quarter Jews appears to have occurred in the haste of rapid segregation, not out of ideological adherence. In the administration's eagerness to separate Jews, whole families, including *Mischlinge* (mixed-race) children and non-Jewish spouses, were included in the registration and subsequent ghettoization. Nazi Party fanatics, who had long pushed for the removal of all with at least one Jewish grandparent, might have been pleased with the inclusion of *Mischlinge*, particularly in light of the "racial" characteristics of the newly conquered peoples. The status of Slavs, far below "Aryans" in the Nazis' constructed hierarchy, shaped the Germans' racial attitude in the East. Children resulting from the "mixed marriage" of a Jew and a Russian or Belarusian did not deserve the same consideration as the product of a union between a Jew and a German. Officials from the SS, the Ministry for the Occupied Eastern Territories, and Ministry of Justice voiced such an attitude at a meeting in Berlin on 29 January 1942. The attendees concurred that on occupied Soviet territory there existed "some difficulties to equate Jewish *Mischlinge* first degree [two Jewish grandparents] with [mixed-race] Jews as one would find in the Reich."[65]

The initial census of "full" and "mixed-race" Jews in Vitebsk tallied only 3,000.[66] Further registration efforts amended the count to between 10,000 and 16,000 Jews. German decrees ordered Jews to sew a ten-centimeter circle of yellow cloth on the front and back of all clothing worn in public.[67] Although the number of registered Jews was less than half the prewar Jewish population, this does not mean that all of the other approximately 19,000 evacuated Vitebsk Jews managed to reach the Soviet interior. The Germans likely captured thousands on their march east. And an unknown number of Jewish refugees from territory to the west of the city were probably counted among the 10,000 plus registered by the Vitebsk Judenrat.

◆ If the populace thought that the Germans meant to instill a sense of order by setting up a Judenrat and registering Jews, the occupiers' violence declared otherwise. Military authorities conducted impromptu round-ups and executions of Jews. Carrying out the bulk of the killings, Sonderkommando (Special Unit) 7a of Einsatzgruppe B,[68] one of four "special-task groups" (A, B, C, and D), was deployed under SS command to murder Jews, Soviet commissars, and Romani peoples on captured Soviet territory. In the days after the census, Sonderkommando 7a murdered selected Jews and captured Soviet officials during three days of executions in the Peskovatik District Jewish cemetery on the northern edge of the city (shown in figure 15).[69] In addition, more than eighty Jews were rounded up in an operation targeting the district west of the train station. The victims were shot in the nearby antitank ditches that the locals had dug in the first weeks of the war.[70]

Killings also occurred in center of the city. Vasily Butrimovich, a Belarusian, reported after the war that he was caught in a round-up of Jews on 18 July, a week after the Germans took the city. Sonderkommando 7a (Butrimovich simply refers to them as "Germans") marched the Jews to the shore of the Western Dvina and pushed them into the water. Although the river level was low during the summer months, the current and slippery bottom produced treacherous conditions in the shallows. Some Belarusians standing on the shore recognized Butrimovich and told the Germans they had made a mistake. No one tried to save the Jews. About 150 Jews were drowned in this massacre.[71] Another witness told investigators after the war that some victims were beaten on the head as they tried to swim or walk in the river shallows. The Germans tied other Jews together before tossing them in the water, giving them slim chance of survival.[72]

Forced-labor recruitment served as an opportunity to kill more Jews just two days later, 20 July. From the assembled men and youths ages fifteen to fifty, the Germans chose several dozen and shot them for their failure to attach yellow patches to their clothing.[73] The largest action committed in the first weeks of the German occupation occurred on 24 July 1941. The German military administration ordered the Judenrat to muster 300 Jews to clear roads. Most were young men, but a few young women may have been present in this group.[74] Members of Sonderkommando 7a and German soldiers marched the work gang to the Ulanovskii hills north of the city. They were told to dig a fresh pit. Sonderkommando 7a shot the Jews in groups of ten to fifteen.[75] Fourteen-year-old Foma Pankov, exploring the nearby antitank ditches, witnessed the killings.[76] To terrorize the city's population into submission as well as to launch an anti-Jewish propaganda campaign, military commanders posted notices around the city reporting the execution of the 300 young Jews as punishment for their alleged participation in setting fire to the city just prior to the Red Army's retreat.[77]

The same day that public notices announced this execution, the military administration ordered all registered Jews to relocate to the right river bank by 27 July and to bring only what they could carry.

The Jewish population remaining in the city was disproportionately young or elderly and female.[78] Most adult males had joined the Red Army or, like Vera German's father, were deployed in labor gangs before the city fell. Among the few records that help to document the ghetto population are the postwar death lists compiled by the Narodyi komissariat gosudarstvennoi bezopasnosti (NKGB, People's Commissariat for State Security). Lists covering Vitebsk's Oktyabrskaya residential district north of the city center reveal whole Jewish families with very particular demographics: mothers and their children; unmarried adult women; grandparents and elderly aunts and uncles. Few men of military draft age are listed among the deceased.[79]

Although the military had constructed a pontoon bridge across the Western Dvina just north of the ruined city bridge, all civilians, including Jews, were forbidden access to it. Gentiles with boats offered to ferry Jews across for payment. Some Jews built rafts. The transit resulted in another massacre as Wehrmacht soldiers used their own watercraft to ram and overturn boats carrying Jews. Those unable to swim were left to drown. German soldiers stood on the shore and beat Jews who made it to the riverbank and dragged themselves from the water. Two to three hundred Jews were murdered during this attempt to cross the river.[80]

The Germans designated the district between the river and the railroad station as the first ghetto (Ghetto I). City residents dubbed it the "Pale of Settlement." Several damaged and partially ruined

(Facing page) 15. Map of Vitebsk based on a German map, *Stadtplan von Witebsk*, from 1940. Soon after taking the city, Wehrmacht command initially designated the entire *Voksal* (train station) district on the right bank of the Western Dvina as an exclusive zone for Jewish habitation (**Ghetto I**). Native residents referred to this area as the "Pale of Settlement." Among the buildings initially used to hold Jews included: **A,** vegetable warehouse; **B,** yeast factory; **C,** flying club; **D,** tobacco factory; and **E,** an apartment house. A few weeks later the Germans herded Jews into the single square block of bombed-out ruins bordering the Western Dvina River (**Ghetto II**).

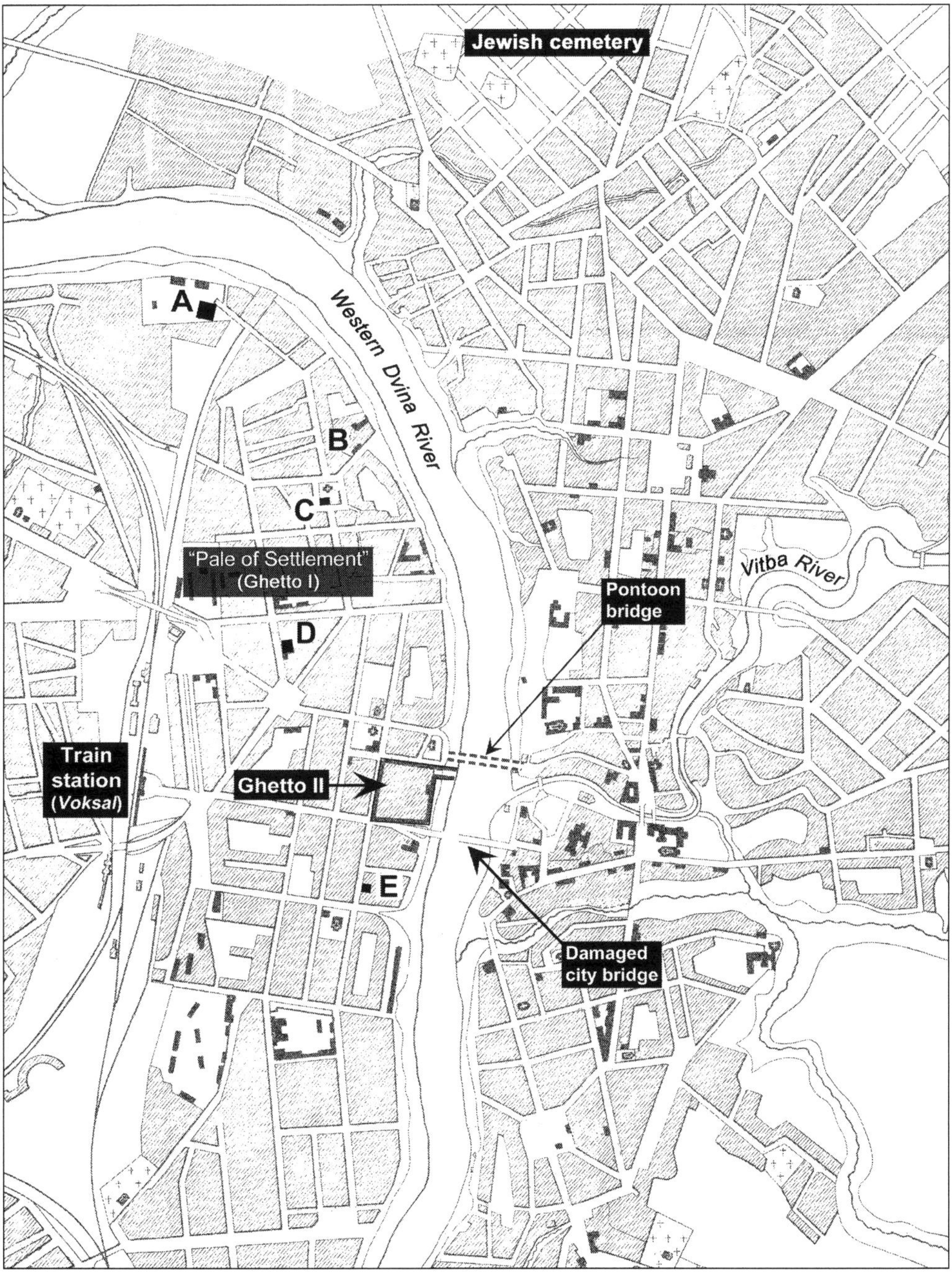

Jewish cemetery
A
B
C
D
E
Western Dvina River
"Pale of Settlement"
(Ghetto I)
Vitba River
Pontoon
bridge
Train
station
(Voksal)
Ghetto II
Damaged
city bridge

structures were initially selected as holding sites: a vegetable warehouse, a yeast factory, a flying club, a tobacco factory, and an apartment house at Komsomolskaya 30.[81] A young Jew, Polina Moisheevna Frumson, was held in the vegetable warehouse along with her mother and brother Motl. "There were no toilets there," she recalled decades later. "It was very hot, and people fainted." Her brother fled and later joined the partisans, but Polina remained behind to look after their mother. Polina recalled her fear that the Germans would rape young women like her. "To conceal our looks, us girls would scrub our faces with coarse river sand," she remembered, an act meant to scar their appearance. Yet it was not a German who tried to rape her, but a Belarusian youth who offered to help her escape. One of Polina's teachers, another Jew also interned in the warehouse, intervened to chase the would-be attacker away.[82]

The Germans held the city's Jews in the five buildings of Ghetto I for several weeks. Sometime between mid-August and early September, a central area was designated for Ghetto II.[83] The second ghetto's location on the riverfront adjacent to the pontoon bridge and damaged city bridge was a puzzling choice. Instead of occupying a spot on the city periphery or near potential killing sites, the single square block of Ghetto II was in the city center. Former *Bürgermeister* Rod'ko told Soviet interrogators after the war that his deputy, Lev Brandt, had chosen that area for Ghetto II.[84] The Feldkommandantur and Ortskommandantur, given their authority over security matters, must have been involved in the selection of the ghetto site. In any event, the ghetto's central location later contributed to its destruction. Fears of epidemics in the city during the buildup and execution of Operation Typhoon, the German strategic offensive to take Moscow, provided the primary motivation for murdering the surviving inhabitants.

The structures on the site of Ghetto II consisted of burned-out shells of houses, multistory apartments, and the local Metal Workers' Club.[85] A crude barbed-wire and wood fence was raised on its perimeter. Extending down to the riverbank was a narrow passage giving ghetto inhabitants access to additional water for drinking and washing.[86]

Warning signs in German and Belarusian were posted on the perimeter fence: "Warning! Precaution! Ghetto!"[87] Under orders by the occupiers, the Vitebsk City Council deployed its local police force to patrol the perimeter in conjunction with German Order Police,[88] a pattern repeated at ghettos in Bobruisk, Borisov, and Polotsk.[89] Ghetto survivor Yuri Zaretski recalled that "outside of the fence, police stood guard, and if someone tried to flee, he was immediately shot."[90]

Ghetto II held between 12,000 and 20,000 Jews, the upper figure quoted by some Soviet investigators after the war. One eyewitness, Vasily Butrimovich, estimated for NKGB postwar investigators that the ghetto initially held about 13,000 Jews.[91] The ruins of Ghetto II could not accommodate all the confined Jews, so most of its inhabitants remained in the open. Fivel Markelis recalled that some "found a piece of tin or plywood to make a kind of a roof to be protected from the rain."[92] Besides shelter, water and food were in short supply. Contaminated water from the river or from a few functioning taps in ruined buildings eventually resulted in a cholera outbreak. Food was scarce throughout the city and even scarcer in the ghetto as the Germans rarely allowed any in.[93] The only nourishment that incarcerated Jews received was smuggled in by youths such as Yuri Zaretski, who later reported that he slipped out of and back into the ghetto almost every day.[94] Taking off his yellow patch, Fivel Markelis also left the ghetto frequently; he polished German soldiers' boots at the train station in exchange for food.[95] An Einsatzgruppe situation report noted the danger of this activity: "In Vitebsk, there were four more cases of liquidating Jews for loitering outside the ghetto and earning their living by begging for food; they, too, had removed their [yellow badges]."[96] But smuggling could not supply sufficient food to feed the ghetto. Jewish forced laborers periodically left the ghetto to clear ruins and bring in limited amounts of food, if they could find any. This lifeline ceased when authorities pressed non-Jews and Soviet POWs into service to replace the Jewish gangs.

Clearly, the Germans' intent was to kill ghettoized Jews through attrition. Although termed a "ghetto," the enclosure in Vitebsk lacked even the most basic elements of shelter, resources, and organization that characterized the ghettos created by the Germans in Warsaw or, as we will see, in Grodno. Indeed, Jews in Vitebsk shared many of the same brutal conditions Soviet POWs faced in Wehrmacht-operated detention camps. One such camp was located in the vacated barracks of the Fifth Railway Regiment, west of the main train station. The Germans surrounded the camp with multiple rows of barbed wire and drove in thousands of captured Red Army troops.[97] The captive soldiers were starved and worked to death. Several Vitebsk residents told investigators after the war that German guards shot weakened and sick POWs at random.[98] One eyewitness recalled emaciated corpses with signs of cannibalistic assaults.[99]

The Germans left Soviet POW camps and civilian prison camps in the region without food for days at time, but local inhabitants sometimes passed food to prisoners.[100] No such aid was possible or even likely for the Vitebsk ghetto, given the food shortage throughout the city. Emergent anti-Jewish attitudes, fostered by German antisemitic propaganda, also dissuaded the local population from providing help. Yuri Zaretski remembered that the Judenrat was powerless to do anything for the ghetto inhabitants.[101] The council was so ineffectual that even an attentive eyewitness like Fivel Markelis could not recall if any such organization existed.[102]

Families clung to each other within the ghetto, a response that strengthened the Germans' hold over their lives. Once incarcerated, few tried to escape. Where could they go? most thought. Some managed to flee during the transfer from the five sites of Ghetto I to the centralized Ghetto II. Inessa Ivanova and her mother, for example, dropped out of a column of Jews being led from an apartment house on Komsomolskaya. The two hid in ruins for several weeks and then fled to the forests northwest of Vitebsk in search of Soviet partisans.[103] In some cases, family members within Ghetto II sacrificed themselves to save loved ones. Fivel Markelis's grandmother, before the war a vibrant seventy-eight-year-old who took care of the household duties while her daughter worked in a factory, refused to eat the food Fivel had smuggled in so that he could survive. "She wanted to die," he later recalled. "She didn't eat a single piece of bread." She slipped into a coma and died the next day.[104] Grandmother Rosental was one of the estimated 5,000 to 10,000 Jews who died of hunger, disease, and exposure in Ghetto I and Ghetto II of Vitebsk during August and September 1941.[105]

Grodno Jews under the Germans

Jews in Vitebsk faced the perils of roundups, shootings, and ghettoization in a rapid sequence of events. The situation in Grodno, although directed in the first weeks of the occupation by a similar German military administration, advanced in the incremental manner that applied in the German-occupied areas of western Poland. Identification of Jews, expropriation of their property, and exploitation of their forced labor were accompanied periodically by the terror of hostage shootings. These actions, in turn, were compounded by ghettoization by the end of 1941. Jews in Grodno responded as was most logical in their confusing situation and as steadfastly connected to their family units as their coreligionists were in Vitebsk.

Registration and official theft, cloaked by the formation of a Jewish Council, began within days of the Germans' arrival. Two Wehrmacht officers approached the lawyer Izaak Gozhanski to organize a Judenrat and serve as elder. Gozhanski demurred, claiming not to know German well enough, and recommended in his place David Brawer, former director of the Tarbut school. Though uneasy about the prospect, Brawer agreed and sought the support of those representatives of the prewar Jewish political movements who remained after the Soviet purge. Ten men consented to serve.[106]

The Germans presented their first demands to the newly constituted Judenrat: a community tax of one million rubles. Threatened arrests of hostages served as leverage.[107] Confiscations of moveable property accompanied the first monetary demands. While forced payment of cash and gold affected adults, particularly among the wealthy, young Jews witnessed the open robbery of household effects. "The Germans wanted some furniture, and one early morning they came in, and we just had new beds; they took away the beds, they took away everything," recalled Ann Lewin. The invaders told the Lewins to keep their mouths shut. "We just stood there until they [took] away those things, and that was that."[108] In some cases, the Judenrat located specific items, even fripperies such as perfume and lace curtains, to satisfy German ultimatums.[109]

A census during the first week of July followed the first expropriations. As in Vitebsk, Jews were commanded to register and submit their identity papers, the latter to be stamped with the word *Jude* (German for "Jew").[110] Because Grodno residents already held Soviet identification cards marked with their nationality, the Germans' task was made all the easier. So-called mixed marriages were uncommon in interwar Grodno, obviating the need for distinctions of "half" and "one-quarter" Jews, as in Vitebsk. Common to both cities, however, was the terror that accompanied registration. A detachment of Einsatzkommando 9 of Einsatzgruppe B arrived in Grodno on 30 June 1941 and remained for more than a week, killing Jewish and Polish elites.[111] Another killing squad, Reserve Polizei-Batallion (Reserve Police Battalion) 131, arrived soon thereafter and targeted vulnerable Jewish inhabitants. Hospital patients and residents of the orphanage and old-age homes were abducted and shot outside the city.[112]

The German military administration commanded all Jews to wear a white armband with a blue six-pointed star.[113] Property theft was transitory, but the armband, required to be worn in public, constantly reminded its bearer of her status and left deep impressions. Children younger than twelve were excluded from this decree, but not teenagers.[114] Chasia Bielicka recalled that she made the first set of armbands for her family with a white sheet and blue ink.[115] This initial marker was replaced a month later by a yellow star sewn onto the front and back of external clothing. "The penalty for not wearing it was death," Feliks Zandman recalled. "They made me feel humiliated."[116] Alexandre Blumstein wrote decades later how he "considered this 'branding' as a rape of my identity."[117]

Further decrees banned Jews from walking on sidewalks and required male Jews to remove their hat when encountering uniformed Germans on the street.[118] "I was constantly reminded of that by many, maybe too many stares of my Polish acquaintances," Daniel Klovsky recalled the experience of walking in the gutter or street.[119] Alexandre Blumstein and his friends coped by remaining indoors as much as possible, reading books or playing chess. The youths also renewed their interest in stamp trading. "I was proud of my collection as I showed my albums to the other boys," he later recalled of this distraction.[120]

While wearing the star and walking in the gutter defined a new and humiliating social space for Jews, additional German edicts widened the social distance between Jews and their neighbors. Jews were barred from theaters, museums, libraries, public transportation, and the market square. Demands to surrender radios, vehicles, and horses followed.[121] Constraints meant to limit Jews' access to food were extended to regulations on the Gentile population. By October, farmers were permitted to sell their produce only in the market; sales elsewhere were punishable by death.[122]

German edicts limiting purchases led to increased reliance on the black market, where high prices further depleted family resources. Some Jews continued to ply their trades, if largely in secret, in exchange for food. Hirshl Grodzienski's father, a barber, began to give haircuts and shaves in his home.[123] Some professionals received a high rate of return for such barter. Dr. Chaim Blumstein never lacked for food during the first months of the German occupation because this bounty was provided by the Polish and Belarusian peasants who continued to be his patients.[124] Most Jews did not have such opportunities. Twenty-eight-year-old Anna Kaletska told an interviewer soon after the war that she had to sell possessions to feed her husband and herself. To add to their burdens, she was pregnant.[125] Chasia Bielicka and her sisters took in sewing work or other odd jobs to supplement their meager rations.[126] Sima Kapulska remembered that her family took "whatever we had—a blouse, a shirt, a piece of linen—and go . . . to the farmers, and they used to give us a little food."[127]

These early stages of the Germans' genocidal policies affected men and women differently. While women acted to save their families from hunger, men such as Chasia Bielicka's father, Yehuda, and brother, Avramele, and Anna Kaletska's husband, Jacob, were pressed into forced labor. Jewish males ages fourteen to sixty who did not hold a craftsman permit were taken by the military or municipality for roadwork or clearing bombing ruins.[128] The work gangs reported each morning at the Great Synagogue at six in the morning and returned exhausted twelve hours later.[129] Some women were recruited as well; for example, Liliana Goldsopl labored with a street-cleaning gang.[130] Young male Jews in particular faced abusive treatment. Given dangerous tasks such as digging up unexploded bombs, some paid with their lives.[131]

Passage of Jewish forced laborers through the city offered local Polish and Belarusian antisemites opportunity to mete out beatings and abuse with the German police's approval.[132] These thugs represented only one particular contingent of the local population, however, and many Jews benefitted from the assistance provided by Gentiles in the first months of German occupation and later during the ghetto period. "Certainly, in Grodno there were the Poles sympathizing with us," Daniel Klovsky recalled.[133] These acts of sympathy were all the more remarkable because the Germans also targeted local Gentiles with separate yet oppressive polices.

Empathy passed through Grodno briefly with the unlikely appearance of the Spanish "Blue Division," volunteers permitted by Franco to assist Hitler in his fight against Bolshevism. Alexandre Blumstein recollected, "Noisy and undisciplined, they did not look very martial."[134] Their presence was a welcome contrast, though, to the Germans' harsh order because the Spaniards interacted with Jews without regard for their "racial" identity. "They associated with the Jewish men without a sign of dislike or hatred," Feliks Zandman recalled decades later.[135] But it was their courting of Jewish girls that made a particular impression. As Liliana Goldsopl remembered, "They were the first Spanish people that I saw, and they would sit on the sidewalk with a guitar and play music [*she laughs*], and here the Germans always marching, always marching." When some Blue Division soldiers saw Liliana and others occupied in street cleaning, they ran up and told the young women, "No, no, no! Don't do it! Don't do it! It's not a job for you!" The soldiers gave them food, augmenting their rations for about a month. She recalled among them a youth named Ricky.

Communicating through their mutual limited knowledge of French, she discovered his complete lack of antisemitic feeling.[136]

The Spanish Blue Division brought a momentary encounter with an outside world obscured first by the Soviet occupation and then by the German invasion. For the most part, only the official news of German victories in the war, disturbing rumors, and rare firsthand accounts circulated among the populace. Leib Reizer, who returned to Grodno in late September 1941, arrived with some of these reports. His flight from his besieged home city on the first day of the invasion had taken him as far as Minsk. The unfolding horrors in the Minsk ghetto brought his thoughts back to the wife and daughter he had abandoned in Grodno. After escaping from his labor gang, Reizer convinced two Dutchmen driving a German supply truck to give him a ride as far as Grodno. Reizer's return trip took him by way of Vilna, where he heard about the mass shootings of Jews in the nearby Ponar forest. Yet the wishful thinking for a swift German defeat that he encountered among many Grodno Jews prevented him from relaying all that he saw and heard.[137] Alexandre Blumstein's uncle, Izaak Kobrowski, had come back from Kovno a few weeks before Reizer made his return to Grodno. Uncle Izaak brought news of mass shootings at Kovno's Seventh Fort.[138] Although his news left his relatives in a somber mood, many others deflected such reports with denials, a response that endured into the ghetto period. "That cannot happen in the Third Reich" was one unattributed response, quoted by editors of the Grodno Yizkor (memorial) book.[139]

Although shootings in Grodno had not yet extended beyond selected community elites, some must have realized that mass shootings were possible. Feliks Zandman narrowly escaped an Einsatzgruppe killing squad in July 1941. He had been in Slonim on 22 June 1941 visiting his grandparents. His quick-thinking grandmother successfully concealed the boy and his grandfather with a blanket during a roundup of Jewish males. Afterward, Feliks cautiously looked out the window to see four trucks drive away loaded with adult Jewish men. Peasants reported later that the Germans had shot them all.[140] His anxieties deepened after they returned to Grodno, where he heard rumors of killings in Lida and elsewhere. "I had started to believe that maybe something really bad might happen to me or my family," Feliks Zandman remembered decades later.[141] His family's response—to sew money into their children's clothing and construct a basement hiding place for valuables—did not seem adequate to stop a bullet.

If flight entered the mind of young Jews during these first months of German oppression in Grodno, they never reported these thoughts in their post-Holocaust memoirs and testimonies. Perhaps subsequent events obscured any such notions. Their actions, however, reveal that most decided to remain in Grodno and stay with their families. Some, such as Feliks Zandman, returned to the city to rejoin loved ones. Leib Reizer, too, returned, his wife and daughter welcoming his presence under the growing danger posed by the German occupation. An exception was Liliana Goldsopl. She had enough of Grodno. "Why I decided—oh!—because they started already the anti-Jewish measures, they wanted us to wear the yellow star, there was already talk about ghetto, and I thought if I have to be in ghetto, I can be with my parents," she recalled about her decision to return to Warsaw. Her aunt remained in Grodno. Liliana hitched a ride on a truck, telling the German driver she was a Pole. From Białystok, she took a train to Warsaw. In time, she joined the Jewish resistance in the Warsaw ghetto.[142]

Germans, Belarusians, and Poles in Grodno

Vitebsk lay firmly under the German military administration, aided by a willing group of local associates. The situation was more complicated in Grodno, where German authorities contended with the infighting of Polish and Belarusian elites. Each of these two groups vied for local hegemony under the occupation order. To further their own agenda, the new rulers manipulated these disputes, turning the rhetoric generated by one faction against the other. The Germans also treated the region around Grodno quite differently from nearly all other territory in the occupied East.

A series of decrees drew Grodno into the Reich, starting with the annexation of Białystok and its environs to East Prussia on 17 July 1941. This Bezirk Bialystok (Białystok District) was enlarged to include

Grodno in September 1941.[143] According to the census dated 29 July 1941, Grodno counted 21,500 Poles; 18,560 Jews; 5,200 Belarusians; 2,060 Russians; 122 Volksdeutsche (ethnic Germans); 48 Lithuanians; and 320 people of other nationalities.[144] The German regional commissar, however, counted an "Aryan" population of around 20,000, comparing favorably to German cities of equal size in Wartheland and West Prussia.[145] As the commissar's colleague, *Landrat* (district councilor) Dr. von Ploetz, told a meeting of his local and regional staff, "We separate not Christians and Jews, but Aryans and Jews."[146] Given Grodno's demographics, these two statements redrew the borders of inclusion.

The case was unusual, given that Nazi racial policy placed Slavs at the bottom of the hierarchy just above Jews, but it was not without precedent. To boost "Aryan" population figures in Danzig–West Prussia and Wartheland, regions of western Poland annexed to the Reich in October 1939, German authorities combed the native Polish population for racial stock suitable for "Germanization."[147] Poles and Belarusians in Grodno were also initially counted as Aryans, at least until German authorities completed similar racial examinations. Nevertheless, the Germans considered Białystok District's Gentile population as potentially dangerous, and they maintained a police boundary limiting transit between the district and the Reich.[148] They also imposed a harsh occupation regime. For example, Dr. von Ploetz declared that acts of sabotage against rail lines would prompt the reprisal killing of one-fifth of the inhabitants of the nearest village.[149] Perhaps one measure of the expendability of Poles and Belarusians was the Germans' willingness to engage the services of these groups' respective elites while treating most of the so-called Aryan population as alien.

Soon after the occupation of Grodno, members of the Polish oligarchy deposed during the Soviet regime emerged from hiding to take their former offices with German endorsement. This remarkable turn of events registered with Grodno's Jews. Hirshl Grodzienski, eleven years old in 1941, remembered it when writing about the first months under German rule.[150] The Poles hoped to leverage German support to reconstitute a Polish state. This plan ran counter to Nazi plans for the East, but the Germans exploited this hope to service their own needs. Local Polish elites in the Białystok District proved to be particularly useful administrators. "These Poles not only have better local knowledge but are significantly better prepared and trained than the 'stubborn' Belarusians," reported an SS assessor in early 1942, adding that these Poles could also speak German.[151]

Belarusian elites were "disappointed and embittered" to live once again under Polish rule and sought numerous ways to discredit the restored local order.[152] Belarusian community leaders alleged that Poles had maintained "friendly relations" with Jews and asserted that Grodno Jews had found themselves "comfortable and free" under a Polish "protectorate."[153] They accused the restored Polish municipality of once belonging to anti-German Polish nationalist parties (largely true) and of desiring the restoration of a "Jewish–English Poland" (completely bizarre).[154] After the Wehrmacht occupation authorities banned the formation of a Belarusian National Committee in late July 1941,[155] several members of this group wrote an ingratiating letter to the Grodno *Landrat* declaring, again, that many Poles in the municipal government were nationalists.[156]

The Poles struck back, but not so strongly as to appear uncooperative. Polish leaders asserted that Belarusians had collaborated with the Soviets.[157] Petty incidents arose as well. The municipal police, exclusively in Polish hands,[158] harassed Belarusians. In one case, a Polish beat cop arrested a Belarusian simply for speaking his ethnic language.[159] Although the pursuit of power and national aspirations fueled many of these conflicts, the clashes were also an economic matter. Belarusian representatives criticized local Polish officials for allocating abandoned Soviet enterprises exclusively to other Poles.[160] The Poles, however, saw only Germans (Reichsdeutsche—Germans from the Reich) filling local handicraft professions and promptly voiced their dissatisfaction. Polish craftsmen would receive a more equitable distribution of these businesses, reassured the district commissar, but only "after the war." Until then, Germans got first dibs.[161]

All this squabbling served German interests. By targeting each other, Poles and Belarusians avoided disputes with the Germans' New Order. And the ruling powers—both the genuine and the pretend—shared a common obsession: the persecution of Jews. The term *Jew* became the universal pejorative. In the same meeting that Landrat von Ploetz implicitly counted most of Grodno's Gentiles as Aryans, he fumed, "One mayor's office has dared to include a Jew on its staff—such a thing cannot exist!"[162] Persecution of Jews became an asset, as in one letter sent to von Ploetz. In seeking a travel permit for Warsaw, a certain Sergiusz Mojnicz of Porzecze, a Pole, openly asserted his former role as a pogromist.[163]

The common interests of German, Polish, and Belarusian leaders shaped the treatment of Jews in other ways. Polish authorities presented the Grodno Judenrat with their own demands for moveable property, but the expropriation of the Jews' property, labor, and money went much further. A matter unrecorded in these exchanges during the first months was growing exploitation of Jewish forced labor. The importance of this resource was demonstrated especially in the scramble to replace Jewish workers after deportations began in November 1942 (examined in chapter 6).

To the Grodno Ghetto

The local German authorities issued a decree in the last days of October 1941 ordering all Jews to move to one of two ghettos on 1 November, shown in figure 16. Ghetto I was located in the *shulhoyf* quarter around the Great Synagogue immediately west of the city center. Ghetto II was situated in the less-developed areas of the Slobodka District on the east side of the city. The preliminary stages to establish a ghetto had occurred at the end of September. First, Jews living on Dominikanska and Orzeszkowej, the main city-center streets, were directed to evacuate their homes. Jewish inhabitants of the newer apartment buildings on the north side of Skidelska Street, the northern border of Ghetto II, were concurrently ordered to relocate as well. Poles moved into the empty dwellings. Another significant preparatory step was the deadline 31 October 1941 for the registration of Jewish craftsmen,[164] linking ghettoization with further economic exploitation.

Rumors circulated for months prior to the final order. Some Jews, such as Chasia Bielicka, felt relief. She learned the news from her

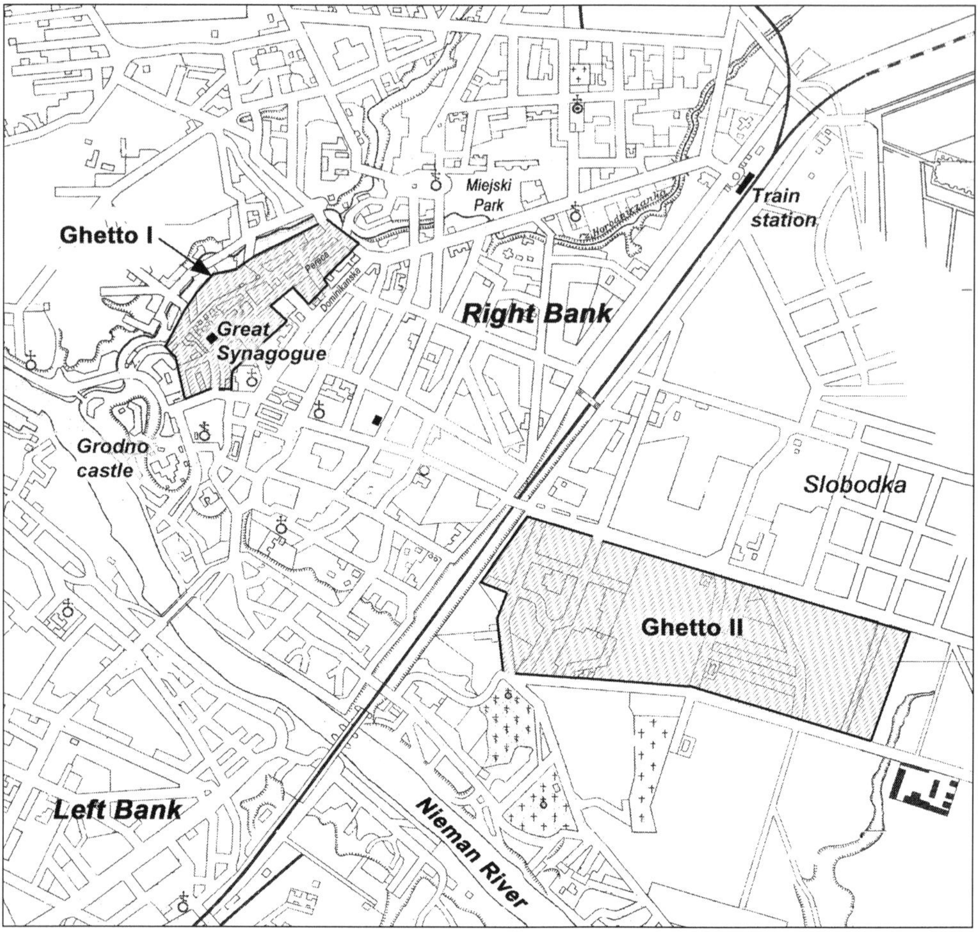

16. Map of Grodno, 1941. Ghetto I and Ghetto II were established by German command on 1 November 1941.

father, who suggested that if Jews were separated from Germans and Poles, they might be protected from abuse.[165] Alexandre Blumstein remembered his family responded the same way. "We reasoned that we would at long last be living among our own kind," he recalled.[166] But not all saw it that way. Sima Kapulska remembered, "My mother cried, and I was frightened to death."[167] Alexandre Blumstein's uncle, Izaak Kobrowski, felt that a ghetto was a trap and reminded the family of the mass shootings he had heard about in Kovno.[168]

Most Jews were too busy with hasty preparations for the forced move to the ghettos to reflect on the meaning of events. The ghettoization decree restricted relocation from 12:00 to 6:00 p.m. on 1 November, forcing Jews to choose quickly what to take and what to leave. Dvorah Bielicka, Chasia's mother, spent all night packing bedding, blankets, kitchen utensils, clothing, food, and soap into bundles for the family to carry.[169] Few had access to horse carts to transport heavy items.[170]

Families debated which ghetto was a safer choice. Ghetto I was supposed to be inhabited by registered craftsmen and their families and thus seemed a better pick; Ghetto II was designated for unskilled labor. According to one survivor's estimate, 65 percent of Grodno's Jews crammed into Ghetto I, even though it covered less dwelling space.[171] Chasia Bielicka's family decided on Ghetto I and took the family sewing machine to assert their claim as skilled workers.[172] Dr. Chaim Blumstein chose Ghetto II to serve community needs because another surgeon was assigned to Ghetto I.[173] Others simply followed the posted instructions. Daniel Klovsky's family already lived in Slobodka, the site of Ghetto II, but his father's trade skills permitted them to live in Ghetto I. It was a bother to lug boxes and satchels across town, but their decision to relocate aided their eventual survival even though they could not know that at the time.[174]

On Saturday, 1 November 1941, a light snow fell on Grodno. "It was the first snow of the season, wet and dirty," Alexandre Blumstein recalled.[175] The Germans photographed these tragic scenes: Jews, identifiable by stars sewn on front and back, pushed carts and carried bundles, luggage, furniture, and mattresses.[176] Abandoning their households was distressing enough, but some Jews also had to witness the plundering of what they left behind. Anna Kaletska recalled shortly after the war how her father-in-law was traumatized when his Polish neighbors pillaged his home of his remaining possessions the moment he vacated it. "He never got well again," she remembered.[177]

"Grodno looked like a beehive that had been ripped open," Chasia Bielicka remembered. "People scurried about, burdened with pots, not knowing where to put them down." A few were able to hire carts to

17. Carts loaded with furniture head toward the Zamkowa Street entrance of Ghetto I, Grodno, in a photograph dated 1 November 1941. Visible on three of the men tending the carts are the yellow stars that the Germans decreed Jews wear on the front and back of their outer clothing. Photograph used by permission of Yad Vashem Photo Archive, Jerusalem, archival signature 1664/1.

carry some of their household possessions (figure 17). Most carried their burdens by hand. Chasia took three loads to the ghetto, but her father carried the heaviest item—their cast-iron sewing machine.[178] "Each of us was wearing as many clothes as he could put on," Feliks Zandman recalled. Feliks, along with his parents, paternal grandparents, and his father's brother, were assigned to Ghetto I; most of his Freydowicz relatives were assigned to Ghetto II.[179] Other extended families found themselves in different ghettos. Zelda Grodzienska went to Ghetto II to be with her sister and mother, while the rest of her siblings dispersed to Ghetto I.[180]

Jews had to pass through a gauntlet at each ghetto's gates as German Order Police, aided by collaborating Polish police, searched at random through their belongings (figures 18 and 19).[181] Leib Bialo recalled how the Germans acted during the move to the ghetto, specifically "the scariness of them, with [their] boots and rifles and

18. On Zamkowa Street in Grodno, Jews move their belongings into Ghetto I under the supervision of the German Order Police, circa 1 November 1941. Photograph used by permission of the United States Holocaust Memorial Museum, Washington, DC, courtesy of the Instytut Pamięci Narodowej (Institute of National Remembrance), Warsaw.

19. German Order Police conduct searches of Jews' belongings near the Zamkowa Street entrance of Ghetto I, circa 1 November 1941. Photograph used by permission of the United States Holocaust Memorial Museum, Washington, DC, courtesy of Jacob Igra.

their loudspeakers."[182] Nearly all Jews had trouble finding quarters for their families in the quickly overcrowded buildings. The Zandmans lodged in a cousin's apartment in Ghetto I. "We lived in one room—my grandparents, parents, Mira, and me," Feliks recalled.[183] The Bielickas found refuge in the *shulhoyf* apartment where Chasia's classmate Sarka lived with her grandparents, and twenty people from Daniel Klovsky's family lived in his grandparents' two-room house. Many families faced similar circumstances. Sima Kapulska's extended family—thirty-eight people in total—packed into the same dwelling with only a few rooms.[184]

Grodno's Jews faced exclusion, abuse, and terror during the first months of the German occupation. Most remained in the familiarity of their homes in these months. Starting in November 1941, however, the ghetto took that comfort away and more. Without private space, no one could escape confrontation with daily violence. Daniel Klovsky, for example, first saw the corpse of a murdered Jew the day after moving to the ghetto. Accompanying his father back to their old home for their remaining possessions, he soon noticed the body of a man lying on the pavement. He never learned what had happened, and as he later recalled, "Soon none in the ghetto asked such a question."[185]

The Annihilation of the Jews in Vitebsk

By the time Grodno's Jews were herded into two ghettos, most of the Jews in Vitebsk's Ghetto II were dead. As thousands succumbed to disease, hunger, and exposure, the Germans conducted waves of executions that took the lives of the rest of the ghetto inhabitants between early August and early October 1941. Ghetto inmates continued to be rounded up periodically for forced labor, but some of these work gangs did not return. "When Germans began to take away some people to work somewhere, and when the people didn't return, we realized that they had been killed," Lev Fleish recalled.[186]

A change in Einsatzgruppen personnel accelerated this process. Einsatzkommando 9 of Einsatzgruppe B, a detachment of which had been in Grodno earlier, arrived in Vitebsk at the end of July or at the latest by 2 August 1941 under the command of doctor of law SS-Obersturmbannführer Alfred Filbert. Einsatzkommando 9 billeted in the same Polytechnic School buildings across the river from the ghetto that had housed Sonderkommando 7a.[187] Unlike Sonderkommando 7a, which operated in the immediate rear areas of the active military front, Einsatzkommando 9 was assigned to secure the army's rear flank.[188] Other than deaths through planned deprivation, the destruction of the Vitebsk ghetto was carried out by this unit with the assistance of the Waffen-SS and the local police.[189] Gas vans were introduced in 1942 to murder Jewish deportees sent to Vitebsk from the surrounding region[190] and thus were not involved in the destruction of the city's native Jewish community.

Several execution sites in the city have been identified, including the Western Dvina, the Jewish cemetery in the Peskovatik District, the Dukhovskii ravine near the aerodrome to the south, and the Ilovsky ravine northeast of the city center (figure 20).[191] Fivel Markelis recalled that multiple executions occurred in the last weeks before the final ghetto liquidation in October 1941, with 150 to 200 people rounded up at each action.[192] Yuri Zaretski has noted that the local collaborationist police entered the ghetto to participate in selections of the Jews to be killed.[193]

Although documents and eyewitness testimony record where, when, and how most massacres transpired, the total numbers murdered in each *Aktion* (the German euphemism for a killing operation) will probably never be known. Also, the exact reasons why the remaining Jews in Vitebsk were murdered from August through October 1941 but not later are not entirely unclear, although an examination of the circumstances facing the German occupiers provides some answers. The broadened scope of mass shootings beginning in August to include Jewish women and children framed the wider scope of events on occupied Soviet territory.[194] The historian Alex J. Kay has shown that squads of Einsatzkommando 9 under Filbert's command were engaged in mass shootings that targeted entire Jewish populations in towns and shtetlekh in Belarus during August and September

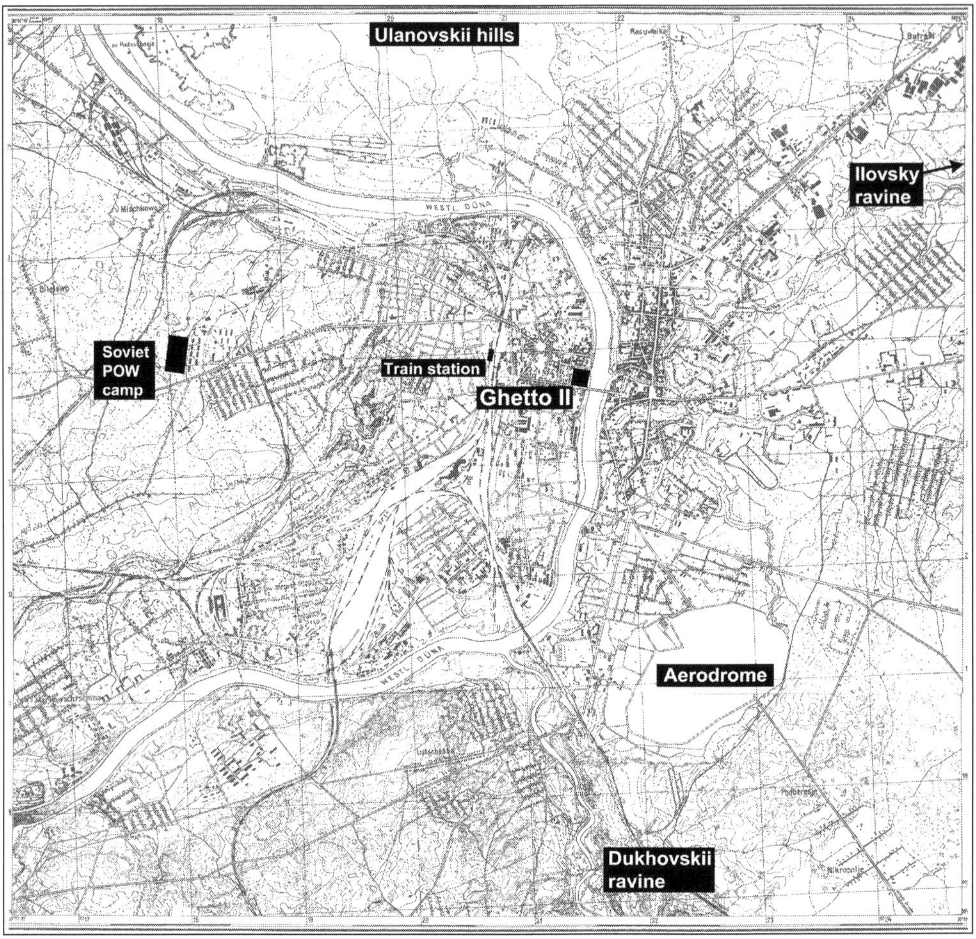

20. Map of Vitebsk based on a German map, *Stadtgebiet Witebsk*, circa 1944. Added notations mark the location of killing sites used in late 1941 on the city perimeter: Ulanovskii hills, Ilovsky ravine, Dukhovskii ravine, and POW camp.

1941.[195] Another historian, Leonid Rein, has suggested that the double curse of being both racial Jews and practicing Bolsheviks raised the importance of the obliteration of the Jews in eastern Belarus.[196]

Other events shaped the immediate situation in Vitebsk. The first stirrings of the Soviet insurgency elevated the Germans' paranoia about the Jewish presence in Vitebsk. In late August, Einsatzgruppe B reported the inflammatory story of a soldier who lost his arm after an explosion, supposedly because a "Jewess" had asked him to open a door, which triggered the blast. The woman was hanged.[197] The Wehrmacht incited a large-scale execution about a week later, handing over 397 Jews in the civilian prison camp to Einsatzkommando 9, accusing them of sabotage.[198] Several massacres across eastern Belarus and occupied Russia were triggered by fear of partisan activity.[199]

The military situation also affected the fate of Vitebsk's Jews. As noted earlier, German armed forces had stalled to the east of Belarus at the end of July. After the fall of Kiev on 19 September 1941, Army Group Center regained sufficient support to resume its advance toward Moscow. On 2 October 1941, German armed forces launched Operation Typhoon, the attack that began the Battle of Moscow. Vitebsk lay at a strategic point along the Wehrmacht's supply lines. No wonder, perhaps, that Einsatzgruppe B declared only six days later (8 October 1941) that it "began the complete liquidation of the Jews in the Vitebsk ghetto owing to the imminent danger of epidemics."[200] To underscore this rationale, other reports of mass shootings in the Vitebsk region during September 1941 gave the same justification.[201]

Such circumstances demonstrate the SS's and Wehrmacht's sense of urgency to eliminate Vitebsk's Jews. In preparation, the Germans had conducted two focused massacres in Vitebsk in the weeks leading up to the October mass shooting to weaken the Jews' capabilities to resist. Einsatzgruppe B reported to Berlin at the end of August, "In Vitebsk, the actions against the Jewish intelligentsia were continued."[202] Mifodiya Fedosenko, a Belarusian from the village Sebyakhi northeast of the Vitebsk city limits, witnessed the murders of 500 Jewish teachers and professionals on 28 August 1941. He saw Jews led in groups of ten or fifteen to the ravine, after which he heard a volley of shots. "At first I thought the Germans were teaching them to shoot," he told Soviet investigators. Later, when the truck left, he crept into the ravine and found a section of antitank ditch, about 20 meters in length, freshly filled in. In a slowly burning bonfire nearby, he found the remnants of clothing and identity cards that confirmed the teachers' and professionals' identity as Jews.[203] Less than a week later, on 3 September 1941, the Germans murdered 332 Jewish adult men in the

Jewish cemetery of the city's Peskovatik District.[204] Among the victims was Fivel Markelis's uncle Yasha.[205]

Concurrent with these mass killings, Wehrmacht *Gefreitor* (private) H. Kilhorn observed a mass shooting of women and children outside the city. He gave the following statement of what he observed in early September to the Wehrmacht propaganda section:

> When I heard the sound of machine guns, a soldier told me that about two kilometers away from the camp was a mass execution of Jews, and that the men had already been shot that morning and now it was the women's turn. Several comrades and I headed to that place . . . on motorcycles. There I saw a group of about 600 women and children, guarded by SS. . . . The women were led in groups of five a distance of 200 meters to the edge of an antitank ditch.[206]

Kilhorn described further how SS men ordered the women to undress; the women screamed in response because they understood that they faced death. Over the course of a half-hour, Kilhorn witnessed the SS shoot between thirty and fifty women; he did not stay to watch the murder of children.[207] Such actions confirmed that the entire Jewish community faced annihilation.

This massacre probably occurred in the Ilovsky ravine on the northeast side of the city. The ravine flanks the Vitba River, a tributary of the Western Dvina. In 1941, the villages of Sebyakhi and Tulovo lay to the north and south, respectively, with the Vitebsk brick factory on the immediate north side of the ravine, along its western edge. Two collective farms lay to the east. Einsatzkommando 9 and a small unit of Waffen-SS, supported by local collaborators, murdered most of the remaining Vitebsk Jews in the Ilovsky ravine beginning on the third day of the Sukkot holiday, 8 October 1941.

The exact date of this massacre has been debated among a number of historical sources. Some accounts cite the end of October or early November.[208] Einsatzgruppe B's own report of the massacre, written on 25 October 1941, gives it as happening on 8–10 October,[209] and several Soviet witnesses (discussed later) recall a mass shooting of Jews in early October. General Schenckendorff visited Vitebsk on 5 October 1941, and some historians have linked his meeting with local security units and inspection of the ghetto to the violent action that unfolded three days later.[210] The Germans murdered ghetto captives in several eastern Belarusian cities during October and November, including Mogilev (2–3 October, 17–19 October, and 23 October 1941), Borisov (20–21 October), Bobruisk (7 November), Polotsk (21 November), and Orsha (26–27 November).

Witnesses recounted specific aspects of the crime to Soviet investigators after liberation. A former Vitebsk policeman, Zupkevich, testified at his trial in 1950 for collaboration that he joined other local policemen assisting the SS to round up and transport Jews to the killing site. The police had orders to tell their victims that they were heading to a labor camp. "The majority of the condemned carried their belongings confidently," he recalled. Up to twenty-five people were loaded on each truck.[211] Vitebsk resident Aleksandr Solenik reported after the war that he saw Jews loaded in open cargo trucks going to the city's east side.[212] Anna Tereshchenko heard that victims were told to undress upon arriving at the ravine edge and led in groups to the ditches. She also described the one-kilometer cordon that the Germans maintained, with positions at 30-meter intervals to keep locals away.[213] Anna Solodukhinya lived near the brick factory at the ravine's west end. Although German guards kept spectators from approaching, Solodukhinya could see and hear enough of the massacre to know exactly what was happening.[214] To Sebyakhi village resident Yevgenia Bavtuto, it appeared that the German gunmen were drunk.[215] Indeed, as discussed in the postwar trial of Alfred Filbert, the Einsatzgruppe commander allowed his men to drink alcohol during their breaks between shootings, which in turn exacerbated their brutality.[216] "I clearly heard the victims' cries, in particular the howl of small children," Mifodiya Fedosenko stated in his testimony.[217] Yevgenia Bavtuto told the NKGB that she went to the killing site sometime after the October action, finding murdered Jews' identity documents and a school notebook in which someone had written nine pages of victims' names.[218]

Postwar NKGB investigators did not lack for witnesses, even if the dates they recorded were sometimes imprecise. Maria Prokhorova, in the company of another witness from the Tulovo collective farm, saw a row of ten "scantily clothed people positioned at the edge of a pit." The Germans shot them with machine guns. As the two witnesses hurried from the area, they saw a woman, bleeding from her wounds, run from the pit. Some of the shooters overtook her in a nearby field and shot her again. Prokhorova stated in her declaration that these shootings occurred in early July 1941, although the place of the events (Ilovsky ravine) imply that this event occurred later. Prokhorova also told postwar investigators that some days later her fellow eyewitness, Kazimir Konstantinovich Boleishets, was forced to bury the bodies from another mass killing. As Boleishets reported to Prokhorova, some of the victims, including children, were merely wounded and still alive when covered with earth. The ground over the filled pits turned for days afterward. "I myself saw hands and feet thrust through cracks in the soil," Prokhorova reported.[219]

One survivor of the killings in the Ilovsky ravine was ghetto captive Fivel Markelis. He told an interviewer of his experience, beginning with selection in the ghetto. "They surrounded our sector, counted the people, and forced them to climb in the trucks and took them away. It was along toward evening. It was October. It was rather cold. . . . There were about 150 or 200 people. There were a lot of [trucks]. I don't know, I didn't count. There were a lot of us." The Jews were told that they were being transferred to another camp and that they should remain calm. But his mother wasn't fooled; she sat in the truck, weeping. He recalled that the local Gentile population witnessed the deportation. "Well, the people stopped and looked at us . . . and by the way, some of them were laughing, I saw them. I don't remember any other reaction of the people. You know, at moments like that one doesn't try to remember anything."[220]

Once their truck reached the ravine, they were ordered to undress even though their clothes were nothing but rags. Their executioners then forced them to stand in three rows on the edge of the pit. "My mother was in front to hide me. . . . She said to me in Yiddish, 'Keep quiet, sonny. Keep quiet.' That was what I did. She was crying. And then . . . there were bursts of machine-gun fire. I felt a push . . . and fell down . . . together with all the others."[221] His mother and the other victims fell on top of him, but Fivel was uninjured. He lay under the bodies for one or two hours, climbing out when darkness fell. No one was around. Covered in blood, he crawled to the Vitba to wash himself. Thus began his renewed odyssey of survival.

Aftermath of Mass Murder

Two months of starvation conditions and periodic massacres had reduced the ghetto population of approximately 13,000 by up to 10,000 souls, leaving, according to the Einsatzgruppe's report, only 3,000 to receive "special treatment" in the Ilovsky ravine.[222] Two months later, another Einsatzgruppe situation report advanced a figure of an additional 4,090 Jews killed.[223] It is unclear whether this number counted additional native Vitebsk Jews, Jews deported from another town, or a recount of the October massacres. Witnesses estimated after the war that 7,000 to 8,000 Jews were murdered at the Ilovsky ravine during those terrible days in October.[224]

The Ilovsky ravine continued as an execution ground well into 1942, largely for Soviet POWs and Jews from outside Vitebsk. One witness told postwar investigators that the Germans conducted small-scale actions at the site through the winter and spring of 1941–42.[225] Another reported in 1944 that she observed groups of men, women, and children, possibly all Jews, escorted to the ravine over the course of about ten days in June or July 1942.[226] Under Aktion 1005, the Germans returned to the ravine in late 1943 and early 1944 with Jewish slave-labor gangs to destroy the evidence of their crimes. The exhumations and cremations lasted for weeks. In a postliberation deposition to NKGB investigators of the Extraordinary State Commission, one eyewitness recalled that "the stench of burning corpses hung over the city."[227]

Remaining Vitebsk residents enduring the third year of the German occupation had other reminders of their vanished neighbors' presence. Some of them had looted Jewish possessions after the Germans posted the orders forming the ghetto. Although the Sicherheitsdienst (SD, Security Service) and Wehrmacht seized valuables and shipped them to the Reich Treasury's War Booty Office,[228] possession of everyday household items was handed over to collaborating municipal and regional authorities to fund local government operations. The Vitebsk City Council carried out a survey to identify belongings not only of Jews but of evacuated Bolsheviks as well. Auditors entered occupied as well as vacant dwellings to complete their task.[229] One inventory from Vitebsk documented extensive looting by the city's Gentiles: 989 beds, 538 couches, 1,141 cabinets, 1,117 tables, and 1,826 chairs.[230]

Property sales commenced in September 1941, concurrent with the suffering of the city's Jewish population in the ghetto. On 12 September 1941, Ivan Bogdanov paid 355 rubles to the Housing Department for furniture, one of dozens of documented transactions over the next few weeks.[231] The city also sought to collect payment for looted belongings. Among the city dwellers possessing Jewish property was A. M. Maslenkov, who had taken some furniture from an abandoned house because, as he reported, his own had been destroyed by fire. Maslenkov requested to purchase the items at the assessed price.[232] Ivan Kovalenko had in his possession a couch, cabinet, and bed taken from an abandoned Jewish home. He petitioned in late October 1941 to buy the items.[233] Discoveries of looted property apparently continued into 1943, when in September one petitioner asked for "permission to sell to me the Jewish things found in my home."[234]

Some Vitebsk Gentiles felt entitled to these possessions based on prewar experiences and prejudices. Sometime in July or August 1941, Konstantya Petrovna Popsuyevich appropriated from a Jewish apartment numerous items: a sewing machine, a kitchen table, a sideboard, a mirror, a full-size bed with mattress, and nine chairs. She justified her theft of "zhidovski veschy" (Jewish things, using the pejorative form) in letters written in Russian and German to the Vitebsk *Bürgermeister* in September 1941:

> I have relatives in Germany, Lithuania, and Latvia. Until 1937, my husband and I corresponded with them, describing our difficult life.

> We were accused by the NKVD of being spies. My husband was sent away and later shot. In 1938, I was robbed by a Jewish commissar and put in prison for a year. After my arrest, my two sons—13 years old and 8 years old—were sent to an NKVD orphanage. I have experienced so much. I have lost my entire family. For that reason I ask your sympathy to allow me to keep the above stated Jewish things.[235]

Popsuyevich's misfortunes were representative of some victims of the Great Terror: foreign contacts leading to suspicion, arrest, and execution; arrest of a spouse sometime thereafter; removal of children to NKVD orphanages; confiscation of property. Yet a key element of this declaration was Popsuyevich's identification of the Soviet official who confiscated her property as a Jew. And she used the derogatory appellation *Zhid* in the Russian-language copy of the letter. The Jewish household items, she argued, were small compensation for her confiscated belongings and shattered family—actions that in her mind were caused by Jews. Her antisemitism endured even after the murder of the city's Jews.

The Jewish property stolen and sold by the Vitebsk City Council was of great value to the original owners. A few Jewish families in the city had enjoyed better furnishings, such as the overstuffed chairs Vera German recalled appointing her family's apartment.[236] Dmitri Khvat's family were sufficiently well off not to share a dwelling with another family, but they still valued the parcels sent by his grandparents to offset Soviet shortages.[237] More typical was the experience of Fivel Markelis. Among his family's valued possessions was his grandmother Rosenthal's cooking pot, which she ransomed from a shop after it had been confiscated by the police.[238]

The sale of such modest possessions involved any and all sellers and takers in a form of collaboration. And those who appropriated Jewish property distanced themselves from their actions when admitting their theft to city officials. Nearly all use a form of the word *nashel*, "found," in their declarations to the city, not "taken," which would imply active participation in theft on their part. Procurers were not just participants, but victims as well. After their homes and possessions were destroyed in the invasion and their Jewish neighbors rounded up and confined, Vitebsk Gentiles grabbed whatever they could. Some may have acted out of material gain and blamed Jews for their alleged plight, but these collaborators paid in coin for the privilege of joining the wider conspiracy of destruction.

Responses to Genocide

As we have seen, young Jews in Soviet Vitebsk possessed a complex identity forged in the multiethnic Soviet city and characterized by inclusion in the life of the state. The purges had shattered their cultural affiliations as the Bolshevized Yiddish culture created in the 1920s and early 1930s became a victim of ideological attacks. In such an environment, the bedrock trust that Soviet Jewish youth retained was in their families. Jewish youth of Polish Grodno, by contrast, grew up in an environment of social, political, and economic marginalization. Compared to their counterparts in Vitebsk, young Jews in Grodno developed an assured ethnic and religious identity reinforced by strong group and community associations. At the core were family connections, both their biological families and their social ties within youth groups.

The violence of the Nazi invasion and occupation stunned everyone. The Germans' anti-Jewish measures were unlike anything that Chasia and Leib in Grodno or Fivel and Vera in Vitebsk had ever experienced. Young Jews in Grodno and Vitebsk responded to war and genocide, forces that tore their societies apart, by focusing their immediate attention on their families. It was the most human of responses. They sought consolation with each other from the first moments of the invasion, huddling together in shelters.

For most in Grodno, flight was unthinkable. "Neither we nor any of the other families thought about getting out of town," Daniel Klovsky recalled decades later. "It was impossible for us, as we all had big families with a lot of children and elderly men."[239] Moishe Kremer had the option to join a workers' transport to flee Grodno, but he remained to aid his wife and child. "How do you just take off and go?" he told an interviewer decades later. "And I stayed. I stayed on."[240]

After the Germans took the city, families remained together through the first weeks and months of the occupation as registrations led first to public markings and then to ghettoization. Some urged escape at this stage. Alexandre Blumstein recalled his uncle Isaak urged other Jews, "Disperse! Go into the forests, there are not enough Germans to hunt you out!" Yet it wasn't that simple, as Alexandre explained. Besides inhospitable weather conditions, hostile peasants, and lack of weapons for protection, his primary reason for staying was family. "Where were we to go with our children, mothers, and grandparents?" he asked.[241] The Germans' policies thus turned family from a support system to a lethal burden.

Jewish families that succeeded in fleeing from Vitebsk continued to rely on each other, but circumstances often drove them apart. When Vera German's family was separated in the chaos, the likelihood of their survival increased. Indeed, all but Vera's brother Yakov survived the war. Those who remained in the city faced terrible dilemmas yet stayed committed to parents and children. The Germans had them trapped. Fivel Markelis slipped out of the ghetto to get food but returned to aid his remaining family members. The youth fled only after his mother was killed by the bullets meant for him as well.[242] Lev Fleish fled, too, leaving the ghetto just before its final liquidation, but he had been separated from his family during their effort to evacuate.[243]

Underlying their success at survival and flight was luck. Vera, Fivel, and Lev lived through the German invasion and initial stages of occupation primarily as a matter of chance. They drew upon their interethnic awareness in efforts to survive. But luck also continued to dictate whether they would live from one day to the next.

By November 1941, nearly the entire Jewish population of Vitebsk had been annihilated. The remaining Jews of Grodno would experience another year of ghetto life, during which German policies continued to punish and exploit them.

6

Exploitation and Annihilation

November 1941 to March 1943

The same day Grodno's Jews were forced into two ghettos, 1 November 1941, Sarah Fishkin in Rubiezewicze wrote in her diary, "Somewhere, far away, there is insistent talk of our 'extermination,' of wiping the Jewish people from the earth." Her fears arose not only from the reports of mass shootings that filtered into her shtetl but also from hearing the "enemy shots that pierce the nocturnal quiet." Sarah also maintained feelings of hope, opening the same diary entry optimistically, "On quiet evenings, as the sun sets, there seems to be hints of an improvement in the present situation for Jews."[1]

Sarah Fishkin's contradictory responses were not unique. The Jews in the Grodno ghetto endured hunger and overcrowding, while the Germans exploited their labor skills. When they heard reports that Warsaw Jews were gassed at Treblinka, most responded with disbelief. They thought, How could this be? What did this mean? Why would the Germans commit such an irrational act, to kill us when we contribute so much through our labor? No matter the conditions or the rumors, most, like Fishkin, could not abandon the notion of "hints of an improvement in the present situation."

Some Grodno Jews, aided by contacts outside the ghetto, looked beyond what was in front of their eyes to assess the wider perspective. They had much to draw upon, including their experiences under the marginalizing atmosphere of Polish rule and the reshaped social order under the Soviets. The Germans, however, presented a new threat—a mortal threat. For Grodno Jews to perceive that danger required a leap that most could not or would not make.

How did they identify and respond to the Germans' policies of annihilation, and what sort of social cooperation marked their actions? For younger Jews, that social unit was Hashomer Hatzair, Dror-Hehalutz or another youth group; for their parents, it was the family.

Survival in the Grodno Ghettos

The Germans kept the Jews of Grodno alive for a year before deciding to murder them. Unlike in Vitebsk, where the Germans coupled starvation and exposure to accelerate death, in Grodno they allotted regular if meager food supplies and two relatively undamaged city districts for Jews to inhabit. The ghettos' survival was hardly a matter of benevolence, however. Minimally paid Jewish labor furnished the German military with a range of necessary goods and services.

As the Germans exploited the Jews, the Jewish masses and their leadership possessed little to no leverage. Yet within this environment, the Grodno Judenräte (councils were organized in both of the city's ghettos) acted decisively to support their community's short-term interests, distributing food supplies equitably and organizing Jews in labor gangs. Council chairman David Brawer traveled to Białystok to study how his counterparts organized Jewish workers in the service of German interests. These work gangs also formed a vital lifeline because their transit outside the ghetto brought them into contact with Gentiles willing to barter or sell food. Others in the ghetto fought to sustain life. Medical personnel successfully contained the spread of disease despite primitive conditions. Family members supported each other emotionally and shared their scant earnings. Young Jews, however, looked beyond the immediacy of mere survival, banding with their comrades and in time working toward the goal of resistance.

Many younger survivors remember their time in the ghetto as a period of relative stability and security, perhaps compared to experiences they shouldered thereafter. "If they would have left us alone in the ghetto, we would have survived, as bad as it was," Vichna

Sidranska later asserted.[2] Feliks Zandman agreed. "I think you could have survived a hundred years there," he reported in an interview, "if you were not murdered."[3] Yet such statements should not be perceived as minimizing the perils. They also illuminate the illusions that many Grodno Jews maintained during the final year in their home city.

Life in the two ghettos was a daily combination of violence and perceived security, of trauma and utter boredom. Gestapo commandants Kurt Wiese of Ghetto I in the *shulhoyf* quarter and Otto Streblow of Ghetto II in the Slobodka District periodically swept through the streets to beat and shoot captives at random.[4] Alexandre Blumstein later recalled an incident soon after Streblow's arrival. "On the second day of his tenure as *Kommandant* of Ghetto II, he whipped a young Jewish policeman who was too slow for his liking."[5] Each commandant reported to the Gestapo chief in Grodno, Heinz Errelis, who arrived in the city in December 1941.[6] Wiese and Streblow were often joined by Karl Rinzler, commandant of the Soviet POW camp at Kielbasin, a few kilometers south of Grodno.[7] Each chose their victims at random. Moishe Kremer later reported that Wiese "was driven through Ghetto I in his Opel Kapitän every day, and for sport, indiscriminately shot Jews caught on the road."[8] As Chasia Bielicka recalled of the three commandants, "Their aim was excellent."[9]

Barbed-wire fences encircled each ghetto, guarded by German Order Police with the assistance of the city's Polish police force. Daily encounters between guards and Jewish labor gangs occurred at the entrance gates, where searches for smuggled food took place. Within the barbed wire, the *Jüdische Ordnungsdienst* (Jewish police) assisted the Germans by patrolling the streets and searching prisoners at the gate.[10] "Like mushrooms after rain, young men with truncheons appeared, recruited by the Judenrat," Leib Reizer recalled about these men wearing blue armbands.[11] Much of the ghetto was repelled by the thought of joining such a force.[12] Chasia Bielicka remembered that the Jewish police were drawn from working-class professions that had required muscle, including "wagoners, market people, and other strong-arm types."[13] Ironically, this was the same class of workers who had defended Grodno's Jews during the pogrom in June 1935 (chapter 2). The use of force needed for arrests and searches called for men capable of "'black' work," as a former Judenrat member declared.[14] And although many of these Jewish police extracted bribes from smugglers,[15] the abundant traffic in supplemental food supplies, much of that food transported through the ghetto gate, could not have occurred without their acquiescence.

◆ With Germans and Poles monitoring the perimeter and Jewish police minding the streets, living quarters offered captives the only privacy. Yet crowding precluded such a luxury, particularly in the greater congestion of Ghetto I (figure 21). Sylvia Mydler and her sister had moved into a cousin's apartment in Ghetto I with their grandparents. "Everybody slept on the floor, on the table, people were scattered all over," she later recalled.[16] Yehuda Rabinovich lived in his aunt's small apartment in Ghetto I, where a dozen people slept in tiers of hastily built bunk beds.[17] Chasia Bielicka and her family crammed into a one-and-a-half-room apartment with a school friend and her grandmother.[18] Bella Ilin, not quite five years old when her family found space in a large hall in Ghetto I, remembered the sheets that her parents hung to separate the sleeping areas of the many inhabitants.[19]

In Ghetto II, close quarters were exacerbated by rudimentary accommodations (figure 22). "Rows of shabby wooden houses like ours extended for maybe a kilometer across the width of the ghetto," Alexandre Blumstein later described.[20] Leib Reizer, along with his wife, Frumke, and five-year-old daughter, Bashele, occupied a small peasant cottage with a clay floor.[21] The Muller family shared a single room.[22] "Conditions were very awful with seven people," Fenia Muller later recalled. A mother and her child from another family lived there as well.[23] Anna Kaletska, her husband, Jacob, and her father-in-law lived in a space three meters by three meters in size. Pregnant at the time of their forced relocation to Ghetto II, Anna gave birth to a daughter on 26 November 1941 in their small room.[24]

In addition to the crowding and primitive conditions, sporadic German requisitions robbed Jews of much of their remaining property. As the first winter of the occupation began, the Germans ordered

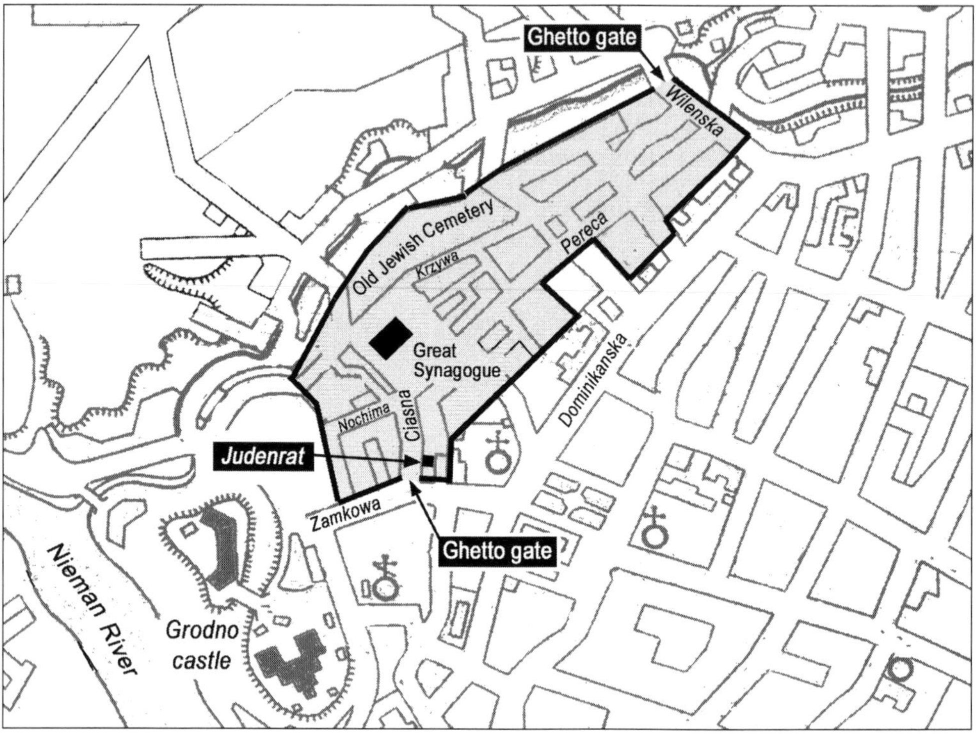

21. Map of Ghetto I in Grodno, located in the *shulhoyf* quarter adjacent to the city center, 1941.

ghetto captives to hand over furs and warm clothing.[25] When they felt the collection was insufficient, they searched from room to room.[26] To avoid these incursions, which typically led to beatings and shootings, the Judenrat formed a requisition department to inventory Jewish property.[27] Later, the Germans ordered Jews to surrender cameras, typewriters, hot plates, and other household appliances.[28]

The Jewish Council's cooperation in property registration angered many in the two ghettos, an emotion that colored survivors' memories. Prompted by the Judenrat's overall actions, Leib Reizer described them as "bureaucrats who were like a plague foisted on the body of the people."[29] Another ghetto survivor expressed more measured opinions of the council soon after the war, yet he admitted that he could not defend all their actions.[30] Consisting primarily of second-rank

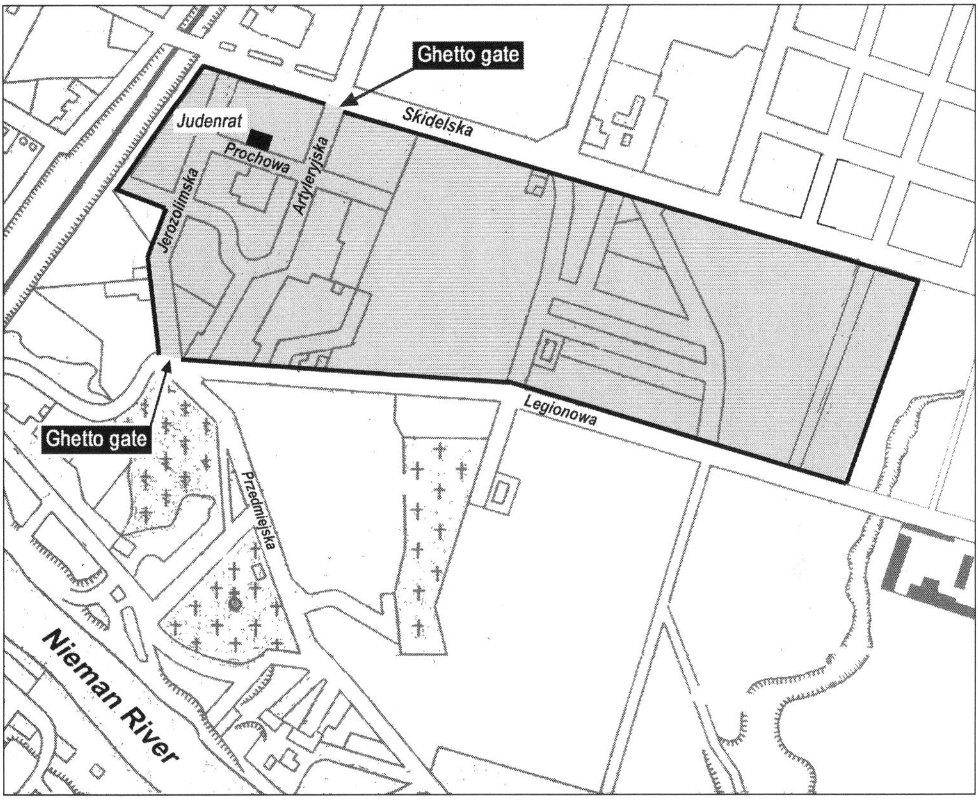

22. Map of Ghetto II in Grodno, located in the Slobodka District across the railroad tracks from the city center, 1941.

community leaders because the top echelon had been deported during the Soviet occupation, the council comprised, as outside observer Chaika Grossman judged them, "good, honest men—the representatives of the Jewish liberal middle class." Her backhanded socialist interpretation was based on the firsthand contacts that some of her Białystok ghetto underground comrades had had with the Grodno Judenrat in its last months. Yet she added, "In other conditions and in other times, they would have contributed to noble missions."[31] Available evidence suggests that these men, including Chairman Brawer, believed they were acting in the best interests of the city's Jews, even if negotiation with the Germans was a losing battle.

Charged with the guardianship of upward of 30,000 people, they sought to improve ghetto conditions in at least one area: through organization of Jewish labor gangs. Jews received the same wage scale as Poles in Grodno, which was 60 percent of the rate that Reich and ethnic German workers without children were paid. Hourly wage rates in the building trades, for example, topped out at 0.39 Reichsmarks per hour for Jews and Poles, among the highest-paying jobs available to them. Yet Jews received only 38 percent of any hourly wage because the Germans' regional commissariat expropriated 50 percent of it, and special taxes took an additional 12 percent.[32] The Judenrat also taxed wages to subsidize ghetto operations, including the purchase of food supplies.

The Judenrat directed part of the tax revenue to purchase building materials for repair and renovation projects to suit the Germans' needs, thereby subsidizing Jewish workers at the highest pay scale.[33] Among younger ghetto inmates who benefitted from this scheme was Leib Bialo, who worked as a plumber in the *Entlausungstelle* (delousing station), a bathhouse for Wehrmacht soldiers on leave from the front.[34] Moishe Kremer did electrical work in the Gestapo headquarters.[35] Yehuda Rabinovich had a job as a locksmith's assistant and handyman with the *Stadtbauamt*, the city maintenance department.[36] Late in the ghetto period, fourteen-year-old Feliks Zandman took on the hard manual labor of mixing mortar for bricklayers.[37]

For many unskilled males fourteen and older, forced-labor gangs offered the sole opportunity to earn a skimpy subsistence wage.[38] Families managed with what they had. "The day my husband was working, we had hope to survive that day," Anna Kaletska recalled soon after the war. "But when people came to the gates of the ghetto and said, 'No more work required,' that was a dark day."[39] Chasia Bielicka's father worked in the municipal storerooms, hauling and stacking goods; his only pay was in bread, which he was permitted to take to his family.[40] Moishe Kremer, before he worked as an electrician, did a variety of manual-labor jobs at the railway yard in Grodno.[41] Jewish laborers faced more acts of violence by Reich German, ethnic German, and Polish guards and supervisors than did skilled workers. To avoid these dangers, some took desk jobs, which paid even less but did not require the same strenuous effort (and associated daily caloric intake). Ann Lewin's brother Arie worked as a bookkeeper for the Judenrat,[42] as did Aaron Zandman, Feliks's father.[43]

Women, who traditionally were not trained in the building trades and were seldom assigned heavy labor, faced their share of debilitating tasks nonetheless. Among these tasks was seasonal work harvesting crops under the watchful eyes of ethnic German and Polish guards. Chasia Bielicka worked in the fields pulling carrots and beets,[44] and many of Zelda Grodzienska's comrades in Hehalutz did similar agricultural work.[45] After Chairman Brawer had visited the Białystok ghetto's Wehrmacht workshops, many women and some men found skilled and unskilled work in factories set up by the Jewish Council in Grodno. Shoe, felt-boot, leather-good, weaving, and metalworking shops supplied German military needs. Women also produced handbags and jewelry for the wives of Gestapo and army officers.[46]

In addition to the Wehrmacht workshops, Jewish men and women also worked in Polish- and German-owned factories.[47] Fenia and Mina Muller were among these laborers.[48] Chasia Bielicka sewed at an underwear factory staffed mostly by Poles as well as in agriculture to take in the harvest. She later found work in the handbag workshop.[49] Vichna Sidranska made slippers for wounded German soldiers.[50] Arie Lewin left his bookkeeping job to work in a German factory, where his sister Ann took a clerical job.[51]

The significance of Grodno's Jews in the wartime economy was measured by the Germans' efforts to replace them as their annihilation policies materialized. In October 1942, after German authorities initiated deportation plans, the Grodno regional commissar requested that East Prussian civilian authorities assist in establishing trade schools for Polish workers "when it is no longer possible to rely on Jewish craftsmen."[52] The local economic office in Grodno requested that factories and other enterprises doing business with the Germans conduct a census of available Jewish and "Aryan" workers. Of particular interest to authorities was these contractors' ability to fulfill production quotas through mid-1943.[53] One German official verified that the census was tied directly with the "loss of tradesmen through the *Judenaktion* [Jewish action; i.e., deportations]."[54]

Debates on the replacement of Jewish laborers continued as deportations began in November 1942. Authorities from the Deutsche Arbeitsfront (German Labor Front), the Nazi-sanctioned labor union, noted in early December 1942 that Jewish craftsmen had been considerably more productive than their Polish counterparts.[55] Of the 12,418 Jews officially remaining in Ghetto I on 9 December 1942, 3,597 were skilled craftsmen, and 2,553 were unskilled laborers. To replace the skilled labor, the regional commissar's economic office estimated that 4,800 Poles were required.[56] The regional commissar addressed the labor issue in a letter to the head of the civil administration in Białystok. "With the removal of all Jews, ghetto industries would come to a standstill," wrote *Landrat* Dr. von Ploetz, specifically mentioning military-clothing production. He requested that the Jewish laborers in Ghetto I be allowed to remain until March or April 1943.[57]

Jews came to realize the pivotal economic role that they played. In the midst of the deportations in January 1943, one Jewish observer noted the key dilemma that their overlords faced—to kill the Jews or to exploit them. Not only did the German administration value Jewish labor and German factory owners recognize how much they relied on skilled Jews, but some in Ghetto I also understood the value of their labor. And yet the "resettlements" rolled on.[58]

Not all Jewish workers participated in the official economy. Many engaged in the "second economy," or black market. Daniel Klovsky's mother, Maria, took in sewing, and Yehuda Rabinovich's mother, Ida, made dresses for the wives of the Gestapo and SS officers. Each received food as payment.[59] Some people banded together to produce items such as artificial honey, soap, sweets, and tobacco products.[60] The Trachtenbergs, neighbors of Feliks Zandman's family, ground seeds to extract oil.[61] The supply of raw materials into the ghetto and the movement of finished goods out depended in part on how the men engaged to clear out latrines put false bottoms in the barrels used to transport human waste.[62]

Work outside the ghetto meant much more than income. Many took jobs because it brought them into contact with Gentiles willing to barter for food. A number of survivors from the ghetto later reported that they either carried food into the ghetto under their clothing or had family members who did so. "You used to go out to work, sometimes you used to organize something, a trade," remembered Leib Bialo. "A piece of silver, a piece of gold, a jacket, or something for a little bit of potatoes or bread or something like this." It was still necessary to smuggle the items through the ghetto gate. "When you came to the gate, if you find a nice guy over there," Leib recalled of some guards—German, Polish, or ghetto police—he might allow the smuggled food to pass through. "But most of them were bad; they used to take everything away."[63]

The Germans, well aware of such smuggling, tried to stop it. The *Kreisbauernführer* (regional farm leader) warned the commander of Reserve Police Battalion 91 of smuggling activities in Grodno. "Repeatedly I have found tons of food pass through the entrances of the two ghettos without any interference from the police," he complained. To regulate what food entered the ghetto, he ordered that all official incoming transports were required to carry documents with his written permission.[64] The case of two Jewish wagon drivers, Jankel Wassermann and Isak Grandzicki, reveals the effort not only to catch smugglers but also to locate the source of illegal food supplies. The two men were captured on 20 October 1942 attempting to smuggle fifteen kilograms of flour into Ghetto I.[65] Under interrogation, Wassermann and Grandzicki admitted to the smuggling but declared they did not know the name of the Pole who sold it to them.[66] Although eligible for the death penalty, the two men were sentenced to serve time in a forced-labor camp.[67]

The World outside the Ghetto

Smuggled food was not the only lifeline. News and rumor framed an uncertain future. "News was one of the things we hungered for," Feliks Zandman recalled. "We lived on rumor."[68] Most official war news reported German victories, but some glimmers of hope appeared.

American entry into the war brought a rare moment of collective joy. Many concluded that between the Soviet Union, Great Britain and its empire, and America, the Germans were bound to collapse. Other rumors in December 1941 told that the German assault in Russia had stalled short of Moscow.[69] Only months later did hints of the situation emerge. Jewish labor gangs saw trains and trucks filled with German wounded, and carpenter Leib Reizer hammered together more and more coffins in his job at the Wehrmacht military hospital. The war must not be going well for the Germans, he inferred.[70]

Other reports shook the ghetto. Whole Jewish communities in western Belarus had been massacred, it was said. News from ghettos in the German General Government was equally disconcerting. A Jewish courier arrived from Warsaw in the late summer of 1942 to report about the Great Deportation, in which tens of thousands of his neighbors were sent into the unknown. What happened to them? What did this mean? Leib Reizer, who had heard eyewitness accounts of mass shootings in Minsk and Vilna during his frenzied flight from Grodno the previous year, could not comprehend what the Warsaw escapee's story meant. "Our healthy common sense could not digest the naked truth, or we were not psychologically prepared for such a catastrophe," Reizer reflected after the war.[71] We will see how some young people in Grodno became the frequent recipients of these reports. Only when numerous messengers delivered the same news did the Jews in Grodno conclude that a catastrophe was unfolding for Jews. Until then, many responded with denial. The city lay within the Białystok District, newly annexed to the Reich. Surely, they would not kill German Jews, a witness recalled overhearing.[72]

New chatter spread in early fall 1942 speculating on the future of the Grodno ghettos. "There were persistent rumors about the Jews of Grodno being sent somewhere to work," Leib Reizer recalled. "As time went on, more and more 'reliable' people spoke of it." He also heard stories about a camp named Treblinka. The Germans told Jews arriving there that they could take a shower and even gave them soap and a towel, but the deportees were instead taken to a building and gassed. The inherit irrationality of such a scenario initially caused

Reizer to discount its veracity.[73] But the rumors persisted, often from very credible sources. Someone heard Polish railroad workers talk about the camp. "The ones who operated the locomotives," Leib Bialo recalled. "And once in a while when they get drunk, you know, they speak up, and they told us the stories [of] what's going on, but nobody would believe."[74]

Nobody believed. And why would they? The Germans had permitted them to live. They had food and shelter and received income, however meager, for their labors. Their work had value, they believed. Conditions were bad, but bartering for food and smuggling made up for the shortfalls in daily sustenance. And at least their families were still together. Why would the Germans keep them alive only to kill them?

The false security offered by the ghetto explains the low occurrence of flight. Life on the outside offered many risks, not least of which was the eagerness of some Poles and other locals to turn in Jews and curry favor with the Germans. Yet a few, mostly young people, did attempt to flee. Alexandre Blumstein later recalled stories of young men and women escaping from Ghetto II to join resistance groups active in the surrounding forests.[75] Fenia Muller's Hashomer Hatzair cell discussed the possibility of flight. "There were seven of us," she remembered. Fenia and one of her brothers, however, remained in the ghetto with their family. The other five members of the cell fled to the forest; as far as she knew, only one survived until the end of the war.[76] Leib Bialo also remained in the ghetto. "The reason is we had a lot of reports that the people who run out from the ghettos," he remembered later, "a lot of them were killed by the Poles, squealed on them."[77]

Leib Bialo's statement reveals a key danger of the world outside the ghetto. Polish informers presented Jews with the real danger of exposure. "They [had] a yen to recognize a Jew for a mile," Leib reflected decades later about these Poles, his former neighbors.[78] Yehuda Rabinovich remembered how "the Poles used to go and point out to the Germans, 'This is a Jew!'"[79] The fear of encountering a hostile Gentile kept many from planning an escape. Alexandre Blumstein recalled hearing that Poles and Lithuanian peasants were openly hostile to Jews and their plight, whereas Belarusians were "indifferent at best."[80]

Responses among Jewish Youth

While their parents were occupied with labor duties or struggled to maintain the household, children and young adults were initially left with nothing to do. The Germans had banned schools, so many of the Jewish youth gathered in the social space of the street as they adjusted to ghetto life.[81] "Sometimes I would go out with friends and do nothing," Feliks Zandman recalled, which for his circle included such mischief as smoking cigarettes.[82] Although some parents arranged for private lessons, most children created their own activities within the confines of the barbed wire. Bella Ilin and her older cousin Izia engaged in various forms of mischief, from bouncing on beds in the hall they occupied with dozens of others to sneaking out to roam the ghetto. "It was all an adventure somehow," she recalled of her five-year-old self. But the ghetto was no playground. Bella felt anxious whenever she and her cousin approached the barbed-wire fence. One time they wandered into the old Jewish cemetery and found a child's naked, frozen corpse. "I remember the horror of that, and that was probably the only horrid scene I saw during my whole period there," she told an interviewer, noting that her parents tried hard to shelter her from the ghetto environment.[83]

Adolescents and young adults grew anxious in a very different way. At first, after months of almost daily encounters with the threatening German occupiers, the newfound isolation of the ghetto offered comparative safety. In time, however, the imposed inactivity proved stultifying. Chasia Bielicka passed the first days and weeks by reading.[84] She was not alone among the idled youth. Many of her former comrades in Hashomer Hatzair responded by sharing their boredom. "Unless we were working," Chasia remembered, "we gathered and grouped—not only to do things at some appointed time, but also just to be together." Their initial meetings, in the cellar below Eliahu Tankus's family home, were social. This cellar stayed warm because the ground floor housed a bakery. "It was there, in the cellar, that we experienced the few kind moments of our lives in the ghetto," Chasia later recalled, "moments of togetherness, intimacy, and the ability to sit and talk quietly about anything."[85]

They were not content to sit out the German occupation, however. "Eliahu Tankus, Shaikele Matus, Gedalyahu Browarski, Cyla Szachnes, Mirjam Pupko, Moni Burla, and I became an *Aktiv* [group]," Chasia recited in her memoir, recording her comrades' names to honor their memory. Their first mission was the education of aimless children and teens. "Nobody was looking out for them," she noted. The Hashomer *Aktiv* gathered children covertly at the former Yavneh school located near the entrance gate to Ghetto I. "We spoke with them about the Jewish festivals that we were not celebrating, told them about *Eretz Israel*, and taught them Hebrew songs," Chasia recalled of their education efforts, which had the additional goal of recruiting new members to the movement. Soon she obtained a pass to carry her work to Ghetto II.[86] Dror-Hehalutz, a Zionist youth movement with nearly as many members as Hashomer, began tutoring sessions as well.[87] Other groups, including Tsukunft and the Komsomol, joined in this effort.[88]

Such initiatives raised group members' confidence. The historian Yehuda Bauer has noted that "cultural, educational, religious, and political activities taken to strengthen morale" constituted a form of resistance.[89] In Grodno, these activities were a significant step toward greater efforts, although numerous factors typically shaped and fostered the development of armed resistance: the collective realization of danger, effective leadership, environmental conditions that aided concealment, logical planning with realistic goals, acquisition of weapons, and choice of appropriate timing for action.[90] In addition, effective resistance was a social process. As the sociologist Nechama Tec has observed, "Resistance required cooperation, a sense of belonging to something greater than oneself."[91] Youth-movement leaders and their followers in Grodno sought to fulfill ambitious goals, and at the core of these efforts lay forging links of intra- and intergroup teamwork.

The process of recognizing that the Germans intended to kill each and every Jew began in Grodno concurrent with the formation of the two ghettos. At the end of October 1941, Bella Chazan from Vilna brought word of the killings in the Ponar forest outside the city. Chazan, a Hehalutz member, later met with Judenrat chairman David Brawer; he received her report with disbelief.[92] Couriers from cells in other ghettos followed. As Chaika Grossman, active in the Hashomer Hatzair underground movement in her native Białystok, later recalled, "Grodno," initially a stopover for messengers, "was for us an important link because it connected the three resistance centers: Vilna, Białystok, Warsaw."[93] These contacts spurred Grodno's youth to join active resistance.

And more messengers came. Hashomer Hatzair member Tosia Altman, a courier with the Warsaw and Vilna ghetto underground movements, arrived in Grodno sometime in January 1942 to bring word of Abba Kovner's manifesto calling on Jews to resist the Germans' mortal threat.[94] Upon hearing her reports of the emerging resistance networks in Warsaw, Vilna, and Białystok, those meeting with Altman felt empowered to join the coordinated effort. "Now it was our turn," Chasia Bielicka later recalled of that moment.[95]

But their turn to do what? Hashomer was one group with, at most, a little more than 100 members. What of Dror-Hehalutz, the Bund, and the Communists? And what about weapons? Additional direction arrived some weeks after Tosia Altman's visit, when Hashomer leader Edek (Eliahu) Boraks of Białystok slipped into the ghetto. "What you're doing with the children is a holy labor," Chasia remembered Boraks telling those assembled, "but you ought to start thinking about a fighting underground."[96] Youth groups in other ghettos were making progress despite the difficulty of organizing resistance activities, he explained.

Although Boraks meant to inspire them, his visit served to highlight how far behind in the resistance the young Grodno Jews were and how few their numbers. Progress appeared possible when the leaders of the Zionist party Poalei Tsiyon–Left brought together the movement leaders from Hashomer Hatzair, Dror-Hehalutz, the Bund, Betar, the Communists, and the Komsomol.[97] Ultimately, however, only Hashomer and Dror-Hehalutz agreed to mutual cooperation.[98] In the interim, other couriers passed through Grodno. Irena Adamowicz, a Polish Gentile and key intermediary with the Armia Krajowa (Polish Home Army), brought updated reports from Warsaw and Vilna.[99] Mordechai Tenenbaum and Tema Schneiderman arrived in the late summer of 1942 to meet with Hashomer and Dror-Hehalutz. They confirmed the stunning news of the Great Deportation from the Warsaw ghetto to Treblinka. How could the Grodno Jews respond? Join the partisans or rise up within the ghetto? Tenenbaum and Schneiderman listened to their ideas. They counseled that the ablest fighters join the growing resistance movement in the Białystok ghetto; the rest should chance flight to the forests.[100]

This advice was exasperating. Was there no action, no duty that they could fulfill in their home city? Must they abandon their families and everything they knew? Their frustration was imprinted on recollections retold decades later, such as those of Hehalutz member Zelda Grodzienska. "We all got together, whoever wanted to, and we tried to see how we can help ourselves or how we can escape or how we can arm ourselves against the Germans," Zelda recalled in the early 1980s, her memories tumbling from self-help to escape to armed resistance. And her narrative reveals precipitous clefts. "So we got a few guns and other homemade things and a—we tried to sabotage here and there wherever we could—we tried to raise a little garden with vegetables to help ourselves and help others in need."[101] Guns and gardening? Indeed, with the arrival of spring in 1942, young people joined others in planting gardens.[102] The activity provided an outlet for their energies and developed social cooperation. It also offered young people some of the few moments of hope they had. "When you work the soil and eat its fruits, you also gain confidence," recalled Chaika Grossman of the gardening activities among the youth of the Białystok ghetto.[103]

Yet Zelda's recollections—contrasting resistance with agriculture—also reveal the exasperation of underground members. They had lived under Polish rule, endured the Soviet occupation and annexation, and survived a year under the Germans, only to face a no-win scenario. Planting beds provided a respite, but not a solution. They received little support from their elders. "Your shoulders are too young to bear this responsibility," Chasia Bielicka's father told her when he learned of her desire to join the nascent ghetto underground. "You don't really understand where you want to take us."[104] When the Judenrat did little to support resistance, youth groups responded as they had in the previous decade under Polish rule: they sought ways to achieve their goals without regard for the opinion of community leaders.

If they wished to act, they had much to learn and acquire. Some took on special roles. Dodik Rozowski of Hashomer applied his skills as a graphic artist to prepare forged papers.[105] Metalworkers sharpened metal rods and fashioned brass knuckles. Eliahu Tankus led the effort to collect gold and jewelry to exchange for the firearms left behind by the Polish and Soviet armies and acquired by local peasants.[106] Chasia Bielicka recalled that when the first pistol arrived, the members of the *Aktiv* treated it as a sacred moment. "We passed the gun around," she recalled. "Each of us kissed it and recited the *shehecheyanu* blessing: thank you, almighty God, for allowing us to live until this moment."[107] From what she reports, the appearance of the weapon gave their underground group a sense of hope, permitting them to plan for a future. Yet one gun did not make a revolt. They had much to do, and no amount of planning prepared them for the onslaught to come.

Deportations from Ghetto II

The "peace" of the ghetto was shattered when the Germans multiplied the guard force at the perimeter of each ghetto on Monday, 2 November 1942. "Every few steps stood an armed German, with his gun ready," Anna Kaletska remembered.[108] As on any other work day, Jewish workers gathered at the gates for their labor assignments. On this day, Commandants Wiese and Streblow appeared at their respective ghettos, each firing his pistol at random into the gathered work gangs. Twelve were killed, and forty wounded.[109] Notwithstanding this violence, frantic speculation arose among the imprisoned Jews regarding the ghetto encirclement. "People gathered in small groups, talking, talking, and talking more," Leib Reizer recalled, "and voiced wild hypotheses, wanting to deceive themselves."[110] Rumor took a turn on 4 November when the Judenrat posted notices throughout the ghettos declaring that the Germans intended to resettle large numbers of Grodno's Jews in labor camps in Upper Silesia. Adults were to pack one set of working clothes, one set of dress clothes, a towel, a bowl and spoon, toothbrush, shoe brush and clothes brush, and food for three days.[111] "Why would it be worth their while to write that they're sending us to work?" Reizer recalled someone responding. "If they wanted to kill us, they could do that outside the town."[112]

Such denial in the face of new and potentially threatening conditions was made easier by German lies. "Have no care, this will become a labor *lager* [camp], my word of honor," Gestapo chief Errelis reportedly told the Judenrat.[113] The Germans' preparations for deportations had begun a few weeks prior to this, in early October 1942, when the chief of the Sicherheitspolitzei (Sipo, Security Police) in the Białystok District, Dr. Wilhelm Altenloh, ordered the liquidation of the region's ghettos.[114] With great thoroughness, German civilian administrators in the Białystok District had spent the summer of 1942 in pursuit of religious community records to assess "proof of descent" among the local population in order to identify all Jews.[115] They also utilized the Jewish administration. After surrounding the ghetto, the Gestapo pressed the Judenrat's statistical department to assemble deportation lists.[116]

The latter effort included identification of "useful" laborers in Ghetto II. The relocation of some 4,000 Jews to Ghetto I occurred on 9–10 November.[117] Among the valued ghetto prisoners was Dr. Chaim Blumstein, who was transferred to the hospital housed on the Great Synagogue's second floor. His family found refuge in another physician's apartment in Ghetto I.[118] On the first day of the relocation, the Germans once again took the opportunity to fire into the crowd of Jews. Seven died of their wounds.[119] Despite the violence, some recognized the urgency to join the group moved to Ghetto I. Zelda Grodzienska heard rumors that anyone remaining in Ghetto II was doomed, so she slipped into a group headed for Ghetto I. She told her mother, Fruma, about the danger, and her mother followed soon thereafter.[120] Leib Reizer, often incensed by the inequalities of the Jewish social order, sneaked his family into the queue for Ghetto I

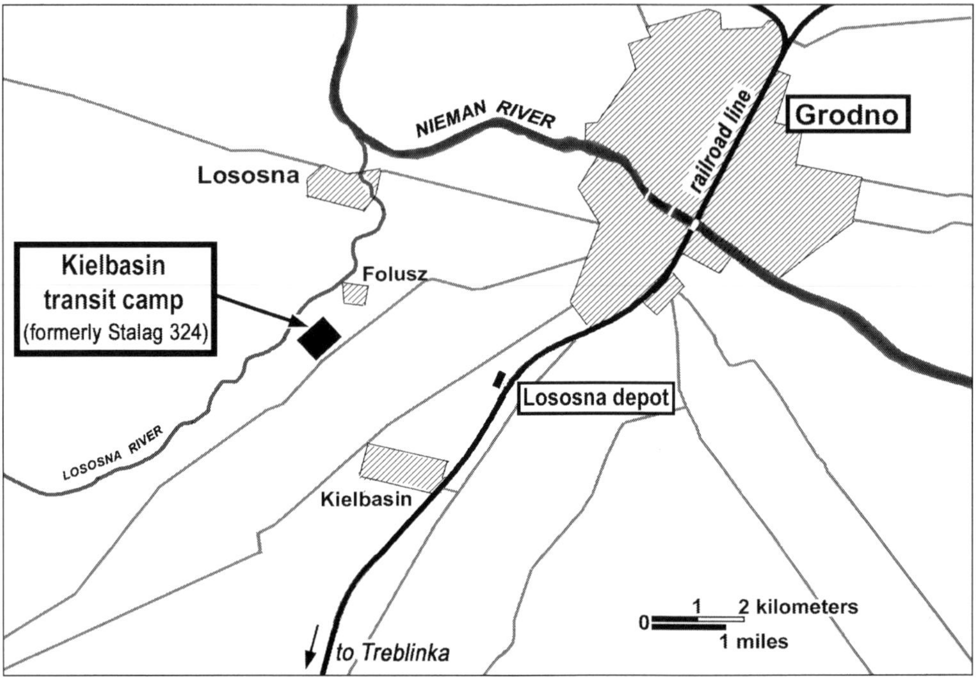

23. Map of Kielbasin transit camp in relation to Grodno and the railroad line to Treblinka, 1941–43.

after he heard that the Jewish Council had transferred several prominent inhabitants.[121]

To make room for laborers transferred from Ghetto II, several thousand others were deported from Ghetto I to the transit camp at Kielbasin (also known as Kolbasin or Kolbasino) (figure 23).[122] The Gestapo requisitioned the former Stalag 324, located about five kilometers south of the city center and established for Soviet POWs, to hold Jewish deportees from Grodno and the surrounding region. The Soviet POWs had died by the thousands at Kielbasin from starvation, disease, exposure, or murder by the German guards. Jews and Gentiles working nearby frequently saw cartloads of corpses from this camp and others set up around the city.[123] Kielbasin lacked barracks structures; its only shelter consisted of ninety-six *zemlyanki* (dugouts), approximately six meters by twenty-five meters in size, built hastily by Soviet POWs in the autumn of 1941.[124] Upon Kielbasin's use as a transit camp for Jews, up to 300 deportees were crowded into each dugout. Typhoid and dysentery became rampant during the winter of 1942–43. Queues for toilet facilities were hundreds of meters long, but Jews caught relieving themselves anywhere else were shot.[125]

With valued labor protected for the time being in Ghetto I, deportations commenced from Ghetto II on 15 November 1942.[126] The Jewish police joined with the German Order Police and the Gestapo in their house-to-house searches rounding up Jews. Deportees were given one hour to pack a bundle and assemble at the ghetto gate. Told they would be sent to a labor camp, the deported were marched that night to the main train station to board passenger trains. The transport traveled first to Treblinka, where it waited for two days before it was rerouted to Auschwitz.[127]

Among the deportees were the Mullers—the children Fenia, Mina, Bluma, William, and Dovid; their parents, Josef and Sonya; and extended family members. The train carrying nearly 1,000 men, women, and children arrived at the railway yard about a kilometer from Auschwitz II (also called Birkenau or Auschwitz-Birkenau). "The young ones that could work and walk should stand on one side," Mina Muller recalled of the process of selection, "and the others go on trucks." Fenia, Mina, Bluma, and William were placed with the group to be inducted into the camp as slave laborers, which numbered 165 men and 65 women. The remaining men, women, and children, including the rest of the Muller family, were driven to the gas chambers and murdered.[128]

Three more deportations followed from Ghetto II, all destined for Auschwitz-Birkenau. Two thousand Jews were herded onto cattle cars in the midst of a snowstorm on 21 November 1942. Upon arrival on 25 November, 305 men and 128 women were selected for slave labor; the rest were murdered in the gas chambers.[129] Two last transports from Grodno, each containing about 1,000 men, women, and children, reached Auschwitz-Birkenau on 2 and 8 December; less than a quarter survived the selections.[130] Leib Bialo's family was taken on the last transport. "My father and mother and brother, they were taken on

Hanukkah," he recalled decades later, noting that their deportation had occurred "on the second candle."[131]

The thoroughness of the initial deportations separated other families as well. Chasia Bielicka's aunts Rosa and Ita, uncles Chaim and Yaakov, and their respective families were deported into the unknown.[132] One of Michael Kremer's brothers, his sister, and his mother vanished on a transport; his father and two other brothers were transferred to Ghetto I.[133] Children lost playmates. Alexandre Blumstein's best friend was placed on one of the first deportation lists. "Why am I left? Why do I have a father who can protect me, and he doesn't?" Alexandre later recalled pondering.[134]

Resistance and Flight

For the approximately 15,000 Jews in Ghetto I, worsened conditions accompanied heightened terror. Water was available a mere three days a week, and electricity was cut off entirely.[135] Hunger grew worse as the Gestapo cracked down on food smugglers. With the influx of skilled workers from Ghetto II, crowding increased. Despite the close quarters, most of the ghetto's inhabitants stayed indoors, and not just to avoid the cold. The street ceased to be a gathering space as incursions from large and small contingents of Gestapo meted out violence. Equipped with newly installed floodlights, the streets blazed with light when the Germans carried out actions in the ensuing weeks and months.[136]

Just before the "useful" Jews in Ghetto II were relocated across town (9–10 November), Ghetto I inhabitants were terrorized by a public hanging on 7 November 1942. Lena Prenska and her neighbor, a Warsaw refugee named Druker, had been captured outside the ghetto posing as Poles. Their landlord in the ghetto, Moishe Shpindler, was arrested as well for failing to report their absence. Commandant Kurt Wiese stage-managed their execution. Three steel beams projecting from the unfinished facade of the Tankus family home proved ideal gallows. Insisting the ghetto captives witness the spectacle, Wiese mustered them into the adjacent street.[137] Decades later, many surviving eyewitnesses remembered Lena Prenska's defiance. "I saw Kurt Wiese put the noose around the neck of [Lena] Prenska; she spat in his face," an eyewitness later recalled for a West German court trying Wiese for his crimes.[138] The ghetto commandant kicked the bench from under the feet supporting the three, then wiped his face.[139]

The deportations from Ghetto II and renewed terror roused some in Ghetto I to take action. A few constructed hiding places behind false walls, below floors, and in attics or cellars. Others investigated escape. Male heads of families often explored such strategies, largely with the aid of contacts outside the ghetto. Their spouses held veto power, however. Vichna Sidranska's father, Mates, wanted to take his family into hiding after the deportations from Ghetto II, but her mother, Doba, was against it because winter had set in.[140] Leib Reizer, who had fled Grodno alone at the outbreak of war in June 1941 and later returned, sought to escape a second time with his wife and daughter. From his comrades in an underground Communist resistance cell, he learned of a Soviet partisan detachment led by Kostia Buchko active in the Nacza forest 100 kilometers to the northeast of Grodno. The Belarusian commander took able-bodied Jews for his fighting forces, particularly if they brought weapons and ammunition. Reizer sent a message through a courier to verify that his wife and daughter would be welcomed as well.[141]

Other parents made plans for their family's escape. Dr. Chaim Blumstein, with his wife's agreement, looked to take his family into hiding with the help of a Polish colleague, Dr. Antoni Docha. In November 1942, as Ghetto II remained surrounded day and night by German Order Police, the elder Blumstein slipped across the fence and traveled to Dr. Docha's village 30 kilometers distant to make arrangements. "Father's self-control, his Aryan looks, and his flawless Polish," his son Alexandre later recalled, were qualities that aided him in this dangerous mission.[142] Ephraim and Anya Ilin secretly decided to send their daughter, Bella, outside the ghetto. Her older cousin, Rachela Tarlowski, was to be sent with her as caretaker because Anya did not want her daughter to be alone. Bella knew nothing of these plans before the day came to sneak through the perimeter fence. "I think everything was kept from me, maybe because I would talk about it," she recalled more than fifty years later.[143]

Whereas some parents looked to go into hiding, particularly if they had young children, adolescents and young adults wanted to fight. An assassination attempt on Otto Streblow failed when the Ghetto II commandant shot the two assailants before they could raise their weapon.[144] Hashomer Hatzair and Dror-Hehalutz embarked on other preparations, such as fabricating steel rods into pikes and metal scraps into brass knuckles. They fashioned prototype Molotov cocktails, filling lightbulbs with flammable liquids.[145] Fighters took slats from fences to permit passage across ghetto courtyards unhindered.[146]

But when would they have a chance to strike at the Germans? Would the Grodno underground ever be ready? Underground leaders in Białystok sent Zerah Zilberberg to assess the situation in January 1943.[147] He sneaked into the ghetto and met with David Brawer to convince the Judenrat chief to keep underground members off deportation lists. The latter agreed, provided that the underground in Grodno not carry out any act of resistance until the final ghetto liquidation, an inflexible position that limited the resisters' opportunities.[148] Zilberberg's mission was further compromised by his failure to forge alliances with the Bund, Betar, and the Communists.[149] Bund and Betar members were too disorganized to support resistance efforts, and the Communists wanted to escape to the forests and join the partisans. Zilberberg subsequently met with underground members to render his advice. Abandon Grodno and join resistance forces in Białystok, he told them.[150] As the Germans carried out their final deportations, some underground members accepted this judgment, but others chose to stand and fight.

Deportations from Ghetto I

The Germans deported most of the remaining 15,000 Jews in Ghetto I in two waves: mid-January 1943 (remembered by survivors as the "Deportation of the Ten Thousand") and mid-February 1943. These two events were marked by heightened levels of violence by the Germans and their local ethnic German and Polish collaborators. The

Jewish police, too, participated in the ferociousness based on promises that they and their families would be protected from deportation. The Gestapo carried out smaller-scale roundups for transport from Ghetto I in mid-December 1942, marching Jews south of Grodno to Kielbasin. Feliks Zandman, deported with his parents, sister, and paternal grandparents, later recalled that they were marched four abreast in a long column toward Kielbasin, flanked by German Order Police and ethnic German collaborators. "Sing, goddamnit! All of you sing!" one of them howled. After what seemed like hours, they arrived at the transit camp. Nearly a week later, during which time he witnessed the murder of his cousin Rifka Freydowicz by Commandant Karl Rinzler, Feliks escaped on the back of an empty food wagon and returned to Ghetto I.[151]

The rest of Feliks's family came back from Kielbasin only a week later when the Germans closed the camp in early January 1943. A shortage of railway carriages influenced their decision to move the remaining 2,000 to 3,000 Jews, many from smaller communities surrounding Grodno, to Ghetto I.[152] Most of these prisoners were in greatly debilitated condition. "I watched a procession of pitiful figures dressed in tatters, dragging their frozen feet in the snow and mud," remembered Alexandre Blumstein.[153]

Despite the arrival of this ragged remnant, some in the ghetto responded to the closing of Kielbasin with hope. Maybe the worst was over, they thought. Others felt relief when news spread that British foreign minister Anthon Eden had read in Parliament a declaration dated 17 December 1942 from the United Nations condemning Germany's murder of Jews.[154] Help was imminent, a few believed.

This optimism did not last long because the Germans had since mid-December 1942 already put plans in motion for the deportation of 30,000 Jews from the Białystok District to Auschwitz-Birkenau.[155] In Grodno, the Gestapo ordered the Judenrat to draw up further deportation lists. Implementation began on 18 January, when the targeted Jews received notices that informed them they were to be sent to munitions factories for labor duties.[156] Jewish policemen, in tandem with the Gestapo, roamed from dwelling to dwelling to round up those on the deportation lists. One eyewitness recalled the cruelty of his coreligionists: "Why, if you saw such Jews, you'd think they were worse than the Gestapo."[157]

Over the course of several days, thousands of ghetto inhabitants passed through the deportation assembly point in the Great Synagogue. Moishe Kremer testified more than twenty years later at Kurt Wiese's trial that the commandant shot Jews at random in and around the building.[158] Alexandre Blumstein's father, Chaim, and older brother, Tolo, told him that the prayer hall was filled to capacity. All able-bodied persons were marched to the deportation trains at the Lososna depot, nearly four kilometers to the south. Those who could not walk were transported on wagons.[159] The action continued for five days, with a transport departing each day for Auschwitz-Birkenau. They reached the concentration and annihilation camp on five successive days, 20–24 January 1943. Some 11,650 men, women, and children passed through selection, with 1,096 men and 703 women registered as slave laborers in the camp. The remaining Jews were killed in the gas chambers.[160]

Many hid in attics and cellars in the Grodno ghetto during the January action. As many as 1,500 people on the transport list could not be found, so the Gestapo threatened the Jewish police that they and their families would be taken unless others were seized to fill the quota.[161] Leib Reizer took his family to the Great Synagogue attic, a space discovered by his brother, Shlomo, during his work in the ghetto hospital on the second floor. When the roundups extended into a third day, and the attic hiding place became less secure, the group sneaked into the cellar below the ghetto soup kitchen and hid there with a dozen others until it was safe to emerge on the sixth day.[162]

For the 5,000 Jews remaining in Ghetto I, the transports meant the loss of more family and friends. Most of Zelda Grodzienska's remaining family members were deported.[163] Alexandre Blumstein played games with friends Shurik, Rita, and Shula on the eve of the action. Shurik was deported; Rita committed suicide rather than leave the ghetto.[164] Following the January actions, the Gestapo reduced Ghetto I to half its size, declaring the rest a no man's land.[165] As the ghetto diminished, the remaining Grodno Jews heard fresh rumors that were as confusing as they were disturbing. "People in the ghetto talked of the Jewish belongings, which [the Germans] had taken from Treblinka to Białystok," reported an eyewitness deported to the Białystok ghetto in late January 1943. The rumors originated from railway workers who had unloaded seven train cars from Treblinka filled with thousands of small bundles of clothing headed for the rag man. The owners, they guessed, no longer needed them.[166]

Yet others chose to believe the Germans' lies. "We know about Treblinka, what they do with the Jews; they are taken for work," was one rejoinder to atrocity tales. Indeed, there had been a labor camp named Treblinka in operation since late 1941, located about two kilometers from the annihilation camp built more than a year later. Moreover, stories circulated that Auschwitz was merely a labor camp. To substantiate these claims, the Gestapo showed letters purported to have been sent by deportees to the Jewish Council, and council members, complicit in the deception, promoted the belief that the letters were genuine.[167] Other conditions indicated a renewed calm. Food rations increased, and labor duties resumed.[168]

New orders to the Judenrat on 11 February 1943 broke the seeming quiet: all Jews were to be sent to labor camps.[169] The deportation action began on 13 February and continued for four days. The day began normally. Labor gangs lined up and were marched to their places of work. The ghetto was sealed later that morning. Vichna Sidranska's family was among those notified to gather their belongings hastily and proceed to the Great Synagogue. Her father, however, had left with the laborers before dawn; Vichna never saw him again. When Vichna, with her mother and brother, reached the Great Synagogue, hundreds of others had already been herded into the prayer room, and hundreds more followed throughout the day. At 4:00 a.m. the next morning, Commandant Wiese entered the synagogue and ordered all the assembled Jews out of the building. Amid shouts and gunshots, German Order Police and Polish police officers marched the deportees in the cold predawn air toward the Lososna depot, where they were loaded onto trains.[170]

The February action presented the ghetto underground movements with one last challenge: resist, flee, or submit and die. Many resistance members were captured and deported to Treblinka. Among them was Zelda Grodzienska, who had taken refuge with friends from Hehalutz after the deportation of most of her family. Their hideout was raided in the middle of the action, and although Zelda initially escaped, she was soon rounded up and sent to the Great Synagogue. "We were taken from there the next day to the train station and put on the train with a lot of shooting and a lot of beating," she recalled later. "From there we were sent to Treblinka."[171]

Some members of the resistance saw the deportations as the signal for an armed uprising. The news that Wiese had shot Dr. Brawer dead seemed another indicator that their time had come. Despite Zerah Zilberberg's counsel to join the underground in Białystok, a few formulated a plan to join the deportees in the Great Synagogue and lead a mass uprising. Zilberberg joined in this effort, perhaps because he thought they needed leadership. Their plan was to open fire on the Germans, break the windows behind the Torah ark, and lead the people in a mass escape. Chasia Bielicka reflected decades later on the fanciful plan: "Who was going to leap to 'freedom' from that location? Women with babies in arms? Fathers with two or three children clutching each of their hands? Exhausted old people?"[172] No wonder the plan collapsed immediately when the German Order Police opened fire on the fighters. Twelve succeeded in escaping, including Zilberberg, who traveled to Białystok to report on events. The rest, however, were soon captured and killed by the Germans.[173]

Four thousand Grodno Jews were deported to Treblinka during the February action. A month later, nearly all of the remaining 1,000 ghetto prisoners were deported to the Białystok ghetto. Among them was B. Borowski, who told a transcriber for the Białystok ghetto archive about the mixed responses of Grodno Gentiles to the departure of the "last" Jews on 12 March 1943. "Along the street stood many Poles and Germans, watching them lead the last Jews out of Grodno. Others looked at us from windows. Some wept; others laughed."[174]

Daniel Klovsky's family was deported in March as well, as were Chasia Bielicka's mother and younger sister, Zipporka.[175] Although the Gestapo posted notices on 13 March declaring Grodno to be cleansed of Jews, about a dozen Jewish tradesmen, including Moishe Kremer, remained engaged in completing construction projects. In May, Kremer requested to join his wife and child, who had been deported to Białystok in March.[176] The remaining Jewish workers were transferred to a prison in Łomza in August 1943.

Grodno was "cleansed" of Jews, but the city's two ghettos remained filled with the hastily abandoned effects of the deported. The German-appointed *Bürgermeister* issued an order to inventory and store Jewish property, but the city lacked adequate personnel, and the work dragged on into late 1943.[177] Unlike the household effects in Vitebsk, the intended destination for Grodno's looted Jewish property was the Reich.[178] Anything that was not suitable "for German purposes" was sold to the local population.[179] In the meantime, locals tried to pilfer whatever they could carry. Three looters caught in the vacant portions of Ghetto I in February 1943 were arrested and executed as an example to the rest of the population.[180] Even after sorted and cleaned items were warehoused, theft remained a serious problem.[181]

Steps to Survival

When Yehuda Rabinovich returned to Ghetto I with his labor gang on 13 February 1943, he heard the shooting that signaled another round of deportations. He jumped from the column of workers and made his way to the city theater, one of the buildings in Grodno at which he had worked as a locksmith. The caretaker, Kuchinski, gave him refuge. Yehuda remained at the theater in hiding, aided by Kuchinski and others for the next seventeen months. In doing so, however, he left his mother, Ida, behind in the ghetto; she was subsequently deported to Treblinka.[182] Feliks Zandman escaped from his labor gang the same day. After unsuccessful attempts to find refuge in and around Grodno, he traveled some 10 kilometers west to Lososna, where the Freydovicz family had a summer house. Jan and Janova Puchalski, caretakers of the village's summer homes, readily agreed to hide Feliks. He was later joined by his uncle, Sender Freydovicz. The rest of his family were deported and murdered at Treblinka.[183]

Ephraim and Anya Ilin took action sometime before the January deportations from Ghetto I. They placed their only child, Bella, in the care of her older cousin, Rachela Tarlowski, and sent them out of the ghetto. "I just remember darkness, I remember wire, and I remember my having to crawl under the wire," Bella noted decades later. Both were mere children, but Rachela was old enough to take Bella to the meeting point where Krystyna Cywiński, a friend of Ephraim from before the war, sheltered them in her home. Ephraim escaped soon thereafter and survived in hiding apart from his daughter. Anya did not leave the ghetto in time. Decades later, Bella still did not know what happened to her mother. Was she unwilling to leave her elderly in-laws behind? Was she caught in a roundup and unable to get away?[184]

The Blumstein family began their flight from the ghetto in late January 1943. In preparation, they occupied an unused room of the Ghetto I Judenrat building that fronted on the "Aryan" side. Alexandre and his mother, Estera, escaped the ghetto at night through a window with the assistance of a Jewish policeman, and the two made off to the Grodno home of Dr. Docha's gardener. They later journeyed to the peasant family that had agreed to shelter them. Chaim Blumstein and his elder son, Tolo, returned to their duties at the ghetto hospital in the Great Synagogue.[185]

With Dr. Blumstein and son was the doctor's mother, who had long since lapsed into senility and was unable to comprehend the events of the previous year and a half under German rule. During the February actions, Dr. Blumstein faced a horrible dilemma when he and his elderly mother were placed on the deportation list. He was pulled out of the gathered deportees to continue his services in the ghetto hospital. His mother, screaming, "Motek, where are you?" as he stood by helpless, was marched away with the rest. Many families tried to stay together during the deportations, but those who wanted to escape realized the terrible necessity to abandon physically or mentally debilitated relatives. To do otherwise imperiled the entire family. So it was for Dr. Blumstein. As his younger son, Alexandre, later described his father's painful decision, "Father sobbed convulsively, but did not squander this unexpected opportunity."[186] Such were the stakes of survival. Chaim and Tolo Blumstein made their break from a subsequent deportation column as it wound its way through the ghetto. After they, too, escaped through the Judenrat building, the family was reunited at their hiding place.[187]

Leib Reizer also escaped with his family, taking with him the price of admission to a partisan otriad: two pistols and 200 bullets. With two teenage accomplices, Beryl Lipski and another youth named Pinye, Leib broke into the Wehrmacht hospital gun magazine on the night of 7 February 1943 and grabbed what they could. The three met up with Leib's wife, Frumke, and daughter, Bashele, as well as with several others who had sneaked thorough the ghetto fence. They joined another group of Jews on Grodno's eastern outskirts and fled into the winter night on horse-drawn sleighs in search of the Buchko partisan camp. In total, twenty-six Jews from Grodno participated in the escape, including extended family members. Other than five-year-old Bashele Reizer, the group ranged from teenagers to middle-aged adults.[188] Some of the runaways, Reizer included, had been active in the Communist underground, while others were members of Poalei Tsiyon–Left.[189]

Others were already engaged in acts of resistance when they took steps to escape. Zerah Zilberberg sent Chasia Bielicka and her comrade Cyla Szachnes to the Białystok ghetto on the eve of the January deportations from Grodno. The two were entrusted with the tools to forge documents.[190] Chasia picked up the illicit implements and placed them in a handbag taken from her workshop. She returned to her parents' apartment after midnight to get only a few extra things because she expected to return to Grodno after a few days. Chasia remembered that her mother awoke and, realizing her daughter was leaving, pleaded, "What will become of the family?" Chasia had to make the agonizing choice whether to remain with family in the ghetto and face deportation, or to escape with her more mobile companions. But Chasia's resolve was firm, given her mission to aid the Jewish underground.

Chasia and Cyla blended into one of the work gangs leaving the ghetto at 4:30 a.m. After dashing into a side street and ripping off their yellow stars, the two young women walked nervously to the station to take a train to Białystok.[191]

Some young people who were not involved in formal resistance efforts held onto dreams of escape to the forests. A group of young men deported from Grodno in mid-February 1943 were determined to break out of the train car using tools smuggled in their clothing. Although told that their destination was another ghetto, they had heard enough German lies to believe they were really headed for Treblinka. Crowded 110 persons per car, the group set to work cutting a hole in the floor while the train was still in the station. "After an hour the train began to move. We took to our work in haste," B. Borowski reported in his testimony collected for the Białystok ghetto archive. They abandoned their escape plan when, indeed, the train stopped in Białystok and all deportees were taken to the ghetto.[192] One who successfully jumped from another deportation train was nineteen-year-old Grigorii (Girsh) Khosid. Deported from Grodno on 13 February 1943, Khosid jumped from the window of the passenger carriage taking his transport to Treblinka. He told an interviewer decades later, "I realized that it was necessary to jump when the train traveled at speed." And so he did, crashing into the snow-covered ground. He recovered his footing and fled as German bullets whizzed by.[193]

Zelda Grodzienska wanted to jump from her deportation train, but she could not get near the small opening of the crowded cattle car webbed with barbed wire. Upon arrival at Treblinka, deportees were greeted by the blows and gunshots from SS men and Ukrainian guards and shouts from Jewish Sonderkommando. It was a cold February day. The guards bellowed for men and women to form separate lines, with children to go with their mothers. Once the women were escorted into another yard, they were told to take off their shoes. More shouts informed that they were headed for showers. After they received food and clothing, they would work in the camp. Decades later, Zelda remembered her terror despite these reassurances. She was certain that all of her family members, deported weeks earlier, were dead. At that instant, she faced what might be her own end.[194] Ahead of her lay the women's undressing barrack, where female deportees' heads were shaved, and beyond that the mouth to the *Himmelstrasse*, the "road to heaven" that led to the gas chamber.

Zelda went no farther, however. She later recalled that the barefoot women and girls ahead of her ran into the undressing barracks to escape the cold.[195] Zelda hesitated, perhaps for a few seconds, perhaps longer. Dazed by what she had just experienced upon arrival, she later remembered hearing an inner voice telling her, "Go back, go back to the line, back to the line." She pushed her way to the back of the group. SS men and Jewish Sonderkommando suddenly took several younger women, Zelda among them, to the barrack opposite the women's undressing barrack.[196]

Vichna Sidranska was on the same deportation transports as Zelda Grodzienska. With Vichna were her mother, Doba; her eleven-year-old brother, Samuel; and a paternal uncle and his family. All except her uncle went to the left, to the women's undressing barrack. She, too, remembered the order to remove her shoes. Unlike Zelda, Vichna entered the women's barrack. "We were told to get undressed," she reported. "We were told to give up any money or any valuables." The women were supposed to hand over the latter items at a deposit window. Vichna took what little jewelry she had and threw it into the sawdust on the floor.[197]

As Vichna began removing her three layers of clothing, she spotted a group of young women being rounded up and placed in a corner of the barrack. Some had had their heads shaved already. Although initially hesitant because she wanted to stay with her mother, Vichna was grabbed by a Sonderkommando and shoved toward the group in the corner. Like Zelda Grodzienska, Vichna was escorted to the other barrack opposite the women's undressing barrack. Sometime later Sonderkommando arrived with clothes for the women who had undressed; Vichna retrieved her mother's coat, finding her gloves and family pictures still in the pockets.

A transport from Białystok arrived several hours later, and more young women were herded into the men's barrack. The combined group totaled 104. They spent a sleepless night as the sounds of the camp surrounded them in the dark. In the morning, the women were loaded onto a cattle car. Three doctors selected from among the male deportees were also aboard. Their destination was Majdanek concentration camp.[198]

For each, these first steps outside of the ghetto marked the beginning of a new stage of survival, one in which they had to act with a greater degree of personal agency. Ephraim and Anya Ilin, Chaim and Estera Blumstein, Yehuda Rabinovich, and Feliks Zandman saw an opening to escape and seized it. Their daring actions are comparable to those of their coreligionists who had fled the Vitebsk ghetto. Chasia Bielicka did the same when she left Grodno on a mission for the underground. Others surely wished to do so but hesitated. B. Borowski and his contemporaries had eleventh-hour desires to escape to the forests via a leap from their deportation train. We only know of their thoughts because they received a temporary reprieve, arriving in Białystok instead of Treblinka. Grigorii Khosid made that leap; he later joined the Bielski partisans.

Zelda Grodzienska, Vichna Sidranska, and some 100 other young women deported from Grodno to Majdanek by way of Treblinka had an uncommon experience. Their survival, however, had little to do with their own actions. Zelda and Vichna were simply in the right place at the right time.

Luck placed Zelda and Vichna with the cohort deported to concentration camps and exploited for slave labor. Luck also shaped the destinies of Yehuda Rabinovich, Feliks Zandman, Bella Ilin, the Reizer and Blumstein families, and anyone else who survived. The windows of opportunity they encountered swiftly closed. As with Zelda and Vichna, being in the right place at the right time determined whether each was able to escape the heavily guarded Grodno ghetto in the midst of its liquidation. And luck would continue to play the dominant role in their lives.

Jewish Grodno had been annihilated. Yet a remnant survived—in camps, in resistance networks, and in hiding. In such diverse settings, these survivors maintained the basic outlines of their Jewish identity. Their experiences stand in stark contrast to Jews raised in Soviet Vitebsk, who immersed themselves completely in new identities to pass as Gentiles until their liberation.

7

Survival

1942 to 1948

In 1942, Sarah Fishkin's family began their observance of Passover, the holiday of deliverance, on 1 April. Their Seder was short. They skipped the Four Questions in the Haggadah—that night in the Rubiezewicze ghetto was not different from any other. Lying in bed afterward, Sarah recalled joyous holiday observances before the war. Her hopes lay flattened under the weight of the Nazi genocide. On that first night of Passover, the tempered optimism expressed in her diary entries a few months earlier had vanished. Now she wrote, "We live without any future; we have no thought of goals, of achievement."[1]

The Nazis sought to degrade and destroy millions of European Jews such as Sarah Fishkin by overturning their social order, entrapping and dividing their families, and humiliating and murdering each individual. A few weeks after Sarah wrote about her family's last Passover, her father and one of her younger brothers were deported to a slave-labor camp. Sarah was transported to another camp soon thereafter. Guards shot her when they liquidated the camp on 28 December 1942.[2]

As 1942 ended, the Germans' genocidal campaign was well advanced. Sarah Fishkin was unable to escape their trap, but chance presented other young Jews with fleeting opportunities for survival. No longer in familiar surroundings, these lucky few found themselves in camps, in hiding, or in resistance groups. Young Jews from Vitebsk and Grodno responded to their situations in sharply contrasting ways. Polish Jews, even when they posed as Gentiles, retained significant aspects of their prewar identities and attendant social ties. Soviet Jews, however, submerged into other selves, expertly mimicking other nationalities. Disparate circumstances shaped the survival of both groups during the Holocaust; distinct, too, were the responses they generated.

Survival Paths

The experiences of Holocaust survivors—that is, those still alive at Nazi Germany's defeat in 1945—fall into a number of patterns. Following initial exposure to increasing degrees of persecution, those whom the Germans selected for slave labor were deported to camps

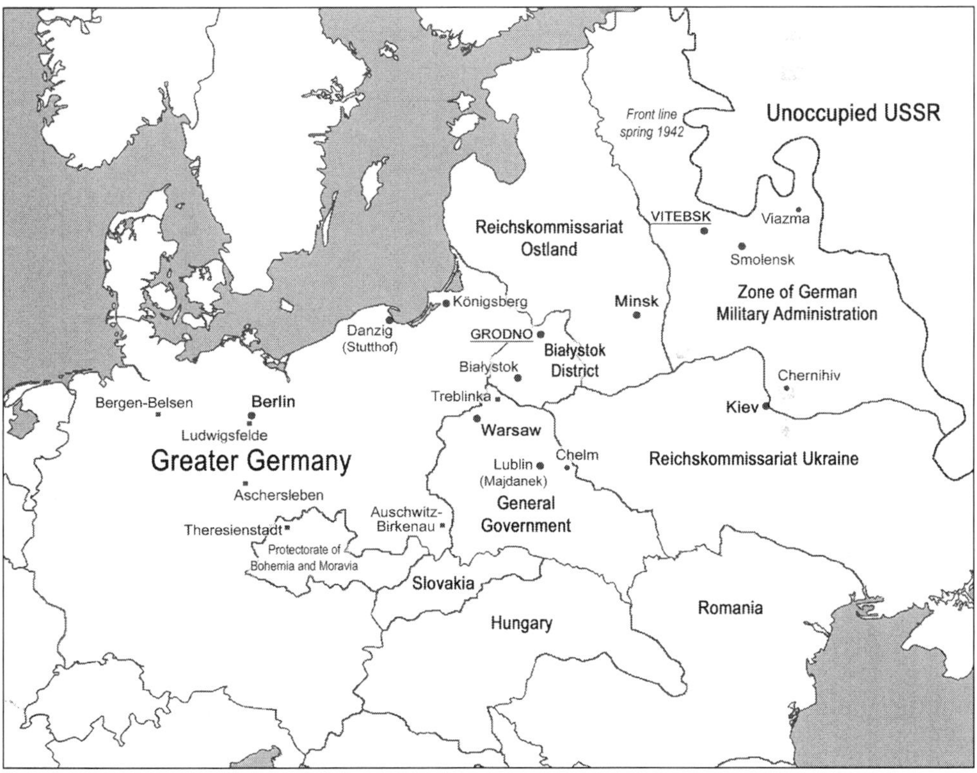

24. Map of German-administered and occupied Europe with Axis countries, circa February 1942. Noted are the cities and concentration camps mentioned in chapter 7.

and suffered through abusive conditions until liberation. Departures from this pattern include Jews who escaped from a ghetto or camp and lived in hiding, usually with the help of Gentiles or, particularly in the wilderness expanses of eastern Europe, with partisan fighters. Some Jews eluded capture altogether and took a false identity, maintaining their cover in territory under Nazi rule or occupation. The lives of these targets of genocide were constantly at risk. Capricious SS officers sent the sick and emaciated or those who appeared so to the gas chambers. Neighbor suspected neighbor of harboring Jews. False papers fell under close scrutiny. Many of the Holocaust survivors' paths from Grodno and Vitebsk follow these patterns, even as German exploitation and annihilation policies transported the survivors across the European continent (figure 24).

In Camps

Luck determined that Zelda Grodzienska and Vichna Sidranska arrived at Treblinka during a window in time when the SS needed slave laborers at another camp. Each was pulled from the group of Grodno Jews headed for the gas chamber. The next day they were transported, along with 102 other women, to Majdanek concentration camp in Lublin.[3] Zelda and Vichna joined hundreds of Jews, women and men, forced to work at the *Flugplatz* (airport) subcamp. Since the previous year, more than one million Jews had been gassed at the three camps organized under Aktion Reinhard (Bełżec, Sobibór, and Treblinka). The SS used the *Flugplatz* camp, a former airfield and factory site, as a central depot for disinfection, repair, sorting, and repackaging of property looted from murdered Jews.[4]

Vichna and Zelda did not know each other before their deportation to Majdanek, and their paths diverged soon after arrival there. Zelda's contacts with the Treblinka prisoners dwindled as the group merged within the *Flugplatz* camp population.[5] Vichna met two others from the transport in her assigned barrack whom she vaguely remembered from Grodno. Former tenants in her grandmother's building, the two adult women, Luba and Riva Kremer, were mother and daughter.[6]

Zelda was assigned to a storage building, which she recalled was "packed with clothes and shoes and whatever." Hour after hour, she sorted the piles into separate bundles of each item: "A dozen of shirts, a dozen of pants, a dozen of socks."[7] Most of the clothing and bedding was handed over to the Main Welfare Office for Ethnic Germans, an SS agency that administered such matters in occupied countries. More valuable items, such as silk underwear and precious metals, were sent to the Reich Economics Ministry in Berlin.[8] Vichna Sidranska was assigned initially to a road-building gang, but later she, too, was transferred to sort the mountains of clothes and other items, including brushes, soaps, and mirrors.[9] Luba Kremer was given the task of searching through clothes and other possessions for money or jewelry. It was heartbreaking work, Luba recalled decades later, and guards watched her the entire time.[10]

The poor conditions in the *Flugplatz* camp led to outbreaks of typhus and typhoid among the prisoners. Vichna and Zelda fell ill with the latter. Each was healed less by the available medical treatment, which was poor, than by fellow prisoners. In Vichna's case, Riva and Luba brought her boiled water. Zelda's comrades found a lemon and passed it to her through the hospital barrack window.

Vichna and Zelda returned to sorting looted property after they recovered. Yet the piles diminished in the early autumn of 1943 as the Aktion Reinhard camps completed their bloody task. "There was no more clothing to sort—there was a feeling that something was going to happen," Vichna recalled. In October, a *kapo* (prisoner overseer) asked for twenty-five volunteers to work in a marmalade plant. Vichna suspected that this was a trap and stayed put. A week later the kapo returned for twenty-five more prisoners for the same factory. This time Vichna agreed. "I said, 'I'm going.' I couldn't take it," she admitted decades later. "The atmosphere in the camp was terrible." Luba and Riva Kremer agreed to go as well. Their destination was a food-processing plant in Milejow, 15 kilometers to the east, where they cleaned carrots, peeled potatoes, and mashed pumpkins.[11] Zelda Grodzienska faced the same dilemma. A *kapo* sought seamstresses for a workshop at Majdanek. Although her fellow prisoners felt it was a trap, Zelda accepted. She had barely begun to learn the trade before she was transferred to the subcamp at Bliżyn, 140 kilometers west of Lublin.[12]

Bliżyn was operated by the SS-run Deutsche Ausrüstungswerke (DAW, German Equipment Works), whose primary function was to manufacture armaments. The camp contained workshops for tailoring, carpentry, tool manufacture, and shoe making. Prisoners also worked in the DAW munitions factory as well as at a nearby quarry, a division of another SS corporation, the building material supplier Deutschen Erd- und Steinwerke (German Earth and Stone Works). The camp population numbered between 2,000 and 4,000 prisoners, all Jews.[13] The camp was unusual, Zelda later recalled, because it held whole families deported from the Radom and Sosnowiec ghettos. Men and women, however, were in separate sections.[14]

Zelda found two familiar faces soon after her arrival. Her distant cousin Eli Grodzienski and his eleven-year-old son had been deported from Grodno to the Białystok ghetto in March 1943. Eli responded to a call for volunteers to work in the tailor shop at Bliżyn. "We knew that we were sort of the last people of our two families left alive," Zelda remembered. They saw each other every other Sunday, when the Germans permitted the inmates of the men's and women's camp to meet on the roll-call square. "We would talk about [our] families and when was the last time we saw anybody."[15]

The experience of seeing people from home reconnected Zelda to a past obliterated only a few months earlier. Now she applied the endurance skills attained in the Grodno ghetto and the *Flugplatz* camp. Having already had typhoid, she endeavored to be watchful for lice. She realized the importance to "organize"—that is, obtain additional food and clothing to supplement the paltry rations doled out by the Germans. She also discovered that her decision to leave the *Flugplatz* had been correct. Another prisoner found a note hidden in a shipment of Jewish clothing declaring that the remaining Jews at the subcamp had been killed.[16] Their murder was part of Aktion Erntefest (Harvest Festival) of 3 November 1943, in which 42,000 Jews from

Majdanek, Poniatowa, Trawniki, and other camps were shot.[17] "So we knew that there was no more camp in Lublin," Zelda recalled, "that all the rest of the women, the friends of mine that came with me among the hundred, were dead."[18]

Not all of the women. At the food-processing plant in Milejow, Vichna Sidranska heard rumors about the preparations for the massacre. One of the *kapos* on a visit to Majdanek to retrieve supplies saw mass graves dug south of the camp and reported this to the prisoners at Milejow. News arrived some days later that the Jews in another camp, Trawniki, had been shot. "We figured, 'Well, if that's happened to them, it'll probably happen to us,'" she recalled. Vichna was instead among fifty Jewish women, including Riva and Luba Kremer, deported to Trawniki to clean up the camp.[19]

Their tasks were gruesome, and they knew what had happened to their predecessors. Although they found multiple stashes of hidden food and additional clothing that aided their immediate survival, they waited to be next. The work, however, stretched out over seven months. After the women cleaned the barracks, the Germans kept them alive to do various tasks—sorting potatoes, dismantling the camp buildings, and helping the Polish prisoners in the bakery. For Vichna, Luba, and Riva, their time in Trawniki, surrounded by the remnants of destroyed lives, consolidated social bonds that remained until the war's end. The labor gang was transported the 35 kilometers back to Majdanek in June 1944, where evacuations from the camp had already commenced because of the Red Army's approach. A few weeks later, Vichna, Riva, and Luba were sent with a thousand other prisoners on a death march headed westward. After several days without food and their only water supplied by puddles in the road, they were loaded on a train and transported to Auschwitz-Birkenau.[20]

Zelda Grodzienska was deported to Auschwitz around the same time as Vichna, late July 1944.[21] Like Majdanek, the subcamp at Bliżyn was evacuated because of advancing Soviet forces. Zelda's arrival at the Birkenau camp mirrors the experience of several others discussed in this chapter. She remembered distinctly the orchestra playing near the disembarkation ramp and the selection of prisoners "unfit" for work who were sent to the gas chamber. Women with children, Zelda noticed, were always sent to the side with the sick and elderly.[22]

After selection, Zelda and the others kept for slave labor were sent to the Central Sauna on the west side of Birkenau. She passed by the Kanada section of the camp, containing the looted possessions of deportees, full to bursting because of the recent influx of more than 400,000 Jews from Hungary in the previous two months. Female prisoners worked outside among the mountains of items. Perhaps her group of forced laborers stood in the yard in front of the Central Sauna for some time as they waited to be "processed," and this was how she saw among the sorting gang a few women from her home city, deported to Auschwitz at the end of 1942 and early 1943.[23]

Zelda recognized another woman in the barbers' room. "One of the women cutting the hair was a friend of mine," she reported in an interview.[24] Vichna Sidranska also met a woman she knew from Grodno.[25] Vichna and Zelda had experienced life under German occupation, the ghetto, and several camps. Yet their experiences in this one building were significant enough for each to remember particular details. In the Central Sauna, they undressed in front of SS men, had their hair shorn, were swabbed with stinging disinfectant, were bathed under water either freezing or scalding, and were inscribed with a tattooed number. To see and talk to someone connected to home might have eased the trauma of entering this particular camp, where human exploitation and destruction existed side by side.

• Zelda and Vichna were prisoners in Auschwitz-Birkenau during the last months of its existence. Leib Bialo had been deported to the camp eighteen months earlier, in January 1943. The SS Building Office at Auschwitz was still designing the Central Sauna at that time, and less-elaborate bathhouses existed in the men's and women's camps in Section I of Birkenau.[26] The importance attached to disinfection procedures reflected the SS's obsession with allaying outbreaks of disease in spite of the appalling conditions of their own making—overcrowding, malnutrition, inadequate clothing, unheated barracks, and insufficient medical care. These conditions' effects on the prisoner population were readily apparent to Leib Bialo. His brother Shloyme had been deported to the camp from Grodno less than two months before him. "When I came to Auschwitz . . . my brother was still alive. I did not recognize him," Leib Bialo recalled. "He recognized me. He looked like a little man [of] sixty years." His brother also introduced Leib to the inmate power structure of the camp. Shloyme had been pressed into duties as a *pipel*, a servant to a *kapo*. "Why, he was only a kid," Leib later recalled. "He must have been about thirteen years old."[27] *Pipels* were often used as sexual slaves, and Leib hinted in testimony recorded fifty years later that his brother endured such abuse. Shloyme Bialo later fell ill with an infection and was sent to the gas chambers.

Leib reconnected with his brother in Birkenau, an experience that revealed another facet of the camp's horrors. He also discovered what had happened to his parents. The smell of bodies cremated in open pits permeated the environment of the camp. "The smoke, you could see [it] for miles and miles," recalled Leib, and the smell "was unbelievable."[28] That was Samuel and Celia Bialo's destiny. They had been deported to Auschwitz when the "temporary" gas chambers in two converted houses were still in use (Bunkers 1 and 2). The gas chambers and ovens of Crematoria II, III, IV, and V had been in operation for about a year by the time Zelda and Vichna were deported to the camp. "We saw the chimneys, we smelled the smoke—the burning of the flesh," Vichna recalled.[29] Zelda remembered, "We knew Jewish lives were going out the chimneys, and every day we thought, 'I'm next.'"[30]

Auschwitz lay at the crossroads for many swept into the concentration-camp world. Moishe Kremer was among the last slave laborers engaged in building projects for the Grodno Gestapo. The twenty-five-year-old electrician rejoined his remaining family members in the Białystok ghetto in May 1943, but they were separated permanently in the ghetto liquidation three months later. The Germans valued Moishe's abilities as well as those of his father, Abram, so they were spared deportation to Treblinka along with about a hundred other tradesmen. Held in a succession of prisons in Białystok, Grodno, and Łomza, this group, known to the Germans as the "Białystok transport," was deported to the Stutthof concentration camp near Danzig in November 1943.[31]

Among the laborers on the Białystok transport were fifteen-year-old Daniel Klovsky and his father, David, a metal craftsman. "When the doors opened, we were blinded by bright searchlights," Daniel remembered of their nighttime arrival at Stutthof. Shouts of snarling SS men and barks of vicious guard dogs accompanied their hurried response to an order to form lines. They were marched through the camp and housed in an austere barrack with plank bunks.[32] Despite all their prior experiences in ghettos and prisons, the Kremers and the Klovskys were unprepared for the terror meted out by the Stutthof SS, nor did they expect the abuse at the hands of the block elders and *kapos*, mostly Poles but some Germans as well.[33] One by one, skilled workers in their group began to die from the harsh conditions. "We spoke to each other in a whisper, 'Look, this man is out,'" Daniel Klovsky remembered of his fellow surviving prisoners' response. "The fear was coming out of those empty plank beds."[34]

Their time in a series of prisons and in Stutthof forged strong communal ties as prisoners that aided their survival at Auschwitz, where they were deported in January 1944.[35] As Daniel Klovsky reflected later, his experiences in Stutthof had dulled any sense of shock he felt during his arrival and processing at the Central Sauna at Auschwitz.[36] They, too, were denuded, sheared, showered, and tattooed. Dressed in camp uniforms, the prisoners were placed in a quarantine barrack in Section BIIa of Birkenau.[37]

The labor of prisoners chosen at Birkenau was exploited on various projects within what the SS called the Interest Zone of KL (*Konzentrationslager*, concentration camp) Auschwitz. The Białystok transport, held in Auschwitz III–Buna, was deployed in the construction of the Buna Werke, IG Farben's synthetic rubber plant. Moishe Kremer was responsible for a gang of ten men installing electrical wiring.[38] David Klovsky installed piping systems.[39] Vichna Sidranska cut sod and carried it to a railroad embankment.[40] Zelda Grodzienska was assigned heavy labor in the railroad yard and in the surrounding farm fields.[41] Leib Bialo was initially assigned the task of gathering the corpses of prisoners who died each night and carting them to a burning pit. As the SS expanded the camp, he was put into a work gang constructing barracks. Prisoners were also deported to other camps, some soon after arrival at Birkenau, others months later. In September 1943, Leib Bialo was deported to the Jaworzno subcamp, 30 kilometers north of Auschwitz. His slave-labor gang worked in the coal mine nearby.[42]

Concentration-camp prisoners at Auschwitz and elsewhere were subject to harsh treatment by the SS guards and the prisoner *kapos*. In the barracks and on slave-labor sites, *kapos* maintained order. "Whatever they said had to be done. And if not, the punishment was very severe, very severe," Leib Bialo remembered.[43] Zelda Grodzienska did not understand how Jews could mistreat other Jews. "Of course, again beaten left and right, even by some of the Jewish [*kapos*], and I'm not judging them—they were supposed to do it, or whatever," she reported long after the war, her conflicted feelings apparent.[44] And marking the start and finish of each day was the monotony and misery of *Appell*, the prisoner roll call, where torture was public spectacle and terror a collective experience. After the war, after Zelda had married Eli and made a new life in America, Auschwitz figured as a crucial nexus in her reflections about survival. "I don't know how, and I don't know why I survived that camp," she declared nearly forty years after leaving Auschwitz. "How could we survive what we survived?" she asked in another interview a decade after that, still pondering the matter.[45] Her question is perhaps unanswerable.

◆ As the Red Army approached Auschwitz in the autumn of 1944, the SS began evacuations. Vichna Sidranska, along with her Grodno companions Riva and Luba Kremer, was among a group of prisoners transported in train wagons to Bergen-Belsen at the end of October or the beginning of November.[46] Zelda Grodzienska followed in a transport around the turn of the New Year.[47] Bergen-Belsen was one of several camps in the German interior to receive evacuated prisoners from the periphery of the collapsing Reich. The prisoner population there soared during the first months of 1945, overwhelming the camp infrastructure. "We came to Bergen-Belsen, there were no barracks. There were tents," Vichna Sidranska remembered.[48] Food rations declined even as the number of inmates rose; clean water was in short supply. Prisoners died in the hundreds each day from starvation and disease. "Even if I wrote ten books, I could not explain or tell wh–how people died in that camp," Zelda Grodzienska described, her hesitancy indicating the horror of the situation. Regarding her situation and that of her fellow prisoners, she later reflected, "We just waited to die."[49]

Vichna Sidranska didn't wait. She accepted a call for volunteers to transfer to the Junkers aircraft factory at Aschersleben working alongside Gentile forced laborers "from all over Europe—a lot of Russian women, Ukrainian women, Polish, men from France, from Holland." The only Germans were the supervisors and the guards. The conditions were appreciably better than at Bergen-Belsen, and even the SS treated them differently. "We knew the war was coming to an end," she later recalled. "The SS women that were in charge started being a little bit nicer toward us." Yet "nicer" merely entailed fewer screamed orders and less-frequent beatings.[50]

Evacuations from Auschwitz followed many paths. On 18 January 1945, SS guards drove out long columns of Buna inmates on a two-day march along snowy roads leading to Gleiwitz. "My heart was pounding madly and I was hardly able to breathe," Daniel Klovsky remembered of the frantic pace they endured.[51] "There were a lot of people with brothers, people they knew, friends or whatever, [who] lost them right there," Moishe Kremer later recalled, speaking from personal experience. His father, Abram, was shot at Gleiwitz along with dozens of other exhausted prisoners.[52]

From Gleiwitz, many of the Buna prisoners were transported in open railroad wagons to Buchenwald. They were given no food, and the only water came from the snow that fell on their bodies. The transports arrived in Weimar during the last week of January.[53] The SS distributed them among the already crowded barracks in the quarantine camp (known as the "Little Camp"). As more transports of evacuated prisoners reached Buchenwald, conditions deteriorated, much as they had at Bergen-Belsen. Some prisoners were deployed into slave-labor gangs in Weimar. Moishe Kremer dug through the ruins of buildings. Looking for bombing victims, he often found instead much needed food.[54]

In Hiding

The SS saw concentration-camp prisoners as numbers, either inscribed as a tattoo in the case of Auschwitz inmates or recorded in registers. As we have seen, Jews from Grodno not only retained their name identities but also sought and maintained communal ties that supported individual survival. Jews in hiding under the care of beneficent rescuers survived under conditions markedly different from their fellow townsfolk in camps. Yet even during long periods of enforced social isolation, young Jews were still able to maintain their individual and communal identities.

Alexandre Blumstein survived in hiding with six other Jews, including his parents, Chaim and Ester, and older brother, Tolo. They had found a hiding place in the home of Edward and Aniela Staniewski, peasant farmers who were patients of Dr. Chaim Blumstein's colleague Dr. Antoni Docha. With the addition of Aniela Staniewski's niece, ten people lived in a hut with a main room measuring five meters by three meters. A small bedroom, shallow attic, and hideout dug into the hard clay floor offered the only additional interior spaces.[55]

Alexandre's contemporary Feliks Zandman found refuge in a place even more confined. Initially, six people lay or sat in a small dugout cellar beneath the bedroom floor in Jan and Janova Puchalski's house, 10 kilometers west of Grodno in the forests around Lososna. Janova Puchalski readily agreed to hide the fifteen-year-old Feliks because his grandmother Tema had once helped her during a time of great need. Feliks's uncle Sender brought four others to the Puchalskis'. Only two, Mottl and Goldie Bass, stayed along with Feliks and Sender because Janova Puchalski reluctantly admitted that she could not feed them all.[56]

Complicating life for the Blumsteins and their fellow hidden Jews was Dr. Docha's effort to convert them all to Christianity. Pressing them on the issue, the good doctor said during one visit, "There are rumors all over the country that I am hiding Jews. We are alive today, but may all be dead tomorrow. There is no salvation for our souls outside the Holy Church and Jesus Christ." Most of those in hiding listened politely when Dr. Docha proselytized, but Dr. Blumstein was shaken by these attempts. "Father was opposed to conversion, with all his body and soul," recalled his son Alexandre. All that had happened to his family and his people deeply depressed the elder Blumstein. "I saw the terrible toll this struggle took on him," Alexandre later remembered.[57]

The boy faced different forms of psychological stress in hiding. "I missed my friends and I was lonely," Alexandre recalled fifty years later. His loneliness turned to despondency when he thought how his friends from the Grodno ghetto had vanished into the abyss of deportation. "Their fate is in the hands of the hangman," he lamented their loss in a poem composed during his first weeks at the Staniewskis' hut.[58]

Whereas Alexandre Blumstein had the luxury of daylight to pass the long hours by writing, Feliks Zandman lived in darkness most of the day. Unlike the Blumsteins and others protected by the Staniewskis, who were able to go outside from time to time, those hidden by the Puchalskis seldom emerged from their cellar. They lit a lamp only to eat or occasionally to play cards. To pass the time, Uncle Sender tried to continue Feliks's education, talking him through the complexities of mathematics, geometry, and trigonometry.[59] Alexandre and Feliks shared one pursuit in common—killing parasites. "I divided my time between killing fleas, losing at chess, and writing my diary," Alexandre remembered. Bedbugs were also a problem for those in the Staniewski hut; however, they managed to keep ahead of the lice.[60] Feliks Zandman and the others beneath the Puchalskis' floor combatted lice, fleas, and worms. "Since we couldn't boil our clothes, we had to delouse them by hand, taking our shirts off and working slowly through the hems and stitches," Feliks recalled.[61]

Such activities kept their minds off their recent traumas in the ghetto and the unknown fates of their families. It also distracted the four lying side by side in the Puchalskis' cellar from other tensions. Early on, Sender Freydovicz laid down strict rules. "We have to make a civilized life down here," Feliks's uncle told Mottl and Goldie Bass. "We want to come out of here alive, and we want to come out as decent people. So the first rule: No sex."[62] Perhaps Sender wanted to prevent himself from pursuing Goldie, or so Feliks later speculated. He may also have wanted to avoid any reminders of normal adult relationships because he had lost his wife and children in the deportations. Sender's frank conversation about sex was not lost on Feliks; he was fifteen at the time and had engaged in kissing girls and, according to his own account, perhaps in a bit more during his time in the ghetto.[63] Alexandre Blumstein was only twelve, still maturing sexually. The presence of three young women in the hut troubled the boy. "I could smell the scent of their bodies and it turned my head," he later recalled. "I fantasized about being alone with one or the other, feeling guilty, sinful, and ashamed of my thoughts." His frustration intensified as he became aware of the young romances developing around him. His brother Tolo disappeared into the barn with Aniela's niece Hela. Two others, a woman named Frania and a man named Hillel Braude, a new arrival to the hut in late 1943, met in the night when all in the hut supposedly were asleep.[64]

◆ Circumstances separated the experiences of Grodno Jews, yet each of these Jews gravitated toward socialization patterns that they had developed in their hometown before the war. Occupation, invasion, and ghettoization in their home city had led to deportations over a period of a little more than three years. Vitebsk Jews faced very different conditions. From the first days of the German occupation, annihilation was the end goal. Under these conditions, survival meant flight from the ghetto, the city, and their identities. The Soviet system had exposed young Jews to Belarusian and Russian culture at the same time as it marginalized them from traditional Jewish culture (chapter 1). Now some harnessed this knowledge to escape annihilation. Lev Fleish and Fivel Markelis passed as Slavs, using a lesser danger to deflect attention from a far greater one. Environment may have shaped the range of responses available to these two young men, but they selected paths that protected them until liberation.

Fourteen-year-old Fivel Markelis's struggle for survival under a false identity began the moment he crawled out of a mass grave in the Ilovsky ravine east of Vitebsk. He had been transported to this killing site from the ghetto in early October 1941 with his mother, Sofia, and other captives. They were told to undress and stand in three rows at the edge of a pit already containing hundreds of corpses. Sofia's body shielded him from the volley of bullets fired by members of Einsatzgruppe B. An hour or two later, as night fell and the executioners departed, he emerged to wash his mother's blood from his naked body in the chilly Vitba.[65]

Fivel made his way to his aunt Lisa's house, nearby on the eastern edge of the city. (She apparently was not a Jew and was married to one of Fivel's relatives.) Slipping through the darkened streets well after curfew, he stayed the night in her garden. In the morning, Lisa hid him in the cellar and gave him food and more clothing. He stayed for a few days but decided it was too risky for his aunt and cousins. Before Fivel left Vitebsk, he went to find his friend Israel, one of a few hundred Jews remaining in the ghetto. They hopped aboard a freight train headed toward Smolensk to get help from another of Fivel's aunts. Finding no aunt and her house a burned-out shell, they pressed on to the east, hoping to cross the front line.[66]

Lev Fleish escaped Vitebsk before the ghetto liquidation. Unlike Fivel Markelis, the nineteen-year-old Lev had no immediate family members in the ghetto. A Russian friend, Liosha Morozov, came across Lev and told him, "You don't look like a Jew. Go away from here if you want to live!" Morozov advised him to join the groups of war refugees roaming the countryside. "They didn't have any documents, and they just were wandering there," Lev recalled. "He told me that I could pretend to be one of them."[67] Using this cover, he also decided to make his way to Soviet-held territory.

Lev's journey took him south toward Mogilev, usually wandering with a group of refugees. The route they followed, south by southeast, avoided the active invasion routes of Army Group Center and Army Group South. He occasionally received food from peasants and villagers. Lev's socialization skills aided his interaction with Gentiles along the refugee route. Even so, he was careful to conceal his Jewish identity. He had discovered in the months after the German invasion that he could not depend on the sympathies of his fellow Soviet citizens because most were, as Lev remembered, "indifferent" to what the Germans were doing to the Jews. Lev took the identity of a former classmate of Tatar descent, Leonid Pavlovich Khalimonov. He elaborated the cover story to include that he had been in an orphanage since the age of four and hence knew few Tatar words or customs. His Tatar Muslim heritage would also explain, should anyone find out, why he was circumcised.[68]

Lev/Leonid was initially given room and board for a few nights in exchange for work, but such acts of hospitality became dangerous for would-be hosts as the Germans consolidated their rule. Strangers without documents exposed such hosts to the scrutiny of the occupation authorities.[69] Fivel Markelis and his companion, Israel, encountered such danger when they sought shelter on the outskirts of Smolensk. Two elderly women living in neighboring houses took them in. Wehrmacht soldiers arrived, searching for Jews, hidden Red Army soldiers, or any males of draft age. Fivel's host told the men who broke down her door that he was her grandson. The woman next door said the same about Israel, but apparently in a less-convincing manner. The men took Israel out and shot him. Fivel stayed in the village only as long as it took for the Germans to leave.[70]

Winter arrived. The snows had grown deeper by the time Fivel reached the village of Strilichevo. Locals talked about Red Army partisans in the nearby forests. They arrived in person a day or two later, capturing the small German post and killing the soldiers. By this time, Fivel had immersed himself in a Belarusian identity, using the false name Valery Domnin. Villagers apparently believed him to be a Gentile. The partisans did as well, accepting Fivel/Valery as an agent to perform reconnaissance on German division headquarters in Anokhovo. And he felt confident not only in this role but also in this identity. "I was a teenager, I was above suspicion," Fivel recalled of his perceived invincibility. The Germans discovered the partisans' location before they could prepare an attack. Most of the fighters were killed in the ambush. Fivel was among those taken prisoner. Because he wore Red Army boots, trousers, and a coat, his new captors mistook him for a soldier and sent him to a POW camp.[71]

Several hundred kilometers to the south, Lev Fleish had found refuge because of his poor health. He lay in a rural clinic in the Chernihiv Oblast of Ukraine, ill with typhus. Despite his lack of proper papers, the chief physician agreed to admit him. He told Lev, "You know, kid, I see who you are"—meaning that he knew he was a Jew. "Of course, I can't guarantee your safety here. As you are not registered as a Jew, stay here, but in any case I'm not responsible for your safety." Although he did not give up Lev's true identity to the Germans or to local collaborators, he was required to report daily that Lev and other patients without documents hadn't run away.[72]

Some of Lev's fellow patients were ready to expose Jews. "Khalimonov, you look like a Jew," one said accusingly. Despite Lev's denials, the man persisted and asked some others in the ward to help pull down Lev's pants. At that moment, another patient, an ethnic Russian, entered the ward and witnessed the commotion. "We want to know whether he's a Jew or not," one said. The Russian shouted, "Stop it, you fuckers, or I'll thrash you all!" Afterward, the doctor moved Lev/Leonid out of the ward and assigned him to more remote quarters in the horse stable.[73]

In May 1942, Lev and some other recovered patients in the clinic without proper papers were turned over to the Germans for deportation as foreign forced laborers. The deployment of workers from occupied Soviet territory to the Reich arose from the need to replace German laborers fighting on the Eastern Front. Labor brought in from central and western European countries was not sufficient to satisfy war industry needs. Through the Reich Ministry for the Occupied Eastern Territories and the Wehrmacht, recruitment began in the first months of 1942, with Ukraine supplying most of the targeted number. Many from the first wave of what came to be known as *Ostarbeiter* (eastern workers) were volunteers, persuaded to sign up by the promise of better food and the assurance they would receive wages. By late spring, however, rumors about the poor treatment of the first transports reduced the number of volunteers and thus necessitated the implementation of compulsory and forceful measures to meet recruitment drives.[74] Lev Fleish later commented on his options at that moment: "I had no place to run because everywhere a strict regime had come to power." Upon departure, Lev received documents with the name "Leonid Pavlovich Khalimonov," giving his false identity official status.[75]

After several days in a cattle car, Lev arrived at a labor-processing center in Berlin. He was sent to Ludwigsfelde, 30 kilometers south of the city, where Daimler-Benz had established an aircraft-motor factory in 1936. During the war, some 12,000 foreign forced laborers, slave laborers, and POWs from France, Italy, Bohemia and Moravia, the Soviet Union, and elsewhere supplemented the 7,000 German workers in this factory. Lev was one of 2,500 Soviet *Ostarbeiter* deported to Ludwigsfelde in 1942 alone.[76]

Lev was housed in the *Ostarbeiter* camp about a kilometer from the Daimler-Benz plant. "The conditions were awful," he remembered. "They gave us food once a day, which was a liter of porridge and 250 grams of bread, half with sawdust." The environment seemed to Lev like a concentration camp, with its rows of barracks, each with a block elder, and the perimeter under guard. The distinction came with the rationale for his captivity—forced labor, not punishment. Lev was engaged in a labor *Kommando* that worked on the grounds of the factory digging trenches and laying cable. He found his work harsh, yet he did not have to contend with the abuse that marked a concentration-camp life. Perhaps Lev/Leonid felt less confident of his false identity in this confined environment because he kept a low profile to avoid exposure. "I tried to be absolutely unnoticeable," he recalled. He shared a barracks room with sixteen Ukrainians. If any suspected him of being a Jew, none said so.[77]

One who did confront Lev was Grishka Timakov, the chief of his labor *Kommando*. Timakov pulled him aside one day and said, "You are a Jew. I'm sure that you are a Jew." Lev denied it, repeating that he was a Tatar. Timakov reported his suspicions to the German camp commandant, who locked up Lev in a punishment barrack and telephoned the Gestapo for further instructions. This occurred in February 1945, and the Red Army had just crossed the Oder. The commandant soon received a reply: "Do whatever you like. We have our own problems." The camp commandant apparently also had problems of his own, what with the Soviets approaching closer day by day. Lev/Leonid was released. As the Soviets loomed, his captors' attitudes softened. "Grishka Timakov began to shake hands with me . . . the commandant's assistant started shaking hands with me."[78]

Lev Fleish successfully concealed his Jewish identity for nearly three years as an *Ostarbeiter* right under the Germans' noses. Fivel Markelis's achievement paralleled Lev's, but also with the added difficulties of surviving both POW and concentration camps. Following his capture under the name Valery Domnin in late November or early December 1941, Fivel was confined to the POW transit camp Dulag (Durchgangslager) 230 in Viazma throughout the winter of 1941–42. The camp consisted of war-damaged buildings with boarded-up windows and no heat. Prisoners slept on the wood floors. "I don't know how thousands of people survived," Fivel remembered, noting also that hundreds died of disease, cold, and malnutrition. The Germans combed through the prisoners looking for Jews, including anyone who looked like what they thought a Jew should look like. "If they were swarthy or had dark hair . . . ," he explained, his voice trailing off. Those pulled out of line were shot immediately in front of the other prisoners.[79]

In early 1942, Fivel/Valery was deported to Stalag 319 in Chelm.[80] Unlike Dulag 230, the POW camp consisted of wooden barracks with a hospital, kitchen, and other support facilities. The barbed-wire fence encompassed a vast area 1,800 meters by 1,600 meters north of the train station and city center.[81] A glass factory lay at the south side of the camp, one of several local industries that employed POWs as slave labor. As in other camps set up to hold Red Army captives, Stalag 319 had been the scene of mass death in the second half of 1941, when the Wehrmacht did little to feed prisoners or treat the sick in the immediate aftermath of the German invasion of the Soviet Union. During the camp's first months of operation, upward of 500 prisoners died each day out of a camp population that had initially swelled to 18,000.[82]

By the time Fivel Markelis arrived at Stalag 319 in the spring of 1942, the Wehrmacht had begun to shift its policies toward Soviet POWs in order to exploit their labor.[83] Fivel remembered conditions to be better than the camp in Viazma. Food was more plentiful: "Actually they gave us enough food not to die of starvation." Russian and Polish doctors treated sick prisoners. During the induction of his transport, the camp administration realized that Fivel was too young to be a Red Army soldier. "They detached me, and I became a displaced person or something of that kind," Fivel later inaccurately described his reassessment as a captive.[84]

For the time being, however, Fivel remained among the POWs. He was assigned to an earth-moving gang to level the camp's grounds. Like Lev Fleish, Fivel tried to remain inconspicuous. He submerged into his Belarusian identity, but at the same time his Jewish origins were so suppressed that he couldn't remember encountering any of his coreligionists among the other inmates. Furthermore, fearing that his origins would be discovered, he kept his distance from others in the camp.[85]

In the first months of 1943, Fivel was deported to a camp near Danzig, most likely Stutthof.[86] Once again, he was assigned to the heavy labor of moving earth. Supervision of prisoner labor was particularly harsh. "If you are an overseer and you command, the people must not respect you, they must dread you," he recalled. The quality and quantity of food at Stutthof were poorer than at Stalag 319. "The soup was very watery," he remembered of their midday meal. "There was a small piece of beet root and a couple of pieces of potato."[87]

Fivel/Valery remained a prisoner in Stutthof until the late summer of 1944, when he was transferred to another camp in Königsberg. Male and female inmates labored in the local shipyards and in a factory that built narrow-gauge railway cars. Male prisoners such as Fivel came from Stutthof, whereas female inmates were deported from Ravensbrück. He remembered many nationalities in the camp: British, Italian, French, German, Polish, and Russian.[88]

The close quarters of the new camp placed Fivel in danger. One of his fellow prisoners noticed he was circumcised. "Are you a Jew?" the camp inmate whispered. Then he reassured Fivel, "I'm a member of the Komsomol," meaning that he would protect him out of Soviet solidarity.[89] Fivel Markelis needed such assurance because the Germans' genocidal campaign continued even in the face of their impending defeat. At the end of January 1945, on the eve of the Red Army's encirclement of Königsberg, the SS marched the remaining 4,500 Jews in the region, mostly women, to the west with no clear destination. Most were shot at the Baltic coastal town Palmnicken a few days later.[90]

As a non-Jewish concentration-camp prisoner, Valery/Fivel remained behind. Within the Red Army encirclement, he was pressed into service to dig trenches and assist other defensive work. One task was to move food supplies from a bomb-damaged warehouse, work that gave him desperately needed access to additional nourishment. His captors grew less interested in maintaining strict discipline as they worried about their futures. "We felt that the liberation would come very soon," he remembered.[91]

◆ Lev Fleish and Fivel Markelis escaped annihilation as Jews by passing as Slavs, making them targets of a different track of Nazi racial policy. Life "in hiding" meant blending into the refugee stream in German-occupied territory and, following their detention under distinct circumstances, enduring the appalling conditions in camps, be they for forced laborers or for punitive detainment. Each of the young men responded with proficiency. Chasia Bielicka from Grodno applied abilities developed before the war and in the ghetto with Hashomer Hatzair, coupling concealment and dedication to aid others through resistance activities.

Chasia Bielicka began her life passing as a Gentile on 16 January 1943, when the leadership of the Grodno underground asked her to carry their document-forging tools to the Białystok ghetto. Hashomer Hatzair was one of several factions in the Białystok resistance aligned in a manner similar to Grodno: Hashomer Hatzair in collaboration with Dror-Hehalutz, then subsequent ties formed with the Communists.[92] Other organizations joined this coalition, including Hanoar Hatzioni (Zionist Youth), Betar, and the Bund.[93] The Białystok ghetto underground, led by Mordechai Tenenbaum, Chaika Grossman, Daniel Moszkowicz, and others, was considerably more advanced than the resistance movement Chasia had left behind. The different factions employed young women to act as couriers to aid the acquisition of weapons, explosives, medical supplies, food, and false documents. Assigned to such courier duties, Chasia slipped out of the ghetto with Jewish workers the day after her arrival and headed to Gestapo headquarters to apply for a *Personalausweis* (identity card) using a forged birth certificate.[94]

Later that month, with her false papers in hand, Chasia left the ghetto to establish her life on the "Aryan" side. "I left behind Chasia Bielicka of Grodno, a member of Hashomer Hatzair, a member of the underground, a Jew," she declared in a postwar memoir. "I took only Halina Stasiuk, a Polish Christian girl from the village of Koszewo." An elderly Polish woman who thought that Chasia was the Polish girl Halina offered her a place to sleep. At the *Arbeitsamt* (labor exchange), Chasia was assigned to the household of an SS officer, Herr Luchterhand, in charge of administering Polish labor. She disliked her employer and his wife immediately. They paid her little, fed her even less, and abused her verbally.[95]

In Resistance Networks

Posing as a Polish servant girl provided the cover necessary for Chasia Bielicka to carry out her assigned task. Like the partisans of the forest, she possessed the essentials—shelter, food, and camouflage—to carry out her true mission: resistance. Chasia's work as a maid and cook buttressed her cover story and protected her from the round-ups for forced-labor duties in Germany. Within a few weeks, she moved into a one-room apartment on the other side of the city, providing necessary distance to run guns or carry messages without risk of running into her employers. The room also served as a crucial way station for underground members passing to and from the ghetto or forest. When the *Arbeitsamt* added work in a German communal kitchen to her daily labor duties, Chasia had access to small bits of food for herself and unexpected guests, a blessing because Frau Luchterhand assiduously monitored the pantry food stocks.

By the time Chasia arrived in Białystok, the Germans had nearly completed the deportation of the region's Jews. Białystok, the largest remaining ghetto, was the subject of dispute among the parties with interests in forced labor, including the Wehrmacht and contractors producing war materiel. The deportations had already had an adverse impact on military-related productivity in Grodno and smaller towns. Under pressure from the SS, however, the more than 41,000 Jews of the Białystok ghetto were scheduled for removal in the first months of 1943.[96] Between 5 and 12 February 1943, some 10,000 Jews were deported in five transports to Treblinka; the Germans shot a further 900 within the ghetto during the *Aktion*.[97] Deportation of the remaining 30,000 Jews was postponed while the SS, Wehrmacht, and employers of Jewish laborers continued their tug of war over the Jews' fate.[98]

Within this context, the Białystok ghetto underground accelerated its pursuit of weapons and ammunition to mount an uprising. Couriers sought contacts beyond the circles of Jewish resistance to coordinate resistance efforts with Soviet and Polish Communist forces (the latter making up the Armia Ludowa).[99] Seventeen young women, according to Chasia Bielicka's count, engaged in this work; only five remained alive at war's end. Besides Chasia, Hashomer Hatzair deployed Rivka Madejska from Vilna; Marila Rozycka from Łódź and Ania Rod and Lisa Chapnik from Grodno represented the Communists; Bronia Winicka of Dror had been a courier between Grodno and Białystok since early 1942 and was posted to the "Aryan" side in Białystok in November of that year.[100]

Connections between the couriers were limited because isolation aided safety. Most carried out their missions alone. Bronia Winicka journeyed to an outlying village to retrieve a revolver and two hand grenades. She brought them back hidden in a loaf of bread. Bronia also smuggled out the Białystok ghetto archives containing Judenrat records, diaries, and testimonies.[101] In practice, some couriers crossed paths during the course of their activities. Lisa and Chasia, for example, worked in adjacent German households as well as in the communal kitchen. Chasia teamed with Chaika Grossman to deliver ammunition to the ghetto because of its physical weight.[102]

This phase of their activities ceased in mid-August 1943. On the afternoon of 15 August, Chasia Bielicka surmised that the large numbers of Ukrainian and Lithuanian police gathered in the vicinity of the ghetto meant a major *Aktion*, perhaps even the ghetto liquidation. As night fell late that summer night, she entered the ghetto to sound the warning. Preparations for battle had already begun. Chasia hoped that the underground leaders would deploy her to a combat unit. "We decided that you have to go out again right away," Chaika Grossman told her. "We need you on the Aryan side." Her task, it was decided, was to coordinate the supply of weapons, ammunition, medical supplies, and other necessities for a long siege. "Get ready and organize the girls on the outside" was the parting instruction she received.[103]

Reluctantly, Chasia obeyed. She made her way to Lisa Chapnik's apartment at dawn, whispering to her, "They're liquidating the ghetto." They went in separate directions to contact the chain of couriers.[104] Fighting broke out midmorning on 16 August between the underground and the German forces. The battle was short-lived. Within twenty-four hours, most of the 200 or so fighters had been killed. Mordechai Tenenbaum and other resistance leader are believed to have committed suicide.[105] The deportations continued for five days, emptying the ghetto of most of its remaining 30,000 Jews. A few thousand managed to hide in the ghetto buildings, but many were captured after a few days. Ukrainian police units swept through the ghetto area over the following months to net the remaining few. But some Jews managed to flee to the forests surrounding Białystok and join partisan units.[106]

Chaika Grossman escaped the ghetto while the deportations were still in progress and met with five other couriers (Rivka Madejska, Ania Rod, Lisa Chapnik, Bronia Winicka, Chasia Bielicka) on the Aryan side to commiserate. Sitting on rocks in a vacant lot, they met as a group for the first time. "We sat alone, lost, cut off," Chasia Bielicka recalled of the encounter. They walked to the edge of the holding area for the deportees, helpless to aid the thousands suffering in the hot August sun before being forced onto trains. Standing among dozens of Polish onlookers, some responding with delight at the Jews' misery, the women resolved to continue their work. "We were totally mobilized," Chasia remembered. The only justification for their lives, she declared, was to carry on the war against the Germans.[107]

These young women's actions mirrored their initial communal responses in the ghetto and during the prewar years, when young Jews with like minds gravitated toward organizations that fit their ideological perspectives. Social ties had played an essential role in group formation during the 1930s. Now ideological differences between Communists and Zionists became insignificant in an overwhelming and unprecedented situation.

They could not move forward independently, however. With the ghetto destroyed and its underground leadership dead, the couriers turned to their connections among Soviet and Polish resistance movements for support, guidance, and cooperation. A number of Jews remained in Białystok passing as Gentiles or in hiding, and the couriers needed to supply them with food. Yet their primary task now was to aid the partisans. In addition to their contacts with other resistance groups, the women developed ties with several Germans committed covertly to anti-fascist causes.[108] One of them was Otto Busse. He had served with a German Reserve Police Battalion on the Eastern Front until he was demobilized and opened a house-painting business in Białystok in 1942. Starting in mid-1943, Busse aided various resistance efforts. He opened his home as a way station to Jews and others in transit to partisan groups. Through his connections in the German civilian administration, he obtained useful military information and passed it on. He also delivered weapons and supplies to the partisans using his personal car.[109]

The couriers' support for the partisans reversed their efforts for the ghetto underground as guns now traveled from Białystok toward the forests and countryside. During one raid on Gestapo headquarters, Chasia and her colleagues did reconnaissance work to identify weaknesses in the guard arrangement. The operation yielded twelve

Mausers.[110] Their actions earned the respect of the Soviet-backed fighters. In recognition, the women were named to the Białystok Anti-Fascist Committee. Lisa Chapnik was appointed chair.[111]

◆ While the couriers of the Białystok underground traveled back and forth to support partisan activities, other Jews sought the forests as a refuge. Leib Reizer, his wife, Frumke, five-year-old daughter, Bashele, and twenty-six other Jews escaped from the Grodno ghetto on the evening of 7 February 1943 in search of the partisans. Riding sleighs, they traveled after dark for several nights to join Kostia Buchko and his partisan otriad positioned in the Nacza forest 60 kilometers northeast of Grodno (figure 25).[112]

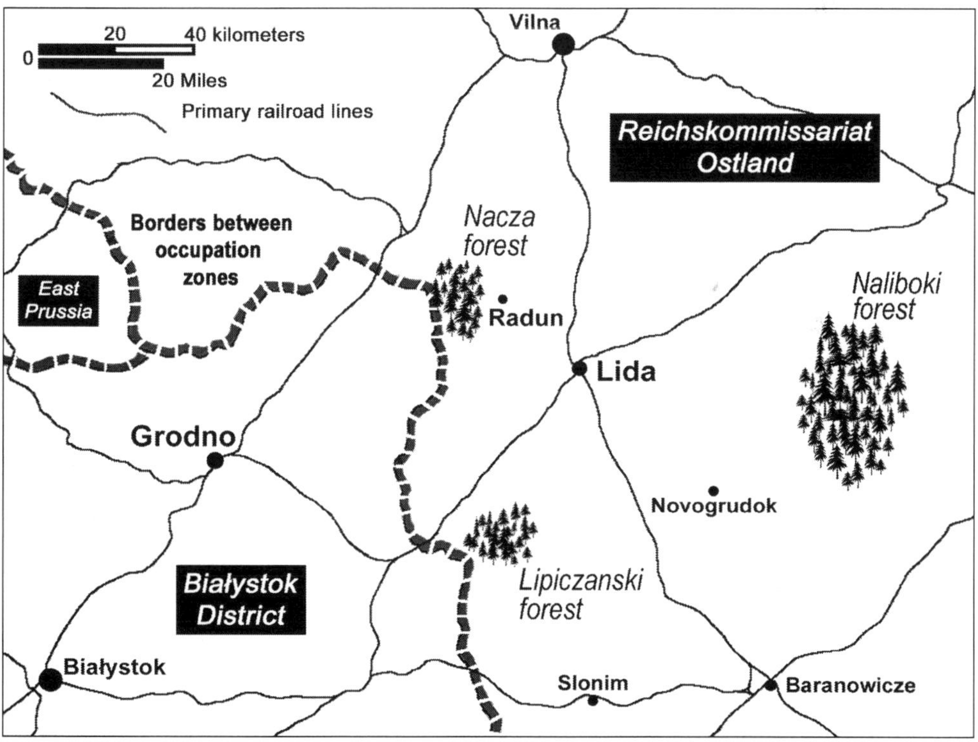

25. Map of northwestern Belarus, showing the locations of the Nacza and Lipiczanski forests in relation to Grodno, 1942–44.

Reizer later wrote obliquely about his partisan experiences fighting the Germans.[113] Most of the time he and his fellow otriad members pursued the partisan fighters' primary task: staying alive. Access to food and secure shelter were most important. Sympathetic peasants shared what they had. From those who were unfriendly, the partisans stole what was needed. Their existence depended on communal effort.

Soon after arriving in the Nacza forest, Leib Reizer discovered the necessity of collective security. A young man, a Gentile, wandered into the forest looking to join the fighting otriad. Experienced partisans found his story suspicious, and under interrogation the youth revealed that the Polish police in Radun had sent him to lure the fighters out. Group leaders shot him, but when they went the next morning to bury his body, all they found was a patch of blood in the snow and footsteps leading away. The entire otriad had to flee. "This was our first lesson as inexperienced partisans," Reizer remembered. "We trudged through the snow until we found another hiding place."[114]

Staying warm through the Belarusian winter was also crucial. Three veteran partisans showed the new arrivals simple techniques previously unknown to them. "We broke off dry twigs and built a fire," he later recalled. "The flames chased away the dark and warmed us a little." As winter gave way to spring, more Jews from the surviving remnants of the Grodno, Lida, and Radun ghettos joined the group. By summer, the group numbered eighty refugees, with two other groups of nearly equal size nearby.[115] Soviet-sponsored partisans under the command of Anton Stankiewicz gathered in the region's armed ghetto escapees and family camps in October 1943, adopting the name "Leninsky Komsomol Battalion."

The Nacza forest camps faced disaster in October 1943.[116] German Order Police, assisted by Lithuanians and Poles, surrounded the forest and killed those in hiding. Leib Reizer and his wife and daughter fled southwest to the forests bordering the Nieman River in search of other Jewish partisan battalions. Other refugee Jews joined them over the following days, increasing the group's number to about twenty. The Orlianski otriad, a Jewish partisan group, allowed Reizer and his family to join their family camp. This group fled south to the

Lipiczanski forest as the New Year approached. The Reizers remained on the move as the Red Army advanced on Belarus in the summer of 1944. Near the Belarusian village of Demianovtsi, they hastily constructed a new bunker as Soviet Katyusha rockets soared overhead. Days passed as they wondered whether the future meant liberation by the Soviets, death by Russian artillery, or murder at the hands of the Germans and their remaining collaborators.[117]

◆ The Reizer family survived thanks to the communal network operating within a partisan detachment. Leib Reizer's memoir reveals little about the reasons why his family and other escapees from the Grodno ghetto were accepted so readily into a series of otriads. Timing may have played a role because by early 1943 resistance networks in the forests were sufficiently strong to accept additional fighters, particularly if they came with weapons. Identity may also have assisted entry: from Reizer's description, Jews operated many of the partisan units that his group encountered.

Daniel Klovsky, who survived in concentration camps with his father, David, is more forthcoming in his recollections about the conditions for his survival protected by the underground network in Auschwitz and Buchenwald. Daniel fell ill soon after their arrival at Birkenau. He was able to conceal his illness from the camp SS with the help of his father and fellow prisoners in the Białystok transport. After their transfer to Buna, longtime prisoners advised David Klovsky to take his son to the *revier* (camp hospital) for treatment. His doctor subsequently declared that without care Daniel would have likely died in a few days.[118]

Daniel remained in the camp hospital for seven months, an extraordinary length of time. He was diagnosed with an abscess in his right lung and spinal tuberculosis as a result of untreated pneumonia. Most prisoners in his condition faced selection for the gas chamber, yet the doctors and staff took extraordinary efforts to care for Daniel and conceal his illness. "I always got an extra portion of soup and bread," he recalled.[119] The hospital was one of several key blocks in Buna dominated by Communist activists.[120] The activists' contacts throughout the Auschwitz camp networks yielded, among others benefits, additional drugs and salves not typically available in a prisoner infirmary. The source of some of these medications was the Sonderkommando in the Birkenau crematoria, which found them among the possessions formerly belonging to gassed deportees.[121]

The underground also went to great lengths to protect certain prisoners. David and Daniel Klovsky benefitted from their relationship to his uncle Izik, David's younger brother. The latter had been a Communist agitator in Grodno during the 1930s and had served time in a Polish prison for his deeds on behalf of the party. One of the camp hospital doctors, Dr. Solomon Lubitch, had been born in Grodno and had heard tales of Izik Klovsky's devotion. Yet the actions of the underground members did more than heal Daniel's body. "Those people were not afraid!" he remembered of these men. "So, the Jews could resist instead of obediently going to death." This realization, Daniel later reflected, raised his morale, which in turn promoted his physical recovery. His father also took strength from the actions of the resistance. "He got his self-respect back," Daniel recalled.[122]

The Klovskys continued to receive assistance from the Communist resistance after their deportation to Buchenwald. A rumor spread on 4 April 1945 that the camp SS intended to deport all Jews from the camp to an unknown destination. Aided by the "Reds," or socialist and Communist political prisoners who had to wear red triangles on their uniforms, the Jews removed their yellow uniform markings and sought shelter in a non-Jewish barrack.[123] When father and son joined a column of Polish prisoners marched from the camp two days later, they also wore red triangles.

Survival Methods and Identities

David and Daniel Klovsky switched the insignias on their camp uniforms to blend into a group of prisoners at a very late stage of the war. Fivel Markelis and Lev Fleish abandoned their prewar identities to endure more than three years in captivity rather than face a worse fate. These two sets of examples reveal significantly different responses to the prospect of annihilation, notwithstanding the fact that each reacted to a distinct situation. The Klovskys sought a way to escape confinement, even at the risk of unfamiliar conditions outside the camp. The surrounding region was in chaos, however, with periodic strafing from Allied aircraft and Allied ground forces approaching by the day. Fivel and Lev chose to pose as Slavs as a grand diversion, aware of the risks this carried. Each took a leap into the unknown prompted by immediate dangers. The Klovskys wore false identities on the surface; Markelis and Fleish immersed themselves into other selves.

The process of survival in camps, in hiding, and in resistance networks required the adjustment of identities. After their violent removal from familiar environments and forced separation from family and friends, individuals applied their skills to navigate new challenges within the narrow opportunities created by sheer luck. The Grodno and Vitebsk Jews examined in this chapter shared remarkable abilities to adapt and endure. How they responded differed according to their prewar socialization. All faced great peril, however, and only fortuitous circumstances far beyond each individual's control permitted a chance at survival.

Social isolation was one of the ongoing challenges to survival. Zelda Grodzienska arrived at Majdanek in a transport of young women from Grodno and Białystok, yet they were dispersed among the prisoners of the *Flugplatz* subcamp. Vichna Sidranska met and maintained contacts with a mother and daughter from her home city, yet the exceptionality of this relationship stands out among the anonymous social order in overcrowded prisoner barracks. Further evidence of the tenuous nature of camp society appeared when each young woman fell ill with typhoid, and they later attributed their survival to the efforts of a few fellow prisoners. Only when the SS deployed smaller groups to other subcamps did Zelda and Vichna seem to form stronger social ties.

Something similar emerged among the members of the "Białystok transport" of Jewish craftsmen from Grodno and Białystok. David Klovsky recalled the prisoner solidarity that had developed by the time the group was in Łomza prison. Moishe Kremer violated rules that forbad prisoners to stand and look out of the prison window. But none of his cellmates gave him up when the guards investigated, even though all of them received beatings.[124] The transport cemented their ties further in Stutthof.

Because this transport of craftsmen was held together in quarantine at Auschwitz-Birkenau, they maintained their unique communal identity. Only in Buna did the group merge into the larger prisoner population. By contrast, the connections that Zelda and Vichna had developed were shattered upon their arrival at Birkenau. Perhaps this was why their encounters with familiar faces from Grodno merited special mention in interviews recorded decades later. (Zelda, of course, had previously encountered her distant cousin Eli and his son at the Bliżyn subcamp.) Their recognition of people tangentially connected to their pasts dispersed the social dislocation that accompanied selection on the disembarkation ramp and processing at the Central Sauna. Perhaps these encounters gave them much needed hope to build or rebuild friendships after the rupture of arrival at Birkenau.

As is apparent from the survival accounts of Grodno Jews in concentration camps, each gravitated toward new social groups for mutual support. Not all such groups were built on companionship. David and Daniel Klovsky traded upon the experiences of David's lost brother, Izik, to form ties with the camp underground. Some succeeded in developing links not only to groups of non-Jewish prisoners but to civilians as well. After Leib Bialo was transferred to the Jaworzno subcamp, his work emptying latrines in the coal mine brought him into contact with ethnic German and Polish workers, who gave him scraps of food and worn clothing. "That's the only reason I survived," he later acknowledged.[125]

Jews in hiding could not develop contacts outside of their place of confinement. Yet they, too, displayed the desire to form or restore social ties. Alexandre Blumstein missed his friends from the ghetto and was haunted by their loss. Furthermore, his sexual frustration indicated a wish for a bond that he saw others experiencing. Feliks Zandman described the efforts that his companions in the cellar took to avoid recollections of lost relatives, efforts that indicate they retained the impulse for human relationships. Leib Reizer and his family formed a series of connections to other Jewish refugees in the forests of Belarus, although most of those connections were shattered through the violence of German counterinsurgency actions. Chasia Bielicka and her fellow couriers passed as Gentiles to fight the Germans. Each may have been affiliated with different ideological movements, yet collectively they found common ground not only in their shared immediate goals but also in the patterns of interdependence learned in the youth groups they belonged to before the war.

When we turn to examine Fivel Markelis and Lev Fleish, young Jews raised in the Soviet system, marked distinctions appear. Zelda, Leib, Daniel, and others from Grodno never ceased to identify by their names even if the SS knew them merely as numbers. Even the Grodno Jews in hiding places maintained appreciable portions of their identities, passing as Gentiles only for transitory periods. Fivel and Lev fled Vitebsk and abandoned their prewar lives in the same instant. Their commitment to their false identities—staying "in character" for well more than three years—had much to do with the circumstances of their eventual capture by the Germans and deportation to camps. Yet the longevity of their feat also reflects the skills they brought to this effort.

During the initial stage of wandering through German-occupied territory, Fivel and Lev shared with their counterparts from Grodno the need as well as the desire for human contact. Access to food and shelter were matters of life and death, yet their contact with Gentiles was driven by more than desperation. Although such connections were typically matters of convenience, and personal interactions were held to a need-to-know basis, these two youths knew how to make their pleas for food or shelter without apparently revealing their origins.

Their strategies shifted after falling into German captivity. Both young men were circumcised, and each made great efforts to conceal their physical distinction from guards and fellow captives, especially on the rare occasions that prisoners had access to bathing facilities. They encountered greater dangers every day in camp from other prisoners. Yet the language and cultural skills acquired in prewar Vitebsk served them well. Fivel had been educated in Belarusian and

Russian as well as Yiddish. He had participated in a prize-winning Belarusian folk dance troupe and had been raised in an interethnic environment. Lev Fleish had many of the same experiences, and to cover any shortfall he created a unique false identity—an orphaned Tatar, raised as a Belarusian even if he didn't completely look like one. And their sense of isolation in camp must have been greater than Jews held as Jews. Even if they did encounter someone from Vitebsk and its environs, acknowledging their common heritage was the last thing they would do.

Other Soviet Jews met German policies of annihilation with similar responses. Fourteen-year-old Stepan Zavgorodnev (introduced in chapter 1) had escaped from the Vitebsk ghetto along with his mother, Maria, and stepbrother, Anatoli, a few days before the final liquidation. Maria and Anatoli were caught without documents and shot; Stepan managed to run away. Realizing how dangerous it was to remain in Vitebsk, where he might be recognized by former neighbors, he fled. He headed south, following a route similar to Lev Fleish's. When he asked for food, he knew not to volunteer anything about his true heritage. "They didn't ask—I didn't tell," he later remembered of those who aided him in his flight.[126]

Stepan pressed onward to Kiev, Poltava, and Kobeliaki in Ukraine over the following months, working odd jobs on farms and in villages in exchange for food and lodging in a hayloft. During his wanderings, he also kept company with another "fugitive" youth, an eighteen-year-old Red Army soldier. The fact that Stepan knew this youth only by his first name, Fedya, reflects the distance that Stepan maintained in their codependent relationship. They were liberated by Red Army forces in early 1942 during the winter offensive, and Stepan subsequently enlisted.[127]

Civilians were not the only Soviet citizens adjusting to conditions. Red Army soldiers David Dodin and Isaak Erukhimov escaped detection as Jews and survived a series of camps. Dodin, born in a small shtetl in 1921 and educated in Vitebsk, was captured and deported to POW camps in Ostrów Mazowiecka, Poland, and Zeithain,

Germany. When questioned in Stalag 304 in Zeithain by a Belarusian collaborator, he easily conversed idiomatically in the interrogator's native tongue. He also successfully rebuffed attempts to expose him as a Jew, responding with indignation when asked to pull his pants down. Attitude as well as skill aided David Dodin's survival.[128] Isaak Erukhimov, a Vitebsk native born in 1924, was captured during frontline fighting in 1943. He ended up in Auschwitz-Birkenau. Using the Russified name "Aleksandr Afanasievich Erukhimov," he remained watchful of informants among the prisoners who reported on "hidden" Jews.[129]

Several cases attest to the ability of young Jewish men from Soviet Vitebsk to masquerade as Slavs, but what of young Jewish women? Among available accounts from young Jewish women, we find patterns of identity suppression similar to that of young Jewish men.[130] Elena Choukmazova, whom we met in chapter 1, posed as a Russian after she escaped from the Smolensk ghetto on the eve of the liquidation. She was in Borisov in early 1943 when caught in a roundup and deported to Germany as an *Ostarbeiter*. She, like Lev Fleish, remained in a forced-labor camp in Germany until the end of the war.[131] Vera German, whose flight from Vitebsk in July 1941 was discussed in chapter 5, was confined to the Liozno ghetto along with her mother, Leya. They escaped the ghetto liquidation and fled toward the front lines in February 1942. Leya and Vera begged for food in populated areas, appealing in the name of Christian charity when necessary. They successfully crossed the front and were later evacuated to Kazakhstan.[132]

Young Jews from Grodno and Vitebsk faced different circumstances during the Holocaust, but they also offered distinct responses. The environments in camps, hiding, and resistance groups shaped their paths, but so did their individual actions. Within narrow windows of survival opened by chance, Grodno Jews preserved some sense of identity and familiar ties. Vitebsk Jews discovered that conditions of a rapidly unfolding genocide merited flight and immersion in another identity. Doing so meant cutting all bonds in order to pass as a Gentile, yet it took skill to maintain their cover and escape detection. When the war ended, some survivors looked around for their shattered prewar worlds and identities but found nothing. They could only go forward.

Liberation: Which Way Forward?

Liberation brought survivors face-to-face with the choice of either returning to a devastated home or seeking a new life elsewhere. Such options were open primarily to survivors who traced their origins to the territories annexed by the Soviet Union in late 1939. Stalin agreed, in order to curry favor with the western Allies and to rid the Soviet Union of potentially "unreliable" minorities, to permit native inhabitants to reclaim their Polish citizenship. Hundreds of thousands of Polish-born persons, many of them Jews, departed for the West in the immediate postwar years.[133]

Grodno remained within the adjusted borders of the BSSR, and to return meant accepting once again a Soviet passport.[134] Until liberated survivors under western Allied custody made this decision, they were classified as displaced persons. Zelda Grodzienska, liberated by the British at Bergen-Belsen, saw no point in returning to her native Grodno. Her entire family was gone, she assumed. Nevertheless, she searched for relatives in the western Allied zones of occupation. Eli Grodzienski found her first, and the two decided to get married. They immigrated to the United States in September 1946 with the assistance of Eli's brother in Los Angeles.[135]

Other survivors from Grodno headed home from the point of liberation. Vichna Sidranska and Luba and Riva Kremer had been transferred from Aschersleben to Theresienstadt in the last weeks of the war; the Red Army liberated them on 9 May 1945. Initially swept up in the repatriation of Soviet citizens, the three women were sent to a camp in occupied Germany to prepare to return. As Jews, they felt threatened among the wholly Slavic population, so they set out for Grodno on their own by hitching rides on Red Army supply trucks. At Białystok, a group of Jewish refugees counseled them not to cross the border into the Soviet Union. "You're crazy, what are you going for?" Vichna remembered one telling her. "If you go in, you're not going to be able to get out." Stay in Białystok, they advised, because the Central Committee of Jews in Poland was extending assistance and collecting names of survivors. Vichna, Luba, and Riva decided to turn back; they settled temporarily in Łódź to figure out what to do next. A few months later, with the assistance of the underground emigration movement Brichah, the three women reached the American occupation zone of Austria. They later immigrated to the United States through contacts with relatives.[136]

David and Daniel Klovsky crossed the border into the Soviet Union, but only after some hesitation. Father and son were liberated by the Americans near Buchenwald and transferred to Soviet custody a few months later. "Did my father and I think of going to the West? I don't think so," Daniel reflected more than fifty years later, after having made a successful life in the Soviet Union. He continued, "My father told me many times that we had the only way—back to Grodno." Fueling this conclusion, Daniel recalled decades later, was the distant hope that some of their family was still alive. Perhaps their positive experiences with the Communist underground movements in Buna and Buchenwald swayed David Klovsky's decision as well. But they waited, not arriving on Soviet soil until the new year in 1947. Ironically, the Klovskys were placed for a few days in Kielbasin, newly rebuilt to process returnees. After interrogation, David and Daniel were permitted to enter Grodno, where they indeed discovered that some surviving cousins had returned as well. Later the same year, David, a widower since his wife's deportation and murder at Treblinka, married the widow of a Jewish partisan. Daniel left Grodno in 1948 to study electrical engineering in Leningrad. David lived out his years in Grodno, dying in 1987.[137] Reflecting on the opportunities to immigrate to Israel or America in the years before or after the collapse of the Soviet Union, Daniel wrote in a memoir published in 2003, "But I did not want to go." His sons grew up as Russians, not Jews, markers of the continued cultural drift that many experienced in the postwar Soviet world. They had no interest in emigration, and Daniel could not leave them behind.[138]

Some survivors returned to Grodno hoping to find relatives, but most were disappointed. Leib Reizer headed back to the city with his wife and daughter after their liberation by the Red Army. When he knocked on the door of their apartment in Ghetto I, he found a Polish woman in residence. Enraged at his audacity when he asked for it back, she went to the provisional authorities of the recently liberated city to report what she perceived to be a crime. The Red Army officer in charge subsequently called Leib and his family into his office. "He looked at us for a moment and told the Polish woman to give back the apartment."[139] Perhaps Leib owed this magnanimity to his status as a partisan fighter. In any event, they did not stay for very long. Nobody else from their extended family had survived, and Soviet rule grew increasingly restrictive. Despite his association with the Communist underground in the Grodno ghetto, he could not see his family making a life there. In 1945, they reacquired their Polish citizenship and migrated westward, subsequently crossing illegally into the American occupation zone. The Reizers immigrated to New Zealand in 1948.[140]

For others, the Soviet Union became their adopted homeland. Ania Rod, Lisa Chapnik, and Chasia Bielicka returned to Grodno in September 1944 and set up house. The three young women enrolled in teachers' college with the assistance of Valentina Ochanina, the director of their prewar Soviet school. The young women formed friendships with Feliks Zandman, Sender Freydovicz, and other survivors who returned looking for lost relatives. After a year in Grodno, Chasia received a letter from Chaika Grossman, who informed her that Hashomer Hatzair had reestablished an *Aktiv* in Warsaw to help members make aliyah to Palestine. Chasia decided to rejoin the movement in the Polish capital; she later led a group of more than 500 children and youths to Israel. Ania Rod and Lisa Chapnik elected to stay. "All her life Lisa had dreamed of living in a Communist country," Chasia remembered of her good friend.[141] Ania and Lisa headed east, enrolling at the Institute for Foreign Language in Moscow to study English. In 1946, the young women were interviewed by *Eynikayt* (Unity), the newspaper of the Jewish Anti-Fascist Committee, about their resistance activities during the war. Lisa married, and both women settled in Ryazan, 200 kilometers south of the Soviet capital. After the Soviet Union was no more, Lisa and Ania immigrated to Israel.[142]

The road to the future for native Soviet Jews was largely a one-way street, unlike the road for their coreligionists born on Polish territory. Even if liberated by the British or the Americans, Soviet citizens faced forcible repatriation under agreements made at Yalta. Liberated by the Red Army at Königsberg, Fivel Markelis was deported to Tula in western Russia, where he was put into a punishment battalion in a coal mine awaiting review of his case. The NKGB officer who finally interviewed him didn't believe he was a Jew. "Why are you still alive?" he was asked suspiciously. It was this officer who redubbed Fivel with the *familiya* (family name) "Markelis-Domnin," fusing his prewar and wartime identities but capped with a new *imya* (first name), "Efim." There was no such Jewish name as "Fivel," he was told. Efim Davidovich Markelis-Domnin was released in 1947. He returned to Vitebsk to find the city still in ruins. Following service in the peacetime Red Army, Fivel/Efim married and settled in Tallinn, Estonia.[143]

Lev Fleish initially experienced less-severe persecution after liberation. He was examined by an NKGB commission in Soviet-occupied Cottbus, Germany, following his liberation and subsequently was drafted into the Red Army. Lev was discharged late in 1946, whereupon he returned to Vitebsk as well. Yet former forced laborers such as Lev had trouble finding work because authorities often suspected them of treason. "I had a 'dirty' biography," he reported later. Only after Stalin's death did his situation improve somewhat.[144] Isaak Erukhimov, a former prisoner of war and concentration-camp inmate, also faced discrimination as a suspected traitor after the war. As for Fivel Markelis, for Isaak the experience of masquerading as a captive left its imprint on his postwar name. He told Soviet investigators that his first name was "Aleksandr" and further Russified his last name to Erofimov.[145]

Aleksandr's name change reflected some Jews' response to the emerging inhospitable environment shaping postwar Soviet life. Already in the 1930s, Jewish culture in its official Soviet Yiddish variant had been in decline, displaced by the elevation of Russian language and culture (chapter 1). The war further advanced the primacy of Russian national identity. Suppression of Jewish identity, however, extended beyond the displacement created by expanding Russian supremacy. In 1942 and 1943, the party and state machinery identified Jewish directors and leading personnel at cultural and academic institutions and replaced them with ethnic Russians. Other fields, such as journalism, also felt the effects of the purge.[146]

Conversely, a resurgence in Jewish identity appeared to be in the works, even if only in its official constructions. Soon after the German invasion, prominent Jewish writers, scientists, scholars, and party officials formed the aforementioned Jewish Anti-Fascist Committee, a counterpart to other committees created to rally the national groups of the Soviet Union. The committee's chair, Yiddish actor and theater director Solomon Mikhoels, traveled to the United States in 1943 with other committee members on a fund-raising drive to support the Soviet war effort.

After liberation of the western borderlands, Yiddish culture resurfaced with the publication of a handful of books and edited collections. Among the writers who came back to Belarus was Hirsh Reles. He had survived the war in the Urals, where he was demobilized from the army late in 1941 to work on a road-clearing crew. When his bosses realized that Reles was a man of letters, they recommended him for the position of editor of the district newspaper, *Stroyitel'* (Builder), in Gremyachinsk.[147] Following the liberation of Belarus, Reles returned to look for his wife and daughter but could find no trace. They probably were murdered in Novogrudok in late 1941.

A much smaller community of Yiddish writers returned to Minsk. Several had been killed fighting with the Red Army. Zelik Akselrod, Reles's literary mentor after the Great Terror of 1937–38, had been arrested during a renewed wave of repression in the spring of 1941. As the NKVD emptied out the prison in Minsk on 26 June 1941, Akselrod was marched away with the political prisoners and shot somewhere along the road between Minsk and Cherven before the Germans arrived.[148] Younger writers took the place of those lost. Chaim Maltinsky edited a new collection of Yiddish writings, *Mit festn trit* (With

Confident Steps), published in Minsk in 1947. Reles contributed several poems.[149]

The climate in Belarus, however, was not amenable to a Yiddish revival. Unable to find sufficient work in the diminished Yiddish literary world, Reles wrote in Russian for a series of newspapers and journals. Only his few remaining friends from before the war knew him as "Hirsh"; he used the formal name "Grigorii" or less-formal "Girsh" or "Grisha" as the byline on his work and in his professional life. These names alone signaled the shift in his identity. Reles is just one case. More sweeping policies affected the situation of Yiddish writers and Soviet Jews in general in the postwar years. In 1946, Reles's colleague Hirsh Kamenetsky joined two other Yiddish writers to approach the first secretary of the Central Committee in Belarus, Panteleimon Ponomarenko, to request the reintroduction of Yiddish education. Ponomarenko, the same official who had closed the Yiddish-language schools in 1938, tersely replied that such a request smacked of Bundism and Zionism and that they had better not ask again.[150]

Words turned into violence with the murder of Jewish Anti-Fascist Committee chairman Solomon Mikhoels by state security agents on the night of 12–13 January 1948. The committee had faced comparatively mild criticism during the war. But its late wartime and postwar initiatives—lobbying for a Jewish Soviet Socialist Republic in Crimea, compiling the *Black Book* to document the annihilation of Jews, and enthusiastically supporting the foundation of a Jewish state in Palestine—were met with mounting distrust by Stalin and the central organs of state security. By the end of 1948, the Jewish Anti-Fascist Committee had been disbanded, and arrests of its leading members began.

Mikhoels's assassination, disguised as a traffic accident, occurred in Minsk. "We all knew very well who planned this death, and who the henchmen were," Reles later recalled.[151] The death reminded some, perhaps, of the loss of Izi Kharik and Moishe Kulbak during the prewar purges. The repression of the Jewish Anti-Fascist Committee and its members coincided with the debut of the anticosmopolitan campaign targeting intellectuals accused of expressing pro-Western thoughts. In this atmosphere, Hirsh Reles lost his position on the editorial staff of the journal *Vozhyk* (Warrior). Yet others helped to ease his departure. He was not officially dismissed, which would have tainted him as an enemy of the people and exposed him to possible arrest. He left on his own accord after his fellow editors tipped him off that he risked facing an investigation. This tactical retreat was the third such instance in his lifetime, the first two being his withdrawals from Minsk to Slutsk during the Great Terror and from Belarus with the Red Army in 1941. With no other writing or editorial work forthcoming, Reles accepted a position teaching Russian language and literature at a night school. And, once again, he survived.[152]

He was fortunate. Hirsh Kamenetsky joined the list of those arrested. Many prominent writers were later tried and shot, such as Itzik Fefer, Dovid Bergelson, and Peretz Markish, all murdered in Moscow in August 1952. Survivors' families faced repression as well. The Red Army had rescued Raisa Gendelev and her grandparents from the Usviaty ghetto in early 1942, and her parents were evacuated from Leningrad around the same period. The reunited family settled first in Lida and then in Minsk after the liberation of Belarus. Then her father, Moishe, was arrested in 1949 on accusations of cosmopolitan chauvinism and collusion with anti-Soviet spies. He was tried and sentenced to a gulag camp.[153]

Tensions eased after the death of Stalin in 1953. Moishe Gendelev was one of tens of thousands of Soviet Jews released under an amnesty in subsequent years.[154] During the Khrushchev thaw, renewed opportunities emerged for Yiddish writers. The literary journal *Sovetish Heymland* (Soviet Homeland) appeared in August 1961, issued under the patronage of the Soviet Writers' Union.[155] From the very first issue, Hirsh Reles published his verses again. His poems, inspired by the Belarusian landscape and rural life, addressed subjects safe enough for official scrutiny. He still taught at the night school until his retirement in 1973. In the 1970s and 1980s, Reles directed his attention to the war, even to his personal loses. He had remarried after the war, to Polina Kopelevna Roskina, and the couple raised one daughter. But his first family remained in his memory. In his poem "In yenem vinkele" (In Every Corner), he wrote:

> The eyes that the enemy's bullet
> shut forever,
> they now gaze gently from the sky,
> when the night is clear.[156]

Other than such instances of literary allusion, Reles never wrote about the loss of Yekha and their daughter, Raisel. After his retirement from teaching, he devoted himself to chronicling the experiences of his literary cohort in Minsk, finding a new audience after the breakup of the Soviet Union in 1991. Reles was a link to a cultural realm that preceded the Jewish revival in the Soviet Union from the 1960s on. And he continued to write and give interviews into the new century. He was among the last Jews of his generation to have witnessed—and survived—all that happened to them.

Conclusion

A Generation Destroyed

After the destruction of World War I and the political restructuring of eastern Europe, the emergent nations granted their citizens, including Jews, liberties and rights previously unknown. But as optimism soured in the face of economic failure and perceived internal threats, old prejudices mixed with new ideologies to revive the local cultures of repression. Jews once again became targets, to differing degrees and for distinct and sometimes unintelligible reasons. Aggression from Nazi Germany outpaced the native hostility within each state, devouring every dimension of civilized society. Instead of safety and security, eastern Europe saw war and genocide; instead of progress, carnage.

The young Jews born between the world wars had no notion of the tragedy and violence that lay ahead. Indeed, in each nation they tried to seek their fortunes as all young people hope to do. In Soviet Vitebsk, they found advocates among the Bolsheviks, who saw all youth as the future. To support the interests of children and adolescents, the Communist Party in Belarus sanctioned schools in the languages of each national group. Education was a principal medium of indoctrination, teaching Bolshevik values and ideologies, and the Soviets made literacy and learning available to all. Many young Jews welcomed these opportunities. "Now we are strong, young, resolute," wrote the twenty-year-old poet Hirsh Reles, the son of a *kheder* instructor, when he attended a teachers' training academy for the Yiddish-language school system. Outside of school, in the streets and parks of the Red city Vitebsk and within Soviet youth organizations, children of all nationalities enjoyed a social familiarity largely unknown across the western border in Poland.

Yet by the late 1930s the party and its divisions of state security grew to perceive Jews as a "nationality" with fatal flaws—not only was religion the core of Jewish heritage, but Jews were also a people spread across borders among the enemies of socialism. The agenda for Yiddish education and culture, originally developed with young people in mind, was sidelined. Party officials in Soviet Belarus closed Yiddish schools and the related institutions training teachers. And some of those who participated in the dismantling of Jewish culture within the party and the ranks of the NKVD were Jews themselves, at least according to their Soviet passports. Nevertheless, young Jews adapted, adding to their knowledge of other cultures acquired in the Belarusian- and Russian-language schools that replaced Yiddish-language instruction in the multiethnic Soviet city. Many parents had tacitly supported these identity shifts resulting from the change in language because the best education was in Russian. But even as Jews acculturated, connections throughout Soviet society were shaken as a result of the Great Terror. Some in Soviet society, for example, blamed Jews for the party's actions, reviving antisemitism despite official suppression of it as "anti-Soviet behavior."

The Jewish youth of Polish Grodno never enjoyed a period of state support. The rebirth of Poland promoted a climate of hostility for ethnic minorities, compounded for Jews by Christian antisemitism. Yet the problems facing Jewish youth extended beyond official and popular exclusions. Economic opportunities were few, and neither the Jewish community nor the youngsters' parents could improve the situation. Many young Jews joined Zionist or Bundist groups to address the problems they confronted and to shape their own futures. They acquired self-sufficiency skills in the context of collective cooperation (and conflict) that served to make them "strong, young, resolute." Even young people who avoided official group affiliation bonded with friends to form their own cliques. These responses among young Grodno Jews reinforced their sense of identity. Membership was limited to Jews primarily because of their exclusion from Polish and Belarusian groups. Indeed, the only group in Grodno to support interethnic membership was the underground Communist Party. But the young Jews in Grodno still achieved a far greater degree of unity and purpose than their coreligionists in Vitebsk, who bent their sense of self to the demands of a changing environment, a process encouraged by the transition to the Belarusian- and Russian-language education. Yet they began this transformation during the purges of the late 1930s, when trust between neighbors was fragile and communal interactions were impeded.

For the young Jews of each city, the Molotov-Ribbentrop Pact of 23 August 1939 initiated a process that brought their two worlds together. Within a month, western Poland fell within the Germans' grasp through invasion, while the Soviets met limited resistance when they occupied the eastern provinces. Rapid sovietization toppled existing community structures. Existing Zionist and Bundist youth groups in Grodno and the rest of the annexed territories were banned. The new Soviet rulers, however, lured young Jews with promises of higher education and equality unknown in interwar Poland. They also opened Yiddish-language primary schools, institutions that no longer existed in eastern Belarus. Some Jewish children and adolescents joined the Pioneers and the Komsomol and heeded the messages disseminated by the party. Many, however, merely followed their friends into these authorized organizations because of the activities and benefits on offer. Still others continued to meet in secret with fellow Zionist or Bund members. Regardless of which avenue they took, young Jews in Grodno maintained their practice of connecting with each other in organizational structures, a response that continued to distinguish them from their more atomized coreligionists in Vitebsk.

The German invasion of the Soviet Union on 22 June 1941 suddenly and violently toppled one oppressive power and replaced it with another, far more destructive authority. Perhaps the first and last collective thought held by the Jew of Grodno in western Belarus and Vitebsk in eastern Belarus was their utter shock at the collapse of the Red Army. Another shared quality, although none was aware of it at the time, was how chance shaped their lives as never before. Although many eyewitnesses recalled their surprise at hearing the first thuds of artillery and at seeing the first German plane, their astonishment had more to do with the Soviet Union's failure to keep them safe. Grodno fell the first day; Vitebsk nearly three weeks later. The two cities were consigned to separate zones of German occupation, and the priorities of local authorities influenced the strategies targeting Jews.

As summer waned in 1941 and the German advance on Moscow stalled, most Vitebsk Jews were dying of disease or starvation in the ghetto set up by the Wehrmacht occupation authority. Renewal of Army Group Center's assault on the Soviet capital prompted the elimination of the perceived hazard presented by a ghetto full of typhus-ridden Jews, a condition of the Germans' own making. The surviving Jewish population was shot outside the city in early October. Escape meant flight, accepting the painful abandonment of older or less-mobile family members, and immersion in another identity. Young Jews typically escaped Vitebsk individually and posed as Russians, Belarusians, Tatars—anyone but themselves. And they proved to be good at it, applying the language and social skills learned in the cultural shifts and political upheavals of the late 1930s. Some maintained the pretense for a few days or weeks, others for years. Young Jews concealed their identities, a concept decried as anti-Soviet in their formative years. Now it saved their lives. While the Germans dictated the policies on occupied Soviet territory that framed these responses, and likely paths to survival constantly shifted, young Jews reacted within the limits of the possible. Luck permitted some to survive.

Such choices were alien to young Grodno Jews. Cooperation among comrades superseded notions of individual impersonation as a natural response to adversity. Family ties held them back as well, but this was also owing to the longer timescale of German policies against captive Grodno Jews. They were not confined to a ghetto until November 1941, by which point most Jews in Vitebsk were already dead. Instead of deprivation, Jews in Grodno and elsewhere in the Białystok District were kept alive as a minimally paid forced-labor pool to support German interests. Yet their "value" as workers was eventually trumped by SS demands for their destruction. As deportations to Treblinka and Auschwitz began in November 1942, Jewish resistance groups accelerated their plans for an uprising, but they could manage only a small and unsuccessful revolt during the last series of roundups from the ghetto.

Cooperation among Grodno Jews did not end with the ghetto liquidation. As we have seen, former group members continued to draw upon ties of solidarity in concentration camps. Within resistance networks, such connections proved vital. Even accounts of Grodno Jews in hiding reference memories from their home environment, particularly of those persons already murdered. Vitebsk survivors, by contrast, shunned making close connections.

The matrix of events was complex, and not all situations were equal. Differences in the Germans' genocidal policies decisively influenced possible survival paths. Chance and randomness created opportunities that played roles as significant as any under the Germans' control. Within these boundaries, Jews took steps toward their own survival. And when we look at the young Jews of Soviet Vitebsk and Polish Grodno, we find that their fundamental responses were completely different. Those born in Grodno looked to each other when facing a mortal threat, whereas their contemporaries from Vitebsk reconstructed their sense of self in their attempts to reach safety.

What did this difference mean for the postwar lives of these survivors? Many young Grodno Jews tried to find family members, but most were unsuccessful. Makeshift family connections among fellow survivors and new community structures took their original families' place, each promoting the exodus that drew many to move forward with their lives somewhere other than Grodno. Vitebsk Jews, if not liberated on Soviet territory, faced compulsory repatriation. Some eventually found that a few family members had survived because more time had been available for flight before the German occupation. Vitebsk survivors demonstrated flexibility once again in adapting to the economically austere and more openly antisemitic postwar environment of the Soviet Union.

We know much more about the patterns of reintegration after liberation from survivors living in the West. Some wrote of their experiences or sat for recorded interviews. The experience of being Polish Jews survived their exile from Grodno, transformed by contacts with the Jewish communities of their destination country but retaining fragments of the traditions learned in childhood. For Soviet Jews, the postwar years continued and compounded the ruptures in Jewish identity that had unfolded before the war and during the Holocaust. Although some facets of community life reemerged—a prayer group here, a small synagogue there—officially sanctioned Yiddish education and cultural life were suppressed and in many cases prosecuted as anti-Soviet. Although Yiddish publications reappeared in the 1960s, this reappearance was a mere shadow of the "glittering epoch" witnessed by Hirsh Reles thirty years earlier.

The arc of history that framed the Jewish experience in the borderlands of Poland and the Soviet Union tells us about identities, responses, and agency among a historically marginalized minority facing oppression and genocide. When new political frontiers split coreligionists into blocs with different interests and goals, the environments of their respective nations reshaped individual and collective identities accordingly, particularly among the youth without any prior firsthand historical knowledge. When their homelands faced catastrophe and their public identities as Jews marked them for death, they pursued courses of action consistent with what they knew and had experienced until that time.

Notes

Bibliography

Index

Notes

Abbreviations

d.	*delo* (folder)
f.	*fond* (record group)
GAGO	Gosudarstvennyi arkhiv Grodnenskoi oblasti (State Archive Grodno Oblast)
GARF	Gosudarstvennyi arkhiv Rossiiskoi federatsii (State Archives of the Russian Federation)
GAVO	Gosudarstvennyi arkhiv Vitebskoi oblasti (State Archive Vitebsk Oblast)
GERO	Grodnenskaya yevreiskaya religioznaya obshchina (Grodno Jewish Religious Community)
l.	*list* (sheet)
NARB	Natsional'nyi arkhiv Respubliki Belarus' (National Archives of the Republic of Belarus)
ob.	*oborot* (reverse side)
op.	*opis* (record subdivision)
USC	Univ. of Southern California
USHMM	United States Holocaust Memorial Museum Archives
VEPU	Vitebskoye evreiskoye pedagogicheskoye uchilishche (Vitebsk Jewish Pedagogical School)
VGU	Vitebskaya gorodskaya uprava (Vitebsk City Council)
YIVO	YIVO Institute for Jewish Research
ZIH	Żydowski Instytut Historyczny (Jewish Historical Institute)

Introduction

1. Vitebsk and its surrounding territory were transferred to the BSSR in 1924.

2. Zvi Y. Gitelman, *Jewish Nationality and Soviet Politics: The Jewish Sections of the CPSU, 1917–1930* (Princeton, NJ: Princeton Univ. Press, 1972), 287.

3. Hirsh Reles, [untitled], *Vitsebski praletarii*, 2 June 1933, f. 2285, op. 2, d. 125, Gosudarstvennyi arkhiv Vitebskoi oblasti [State Archive Vitebsk Oblast] (GAVO).

4. Lev Fleish, Rishon LeZiyyon, Israel, 12 June 1997, Russian language (trans. Oleg and Irina Pyshnenko), interview code 30205, USC Shoah Foundation, Univ. of Southern California (USC), Los Angeles.

5. Batya, "Jedem rok: Urywki z pamiętnika" [One Year: Fragments of a Diary], Akiva youth newspaper, n.d. (c. 1936), trans. Ania Lepak, Grodnenskaya yevreiskaya religioznaya obshchina [Grodno Jewish Religious Community] (GERO), f. 56, op. 1, d. 147, l. 22, Gosudarstvennyi arkhiv Grodnenskoi oblasti [State Archive Grodno Oblast] (GAGO).

6. Zelda (Grodzienska) Gordon, c. 6 Mar. 1984, interview by Univ. of California at Los Angeles, at the 1939 Society website, http://www.the1939society.org/.

7. Fleish interview, USC Shoah Foundation.

8. Debórah Dwork, *Children with a Star: Jewish Youth in Nazi Europe* (New Haven, CT: Yale Univ. Press, 1991), xxxiii.

9. Hugh Trevor-Roper, *History and Imagination* (Oxford: Clarendon Press, 1980), 16.

1. Raised in the Red City

1. Hirsh Reles, Minsk, Belarus, 2003, interview by Ellen Kellman, Brandeis Univ., author's collection.

2. Emmanuel Ioffe, "Patriarkh evreiskoi literaturi v Belarusi" [Patriarch of Jewish Literature in Belarus], introduction to Hirsh Reles [as Grigorii Reles], *V krayu svetlykh beryoz* [In the Country of Bright Birches] (Minsk, Belarus: Izdatel E. S. Gilperin, 1997), 3.

3. Women's first names are too frequently omitted from personal accounts of eastern European Jewish life; thus, Hirsh Reles's mother's name is lost to history.

4. Inyessa Gankina, "Portret na fonye veka" [Portrait against the Background of the Century], *Aviv* (Minsk), Apr.–May 2001, 24.

5. Gleb Lobodenko, "Girsh Reles: 'Nadeyus uspet' . . . '" [Girsh Reles: "I Hope to Have Time"], *Aviv* (Minsk), Mar.–Apr. 2003, 2.

6. Ioffe, "Patriarkh evreiskoi literaturi v Belarusi," 3.

7. Gankina, "Portret na fonye veka," 24.

8. Ioffe, "Patriarkh evreiskoi literaturi v Belarusi," 3; Hirsh Reles, *Di yidish-sovetishe shrayber fun Vaysrusland* [The Yiddish-Soviet Writer from Belarus] (Minsk, Belarus: I. P. Logvinov, 2004), 13.

9. H. Reles, "Fun tsikl lider 'Shtetele'" [From the Verse Cycle "Little Shtetl"], *Vitsebski praletarii*, 8 Jan. 1933, f. 2285, op. 2, d. 125, GAVO.

10. H. Reles, "Zunen signaln" [To the Sun's Motions], *Vitsebski praletarii*, 12 May 1933, f. 2285, op. 2, d. 125, GAVO.

11. H. Reles, [untitled], *Vitsebski praletarii*, 2 June 1933, f. 2285, op. 2, d. 125, GAVO.

12. Reles interview by Kellman, Brandeis Univ.

13. Ioffe, "Patriarkh evreiskoi literaturi v Belarusi," 3; Arkadii Shulman, "Ostrov Relesa" [Isle of Reles], in Girsh [Hirsh] Reles, *Yevreiskie sovetskie pisateli Belorussii* [Jewish Soviet Writers of Belarus] (Minsk, Belarus: Izdatel' D. T. Kolas, 2006), 239–40.

14. Arkadii Zeltser, *Evrei sovetskoi provintsii: Vitebsk i mestechki, 1917–1941* [Jews of the Soviet Provinces: Vitebsk and Surrounding Region, 1917–1941] (Moscow: Rossiiskaya politicheskaya entsiklopediya, 2006), 152. See also Mordechai Altshuler, *Soviet Jewry on the Eve of the Holocaust: A Social and Demographic Profile* (Jerusalem: Center for Research of East European Jewry, Hebrew Univ., 1998), 233.

15. Arkadii Podlipskii, *Evrei v Vitebsk* [Jews in Vitebsk] (Vitebsk, Belarus: UPP "Vitebskaya oblastnaya tipografiya," 2004), 105.

16. Per Anders Rudling, *The Rise and Fall of Belarusian Nationalism, 1906–1931* (Pittsburgh: Univ. of Pittsburgh Press, 2015), 25, 326n62.

17. Zeltser, *Evrei sovetskoi provintsii*, 418.

18. "Dort, vu men hot derlozn groyse durkhraysn" [There, Where One Is Allowed Great Breakthroughs], *Vitsebski praletarii*, 27 Jan. 1933, f. 2285, op. 2, d. 125, GAVO. Similar demographics were present in other Vitebsk factories, such as the Red Metal Worker plant (Zeltser, *Evrei sovetskoi provintsii*, 154).

19. "Arbeterns-shloglerns fun farshaydene natsionalitetn af der fabric 'industrializatsie-fon'" [Shock Workers from Different Nationalities from the Factory "Banner of Industrialization"], *Vitsebski praletarii*, 27 Jan. 1933, f. 2285, op. 2, d. 125, GAVO.

20. Sheila Fitzpatrick, *Everyday Stalinism: Ordinary Life in Extraordinary Times, Soviet Russia in the 1930s* (New York: Oxford Univ. Press, 1999), 139; Wendy Z. Goldman, *Women at the Gates: Gender and Industry in Stalin's Russia* (Cambridge: Cambridge Univ. Press, 2002), 202–5.

21. *Pratakol agul'bava skhoda studentav, vykladchykav, i tekh. persanala yevpedtekhnikuma* [Protocol of General Meeting of Students, Teachers, and Personnel of Jewish Pedagogical Tekhnikum], 23 Nov. 1934, Vitebskoye evreiskoye pedagogicheskoye uchilishche [Vitebsk Jewish Pedagogical School] (VEPU), f. 905, op. 1, d. 128, l. 122–25, GAVO.

22. "Drugi komunal'ny dom na vul. imya Valadarskava" [Another Communal House on Volodarskaya Street], *Vitsebski praletarii*, 16 Nov. 1933, and "Havyadzem in kamunal'nykh damakh chyctatu i ŭzorny napadak" [Constructing at Communal houses—Bright and Examples of Order], *Vitsebski praletarii*, 8 Dec. 1933, f. 2285, op. 2, d. 125, GAVO.

23. "Garshtarkn dem arbiter control af der stalove" [Strengthen the Workers' Control on the Communal Dining Room], *Vitsebski praletarii*, 14 May 1933, f. 2285, op. 2, d. 125, GAVO.

24. Elena (Choukmazova) Zibert, Vitebsk, Belarus, May 1998, Russian language (trans. Oleg Pyshnenko and Irina Pyshnenko), interview code 49456, USC Shoah Foundation.

25. Fleish interview, USC Shoah Foundation.

26. Stepan Zavgorodnev, Kiev, Ukraine, 15 Apr. 1998, Russian language, interview code 43514, USC Shoah Foundation.

27. Arkadii Zeltser, "Interwar Ethnic Relations and Soviet Policy: The Case of Eastern Belorussia," *Yad Vashem Studies* 34 (2006): 87–124.

28. Zeltser, "Interwar Ethnic Relations," 92–93.

29. Zeltser, "Interwar Ethnic Relations," 93.

30. Zeltser, "Interwar Ethnic Relations," 101.

31. Fitzpatrick, *Everyday Stalinism*, 186–87; Sarah Davies, *Popular Opinion in Stalin's Russia: Terror, Propaganda, and Dissent, 1934–1941* (Cambridge: Cambridge Univ. Press, 1997), 85–88, 132.

32. Harvard Project on the Soviet Social System, Schedule A, vol. 11, Case 142, pp. 10–11, at https://iiif.lib.harvard.edu/manifests/view/drs:5228022$12i. This interview of a Belarusian male born circa 1923 took place in 1950. Between 1949 and 1953, with funding from the US Air Force, social science scholars at the Russian Research Center of Harvard University interviewed refugees from the Soviet Union living in the United States and in West Germany. Transcripts of the interviews are available online through the Harvard Library's website.

33. David C. Engerman, *Know Your Enemy: The Rise and Fall of America's Soviet Experts* (New York: Oxford Univ. Press, 2009), 60.

34. "Sud nad antisemitami no delu Barshai" [Trial over Antisemitism in Affair Barshai] and "Prigovor po delu Barshai" [Verdict in Affair Barshai], *Zarya zapada*, 18 and 22 Jan. 1929, f. 2289, op. 2, d. 118, l. 13 ob., GAVO.

35. "S tochki zreniya 'pedagogiki'" [With the Sharp Sight of "Pedagogy"], *Zarya zapada*, 10 Jan. 1929, f. 2289, op. 2, d. 118, l. 13 ob., GAVO.

36. "Dort, vu men hot derlozn groyse durkhraysn."

37. Zeltser, *Evrei sovetskoi provintsii*, 214, 221.

38. Efim Markelis-Domnin (Fivel Markelis), Tallinn, Estonia, 1 May 1997, Russian language (trans. Oleg Pyshnenko and Irina Pyshnenko), interview code 31115, USC Shoah Foundation.

39. Elizaveta (Gurevich) Pototskaia, Odessa, Ukraine, 27 May 1998, Russian language, interview code 46371, USC Shoah Foundation.

40. Zibert interview, USC Shoah Foundation.

41. Markelis-Domnin interview, USC Shoah Foundation.

42. See Fitzpatrick, *Everyday Stalinism*, chap. 6, "Family Problems." For an in-depth examination, see Wendy Z. Goldman, *Women, the State, and Revolution: Soviet*

Family Policy and Social Life, 1917–1936 (Cambridge: Cambridge Univ. Press, 1993), chaps. 3, 6, 8.

43. Zavgorodnev interview, USC Shoah Foundation.

44. Zavgorodnev interview, USC Shoah Foundation.

45. Fitzpatrick, *Everyday Stalinism*, 139.

46. Markelis-Domnin interview, USC Shoah Foundation.

47. See Goldman, *Women, the State, and Revolution*, 126–34, for a discussion of child support from estranged spouses during the 1920s and early 1930s.

48. Zibert interview, USC Shoah Foundation.

49. Vera (German) Kurinets, Penza, Russia, 5 July 1997, Russian language, interview code 33813, USC Shoah Foundation.

50. "Dershlogn zikh an oyfshtayg fun der yidisher avtonomer gegnt" [Accomplishments of the Jewish Autonomous Region], *Oktyabr* (Minsk), 19 July 1934, microfilm of *Oktyabr* issues at YIVO Institute for Jewish Research, New York (YIVO), and Dorot Jewish Division, New York Public Library.

51. Kurinets interview, USC Shoah Foundation.

52. Dmitri Khvat, Jaffa, Israel, 20 Sept. 1996, Russian language, interview code 19847, USC Shoah Foundation.

53. Marx Pipkin, "Istoriya odnovo apkhiva" [History of One Archive], *Mishpokha* 20 (2007): 121.

54. Altshuler, *Soviet Jewry on the Eve of the Holocaust*, 268–69. These overall percentages for Belarus were considerably higher than for the Russian Socialist Federated Soviet Republic, where intermarriage occurred somewhat more often (58 percent of men and 63 percent of women in 1936).

55. Zibert interview, USC Shoah Foundation.

56. Pototskaia interview, USC Shoah Foundation.

57. For discussion of the Yevsektsiya's campaigns during the 1920s, see chapter 1, "Antireligious Propaganda and the Transformation of Jewish Institutions and Traditions," in Anna Shternshis, *Soviet and Kosher: Jewish Popular Culture in the Soviet Union, 1923–1939* (Bloomington: Indiana Univ. Press, 2006).

58. Elissa Bemporad, *Becoming Soviet Jews: The Bolshevik Experiment in Minsk* (Bloomington: Indiana Univ. Press, 2013), 158–59.

59. "Kustar" [Craftsman, pseud.], "Klerikaln manevrirn" [Clericals Maneuver], *Vitebsker arbet*, supplement to *Zarya zapada*, 12 Jan. 1929, f. 2289, op. 2, d. 118, l. 13 ob., GAVO.

60. Sholem Izraelit [pseud.], "Farayn fun medtuer, luftert oys ayere reyen!" (Union of Medical Personnel, Air Out Your Ranks!), *Vitebsker arbet*, supplement to *Zarya zapada*, 12 Jan. 1929, f. 2289, op. 2, d. 118, l. 13 ob., GAVO.

61. Zibert interview, USC Shoah Foundation.

62. Kurinets interview, USC Shoah Foundation.

63. Markelis-Domnin interview, USC Shoah Foundation.

64. Zeltser, *Evrei sovetskoi provintsii*, 426.

65. Markelis-Domnin interview, USC Shoah Foundation.

66. Fleish interview, USC Shoah Foundation.

67. Zavgorodnev interview, USC Shoah Foundation.

68. Kurinets interview, USC Shoah Foundation.

69. Kurinets interview, USC Shoah Foundation.

70. Markelis-Domnin interview, USC Shoah Foundation.

71. Khvat interview, USC Shoah Foundation.

72. "Kayn eyn kind oyser di vent fun der shul" [No Child Excluded from the School System], *Vitsebski praletarii*, 2 June 1933, f. 2285, op. 2, d. 125, GAVO.

73. The BSSR was the only Soviet republic to designate Yiddish as an official state language, as written into the second constitution of 1927. Belarusian, Yiddish, Polish, and Russian were the permissible languages for government transactions, legal proceedings, and public life. See Claire LeFoll, "The 'Belorussianisation' of the Jewish Population during the Interwar Period: Discourses and Achievements in Political and Cultural Spheres," *Eastern European Jewish Affairs* 38, no. 1 (Apr. 2008): 72.

74. Terry Martin, *The Affirmative Action Empire: Nations and Nationalism in the Soviet Union, 1923–1939* (Ithaca, NY: Cornell Univ. Press, 2001), 10–12.

75. Grigory Ioffe, "Understanding Belarus: Questions of Language," *Europe-Asia Studies* 55, no. 7 (Nov. 2003): 1025; Bemporad, *Becoming Soviet Jews*, 84–85.

76. "Undzere dergraykhungen afn kultur-front" [Our Accomplishments on the Culture Front], *Oktyabr* (Minsk), 9 July 1935.

77. Z. Novodvorets, "Di yidishe sovetishe shul in Vaysrusland" [The Jewish Soviet School in Belarus], *Oktyabr* (Minsk), 17 July 1935.

78. A parallel situation existed in Soviet Ukraine, where a teacher observed that "most Jews sent their children to Russian or Ukrainian schools because they felt that Yiddish was a dying language" (Harvard Project on the Soviet Social System, Schedule B, vol. 9, Case 383, p. 5).

79. Elias Schulman, *A History of Jewish Education in the Soviet Union* (New York: KTAV Publishing House, 1971), 160n9.

80. Viacheslav Selimenev and Arkadii Zeltser, "The Liquidation of Yiddish Schools in Belorussia and Jewish Reaction," *Jews in Russia and Eastern Europe* 41, no. 1 (2000): 76; Zeltser, *Evrei sovetskoi provintsii*, 296.

81. Zeltser, *Evrei sovetskoi provintsii*, 277.

82. Zeltser, *Evrei sovetskoi provintsii*, 286.

83. Catriona Kelly, *Children's World: Growing Up in Russia, 1890–1991* (New Haven, CT: Yale Univ. Press, 2007), 66–70.

84. Kelly, *Children's World*, 538.

85. Khvat interview, USC Shoah Foundation.

86. Zavgorodnev interview, USC Shoah Foundation.

87. Pototskaia interview, USC Shoah Foundation.

88. Kurinets interview, USC Shoah Foundation.

89. Kurinets interview, USC Shoah Foundation.

90. Markelis-Domnin interview, USC Shoah Foundation.

91. Leonid Smilovitsky, "Jewish National School in Belorussia, 1920–1930," *Shvut* 4 (1996): 70.

92. K. B. Hadashevich, "Far a bolshevistishn kurs fun geshichte" [Toward a Bolshevik Course in History], *Oktyabr* (Minsk), 3 Feb. 1935.

93. Bemporad, *Becoming Soviet Jews*, 99.

94. *Etiudn tsu der alt-yidisher geshikhte* [Studies in Ancient Jewish History], adapted by A. Yuditski from A. Ranovitsh, *Etiud iber der geshikhte fun der alt-yidisher religie* [Historical Overview of the Ancient Jewish Religion] (Moscow: Melukhe-farlag "Der emes," 1940), 66.

95. Shulman, "Ostrov Relesa," 240.

96. *Pasvedchanne* [Certificate], Vitebsker Kino Tekhnikum, 3 Sept. 1933, VEPU, f. 905, op. 1, d. 969, l. 2, GAVO.

97. A third Jewish Pedagogical Tekhnikum was established in 1925 in Gomel, southeast of Minsk, but in 1929 it was moved to Smolensk in the Russian Socialist Federated Soviet Republic, about 100 kilometers southeast of Vitebsk.

98. Esther Frumkina was born in 1880 with the name "Malkah Lifchitz." Frumkina (her first husband had the last name "Frumkin") was active in the Bund until joining the Bolsheviks in 1921 when the Bund was banned. After her advocacy work with the Yevsektsiya, Frumkina favored the assimilation of the Jewish nationality into the Soviet masses. Like many former Bundists and Yevsektsiya leaders, she did not survive the purges of the 1930s. Frumkina was arrested in January 1938 and deported to a camp in Karaganda, where she died in 1943 (Podlipskii, *Evrei v Vitebsk*, 107–8; Tamar Kaplan Appel, "Esther Frumkin, 1880–1943," Jewish Women's Archive Encyclopedia, n.d., at https://jwa.org/encyclopedia/article/frumkin-esther).

99. *Otchet o naborye uchashchikhsya* [Account of Student Recruiting], n.d. [1935], VEPU, f. 905, op. 1, d. 133, l. 207 and 207 ob., GAVO.

100. *Kharaktaristiki studentov v vypucknikov v 1935 g.* [Characteristics of Students Graduating in 1935], VEPU, f. 905, op. 1, d. 134, l. 34–37, GAVO).

101. *Kharaktaristika* [Characteristics] of Manya Moishevna Izrail, n.d. [c. 1935], VEPU, f. 905, op. 1, d. 134, l. 8, GAVO.

102. *Kharaktaristika* of Monya Yankelevich Glinik, n.d. [c. 1935], VEPU, f. 905, op. 1, d. 134, l. 9, GAVO.

103. Shulman, "Ostrov Relesa," 235.

104. Hirsh Reles quoted in Shulman, "Ostrov Relesa," 236.

105. "Spis rabotnikov Vitsebskava yevreyskava pedagagichnava tekhnikuma" [List of Workers in the Vitebsk Jewish Pedagogical Tekhnikum], n.d. [c. 1934], VEPU, f. 905, op. 1, d. 134, l. 3, GAVO; *Spravazdacha ab pratsi za 1933–34 navuchal'ny god na Vitsebskamu Yavreiskamu Pedagagichnamu Tekhnikumu* [Report about Workers for the 1933–34 Academic Year in Vitebsk Jewish Pedagogical Tekhnikum], 23 July 1934, VEPU, f. 905, op. 1, d. 125, l. 71 and 71 ob., GAVO.

106. "Feskin's 'aynperzonikeyt': Viazoy der direkter fun yidpedtekhnikum kemft mit dezorganizatorn fun lere, pragilshtshikes un flier" [Feskin's "One-Person Rule": How the Director of the Jewish Pedagogical Tekhnikum Fights with Disorganization of Teachers, Truancy, and Absences], *Vitsebski praletarii*, 1 Feb. 1933, f. 2285, op. 2, d. 125, GAVO; "Kayn eyn kind oyser di vent fun der shul."

107. Bafel [Order] no. 207 [from Director Feskin], 2 Mar. 1933, and Bafel no. 208 [from Director Babitski], 31 Mar. 1933, VEPU, f. 905, op. 1, d. 108, l. 42, GAVO.

108. Zalman Moishevich Babitski, "A nayer otriad—yunge kemfer afn front fun der kultur-revoliutsie" [A New Group—Young Fighters on the Front of Cultural Revolution], *Vitsebski praletarii*, 14 May 1933, f. 2285, op. 2, d. 125, GAVO.

109. Bafel no. 14, 26 Oct. 1934, VEPU, f. 905, op. 1, d. 117, l. 6; Bafel no. 37, 11 Nov. 1935, f. 905, op. 1, d. 117, l. 21, GAVO.

110. Bafel no. 14.

111. Zagad [Order] from the People's Commissariat of Enlightenment, 15 Oct. 1934, VEPU, f. 905, op. 1, d. 116, l. 184, GAVO.

112. Bafel no. 241, 8 Oct. 1933, f. 905, op. 1, d. 108, l. 26, GAVO. A little more than two years later, Babitski added the incentive of free bathhouse and laundry tickets to students who received "good" and "very good" scores (Bafel no. 55, 23 Nov. 1935, VEPU, f. 905, op. 1, d. 117, l. 26, GAVO).

113. Bafel no. 241.

114. *Otchetny doklad po boyennoi rabota Vitebskogo Yevpedtekhnikuma za 1934–35 uch. god.* [Accounting Paper for Military Work at the Vitebsk Jewish Pedagogical Tekhnikum for the 1934–35 School Year], n.d. (c., 1935), VEPU, f. 905, op. 1, d. 134, l. 88 and 89, GAVO.

115. Zagad no. 7, 29 Jan. 1936, VEPU, f. 905, op. 1, d. 117, l. 34, GAVO.

116. Prikaz [Order] no. 13, 10 Oct. 1936, VEPU, f. 905, op. 1, d. 117, l. 44 ob., GAVO.

117. Bafel no. 3, 8 Sept. 1934, VEPU, f. 905, op. 1, d. 117, l. 3, GAVO.

118. Moishe Sendaravich Slivko, "Der kurs 'II' muz bakumen di noytike yedies" [Course "II" Must Receive the Necessary Information], *Vitsebski praletarii*, 1 Nov. 1933, f. 2285, op. 2, d. 125, GAVO. Moishe Sendaravich Slivko, born in 1903 in Turek, Poland, had been a craftsman and a member of the Vitebsk branch of the Profintern since 1925 (*kharaktaristika* of Moishe Sendaravich Slivko, n.d. [1935], VEPU, f. 905, op. 1, d. 134, l. 7, GAVO).

119. Reles, *Di yidish-sovetishe shrayber fun Vaysrusland*, 224.

120. Gankina, "Portret na fonye veka," 25.

121. Reles, *V krayu svetlykh beryoz*, 325.

122. Gankina, "Portret na fonye veka," 25.

123. Reles, *V krayu svetlykh beryoz*, 315.

124. Reles, *Di yidish-sovetishe shrayber fun Vaysrusland*, 8.

125. Reles, *Di yidish-sovetishe shrayber fun Vaysrusland*, 9.

126. Reles, *Di yidish-sovetishe shrayber fun Vaysrusland*, 10–14.

127. David Shneer, *Yiddish and the Creation of Soviet Jewish Culture, 1918–1930* (Cambridge: Cambridge Univ. Press, 2004), 217.

128. Ayzik Platner, "Radio un literatur," *Oktyabr* (Minsk), 19 Jan. 1934.

129. Leonid Smilovitsky, "Izi Kharik: Pevets i zhertva epokhi" [Izi Kharik: Singer and Victim of the Epoch], *Mishpokha* 2 (1996): 54.

130. Izi Kharik, *Af a fremder khasene* [At a Stranger's Wedding] (Minsk, Belarus: Melukhe-farlag fun Vaysrusland, 1936), 5.

131. Smilovitsky, "Izi Kharik," 54.

132. Reles, *Di yidish-sovetishe shrayber fun Vaysrusland*, 34–35.

133. Kulbak's return to the Soviet Union because of its cultural and financial support for Yiddish literature mirrors the motives of another literary expatriate, David Bergelson, who settled in Moscow in 1934. See Boris Kolterman, "'Why I Am in Favour of Birobidzhan': Bergelson's Fateful Decision (1932)" (222–35), and other essays in Joseph Sherman and Gennady Estraikh, eds., *David Bergelson: From Modernism to Socialist Realism* (London: Modern Humanities Research Association and Maney, 2007).

134. Gennady Estraikh, "Zelik Akselrod," in *The YIVO Encyclopedia of Jews in Eastern Europe*, 2 vols., ed. Gershon David Hundert (New Haven, CT: Yale Univ. Press, 2008), 1:24.

135. Reles, *Di yidish-sovetishe shrayber fun Vaysrusland*, 43.

136. Leanid Marakov, *Akhvyary i karniki* [Victims and Criminals] (Minsk, Belarus: Vydavets Zmitser Kolas, 2007), 90.

137. Reles, *Di yidish-sovetishe shrayber fun Vaysrusland*, 103.

138. Reles, *Di yidish-sovetishe shrayber fun Vaysrusland*, 116. Ruve Reyzin (born 1911), Leib Talalay (born 1906), and Mote Dekhtiar (born 1909) joined the Red Army and died in combat. Rokhl Boimvol (born 1914) and Ziame Telesin (born 1907) immigrated to Israel in the late 1960s. Pinie Plotner (born 1915) immigrated to the United States in the 1990s and died on 27 November 2009. Lipe Heler (born 1916) died in the Soviet Union in 1986 (Reles, *Di yidish-sovetishe shrayber fun Vaysrusland*, 218–23).

139. Reles, *Di yidish-sovetishe shrayber fun Vaysrusland*, 8.

140. Reles, *Di yidish-sovetishe shrayber fun Vaysrusland*, 135–38. Born in 1914 in Bobruisk, Belorussia, Henekh Shvedik journeyed to Birobidzhan in 1929 and

returned to Minsk two years later. His first book of poems, *Start*, appeared in 1934. He graduated from the Minsk Jewish Pedagogical Tekhnikum in 1937 and worked at the children's newspaper *Pioner Belarusi* and other newspapers. Shvedik was a researcher at the Belarusian Academy of Sciences from 1939 until joining the Red Army in 1941. He died in battle on 11 October 1942 ("Henekh Shvedik [1914–1942]," *Sovetish Heymland* 10 [Oct. 1988]: 168).

141. Shvedik is identified as an NKVD informant in a denunciation report from another informant dated 11 August 1938, Tsentral'nyy komitet Kommunisticheskoi partii Belorussii [Central Committee of the Communist Party of Belarus], f. 4-P [Communist Party], op. 21, d. 1392, l. 38–54, Natsional'nyi arkhiv Respubliki Belarus' [National Archives of the Republic of Belarus] (NARB), translated and published in Viacheslav Selimenev and Arkadii Zeltser, "The Jewish Intelligentsia and the Liquidation of Yiddish Schools in Belorussia, 1938," *Jews in Russia and Eastern Europe* 43, no. 3 (2000): 85–86.

142. Gankina, "Portret na fonye veka," 24.

143. Gankina, "Portret na fonye veka," 25. Reles does not state which year this incident occurred, but it was likely in 1936 or 1937.

144. Ioffe, "Patriarkh evreiskoi literaturi v Belarusi," 8.

145. Lobodenko, "Girsh Reles," 2.

146. H. Reles, "Maydl komiugistke" [Komsomol Maiden], *Shtern*, no. 7 (July 1935): 74, microfilm at YIVO.

147. H. Reles, "Afn tish a bintl blumen" [On a Table a Bunch of Flowers], *Shtern*, no. 2 (Feb. 1936): 20.

148. Ioffe, "Patriarkh evreiskoi literaturi v Belarusi," 4.

149. Robert Conquest, *The Great Terror: Stalin's Purge of the Thirties* (New York: Macmillan, 1968); see also Robert Conquest, *The Great Terror: A Reassessment* (New York: Oxford Univ. Press, 1990).

150. J. Arch Getty, *Origins of the Great Purges: The Soviet Communist Party Reconsidered, 1933–1938* (New York: Cambridge Univ. Press, 1985).

151. Nicolas Werth, "The NKVD Mass Secret National Operations (August 1937–November 1938)," SciencesPo, Mass Violence, and Resistance Research Network, 20 May 2010, at http://www.sciencespo.fr/mass-violence-war-massacre-resistance/en/document/nkvd-mass-secret-national-operations-august-1937-november-1938.

152. James Harris, *The Great Fear: Stalin's Terror in the 1930s* (New York: Oxford Univ. Press, 2016).

153. "On the Trotskyist–Zinovievist Counterrevolutionary Activities among Teachers and Pupils in 1935–1936," Narodnyi komissariat prosvieshcheniia (Narkompros) BSSR [People's Commissariat of Enlightenment BSSR], f. 42, op. 17, d. 9, l. 1–13, NARB, quoted in Leonid Smilovitsky, "Jewish National School in Belorussia, 1920–1930," *Shvut* 4 (1996): 72. Former Bolshevik leader Leon Trotsky (born Leib

Davidovich Bronsteyn, 1879–1940) was expelled from the Communist Party and deported from the Soviet Union after the failure of the Left Opposition against Stalin in the 1920s. An NKVD agent assassinated Trotsky in Mexico in 1940. Grigorii Zinoviev (born Ovsei-Gershon Aronovich Radomyslsky, 1883–1936), former ally (alternatively) of Trotsky and Stalin, was tried twice (January 1935 and August 1936) in show trials. In the second trial, he was charged with forming a terrorist organization that allegedly killed Kirov and attempted to kill Stalin. Zinoviev was found guilty and executed on 25 August 1936.

154. Zagad no. 2, 29 Jan. 1935, VEPU, f. 905, op. 1, d. 117, l. 9, GAVO. The identity of instructor Khanin is not documented in surviving *tekhnikum* files. It is probably not Matsvin Efimavich Khanin, who remained at the *tekhnikum* until its closure in 1937. Based on Memorial [Organization], "List of Purge Victims" (in Russian), n.d., at http://lists.memo.ru, this instructor may have been Abram Joachimovich Khanin. Born in 1893, Abram Joachimovich Khanin was arrested in November 1937 as a Polish spy under the NKVD's national operations and executed the following month.

155. *Anketa* completed by Semyon Beyaminavich Gendelman, n.d. [1935], VEPU, f. 905, op. 1, d. 445, l. 1, GAVO.

156. Zagad no. 2, 29 Jan. 1935.

157. Management of the Preparation of Teachers, People's Commissariat of Enlightenment, to the director of the Vitebsk Jewish Pedagogical Tekhnikum, 20 Aug. 1935, VEPU, f. 905, op. 1, d. 133, l. 175, GAVO.

158. Zagad no. 2, 29 Jan. 1935.

159. Zagad no. 13, 13 Mar. 1935, VEPU, f. 905, op. 1, d. 117, l. 12 ob., GAVO.

160. Zagad no. 19, 9 Apr. 1935, VEPU, f. 905, op. 1, d. 117, l. 14 ob., GAVO.

161. Management of the Preparation of Teachers to the director of the Vitebsk Jewish Pedagogical Tekhnikum, 20 Aug. 1935.

162. Management of the Preparation of Teachers to the director of the Vitebsk Jewish Pedagogical Tekhnikum, 20 Aug. 1935.

163. Reles, *Di yidish-sovetishe shrayber fun Vaysrusland*, 25; Shulman, "Ostrov Relesa," 249–50.

164. Reles, *Di yidish-sovetishe shrayber fun Vaysrusland*, 26–27.

165. Quoted in Ber Boris Kotlerman, *In Search of Milk and Honey: The Theater of "Soviet Jewish Statehood" (1934–49)* (Bloomington, IN: Slavica, 2009), 76.

166. Kotlerman, *In Search of Milk and Honey*, 87–89; Avraham Novershtern, "Moishe Kulbak," trans. Marc Caplan, in *The YIVO Encyclopedia of Jews in Eastern Europe*, ed. Hundert, 1:953. The manuscript for *Benyomin Magidov*, alternatively known as *David Magidov*, has been lost.

167. Reles, *Di yidish-sovetishe shrayber fun Vaysrusland*, 25, 105.

168. Reles, *Di yidish-sovetishe shrayber fun Vaysrusland*, 29.

169. Marakov, *Akhvyary i karniki*, 35–36, 51–52, 82–83, 90. The dates that Kharik and Yudelson died were unknown to their own spouses until the writers were rehabilitated in the late 1950s. Even then, however, Kulbak's widow was told incorrectly that her husband had died in 1940 in a camp. Documents released to his surviving daughter in 1989 gave the date 29 October 1937, as discussed in the text. Many publications in the West until recently listed the date of Kulbak's death as 1940.

170. The Kurapaty forest was used for executions as well as burials. In interviews conducted in the 1980s and 1990s, Zianon Pazniak and Yauhen Shmyhalou have described the executions in the Kurapaty forest: "The shootings began here in 1937. At first, three times a day—at dawn, at 2.00 pm and in the evening, at dusk. They brought a few truckloads of people into the forest and shot them. They threw down the corpses, as ordered, into deep pits which had been dug there, layer upon layer. . . . Sometimes they planted pine saplings on top" (Zianon Pazniak and Yauhen Shmyhalou, "Kurapaty—the Road of Death," in *Kurapaty*, ed. V. Bagdanovich (Minsk, Belarus: "Tekhnalogiya," 1994), 82. The Prosecutor's Office of the BSSR authorized an archaeological examination of the Kurapaty forest in 1988, which found ample evidence of mass graves. The discovery was made public and served as a rallying point for groups supporting succession from the Soviet Union. President Bill Clinton was present for the dedication of a memorial at Kurapaty in 1994. The site remains controversial in Belarus.

171. See Marakov, *Akhvyary i karniki*, 18–90, for short biographies of many of those executed on the night of 28–29 October 1937.

172. During the Great Terror, investigators routinely forced confessions from spouses, usually through torture. Persons under arrest might survive by divorcing their spouse, but their survival was not guaranteed (Hiroaki Kuromiya, *The Voices of the Dead: Stalin's Great Purges in the 1930s* [New Haven, CT: Yale Univ. Press, 2007], 198–99).

173. Marakov, *Akhvyary i karniki*, 51, 83, and 90. Dina Kharik and Zelda Kulbak were sent to gulag camps in Kazakhstan, and Basia Shur to the camp at Karaganda. All were released in late 1945 and 1946 and sought rehabilitation of their murdered spouses after Stalin's death.

174. Kulbak's two children, for example, were sent to different children's homes. Moishe Kulbak's sister Tonya found her niece and nephew and brought them to live with her family in Minsk. Circumstances at the start of the war in 1941 separated the Kulbak children again. Raya, Moishe Kulbak's daughter, survived the war because her summer camp evacuated and outpaced the German invasion. Kulbak's son, Ilya, evacuated Minsk with his aunt Tonya, her children, and his fraternal grandparents (Solomon and Sima Kulbak). The group failed to outrun the Germans, however, and was placed in a small ghetto in Lapichi, Belarus. Ilya and his grandfather were shot by the Germans in January 1942. Tonya and Sima were shot in April 1942 ("The

Story of the Poet, Moshe Kulbak [Recollections by Raya Kulbak]," n.d., at http://www.eliatgordinlevitancom/kurenets/k_pages/kulbak.html). Kharik's two sons did not survive the Holocaust, and the fate of Yudelson's two children is unknown.

175. Werth, "The NKVD Mass Secret National Operations."

176. Kuromiya, *The Voices of the Dead*, 204–16.

177. Timothy Snyder, *Sketches from a Secret War: A Polish Artist's Mission to Liberate Soviet Ukraine* (New Haven, CT: Yale Univ. Press, 2005), 83–95, 115–24.

178. See Kate Brown, *A Biography of No Place: From Ethnic Borderland to Soviet Heartland* (Cambridge, MA: Harvard Univ. Press, 2004), chaps. 4 and 5; Martin, *The Affirmative Action Empire*, 322–33.

179. Nikita Petrov and Arsenii Roginskii, "The 'Polish Operation' of the NKVD, 1937–8," in *Stalin's Terror: High Politics and Mass Repression in the Soviet Union*, ed. Barry McLoughlin and Kevin McDermott (New York: Palgrave Macmillan, 2003), 154. Similar NKVD investigation and arrest operations targeted suspected German and Latvian intelligence agents. NKVD Order no. 00439, "About Repression Operations against German Citizens Suspected of Espionage," 25 July 1937, and NKVD Telegram no. 49990, "About the Operation for Repression of Latvians," 30 Nov. 1937, are discussed in Paul R. Gregory, *Terror by Quota: State Security from Lenin to Stalin (an Archival Study)* (New Haven, CT: Yale Univ. Press, 2009).

180. Those purged from the staff of *Orka* included Henrik Kharski, chief editor, executed 14 October 1937; Kazimir Dauksha, editor, and Piotr Piasko, journalist, both executed 26 October 1937; and Romuald Brzhasovski, journalist, executed 29 November 1938 (Marakov, *Akhvyary i karniki*, 116, 131, 133, and 369). *Orka* was shuttered in August 1938 (Selimenev and Zeltser, "The Liquidation of Yiddish Schools in Belorussia and Jewish Reaction," 74n2).

181. Petrov and Roginskii, "The 'Polish Operation' of the NKVD," 159.

182. People's Commissar for Internal Affairs Nikolai Yezhov, letter accompanying Order no. 00485, quoted in Petrov and Roginskii, "The 'Polish Operation' of the NKVD," 156.

183. Tatiana Sergeievna Protko, *Stanovleniye sovetskoi totalitarnoi sistemy v Belarusi (1917–1941 gg.)* [Creation of the Soviet Totalitarian System in Belarus (1917–1941)] (Minsk, Belarus: Tesei, 2002), 336.

184. Reles, *Di yidish-sovetishe shrayber fun Vaysrusland*, 29.

185. Marakov, *Akhvyary i karniki*, 83.

186. Marakov, *Akhvyary i karniki*, 23, 90.

187. Marakov, *Akhvyary i karniki*, 51; Verdict of the Military Board of Supreme Court of the USSR for Kulbak Moishe Solomonovich, 28 Sept. 1937, at http://www.eliatgordinlevitan.com/kurenets/k_pages/kulbak.html.

188. The executed editors included editors in chief Eli Osherovich and Noakh Kabakov, deputy editor Havum Kabakov, and business editor Yakov Mendelson

(Selimenev and Zeltser, "The Jewish Intelligentsia," 80n7; Marakov, *Akhvyary i karniki*, 300, 352).

189. Gennady Estraikh, *In Harness: Yiddish Writers' Romance with Communism* (Syracuse, NY: Syracuse Univ. Press, 2005), 169. Litvakov stood accused of collaborating with rivals Dunets and Bronshtein in an anti-Soviet conspiracy.

190. Marakov, *Akhvyary i karniki*, 291. Okun had been arrested on 28 February 1938.

191. A biographical sketch in a collection of Kharik's work published in 1962 noted that the Yiddish writer "was shot in 1937—exactly when and where no one knows" ("Biografishe shtrikhn" [Biographical features], in *Oysgeklibene shriftn: Dovid Hofshteyn, Izi Kharik, Itsik Fefer* [Collected Works: Dovid Hofshteyn, Izi Kharik, Itsik Fefer], ed. Shmuel Rozshanski [Buenos Aires: Literatur-gezelshaft beym YIVO in Argentine, 1962], 60). A collection of Kulbak's writings states that Kulbak was arrested in 1937, sent to an insane asylum, and disappeared in 1940 ("Biografishe shtrikhn" [Biographical features], in *Oysgeklibene shriftn: Moishe Kulbak* [Collected Works: Moishe Kulbak], ed. Shmuel Rozshanski [Buenos Aires: Literatur-gezelshaft beym YIVO in Argentine, 1976], 10).

192. Alfred A. Greenbaum, "Soviet Jewry during the Lenin–Stalin Period," *Soviet Studies* 16, no. 4 (Apr. 1965): 420.

193. "Yakub Kolas: Personality and Work," n.d., at http://archives.gov.by/eng/index.php?id=109695; "Belarusian Homer," n.d., at http://www.democraticbelarus.eu/node/5810. "Yanka Kupala: Personality and Work," n.d., http://archives.gov.by/eng/index.php?id=856629; "Yanka Kupala: Belarusian Treasure-Seeker," n.d., http://www.democraticbelarus.eu/node/5811. Yanka Kupala died in 1942 when he fell down the staircase of his Moscow hotel. His death may have been a politically motivated murder, suicide, or simply an accident.

194. Protko, *Stanovleniye sovetskoi totalitarnoi sistemy v Belarusi*, 600.

195. *Pamyats': Vitsebsk* [Memory: Vitebsk], vol. 1 (Minsk, Belarus: Belaruskaya entsyklapedyya, 2002), 286.

196. Of those listed in *Pamyats': Vitsebsk* as being executed, about 10 percent were Jews, just less than half their proportion among the total urban population (287–384).

197. Markelis-Domnin interview, USC Shoah Foundation.

198. Zavgorodnev interview, USC Shoah Foundation. Mikhail Yeines survived his interrogation and eight years of imprisonment. Released after the war ended, he was later exonerated (or "rehabilitated," in Soviet parlance) and died many years later in a small Soviet apartment.

199. Khvat interview, USC Shoah Foundation.

200. *Pamyats': Vitsebsk*, 366–67; Memorial [Organization], "List of Purge Victims."

201. Memorial [Organization], "List of Purge Victims."

202. *Pamyats': Vitsebsk*, 337.

203. *Pamyats': Vitsebsk*, 376; Memorial [Organization], "List of Purge Victims."

204. Pipkin, "Istoriya odnovo apkhiva," 121.

205. Zagad no. 43, 4 Jan. 1937, VEPU, f. 905, op. 1, d. 168, l. 3, GAVO.

206. Protko, *Stanovleniye sovetskoi totalitarnoi sistemy v Belarusi*, 333.

207. Zagad no. 459 from People's Commissariat of Enlightenment, 8 July 1936, VEPU, f. 905, op. 1, d. 149, l. 59–60, GAVO.

208. Kelly, *Children's World*, 95–96.

209. Inspector L. Glaz, People's Commissariat of Enlightenment, to Director Babitski, 16 Sept. 1936, VEPU, f. 905, op. 1, d. 149, l. 46 and 46 ob., GAVO.

210. Zeltser, *Evrei sovetskoi provintsii*, 296.

211. Zagad no. 791 from People's Commissariat of Enlightenment, 17 Aug. 1936, VEPU, f. 905, op. 1, d. 149, l. 64 and 65, GAVO. More than half of the twenty-eight graduates received placement teaching classes 1 through 4; the remainder were assigned jobs teaching Yiddish language and literature, history, mathematics, and geography. One graduate was assigned a position teaching Belarusian language and literature.

212. Director Babitski to the director of the Khotim HSSh., 22 Aug. 1936, VEPU, f. 905, op. 1, d. 147, l. 48, GAVO.

213. Deputy Commissar Serafimov, People's Commissariat of Enlightenment, to the director of the Vitebsk Jewish Pedagogical Studies, 17 June 1937, VEPU, f. 905, op. 1, d. 168, l. 25, GAVO.

214. Zagad no. 73, Dzyakov, People's Commissar of Enlightenment, to the directors and chiefs of education sections of pedagogical *tekhnikums*, 10 Jan. 1937, VEPU, f. 905, op. 1, d. 148, l. 17, GAVO.

215. Inna Gerasimova, "Evreiskoye obrazovaniye v Belarusi v 20-30-kh godakh" [Jewish Education in Belarus in the 1920s and 1930s], in *Evrei Belarusi*, vol. 2, ed. Inna Gerasimova (Minsk, Belarus: PKP "ARTI-FEKS," 1998), 69.

216. Central Committee of the Communist Party (Bolsheviks) of Belarus, Protocol no. 3, paragraph 255, of the Meeting of the Bureau of CC CPB of July 3, 1938, f. 4-P [Communist Party], op. 3, d. 575, l. 287, NARB, translated and published in Selimenev and Zeltser, "The Liquidation of Yiddish Schools in Belorussia and Jewish Reaction," 84. The planned closure of Yiddish schools in Smolensk Province, which neighbored Vitebsk, began with resolutions passed by the provincial executive committee in August 1938. This policy was not universally adopted across the Soviet Union, however, and the number of Yiddish-language schools in Ukraine was reduced but not eliminated (Selimenev and Zeltser, "The Liquidation of Yiddish Schools in Belorussia and Jewish Reaction," 77).

217. Gomel'skii inspektoriat narodnogo obrazovaniya okruzhnogo ispolnitel'nogo komiteta Soveta rabochikh, krest'ianskikh i krasnoarmeiskikh deputatov

[Inspector's Office of Public Education of the Executive Committee of the Council of Worker, Peasants, and the Red Army, Gomel Area], f. 633, op. 2, d. 18, l. 22, GAGO, cited in Gerasimova, "Evreiskoye obrazovaniye v Belarusi," 71.

218. Markelis-Domnin interview, USC Shoah Foundation.

219. Kurinets interview, USC Shoah Foundation.

220. See the denunciation reports of Jewish pedagogues in Selimenev and Zeltser, "The Jewish Intelligentsia," 93–95.

221. Arkadii Shulman, "Evreiskii Gorodok" [Jewish Gorodok], in *Mesto yevo uzhe ne uznaet evo* [Places That No Longer Know Them] (Minsk, Belarus: Medisont, 2007), 108.

222. Shulman, "Ostrov Relesa," 236.

223. Selimenev and Zeltser, "The Jewish Intelligentsia," 78–79.

224. Denunciation report from an agent, 11 August 1938, Tsentral'nyy komitet Kommunisticheskoi partii Belorussii, f. 4-P [Communist Party], op. 21, d. 1392, l. 38–54, NARB, translated and published in Selimenev and Zeltser, "The Jewish Intelligentsia and the Liquidation of Yiddish Schools in Belorussia, 1938," 85–86.

225. Estraikh, *In Harness*, 170.

226. H. Reles, "Fun shtetl" [From a Shtetl], *Shtern*, no. 1 (Jan. 1938): 15.

227. H. Reles, "In lazaret" [In Hospital], *Shtern*, no. 1 (Jan. 1938): 16.

228. Reles interview by Kellman, Brandeis Univ.

229. Shulman, "Ostrov Relesa," 229.

230. Hirsh Reles, *Onheyb* [Beginning] (Minsk, Belarus: Melukhe-farlag fun Vaysrusland, 1939).

231. Shulman, "Ostrov Relesa," 248.

232. "Farzamlung fun di yidishe Sovetishe shrayber fun VSSR" [Gathering of Soviet Yiddish Writers from the BSSR], *Oktyabr* (Minsk), 3 Aug. 1938.

233. Zelik Akselrod and Hirsh Kamenetsky, eds., *Ordentregerishe Vaysrusland* [Belarus, the Common Porter] (Minsk, Belarus: Melukhe-farlag fun Vaysrusland, 1939). Hirsh Reles's poems were not included in the collection.

234. O. Margolis, *Viazoy lebn Yidn in Sovetnland* [How Jews Live in the Soviet Union] (Moscow: Melukhe-farlag "Der emes," 1940), 85.

235. Reles interview by Kellman, Brandeis Univ.

236. Francine Hirsch, *Empire of Nations: Ethnographic Knowledge and the Making of the Soviet Union* (Ithaca, NY: Cornell Univ. Press, 2005), 294.

237. Davies, *Popular Opinion in Stalin's Russia*, 124.

238. Wendy Z. Goldman, *Inventing the Enemy: Denunciation and Terror in Stalin's Russia* (New York: Cambridge Univ. Press, 2011), 248.

239. Zavgorodnev interview, USC Shoah Foundation.

240. Reles, *Di yidish-sovetishe shrayber fun Vaysrusland*, 25, 105.

241. Zeltser, "Interwar Ethnic Relations and Soviet Policy," 100.

242. Z. I. Dykman, "A Guest in My Own Village," 3 Jan. 1939, Tsentral'nyy komitet Kommunisticheskoi partii Belorussii, f. 4-P [Communist Party], op. 21, d. 1392, NARB, translated and published in Viacheslav Selimenev and Arkadii Zeltser, "Kolyshki—a Shtetl in the Late 1930s," *Jews in Russia and Eastern Europe* 45, no. 2 (2001): 51.

243. Mordechai Altschuler, "The Distress of Jews in the Soviet Union in the Wake of the Molotov-Ribbentrop Pact," *Yad Vashem Studies* 36, no. 2 (2008): 76.

244. Research on the period provides contradictory answers to the Great Terror's typical effect on families. Sheila Fitzpatrick concludes that families grew somewhat closer together or were unaffected (*Everyday Stalinism*, 140). Orlando Figes asserts that the purges undermined internal family confidences (*The Whisperers: Private Life in Stalin's Russia* [New York: Metropolitan Books, 2007], 300).

245. After the Spanish Civil War erupted in 1936, *Oktyabr* readers received reports on the conflict between leftist and fascist forces in almost every issue, and by 1937 a separate column, "Af di frontn in Shpanie" [On the Spanish Front], headlined the front page.

246. "A kegngaz far kinder" [A Gas Mask for Children], *Oktyabr* (Minsk), 9 July 1935.

247. "Dos alte milkhome lid" [The Old War Song], *Oktyabr* (Minsk), 3 July 1935.

248. "Di gesheienishn in Palestine" [Events in Palestine], *Oktyabr* (Minsk), 4 Nov. 1938.

249. "Di blutiker Hitler—Premier in Daytshland" [The Bloody Hitler—Prime Minister in Germany], *Oktyabr* (Minsk), 1 Feb. 1933.

250. *Vitsebski praletarii*, 17 Nov. 1933, f. 2285, op. 2, d. 125, GAVO.

251. "Di KomPartay rufn tsu an algemaynem shtreyk kegn der fashistisher Hitler-regirung" [The Communist Party Call for a General Strike against the Fascist Hitler Government] and "Revoliutsionere protest-demonstratsies in gants Daytshland" [Revolutionary Protest Demonstrations in all of Germany], *Oktyabr* (Minsk), 2 Feb. 1933; "Kryvavaya sutychka pamizh pabochymi i natsyyanal-satsyyalistami ŭ Breslaŭli" [Crooked Clashes between Workers and National Socialists in Breslau] and "Ablavy, aryshty i katarzhnyya prysudy" [Round-ups, Arrests, and Floods of Verdicts], *Vitsebski praletarii*, 12 and 27 Apr. 1933, f. 2285, op. 2, d. 125, GAVO.

252. "Organizirter fashistisher anti-yidisher boikot" [Organized Fascist Anti-Jewish Boycott], *Oktyabr* (Minsk), 1 Apr. 1933; "Der anti-yidisher boikot viklt zikh fanander" [The Anti-Jewish Boycott Escalates], *Oktyabr* (Minsk), 2 Apr. 1933.

253. "Pratim vegn der neyer pogrom-khvalie in Daytshland" [Details about the New Pogrom Wave in Germany], *Oktyabr* (Minsk), 17 July 1935; "Di pogrom-khvalie in Daytshland doyert" [The Pogrom Wave Continues in Germany], *Oktyabr* (Minsk), 24 July 1935.

254. "Vayterdike farsharfung fun der inerlekher politisher lage in Daytshland" [Successive Intensifications of the Domestic Political Situation in Germany], *Der*

emes (Moscow), 24 July 1935, microfilm at Dorot Jewish Division, New York Public Library.

255. "Mitlalterlekhe gezetsn in Hitler-reykhstag" [Medieval Laws in Hitler's Reichstag], *Oktyabr* (Minsk), 17 Sept. 1935.

256. Harvard Project on the Soviet Social System, Schedule A, vol. 11, Case 142, p. 30, at https://iiif.lib.harvard.edu/manifests/view/drs:5228022$30i. *Oktyabr* and *Der Emes* regularly printed stories tracking Germany's rearmament. The young teacher mentioned in the text stated later in his Harvard Project interview: "Before the war, for example, there were conversations about Hitler's rearmament, about the crusade against the Soviet Union, and so forth. Since my father was in contact with Jews, he got most of his information from them."

257. "Yidishe pogromen in Daytshland" [Jewish Pogroms in Germany], *Oktyabr* (Minsk), 11 Nov. 1938.

258. "Yidishe pogromen in Daytshland."

259. "A khvalie fun yidishe pogromen in Daytshland" [A Wave of Jewish Pogroms in Germany], *Oktyabr* (Minsk), 12 Nov. 1938.

260. "Yidishe pogromen in fashistishn Daytshland" [Jewish Pogroms in Fascist Germany], *Oktyabr* (Minsk), 14 Nov. 1938; "Yidishe pogromen in Daytshland" [Jewish Pogroms in Germany], *Oktyabr* (Minsk), 15 Nov. 1938.

261. "Ayntslheytn fun di yidishe pogromen in Daytshland" [Particulars of the Jewish Pogroms in Germany], *Oktyabr* (Minsk), 15 Nov. 1938.

262. *Vitsebski praletarii* carried an article in February 1933 outlining the distribution of 900 copies of *Oktyabr* and 200 copies of *Shtern* in Vitebsk (B. Vaserman, "Vitebsk muz gebn nit vayniker vi 900 ekz. 'Oktyabr' and 200 zshurnaln 'Shtern'" [Vitebsk Must Be Given Not Fewer Than 900 Copies *Oktyabr* and 200 Journals *Shtern*], *Vitsebski praletarii*, 18 Feb. 1933, f. 2285, op. 2, d. 125, GAVO).

263. Khvat interview, USC Shoah Foundation.

264. Joseph Stalin, speech to the Politburo, 19 Aug. 1939, in *The Rise and Fall of the Soviet Union, 1917–1991*, ed. Richard Sakwa (London: Routledge, 1999), 235.

265. "Rede durkh radio fun Forsitser funem Rat fun di Folks-Comisarn fun FSSR, Khaver V. M. Molotov, dem 17th Sentiaber 1939 yor" [Radio Speech of the Chairman of the Council of the People's Commissariat of the USSR, Comrade V. M. Molotov, 17th Sept. 1939], *Shtern*, no. 9 (Sept. 1939): 1–3. *Shtern*'s editors felt the speech was significant enough to publish a Yiddish-language translation of it.

2. Responses to Exclusion and Violence

1. "L. Zh." [Lev Zhubov], "Meyn oytobiografie" [My Autobiography], 1939, no. 3554, pp. 30–32, Record Group 4, Autobiographies of Jewish Youth, box 5, YIVO. The Yidisher visnshaftlekher institut (Jewish Scientific Institute, known by the initials YIVO) was founded in Berlin in 1925 and became the leading scholarly

institution for Yiddish language and eastern European Jewish history and culture. YIVO moved its headquarters to Vilna in 1927.) YIVO organized a series of essay contests in 1932, 1934, and 1939 to study how young people coped with antisemitism and limited economic opportunities in Poland. During the same period, it established branch offices in New York and Buenos Aires (the latter known as the Fundacion IWO). New York became the organization's headquarters with the start of World War II. Some 300 of the essays surfaced in Germany after the war among YIVO's surviving Vilna archives. YIVO had guaranteed the respondents that their essays would remain anonymous. That commitment is honored here through the use of pseudonyms, either provided by the writers themselves or, as in the case with "Lev Zhubov," derived from the name inscribed on his YIVO essay.

2. Jacob Lestschinsky, "The Jews in the Cities of the Republic of Poland," in *East European Jews in Two Worlds: Studies from the YIVO Annual*, ed. Deborah Dash Moore (Evanston, IL: Northwestern Univ. Press, 1990), 113, table 5. The Grodno *kehilah* administration stated in a letter in 1938 that 25,000 Jews, or 46 percent of the total population, inhabited the city (Grodno *kehilah* administration to Bernard Herzer, 17 Jan. 1938, trans. Ania Lepak, GERO, f. 56, op. 1, d. 135, l. 75, GAGO).

3. Lestschinsky, "The Jews in the Cities of the Republic of Poland," 113.

4. Zelda (Grodzienska) Gordon, Beverly Hills, CA, 15 July 1994, interview code 15, USC Shoah Foundation.

5. Iosif Moisevich Zbar, Hrodna (Grodno), Belarus, 24 Oct. 1997, Russian language (trans. Oleg Pyshnenko and Irina Pyshnenko), interview code 50572, USC Shoah Foundation.

6. Zbar interview, USC Shoah Foundation.

7. "Oytobiografie" [Autobiography], 1934, no. 3555, p. 22, Record Group 4, box 5, YIVO.

8. "Oytobiografie fun Hanan L. in Grodne" [Autobiography of Hanan L. in Grodno], 1934, no. 3553, p. 5, Record Group 4, box 5, YIVO. Between 100 and 170 homes were reported destroyed (Louis Cohan, American Jewish Joint Distribution Committee [JDC] Warsaw, to JDC Paris, 31 July 1921; and Komitet pogorzelcow przedmiesciu Grodno [Committee of the Fire Victims in Grodno] to the Zarzad gminy Zydowskiej [Council of the Jewish Community], 21 Apr. 1922, File 408, Countries and Regions; Poland: Localities, Chomsk to Jezierzany, American Jewish Joint Distribution Committee Archives, New York(JDC Archives).

9. Anonymous autobiography ["Yankl"], 1934, no. 3556, pp. 1–3, Record Group 4, box 5, YIVO.

10. Alexandre Blumstein, *A Little House on Mount Carmel* (London: Valentine Mitchell, 2002), 2–3.

11. Grodno was located in the Białystok District after 1921, not in one of the six administrative districts of which the Kresy was composed. However, the city is

commonly considered part of the Kresy because it possessed many characteristics shared with other eastern borderland urban areas, including an endemic economic malaise and a population diversity that included Belarusians and/or Ukrainians.

12. Jacob Lestschinsky, "Der yidisher handl inem kleynem shtetl fun Poyln" [Jewish Trade in the Small Towns of Poland], *Di yidishe ekonomik* 1 (May 1937): 12, table 2. Jacob Lestschinsky (1876–1966) pioneered the economic and demographic study of eastern European Jewish life and established the economic-statistical department of YIVO. He immigrated to the United States in 1938 and then to Israel in the 1950s.

13. The sociologist Jan Gross profiles Jedwabne in *Neighbors: The Destruction of the Jewish Community in Jedwabne, Poland* (Princeton, NJ: Princeton Univ. Press, 2001), describing the massacre of the shtetl's Jewish population by their Gentile neighbors in July 1941.

14. Menachem Linder, "Der hurbn funem yidishn handl in Białystoker raion" [The Destruction of Jewish Trade in the Białystok District], *Di yidishe ekonomik* 1 (June 1937): 17, tables 2 and 3. Menachem Linder's study carefully avoids discussion of the reason for the rapid growth of Gentile-owned shops, such as government-backed low-interest loans. By avoiding criticism of official policies, he avoided government censors. Linder, born in 1911, contributed to the Oyneg Shabbes Archive in the Warsaw ghetto. He was shot by the Germans on the night of 17–18 April 1942 along with fifty-one other Jews.

15. Linder, "Der hurbn funem yidishn handl in Białystoker raion," 14.

16. Sima (Kapulska) Grozalsky, Hollywood, FL, 20 Mar. 1997, interview code 27452, USC Shoah Foundation.

17. Elka (Fomin) Ekstein, North Borwin, Victoria, Australia, 21 Oct. 1996, interview code 21518, USC Shoah Foundation; Elka Ekstein, *Chutzpe un Draystkayt: A Teenager with Chutzpah and Tenacity in the Holocaust* (Victoria, Australia: Makor Jewish Community Library, 2006), 4, 6.

18. Leo (Leib) Bialo, Lyndhurst, OH, 27 Jan. 1997, interview code 25406, USC Shoah Foundation.

19. "L. Zh.," "Meyn oytobiografie," 44–45.

20. See Ezra Mendelsohn, *The Jews of East Central Europe between the World Wars* (Bloomington: Indiana Univ. Press, 1983), 73–76; Emanuel Melzer, "Antisemitism in the Last Years of the Second Polish Republic," and Jerzy Tomaszewski, "The Role of Jews in Polish Commerce, 1918–1939," in *The Jews of Poland between Two World Wars*, ed. Yisrael Gutman, Ezra Mendelsohn, Jehuda Reinharz, and Chone Shmeruk (Hanover, NH: Univ. Press of New England, 1989), 126–37, 141–57.

21. Ann (Lewin) Lazar, [no city], CA, 6 Mar. 1997, interview code 27890, USC Shoah Foundation.

22. Bialo interview, USC Shoah Foundation.

23. Vivian Chakin (Vichna Sidranska), Los Angeles, CA, 21 Nov. 1995, interview code 7457, USC Shoah Foundation.

24. Fenia (Muller) Rantz, [no city], FL, 14 Oct. 1996, interview code 22686, USC Shoah Foundation.

25. Rita (Rivke Altshuler) Kesselman, 13 Apr. 1989, interview by Holocaust Center of the Jewish Federation of the North Shore, Peabody, MA, 1989, HVT-1432, Fortunoff Video Archive of Holocaust Testimonies, Yale Univ., New Haven, CN.

26. Bialo interview, USC Shoah Foundation.

27. In this particular instance, the attacker was caught. A policeman heard young Taub's cries for help and arrested Patignovski: "Yidisher yungerman geshlogen in gas biz blut, fun a khuligan" [Jewish Youth Beaten until Bloody in Street by a Hooligan], *Grodner moment*, 14 Nov. 1933, GERO, f. 56, op. 1, d. 82, l. 218, GAGO.

28. Yehuda (Rabinovich) Rabin, Melbourne, Australia, 4 Feb. 1997, interview code 26578, USC Shoah Foundation.

29. Daniel Klovsky, *The Road from Grodno* (Samara, Russia: n.p., 2003), 9–10.

30. Mina (Muller) Utianski, North Miami Beach, FL, 17 July 1996, interview code 17402, USC Shoah Foundation.

31. Bronia (Winicka) Klibanski, 11 Apr. 1979, interview by the Holocaust Survivors Film Project, Jerusalem, 1979, HVT-76, Fortunoff Video Archive of Holocaust Testimonies, Yale Univ.

32. Bialo interview, USC Shoah Foundation.

33. "Wykaz—Bóżnic na terenie Gminy Wyznaniowej Żydowskiej w Grodnie" [List—Synagogues within the Jewish Religious Community in Grodno], n.d. [c. 1930s], GERO, f. 56, op. 1, d. 82, l. 345 and 345 ob., GAGO.

34. Grodno Relief Association of Greater Boston to the Grodno *kehilah* administration, 20 Dec. 1938, GERO, f. 56, op. 1, d. 149, l. 88, GAGO; Grodno *kehilah* administration to United Grodner Relief, 16 Apr. 1935, GERO, f. 56, op. 1, d. 82, l. 288, GAGO; Grodno *kehilah* administration to Isidor Heller, Los Angeles, 23 Feb. 1938, GERO, f. 56, op. 1, d. 149, l. 51 ob., GAGO; Federation of Jewish Philanthropies, Altoona, PA, to the Grodno *kehilah* administration, 2 June 1937, GERO, f. 56, op. 1, d. 149, l. 36, GAGO.

35. "Berikht fun revisions komisie baym kehilah rat" [Report of the Revisions Commission of the *Kehilah* Council], n.d. [Oct. 1933], 9, GERO, f. 56, op. 1, d. 135, l. 17–41, GAGO.

36. The TOZ was established in Poland in 1921 to foster the health of Jewish children and adults.

37. JDC officials described the Jewish Orphan Asylum in Grodno as "a very big beautiful house . . . built before the war by the family J. L. Shereshewsky" and home to fifty-seven boys and thirty-eight girls at the end of 1926 (Dr. Bernhard Kahn, chairman of the European Executive Council of the JDC, Berlin, to J. C. Hyman,

JDC, New York, 23 Jan. 1927, Record Group 338a, Organizations, Jewish Orphan Asylum, Grodno, JDC Archives).

38. "Protokol fun der virtshaftlikher Komisie" [Protocol of the Economic Commission], 16 Jan. 1933, GERO, f. 56, op. 1, d. 82, l. 119–120 ob., GAGO.

39. "Kehilah farvaltung nit derlangt keyn recurs af di oysshtraykhungen iz biudzshet" [*Kehilah* Administration Has Not Reached a Conclusion on the Changes in Budget], *Grodner moment*, 7 Dec. 1937, GERO, f. 56, op. 1, d. 135, l. 170, GAGO. Grodno city government still provided a substantial grant of 40 percent for Jewish schools during the 1935–36 school year, such as the Talmud Torah school ("Protokol fun der revizie in der farshtelter shule Talmud Torah dem 21 June 1936" [Protocol of the Improvement in the Operation of the Talmud Torah School on 21 June 1936], GERO, f. 56, op. 1, d. 136, l. 33, GAGO).

40. "Shtime far der liste 4—Arbeter un folks-mentshn" [Voices for List 4—Workers and People's Representatives], campaign literature edited by L. Strupinski and printed by M. Dana, Grodno, n.d. [1936], Record Group 1400, Bund Archives, mg-2, box 1198, folder 278, YIVO.

41. "Członkowie Rady Gminy" [Members of the Community Council], n.d. [Aug. 1939], GERO, f. 56, op. 1, d. 164, l. 8 ob., GAGO.

42. Aaron Zakhari, "Grodner tipn in mayn zikorn" [Grodno Characters in My Memory], in *Grodner opklangen* [Grodno Echoes] (Buenos Aires: n.p., Sept. 1975), 36, Record Group 1400, m-14, box 586, folder 35 (Grodno), YIVO.

43. Rantz interview, USC Shoah Foundation; Utianski interview, USC Shoah Foundation.

44. Gordon interview, USC Shoah Foundation.

45. Ekstein interview, USC Shoah Foundation; Ekstein, *Chutzpe un Draystkayt*, 2.

46. Ekstein, *Chutzpe un Draystkayt*, 2–5.

47. "L. Zh.," "Meyn oytobiografie," p. 3.

48. Michael (Moishe) Kremer, Hollywood, FL, 16 Mar. 1997, interview code 27415, USC Shoah Foundation.

49. Sidney Sisun, Woodmere, NY, 8 Oct. 1996, interview code 20823, USC Shoah Foundation.

50. Chakin interview code, USC Shoah Foundation.

51. Felix [Feliks] Zandman, with David Chanoff, *Never the Last Journey* (New York: Schocken Books, 1995), 7.

52. Bella (Ilin) Shulman, Melbourne, Australia, 30 Nov. 1997, interview code 35750, USC Shoah Foundation. Bella Shulman was little more than a toddler when the war began, so her testimony provides fragmentary but significant information about her parents' and grandparents' experiences as well as her own.

53. Grozalsky interview, USC Shoah Foundation.

54. Rabin interview, USC Shoah Foundation. Berkalt, a young woman born in Białystok in 1922, explained in her YIVO autobiography that her mother successfully took her estranged husband to court to receive child support (Berkalt, "Oytobiografie" [Autobiography], 1939, no. 3534, pp. 1–3, Record Group 4, box 3, YIVO).

55. "Oytobiografie fun Hanan L. in Grodne" [Autobiography of Hanan L. in Grodno], 1934, no. 3553, pp. 5–7, Record Group 4, box 3, YIVO.

56. Anonymous autobiography ["Yankl"], 5.

57. *Cholent* is a traditional stew of meat, potatoes, beans, and barley, simmered overnight and eaten for lunch on Shabbat.

58. Leib Reizer, "Grodner bildlekh" [Grodno Images], in *Grodner opklangen*, 33.

59. Chasia Bornstein-Bielicka, with Neomi Izhar, *One of the Few: A Resistance Fighter and Educator, 1939–1947*, trans. Naftali Greenwood (Jerusalem: Yad Vashem, 2009), 31.

60. Shulman interview, USC Shoah Foundation.

61. The Grodno yeshiva Shaar Hatorah, under the guidance of Rabbi Shimon Shkop, is not discussed here because most of its students were not native to Grodno. From 300 students in 1928, the yeshiva's enrollment dropped to 200 by 1937 owing to successive budget shortfalls (Israel Davidson, Jewish Theological Seminary of America, to Dr. Cyrus Adler, JDC, 5 Dec. 1928, Record Group 354, Individual Yeshivot, Shaar Hatorah, Grodno, 1928–29, JDC Archives; Rabbi Shimon Shkop to Dr. Bernhard Kahn, JDC Paris, 9 June 1938, and "Information on European Yeshivoth," Mar. 1939, Record Group 833, Poland, Cultural and Religious, Yeshivot and Seminaries, Miscellaneous, JDC Archives).

62. Jack Jacobs, *Bundist Counterculture in Interwar Poland* (Syracuse, NY: Syracuse Univ. Press, 2009), 39.

63. This figure is based on the autobiographies and testimonies cited in this chapter.

64. Students who went to gymnasium left the elementary school after the sixth year; those who did not intend to advance their education further attended a seventh year.

65. Ekstein, *Chutzpe un Draystkayt*, 7.

66. Bialo interview, USC Shoah Foundation.

67. Rabin interview, USC Shoah Foundation. The Tsentrale yidishe shul-organizatsie was established in 1921 by Bund and Poalei Tsiyon members to create a network of secular Yiddish schools that were socialist in orientation.

68. "L. Zh.," "Meyn oytobiografie," p. 23.

69. Gordon interview, USC Shoah Foundation.

70. "Grodno: Between the World Wars," in *Lost Jewish Worlds: The Communities of Grodno, Lida, Olkieniki, Vishay*, ed. Shmuel Spector and Bracha Freundlich (Jerusalem: Yad Vashem, 1996), 61–62. Besides the Tarbut gymnasium, the secular Re'ali

gymnasium gave lessons in Polish to those fortunate Jewish youths able to continue their education ("Grodno: Between the World Wars," 65).

71. Zandman, *Never the Last Journey*, 19–20.

72. Adina Bar-El, "Tarbut," in *The YIVO Encyclopedia of Jews in Russia and Eastern Europe*, ed. Hundert, 1:1842.

73. "Oytobiografie fun Hanan L. in Grodne," p. 10.

74. "Grodno: Between the World Wars," 62.

75. Sisun interview, USC Shoah Foundation.

76. Grozalsky interview, USC Shoah Foundation.

77. "L. Zh.," "Meyn oytobiografie," 15.

78. Kremer interview, USC Shoah Foundation.

79. Anonymous autobiography ["Yankl"], 7.

80. "L. Zh.," "Meyn oytobiografie," 7.

81. Rantz interview, USC Shoah Foundation.

82. Utianski interview, USC Shoah Foundation.

83. Bornstein-Bielicka, *One of the Few*, 29.

84. Max Weinreich, *Der veg tsu undzer yugnt* [The Way to Our Youth] (Vilnius, Lithuania: Yidisher visnshaftlekher institut, 1935), 198.

85. The Polish writer and Grodno native Eliza Orzeszkowa (1841–1910) wrote several popular novels examining social conditions in western Imperial Russia, including *Meir Ezofowicz* (1878), which describes the conflict between Hasidim and Mitnagdim in the eighteenth and nineteenth centuries.

86. Blumstein, *A Little House on Mount Carmel*, 7–8.

87. Chakin interview, USC Shoah Foundation.

88. Lazar interview, USC Shoah Foundation.

89. Blumstein, *A Little House on Mount Carmel*, 9.

90. Weinreich, *Der veg tsu undzer yugnt*, 208.

91. Hannah, "Matura . . . a co dalej?" [Diploma . . . and What Then?], Akiva youth newspaper, trans. Ania Lepak, n.d. [c. 1936], GERO, f. 56, op. 1, d. 147, l. 35, GAGO.

92. Bornstein-Bielicka, *One of the Few*, 49.

93. Zandman, *Never the Last Journey*, 15.

94. Blumstein, *A Little House on Mount Carmel*, 8.

95. Bialo interview, USC Shoah Foundation.

96. This trade school had roots that predated the Russian Revolution of 1905 but functioned legally only after that date. It operated outside of Russia after the Bolshevik Revolution.

97. "Geshikhte fun der Kehilah fun ir antshtayung in 14-tn yorhundert biz der baneyter Poylisher hershaft" [History of the Community from Its Origin in the 14th Century until the Revival of Polish Rule], in *Grodne*, ed. Dov Rabin (Jerusalem: Hevrat Entsiklopedyah shel galuyot, 1973), 658.

98. "Formularz statystyczny dla seminarjów nauczycielshich rok szkolny 1935/36" [Statistical Form of Teacher's Seminar for 1935–36 School Year], GERO, Chastnaya yevreiskaya uchitel'skaya seminariya obshchestva "Tarbut" [Grodno Private Jewish Teachers' Seminary "Tarbut"], f. 219, op. 1, d. 71, l. 65 ob., GAGO.

99. "17-ter aroysloz fun der Mener-hantverker-shule" [17th Graduating Class of the Men's Craftsmen School], *Grodner moment*, 27 June 1939, microfiche BC 545, Biblioteka Narodowa, Warsaw.

100. Rabin interview, USC Shoah Foundation.

101. Rantz interview, USC Shoah Foundation.

102. Sisun interview, USC Shoah Foundation.

103. "Grodno: Between the World Wars," 43.

104. Kremer interview, USC Shoah Foundation.

105. Kremer interview, USC Shoah Foundation.

106. Mendelsohn, *The Jews of East Central Europe between the World Wars*, 79.

107. "Der yidisher yishuv in Erts-Isroel gegn di Arabishe hetses un mordn" [The Jewish Community in Palestine against Arabian Agitation and Murders], *Grodner moment*, 8 Jan. 1933, GERO, f. 56, op. 1, d. 61, l. 40, GAGO; "Moyre far naye unruen in Erts-Isroel" [Fear of New Unrest in Palestine] and "Abshteln ingantsn di alie" [Stop Entirely the Aliyah], *Grodner kurier*, 6 Nov. 1933, GERO, f. 56, op. 1, d. 82, l. 215, GAGO.

108. Bornstein-Bielicka, *One of the Few*, 54.

109. Zandman, *Never the Last Journey*, 22.

110. Utianski interview, USC Shoah Foundation.

111. Bialo interview, USC Shoah Foundation.

112. "Daytshe prese shturemt" [German Press Rages], *Grodner lebn*, 9 Nov. 1938, microfiche BC 223, Biblioteka Narodowa, Warsaw.

113. "*Eretz Yisrael* vet nit tseteylt vern" [Palestine Will Not Be Divided], *Grodner lebn*, 10 Nov. 1938, microfiche BC 223, Biblioteka Narodowa, Warsaw.

114. Kremer interview, USC Shoah Foundation.

115. Rantz interview, USC Shoah Foundation.

116. Blumstein, *A Little House on Mount Carmel*, 5. Estera Blumstein had left her parents behind in Ukraine and was unable to visit them because of the closure of the border.

117. Kh. Rasner, "Di kleyn-industri zukht naye abzats-merk" [Small Industry Searches for a New Start], *Grodner moment*, 14 Nov. 1933, GERO, f. 56, op. 1, d. 82, l. 218, GAGO.

118. Yisrael Gutman, "Youth and Resistance Movements in Historical Perspective," interview by Daniel Blatman, *Yad Vashem Studies* 23 (1993): 18.

119. "Di baneyte Poylishe hershaft" [Revived Polish Rule], in *Grodne*, ed. Rabin, 666.

120. "Di baneyte Poylishe hershaft," 669.

121. See "Di baneyte Poylishe hershaft," ed. Rabin, 674; "Grodno: Between the World Wars," 74; "Berikht fun revisions komisie baym kehilah rat," 9.

122. The historian Alina Cała has noted in her study of Polish-language YIVO youth autobiographies that joining organizations had less to do with principles than with popularity: "The joining of a party, which usually occurred as early as primary or secondary school, was seldom motivated by conscious political choice. It was decided by peer pressure or by other, non-ideological considerations" ("The Social Consciousness of Young Jews in Interwar Poland," in *Polin*, vol. 8: *Jews in Independent Poland, 1918–1939* [Portland, OR: Littman Library of Jewish Civilization, 1994], 58).

123. Batya, "Jedem rok: Urywki z pamiętnika" [One Year: Fragments of a Diary], Akiva youth newspaper, n.d. [c. 1936], trans. Ania Lepak, GERO, f. 56, op. 1, d. 147, l. 19, l. 21, l. 22, GAGO.

124. Zandman, *Never the Last Journey*, 20, 21.

125. Bialo interview, USC Shoah Foundation.

126. Rantz interview, USC Shoah Foundation; Utianski interview, USC Shoah Foundation.

127. Klibanski interview, Holocaust Survivors Film Project, Fortunoff Video Archive.

128. "L. Zh.," "Meyn oytobiografie," 15–17. The drive to collect social history was part of the movement originated by Simon Dubnow (1860–1941) and his contemporaries to remedy the imbalance in Jewish historiography, which traditionally focused on the deeds of rabbis and the wealthy. See Samuel D. Kassow, *Who Will Write Our History? Rediscovering a Hidden Archive from the Warsaw Ghetto* (New York: Vintage Books, 2009), 9.

129. "Oytobiografie fun Hanan L. in Grodne," 14–15.

130. Weinreich, *Der veg tsu undzer yugnt*, 269.

131. "A briv in redaktsie" [Letter to the Editor], *Grodner shtime*, 4 Feb. 1938, GERO, f. 56, op. 1, d. 59, l. 43 ob., GAGO.

132. Bornstein-Bielicka, *One of the Few*, 59–60.

133. Organizations that shared Zionist House/Movement House included the General Zionists and Poalei Tsiyon-Left, their associated youth organizations, the Eretz Yisrael Office for Emigration, and the Brener Library ("Grodno: Between the World Wars," 76). Chasia Bielicka recalled decades later, "The Movement House had been put together from a series of Polish apartments no longer habitable. Several interior walls had been torn down to create one cavernous space" (*One of the Few*, 57). Photographs of this meeting room are available in the archives at Yad Vashem and Bet Lohamei ha-Getta'ot (Ghetto Fighters' House). It is also described in Yankl's YIVO youth autobiography (anonymous autobiography ["Yankl"], 11).

134. Utianski interview, USC Shoah Foundation.

135. "Oytobiografie fun Hanan L. in Grodne," 16–17; anonymous autobiography ["Yankl"], 17.

136. Kremer interview, USC Shoah Foundation.

137. Kremer interview, USC Shoah Foundation.

138. *Kehilah* records in the Grodno branch of the Belarusian State Archives contain almost no items illuminating the community's response to the pogrom.

139. "Z nożem w plecach" [Stabbed in the Back], *Kurier Grodzieński*, 6 June 1935, trans. Ania Lepek, microfiche 95103, Biblioteka Narodowa, Warsaw.

140. "Der blutiger Shvues in Grodne" [The Bloody Shavuot in Grodno], *Forverts* (New York), 29 June 1935, Record Group 1400, m-14, box 586, folder 35 (Grodno), YIVO. The *Forverts* article refers to the gathering at the dance hall as a "dance class." Ann (Lewin) Lazar reported in an interview (USC Shoah Foundation) that the fight occurred at a "dancing school."

141. "Oświadczenie w sprawie ostatnich wydarzeń" [Statement on Past events], *Kurier Grodzieński*, 9 June 1935, trans. Ania Lepek, microfiche 95103, Biblioteka Narodowa, Warsaw.

142. Utianski interview, USC Shoah Foundation.

143. Mendelsohn, *The Jews of East Central Europe between the World Wars*, 69.

144. Joanna Beata Michlic, *Poland's Threatening Other: The Image of the Jew from 1880 to the Present* (Lincoln: Univ. of Nebraska Press, 2008), 116.

145. Cited in Michlic, *Poland's Threatening Other*, 116.

146. "Der blutiger Shvues in Grodne."

147. "Oświadczenie w sprawie ostatnich wydarzeń."

148. "Der blutiger Shvues in Grodne."

149. "Der blutiger Shvues in Grodne."

150. Photographs taken in the days after the pogrom illustrate that attackers targeted Jews' businesses. See photographs NY 01839–NY 01848, among others, at the JDC New York; catalog nos. 1212–24 at YIVO (New York); and catalog nos. 1366/405 and 1366/406 at Yad Vashem (Jerusalem).

151. Kremer interview, USC Shoah Foundation.

152. "Der blutiger Shvues in Grodne."

153. "Der blutiger Shvues in Grodne."

154. Klovsky, *The Road from Grodno*, 11. Klovsky does not specify if this was his memory or that of another witness.

155. Klovsky, *The Road from Grodno*, 11. Lev Zhubov wrote in his YIVO autobiography that he observed police presence only in the early morning hours ("L. Zh.," "Meyn oytobiografie," 31).

156. Bialo interview, USC Shoah Foundation.

157. Klovsky, *The Road from Grodno*, 10.

158. Utianski interview, USC Shoah Foundation; Rantz interview, USC Shoah Foundation.

159. Lazar interview, USC Shoah Foundation.

160. "Der blutiger Shvues in Grodne."

161. Batya, "Jedem rok," l. 21.

162. Rantz interview, USC Shoah Foundation.

163. Batya, "Jedem rok," l. 21.

164. "L. Zh.," "Meyn oytobiografie," 31. See also "Grodno: Between the World Wars," 47.

165. Bornstein-Bielicka, *One of the Few*, 62.

166. "Grodno: Between the World Wars," 50.

167. V. I. Krivut, *Molodyozhniye organizatsii no territorii zapadnoi Belarusi (1929–1939 gg.)* [Youth Organizations in Western Belarus (1929–1939)] (Minsk: Belarusskaya nauka, 2008), 63, 64, 158.

168. "Der blutiger Shvues in Grodne."

169. "Di baneyte Poylishe hershaft" (655) reported forty injured. "Grodno: Between the World Wars" (50) stated that "forty to fifty Jews were injured." The author of the *Forverts* article "Der blutiger Shvues in Grodne" estimated that more than fifty were injured. Writing in 1939, Lev Zhubov recalled that "tens of Jews" were injured ("L. Zh.," "Meyn oytobiografie," 32).

170. "Der blutiger Shvues in Grodne."

171. "Grodno: Between the World Wars," 50. *Kurier Grodzieński* reported on 10 June 1935: "Yesterday at 6.30 p.m. in the Jewish Hospital died Israel Berezowski (Brygidzka 13) who was beaten on the 7th of June on Batory Square" ("Pierwszą ofiarą ustawy o bestialskie" [First Victim of Bestial Act], *Kurier Grodzieński*, 10 June 1935, microfiche 95103, Biblioteka Narodowa, Warsaw, trans. Ania Lepek).

172. "Zaktualizowane liczba ofiar" [Updated Number of Victims], *Kurier Grodzieński*, 16 June 1935, microfiche 95103, Biblioteka Narodowa, Warsaw, trans. Ania Lepek.

173. "Grodno: Between the World Wars," 50.

174. "Grodno: Between the World Wars," 50.

175. United Grodner Relief to Grodno *kehilah* administration, 4 May 1936, GERO, f. 56, op. 1, d. 135, l. 79, GAGO, and 17 Feb. 1937, GERO, f. 56, op. 1, d. 149, l. 5, GAGO.

176. When United Grodner Relief again forwarded money ($8), a dispute erupted between the surviving Shapiros (Leib's siblings, three brothers and a sister) and Leib's widow. A *kehilah* representative mediated the dispute, dividing the $8 in five nearly equal portions after the money was converted to zlotys. Eight dollars

converted to 42 zlotys, 20 groshen, out of which each of the three Shapiro brothers received 8 zlotys; Leib's sister, Reizl, received 9 zlotys; and Leib's widow 9 zlotys, 20 groshen (Grodno *kehilah* administration to United Grodner Relief, 19 Apr. 1938, GERO, f. 56, op. 1, d. 149, l. 64 ob.–1. 65 ob., GAGO). In another disbursement of money in early 1939, the Shapiros received 70 zlotys (approximately $13) (United Grodner Relief to Grodno *kehilah* administration, n.d. [early 1939], GERO, f. 56, op. 1, d. 149, l. 118 ob., GAGO).

177. "L. Zh.," "Meyn oytobiografie," 32.

178. "Der blutiger Shvues in Grodne."

179. Utianski interview, USC Shoah Foundation.

180. Grozalsky interview, USC Shoah Foundation.

181. Zandman, *Never the Last Journey*, 17–18.

182. Blumstein, *A Little House on Mount Carmel*, 6.

183. By the end of 1937 in Poland, pogroms had erupted in Przytyk, Mińsk Mazowiecki, Brześć nad Bugiem, and Częstochowa (Melzer, "Antisemitism in the Last Years of the Second Polish Republic," 129).

184. The precise date of the bombing could not be determined from available documents. See Chairman and Secretary of TOZ, Grodno Department, to the Grodno *kehilah* administration, 22 Nov. 1936, and *Protokol fun der gezelshaftlekher baratung in Ved hakahal dem 29-tn November 1936* [Protocol of the Communal Conference of the *Kehilah* on 29 November 1936], GERO, f. 56, op. 1, d. 135, l. 141–44, GAGO.

185. Nearly a full year to the day after the Grodno pogrom (6 June 1936), Prime Minister Sławoj-Składkowski famously declared *owszem*—"of course"—in support of aggressive economic policies against businesses owned by Jews ("Grodno: Between the World Wars," 39; Mendelsohn, *The Jews of East Central Europe between the World Wars*, 71).

186. Mendelsohn, *The Jews of East Central Europe between the World Wars*, 73.

187. Yisrael Gutman, "Polish Antisemitism between the Wars: An Overview," in *The Jews of Poland between Two World Wars*, ed. Gutman et al., 107–8.

188. "Grodner yidishe kemfer far Poylns umophengikayt" [Grodno Jewish Fighters for Poland's Independence], *Grodner moment*, 12 Mar. 1939, microfiche BC 545, Biblioteka Narodowa, Warsaw; and "Haynt der 25-ter yortog zint dem ershtn aroysmarsh fun di legionen tsum kamf" [Today the 25th Anniversary since the First March of the Legions to Fight], *Grodner moment*, 6 Aug. 1939, GERO, f. 56, op. 1, d. 164, GAGO.

189. "Haynt letster tsaykhnungs-tog fun der 2-ter rote fun der luftshuts-halvoe" [Today Last Response Day of the 2nd Group of Air Defense Loan], *Grodner moment*, 5 June 1939; "Masn Yidn hobn nekhtn eyngetsolt in di yidishe benk di 2-te rote

fun der luftshuts-halvoe" [Many Jews Contributed Yesterday to the Jewish Group's Second Installment of the Air Defense Fund], *Grodner moment*, 6 June 1939; "Der yidisher komitet far der luftshuts-halvoe apelirt tsu der yid. bafelkerung" [The Jewish Committee for the Air Defense Fund Calls Out to the Jewish Population], *Grodner moment*, 27 June 1939; "Di yidishe bafelkerung hot fulshtendig erfilt ir glikht legabe der luftshuts-halvoe" [The Jewish Population Has Completely Fulfilled Its Obligation for the Air Defense Fund], *Grodner moment*, 9 July 1939, all microfiche BC 545, Biblioteka Narodowa, Warsaw.

190. "Vi azoy der kehilah-rat hot bashlosn tsu shenkn an eroplan far der Poylisher armey" [How the *Kehilah* Council Decided to Donate an Airplane to the Polish Army], *Grodner moment*, 6 Aug. 1939, GERO, f. 56, op. 1, d. 164, GAGO.

191. "Protokol fun zitsung fun kehilah rat dem 3-tn Avgust 1939" [Protocol of Meeting of the *Kehilah* Council on 3 August 1939], 2, GERO, f. 56, op. 1, d. 164, l. 3–4 ob., GAGO.

192. "Protokol fun zitsung fun kehilah rat dem 3-tn Avgust 1939," l. 4.

193. "Yidishe shul-kinder hobn baygeshteyert afn pulemiat" [Jewish Schoolchildren Contributed for Guns], *Grodner lebn*, 31 Oct. 1938, microfiche BC 223, Biblioteka Narodowa, Warsaw.

194. Bialo interview, USC Shoah Foundation.

195. Zandman, *Never the Last Journey*, 17. Women's political opinions are seldom recorded in the memoirs and testimonies of eyewitnesses. Women participated in Jewish political movements, although they lacked voting rights in Polish and *kehilah* elections.

196. Gutman, "Youth and Resistance Movements in Historical Perspective," 4.

197. Avraham Barkai, "Jewish Life under Persecution," in *German-Jewish History in Modern Times*, vol. 4: *Renewal and Destruction, 1918–1945*, ed. Michael A. Meyer (New York: Columbia Univ. Press, 1998), 247–48.

198. Yehuda Bauer, *The Death of the Shtetl* (New Haven, CT: Yale Univ. Press, 2009), 26.

199. Mendelsohn, *The Jews of East Central Europe between the World Wars*, 60.

200. "Kolinie fun 'TOZ'" [Colony of "TOZ"], *Grodner moment*, 13 June 1939, microfiche BC 545, Biblioteka Narodowa, Warsaw.

201. "Haynt vet shpiln muzik in shtat-gortn" [Music Will Be Played Today in the City Garden], *Grodner moment*, 17 July 1939, microfiche BC 545, Biblioteka Narodowa, Warsaw.

202. Bornstein-Bielicka, *One of the Few*, 64.

203. Bornstein-Bielicka, *One of the Few*, 19–20.

204. Gordon interview, USC Shoah Foundation.

205. Shulman interview, USC Shoah Foundation.

206. Y. H.-N., "Zumer . . ." [Summer . . .], *Grodner moment*, 15 June 1939, microfiche BC 545, Biblioteka Narodowa, Warsaw.

207. Y. H.-N., "Zumer. . . ."

3. Red Revolution in Grodno

1. Sarah Fishkin diary, 17 Sept. 1939, unaccessioned records, YIVO.

2. Simeon Osherovitch, "Togbukh fun Sarah Fishkin: Araynfir un ufklerung" [Diary of Sarah Fishkin: Introduction and Background], in *Yizkhor-bukh Rubizivitsi, derevne un svive* [Memorial Book Rubiezewicze, the Village and Surroundings], ed. Dovid Sztokfisz (Tel Aviv: n.p., 1968), 181–82.

3. Klovsky, *The Road from Grodno*, 15.

4. Lazar interview, USC Shoah Foundation.

5. Tzevi Aviram (Hershl Abramovich), "Epizodn un refleksn" [Episodes and Reflections], in *Grodner opklangen*, 19, Record Group 1400, box 586, folder 35 (Grodno), YIVO; "Der umkum fun Grodner kehilah" [The Destruction of the Grodno Community], in *Grodne*, ed. Rabin, 676.

6. Chakin interview, USC Shoah Foundation.

7. Zandman, *Never the Last Journey*, 27.

8. Kremer interview, USC Shoah Foundation.

9. Aviram, "Epizodn un refleksn," 19.

10. Zandman, *Never the Last Journey*, 27.

11. Rantz interview, USC Shoah Foundation.

12. Mikhal Rayak and Tzevi Rayak, *Khurbn Glubok, Sharkoystsene, Dunilovitsh, Postav, Droye, Kazan* [Destruction of Glubokie, Szarkowszczyzna, Dunilowicze, Postawy, Druja, and Kaziany] (Buenos Aires: n.p., 1956), 34.

13. Gordon interview, USC Shoah Foundation.

14. Utianski interview, USC Shoah Foundation; Rantz interview, USC Shoah Foundation.

15. Berachah (Friedman) Barabik, "Gviet adot" [Testimony], in *Sefer Sokolkah: Dos bukh fun Sokolke* [Book of Sokolka], ed. Ester Miszkinski, David Yardeni, Ben-Zion Hasid, and Yekutiel Chinski (Jerusalem: n.p., 1968), 526.

16. Bornstein-Bielicka, *One of the Few*, 73–74.

17. Lazar interview, USC Shoah Foundation.

18. Kremer interview, USC Shoah Foundation.

19. Leah Katzenlenberg, "Af dem vaynt mayn hartz" [From the Cry of My heart], in *Disnah: Sefer zikaron li-kehilah* [Disna: Memorial Book of the Community], ed. Dov Bernsthayn (Shalom Tsirlin) (Tel Aviv: Irgun yotśe Disnah be-Yiśráel uve-Ar. ha-B., 1969), 141–42.

20. Rabin interview, USC Shoah Foundation.

21. Josef Shapiro, "In geto Dokshitz" [In Dokshitzy Ghetto], in *Sefer-Yizkor Dokshitz-Parafyanov* [Memorial Book Dokshitzy-Parafianow] (Tel Aviv: n.p., 1970), 210.

22. Aviram, "Epizodn un refleksn," 19.

23. Zandman, *Never the Last Journey*, 28.

24. Jan Siemiński, *Grodno Walczące: Wspomnienia harcerza* [Grodno Fighters: Memories of Scouts] (Białystok, Poland: Towarystwo Literackie im. Adam Mickiewicza, Oddział Białstocki, 1992), 51.

25. Quoted in Jerzy Jadeszko, "Obrona Grodna we wrześniu 1939 roku" [Grodno Defense in September 1939], in *Agresja sowiecka 17 września 1939 roku na Kresach Wschodnich i Lubelszczyźnie* [Soviet Aggression 17 September 1939 in the Eastern Borderlands and the Lublin Region], vol. 1, ed. Tomasza Rodziewicza (Lublin, Poland: Towarzystwo przyjaciół Grodna i Wilna, 2011), 71–72.

26. "Der umkum fun Grodner kehilah," 677.

27. "Grodno under Soviet Rule," in *Lost Jewish Worlds*, ed. Spector and Freundlich, 88.

28. Dovid Berezovski to Jacob Mogil, 17 Nov. 1939, *Grodner veker* (Mar. 1940), 1, Record Group 996, United Grodner Relief, box 1, YIVO.

29. Klovsky, *The Road from Grodno*, 17.

30. Bornstein-Bielicka, *One of the Few*, 75.

31. Bialo interview, USC Shoah Foundation.

32. Berezovski to Mogil, 17 Nov. 1939.

33. Tadeusz Piotrowski, *Poland's Holocaust: Ethnic Strife, Collaboration with Occupying Forces, and Genocide in the Second Republic, 1918–1947* (Jefferson, NC: McFarland, 1998), 145.

34. Quoted in Piotrowski, *Poland's Holocaust*, 145.

35. Piotrowski, *Poland's Holocaust*, 145–46.

36. "Pamyatka ocherednyye voprosy raboty na 18-ye sentyabrya 1939 goda" [Memorandum of Immediate Questions for Work on 18 September 1939], 18 Sept. 1939, Fondi mestnikh organov Kommunisticheskoi partii Belorussii, Gorodskiye komiteti KPb, Glubokskii [Records of Local Communist Party Organizations of Belarus, Glubokie], f. 7045-P, op. 1a, d. 2, l. 15, GAVO.

37. Lazar interview, USC Shoah Foundation.

38. Aviram, "Epizodn un refleksn," 19.

39. Chakin interview, USC Shoah Foundation.

40. Kremer interview, USC Shoah Foundation.

41. "Ukaz prezediuma verkhovnogo soveta BSSR, O natsionalizatsii promishlennikh predpriyati i uchpezhdenii na territorii zapadnikh oblastei BSSR" [Decree from the Supreme Presidium of Soviets of the BSSR, Concerning Nationalization of Industrial Enterprises and Establishments on the Territory of the Western Oblasts of the BSSR], n.d. [c. Nov. 1939], Ispolnitel'nyi komitet Belostokskogo gorodskogo

Soveta deputatov trudiashchikhsia, g. Belostok [Executive Committee, Białystok Municipal Council of Workers Deputies, f. 292, op. 1, d. 1, l. 1–3, GAGO.

42. Blumstein, *A Little House on Mount Carmel*, 15.

43. Chakin interview, USC Shoah Foundation.

44. "Postanovlenie no. 672, O munitsipalizatsii i natsionalizatsii stroyenii na territorii zapadnikh BSSR" [Order no. 672, on the Municipalization and Nationalization of Buildings on the Territory of Western Belarusian Soviet Socialist Republic], 10 May 1940, f. 292, op. 1, d. 10, l. 7 and 7 ob., GAGO.

45. Aviram, "Epizodn un refleksn," 19.

46. Shulman interview, USC Shoah Foundation.

47. Bornstein-Bielicka, *One of the Few*, 81, 85.

48. "Agreement between the Government of the USSR . . . and the American Society for Jewish Farm Settlement in the USSR," July 1938, Record Group 358, Joseph A. Rosen Papers, box 1, folder 9, YIVO. The Agro-Joint was established in 1924 primarily to subsidize Soviet efforts to turn urban Jews into farmers; the organization also funded clinics and technical schools (Michael Beizer, "American Jewish Joint Distribution Committee," trans. I. Michael Aronson, in *The YIVO Encyclopedia of Jews in Eastern Europe*, ed. Hundert, 1:41–42). For an examination of the fate of Agro-Joint employees during the purges in the 1930s, see Mikhail Mitsel, "The Final Chapter: Agro-Joint Workers—Victims of the Great Terror in the USSR, 1937–40," *East European Jewish Affairs* 39, no. 1 (Apr. 2009): 79–99.

49. Avraham Zak, *Knekht zenen mir geven* [We Were Slaves], 2 vols. (Buenos Aires: Tsentral farband fun Poylishe Yidn in Argentine, 1956), 1:79.

50. "Grodno under Soviet Rule," 99. Noakh Bass, a Zionist, was eventually released but was rearrested on 19 June 1941; his deportation train was destroyed by German bombs in the first days of the German invasion. The fate of Leib Shifres, a Bundist, is unknown.

51. "Der umkum fun Grodner kehilah," 677–78; "Grodno under Soviet Rule," 92.

52. Chakin interview, USC Shoah Foundation.

53. Bornstein-Bielicka, *One of the Few*, 85.

54. Shalom Cholawsky, *The Jews of Bielorussia during World War II* (Amsterdam: Harwood Academic, 1998), xxvi.

55. "Grodno under Soviet Rule," 99.

56. Bornstein-Bielicka, *One of the Few*, 80.

57. "Der pleytim-komitet apelirt tsu der yidisher bafelkerung vegn brengen teykef betgevant" [The Refugee Committee Calls on the Jewish Population to Bring Bedding Immediately], *Grodner moment*, 24 July 1939, microfiche BC 545, Biblioteka Narodowa, Warsaw. The number rose to sixteen refugees by August 1939 ("List of 110 Centers at Which Refugees Are Staying," 8 Aug. 1939, File 874, Reports and Memos on Refugee Problems in Poland, 1934, 1937–39, JDC Archives.

58. Lucien Feigenbaum, White Plains, New York, 11 June 1996, interview code 16030, USC Shoah Foundation.

59. Ruth (Rozalia Herbshteyn) Hollander, Phoenix, AZ, 6 Jan. 1996, interview code 33260, USC Shoah Foundation.

60. Joseph Ceder, Far Rockaway, NY, 12 May 1996, interview code 15128, USC Shoah Foundation.

61. Dora (Blum) Huze, Melbourne, Australia, 13 June 1997, interview code 32477, USC Shoah Foundation.

62. Liliana (Goldsopl) Paczynski, Ottawa, Canada, 25 Sept. 1996, interview code 20082, USC Shoah Foundation.

63. Ceder interview, USC Shoah Foundation.

64. Huze interview, USC Shoah Foundation.

65. Ceder interview, USC Shoah Foundation.

66. Huze interview, USC Shoah Foundation.

67. Ceder interview, USC Shoah Foundation.

68. Hollander interview, USC Shoah Foundation.

69. Paczynski interview, USC Shoah Foundation.

70. Ceder interview, USC Shoah Foundation.

71. "Grodno under Soviet Rule," 105.

72. Branches of the Komitet pomoshchi bezhenstam (Kompobez, Committee to Help Refugees) were set up across the Kresy during the last months of 1939 ("Grodno under Soviet Rule," 105).

73. "Protocol no. 22, Zasedaniya vremennovo upravleniya goroda Belostoka" [Meeting Minutes, Session of the Provisional Administration of the City of Białystok], 25 Oct. 1939, f. 292, op. 1, d. 32, l. 17, GAGO.

74. Gordon interview, USC Shoah Foundation.

75. Bornstein-Bielicka, *One of the Few*, 88.

76. Hollander interview, USC Shoah Foundation.

77. Paczynski interview, USC Shoah Foundation.

78. Blumstein, *A Little House on Mount Carmel*, 12.

79. Ceder interview, USC Shoah Foundation.

80. Huze interview, USC Shoah Foundation.

81. Bornstein-Bielicka, *One of the Few*, 83.

82. Zandman, *Never the Last Journey*, 30.

83. Zak, *Knekht zenen mir geven*, 1:196. Avraham (Avrom) Zak (born in Amdur, Belarus, in 1891) was a Yiddish poet, writer, and journalist from the Grodno area who moved to Warsaw in 1919. When he fled to Soviet-occupied territory in 1939, he left behind a wife and children, who did not survive the Holocaust. His memoirs, *Knekht zenen mir geven* and *Oyf shlakhn fun hefker* (On the Road of Abandonment) (Buenos Aires: Farlag Yidnbukh, 1958) chronicle his life on Soviet territory. He returned to

Poland in 1946 and immigrated to Argentina in 1952. Zak died in Buenos Aires in 1980 (Mikhail Krutikov, with Khayim Beider, "Yiddish Writers: Avrom Zak," in *The YIVO Encyclopedia of Jews in Eastern Europe*, ed. Hundert, 2:2083).

84. Kremer interview, USC Shoah Foundation.

85. "Material k otchetu gorkoma KP (b), Sostoyanie narodnovo obrazovaniya na 20/III 1940" [Matters to Report to the City Commissariat Communist Party (Bolshevik), Condition of People's Education on 20 Mar. 1940], 1–2, file 2853, Record Group M.41, Archives in Belarus, Yad Vashem, document originals held in the Communist Party Archive branch in Hrodna (Grodno), Belarus.

86. "Fakul'turnom stroi'tel'stve" [Academic Development], n.d. [c. late 1940], file 2862, Record Group M.41, Yad Vashem, document originals held in the Communist Party Archive branch in Hrodna (Grodno), Belarus; "Doklad na obshchegorodskom sobranii intelligentsia goroda, posvyashchenny vyboram v mestnye organy vlasti Grodno" [Report in the Municipal Meeting of the City's Intelligentsia, Initially Elected to the Organs of Power in Grodno], 31 Oct. 1940, 10, file 2862, Record Group M.41, Yad Vashem, document originals held in the Communist Party Archive branch in Hrodna (Grodno), Belarus.

87. "Material k otchetu gorkoma KP (b), Sostoyanie narodnovo obrazovaniya na 20/III 1940," 1.

88. Zandman, *Never the Last Journey*, 30.

89. Bornstein-Bielicka, *One of the Few*, 81.

90. Bornstein-Bielicka, *One of the Few*, 92.

91. Rabin interview, USC Shoah Foundation.

92. Blumstein, *A Little House on Mount Carmel*, 14.

93. Zak, *Knekht zenen mir geven*, 1:81–82. Zak wrote that Shapiro was a shoemaker from Minsk, but it is more likely that he was an official with the Belarusian Commissariat of Enlightenment and had formerly worked in that trade.

94. Zandman, *Never the Last Journey*, 29.

95. Zak, *Knekht zenen mir geven*, 1:79–80.

96. "Postanovlenie, Biuro belostokskogo OBKOMA KP (b) Belorussii, O ispolnenii Belostokskom gorkomom KP (b) B" [Resolution, Office of Białystok Regional Committee of the Belarusian Communist Party (Bolshevik), on the Realization of the Białystok City Committee of the Belarusian Communist Party (Bolshevik)], 28 Nov. 1940, file 2851, Record Group M.41, Yad Vashem, document originals held in the Communist Party Archive branch in Hrodna (Grodno), Belarus.

97. Shulman, "Ostrov Relesa," 247.

98. Zandman, *Never the Last Journey*, 30.

99. Lazar interview, USC Shoah Foundation.

100. Bornstein-Bielicka, *One of the Few*, 93.

101. "Doklad na obshchegorodskom sobranii intelligentsia goroda," 11.

102. Zak, *Knekht zenen mir geven*, 1:82.

103. "Material k otchetu gorkoma KP (b), Sostoyanie narodnovo obrazovaniya na 20/III 1940," 3.

104. "Fakul'turnom stroi'tel'stve."

105. "Postanovlenie, Biuro Belostokskogo OBKOMA KP (b) Belorussii, O faktakh izvrasheniya Leninsko-Stalinskom natsional'noi politiki v shkol'nom stroitel'stve" [Resolution, Office of Białystok Regional Committee of the Belarusian Communist Party (Bolshevik), on the Factual Distortion of Lenin–Stalin Nationality Politics in School Development], 11 Oct. 1940, file 2851, Record Group M.41, Yad Vashem, document originals held in the Communist Party Archive branch in Hrodna (Grodno), Belarus.

106. "Postanovlenie, Biuro Belostokskogo OBKOMA KP (b) Belorussii, O perevode Pol'skikh i Yevreiskikh shkol v Russkie i Belorusskie v Sopotskinskom, Dombrovskom, i Belostokskom raionom" [Resolution, Office of Białystok Regional Committee of the Belarusian Communist Party (Bolshevik), on the Transfer of Polish and Jewish Schools to Russian and Belarusian in Sopotskin, Dombrov, and Białystok Raions], 27 Sept. 1940, file 2851, Record Group M.41, Yad Vashem, document originals held in the Communist Party Archive branch in Hrodna (Grodno), Belarus.

107. "Grodno under Soviet Rule," 94.

108. Bornstein-Bielicka, *One of the Few*, 92.

109. "Der umkum fun Grodner kehilah," 677.

110. Zak, *Knekht zenen mir geven*, 83.

111. Klovsky, *The Road from Grodno*, 17.

112. Zandman, *Never the Last Journey*, 29.

113. "Postanovlenie TsK KP (b) Belorussii, O sozdanii Pionerskikh organizatsii v novykh oblastyakh BSSR" [Resolution of the Central Committee of the Belarusian Communist Party, on the Creation of Pioneer Organizations in the New Oblasts of the BSSR], 11 Dec. 1939, f. 7045-P, op. 1a, d. 2, l. 15, GAVO.

114. Y. Fradlin, "Pinsker Yidishe Mitlshul Num. 5" [Pinsker Jewish Middle School No. 5], *Oktyabr* (Minsk), 2 Feb. 1941.

115. Klovsky, *The Road from Grodno*, 18.

116. Blumstein, *A Little House on Mount Carmel*, 18.

117. Bornstein-Bielicka, *One of the Few*, 95.

118. "Grodno under Soviet Rule," 100.

119. Bornstein-Bielicka, *One of the Few*, 90.

120. Bornstein-Bielicka, *One of the Few*, 92, 94, 95.

121. "Ukaz prezediuma verkhovnogo soveta BSSR"; "Shto proiskhodilo v promishlennosti" [What Happened in Industry], n.d. [c. mid-1940], file 2862, Record Group M.41, Yad Vashem, document originals held in the Communist Party Archive branch in Hrodna (Grodno), Belarus.

122. "Doklad na obshchegorodskom sobranii intelligentsia goroda," 3.

123. "Doklad na obshchegorodskom sobranii intelligentsia goroda," 7.

124. "Spisok, Rabochikh i sluzhashchikh tabachnoi fabriki g. Grodno" [List of Workers and Employees in Tobacco Factory, Grodno], n.d. [c. 1940], file 2863, Record Group M.41, Yad Vashem, document originals held in the Communist Party Archive branch in Hrodna (Grodno), Belarus. Most factory directors were full or candidate party members brought in from eastern Belarus and primarily of Belarusian or Russian nationality. Out of twenty-five factory directors, only six were Jews and one a Pole ("Spisok direktorov predpruyatii g. Grodno na 25-e yanvarya 1941 g." [List of Directors of Enterprises in Grodno on 25 January 1941], file 2863, Record Group M.41, Yad Vashem, document originals held in the Communist Party Archive branch in Hrodna (Grodno), Belarus.

125. The Soviet Citizenship Law was extended to the newly acquired territories formerly in eastern Poland on 29 November 1939, and all those residing in "western Ukraine" as of 1 November 1939 and "western Belarus" on 2 November 1939 were eligible. These were the dates when the newly constituted People's Assemblies in each region voted to approve unification with the Soviet Union.

126. Bialo interview, USC Shoah Foundation.

127. Bialo interview, USC Shoah Foundation.

128. Gordon interview, USC Shoah Foundation.

129. Grozalsky interview, USC Shoah Foundation.

130. Ekstein, *Chutzpe un Draystkayt*, 9.

131. "Grodno under Soviet Rule," 101.

132. Klovsky, *The Road from Grodno*, 18.

133. Aviram, "Epizodn un refleksn," 20.

134. Berezovski to Mogil, 17 Nov. 1939.

135. Employees lists in the files of the Executive Committee, c. late 1939 and early 1940, f. 292, op. 1, d. 31 and d. 32, GAGO. Percentages varied between departments, with some employing Jews in higher numbers and others not at all. Exact figures are not easily discerned, however, because nationality was not always noted. In such cases, I identified Jews based on their names.

136. [List of Employees from Industrial Department, Białystok] (orig. title not given), f. 292, op. 1, d. 32, l. 56 and 56 ob., GAGO.

137. Zandman, *Never the Last Journey*, 29.

138. "Grodno under Soviet Rule," 89.

139. Barabik, "Gviet adot," 527.

140. Ceder interview, USC Shoah Foundation.

141. Bornstein-Bielicka, *One of the Few*, 88.

142. "Grodno under Soviet Rule," 105.

143. "Grodno under Soviet Rule," 106.

144. Huze interview, USC Shoah Foundation.

145. "Grodno under Soviet Rule," 102.

146. "Grodno under Soviet Rule," 103.

147. Bornstein-Bielicka, *One of the Few*, 83.

148. Kremer interview, USC Shoah Foundation.

149. "Grodno under Soviet Rule," 91.

150. Bornstein-Bielicka, *One of the Few*, 83.

151. Klovsky, *The Road from Grodno*, 17.

152. Sisun interview, USC Shoah Foundation.

153. Zandman, *Never the Last Journey*, 28; Kremer interview, USC Shoah Foundation; Sisun interview, USC Shoah Foundation.

154. G. Goldshmit, "Dos shtetl Indur" [The Shtetl Indura], *Oktyabr* (Minsk), 1 Jan. 1941.

155. Zandman, *Never the Last Journey*, 29.

156. [Register of Members of the Communist Party (Bolshevik) of Belarus Transferred to Glubokie] (orig. title not given), n.d. [c. 1940], f. 7045-P, op. 1a, d. 8, GAVO; [List of Party Personnel Records in Dokshitzy] (orig. title not given), n.d. [c. 1940], Kommunisticheskoi partii Belorussii, Gorodskiye komiteti KPb; Dokshytsy [Records of Local Communist Party Organizations of Belarus, Dokshitzy], f. 7046-P, op. 1a, d. 10, GAVO; [Curriculum Vita of Personnel Sent to Western Belarus] (orig. title not given), n.d. [c. 1939 and 1940], Fondi mestnikh organov Kommunisticheskoi partii Belorussii, Gorodskiye komiteti KPb, Vitebskii [Records of Local Communist Party Organizations of Belarus, Vitebsk], f. 102-P, op. 1, d. 595, GAVO.

157. Protko, *Stanovleniye sovetskoi totalitarnoi sistemy v Belarusi*, 600–601.

158. Zandman, *Never the Last Journey*, 29.

159. Bornstein-Bielicka, *One of the Few*, 90.

160. Bornstein-Bielicka, *One of the Few*, 86.

161. Chaika Grossman, *The Underground Army: Fighters of the Białystok Ghetto*, ed. Sol Lewis, trans. Shmuel Beeri (New York: Holocaust Library, 1987), 5.

162. Zak, *Knekht zenen mir geven*, 1:191.

4. Faith in Soviet Security

1. Reles, *Di yidish-sovetishe shrayber fun Vaysrusland*, 128.

2. Zak, *Knekht zenen mir geven*, 1:74.

3. Zak, *Knekht zenen mir geven*, 76.

4. Blumstein, *A Little House on Mount Carmel*, 16.

5. Zak, *Knekht zenen mir geven*, 1:74–75.

6. Władysław Krupa, "Osada Budowla, District Grodno," in *Stalin's Ethnic Cleansing in Eastern Poland: Tales of the Deported, 1940–1946*, ed. Teresa Jeśmanowa (London: Association of the Families of the Borderland Settlers, 2000), 731–32.

7. NKVD major Lavrentii Tsanava, Minsk, to People's Commissar of Internal Affairs Lavrentii Beria, Moscow, telegram, 11 Feb. 1940, Situation Report no. 6 NKVD of BSSR to evict settlers and foresters, in *Deportation of Polish Citizens from Western Ukraine and Western Belarus in the Year 1940* (Moscow: Federal Security Service of the Russian Federation, Ministry of Internal Affairs; Warsaw: Republic of Poland Institute of National Remembrance, Commission for Prosecution of Crimes against the Polish Nation, 2003), 27.

8. Tadeusz Piotrowski, introduction to *The Polish Deportees of World War II: Recollections of Removal to the Soviet Union and Dispersal throughout the World*, ed. Tadeusz Piotrowski (Jefferson, NC: McFarland, 2004), 4.

9. Katherine R. Jolluck, *Exile and Identity: Polish Women in the Soviet Union during World War II* (Pittsburgh: Univ. of Pittsburgh Press, 2002), 6.

10. Jan Malanowski, "Sociological Aspects of the Annexation of Poland's Eastern Provinces to the USSR in 1939–41," in *The Soviet Takeover of the Polish Eastern Provinces, 1939–41*, ed. Keith Sword (New York: St. Martin's Press, 1991), 79.

11. Zandman, *Never the Last Journey*, 31.

12. Zandman, *Never the Last Journey*, 31–32.

13. Paczynski interview, USC Shoah Foundation.

14. Sara Bender, *The Jews of Białystok during World War II and the Holocaust*, trans. Yaffa Murciano (Lebanon, NH: Brandeis Univ. Press, 2008), 54; Ben-Cion Pinchuk, "Jewish Refugees in Soviet Poland, 1939–1941," *Jewish Social Studies* 40, no. 2 (Spring 1978): 150.

15. Zak, *Knekht zenen mir geven*, 1:77.

16. Bender, *The Jews of Białystok*, 55.

17. Ceder interview, USC Shoah Foundation.

18. Jolluck, *Exile and Identity*, 15.

19. Max (Markiewitz) Martel, Los Angeles, CA, 7 Feb. 1995, interview code 817, USC Shoah Foundation. Max Martel was released in 1942 and later immigrated to the United States.

20. Hollander interview, USC Shoah Foundation.

21. Huze interview, USC Shoah Foundation. The Huzes were released with other amnestied Poles in the second half of 1941. They migrated first to Uzbekistan and then to Kyrgyzstan, a route that many released Polish citizens followed. After the war, the couple returned to Łódź and subsequently emigrated from Poland to Australia (Huze interview, USC Shoah Foundation).

22. Jan T. Gross, *Revolution from Abroad: The Soviet Conquest of Poland's Western Ukraine and Western Belorussia*, exp. ed. (Princeton, NJ: Princeton Univ. Press, 2002), 193.

23. Jolluck, *Exile and Identity*, 15.

24. Z. S. Siemaszko, "The Mass Deportations of the Polish Population to the USSR, 1940–1941," in *The Soviet Takeover of the Polish Eastern Provinces, 1939–41*, ed.

Sword, 217. These figures do not include Polish army POWs, civilians convicted of crimes under Soviet law, or other categories of politically repressed individuals and groups, which account for nearly another 450,000 people (Siemaszko, "The Mass Deportations of the Polish Population," 217–18).

25. Chakin interview, USC Shoah Foundation.

26. Lazar interview, USC Shoah Foundation.

27. Paczynski interview, USC Shoah Foundation.

28. Zandman, *Never the Last Journey*, 31–32.

29. Bornstein-Bielicka, *One of the Few*, 86.

30. Blumstein, *A Little House on Mount Carmel*, 18.

31. "Vos vet gebn oystrikenen di sumpn der sotsialistisher landvirtshaft tsum 1947 yor?" [What Will Yield from the Drainage of the Swamps under Socialist Agriculture toward the Year 1947?], *Oktyabr* (Minsk), 28 Mar. 1941.

32. Jews were not the only targets of cultural propaganda; authorities initially allowed Lvov to become a center for Polish culture. This was unusual, considering the suppression of Polish identity just a few years earlier in the western Soviet borderlands (Bogdan Czaykowski, "Soviet Policies in the Literary Sphere: Their Effects and Implications," in *The Soviet Takeover of the Polish Eastern Provinces*, ed. Sword, 105–6).

33. "Rekomendirt Yidishe shrayber tsu der Stalin-premie" [Nominations of Yiddish Writers for the Stalin Prize], *Oktyabr* (Minsk), 1 Jan. 1941.

34. Pinchuk, "Jewish Refugees in Soviet Poland," 148; Moishe Grosman, *In farkishuftn land fun legendarn Dzshugashvili: Mayne zibn yor lebn in Ratnfarband, 1939–1946* [In the Enchanted Land of the Legendary Jugashvili: My Seven Years in the Soviet Union] (Paris: Emes un Frayhayt, 1950), 46; Sheyne Miriam Broderzon, *Mayn laydns-veg mit Moishe Broderzon: Di milkhome hot gedoiert far undz zibetsn yor* [My Road of Suffering with Moishe Broderzon: For Us the War Lasted Seventeen Years] (Buenos Aires: Tsentral-farband fun Poilishe Yidn in Argentine, 1960), 26.

35. Ioffe, "Patriarkh evreiskoi literaturi v Belarusi," 5; Reles interview by Kellman, Brandeis Univ.

36. Broderzon, *Mayn laydns-veg mit Moishe Broderzon*, 26. The Broderzons successfully fled Białystok during the German invasion in June 1941 and settled in central Asia. In 1944, they relocated to Moscow, where Moishe Broderzon taught at the drama school of the state Yiddish theater. He was arrested during the postwar suppression of Jewish culture and sentenced to ten years in a labor camp. When he was released in September 1955, the Broderzons returned to Warsaw, where Moishe died in June 1956. Sheyne Miriam Broderzon left Poland thereafter.

37. Grosman, *In farkishuftn land fun legendarn Dzshugashvili*, 46, 47.

38. Broderzon, *Mayn laydns-veg mit Moishe Broderzon*, 26.

39. Broderzon, *Mayn laydns-veg mit Moishe Broderzon*, 25–26.

40. David Lederman, *Fun yener zayt forhang* [From Those Times Past] (Buenos Aires: Tsentral-farband fun Poylishe Yidn in Argentine, 1960), 126.

41. Gross, *Revolution from Abroad*, 206n. Gross's source for this information was Hirsh Smolar (1905–93), secretary of the Jewish section of the Belarusian Writers' Union in Białystok and later a leader in the Minsk ghetto resistance.

42. Grosman, *In farkishuftn land fun legendarn Dzshugashvili*, 26–27.

43. Broderzon, *Mayn laydns-veg mit Moishe Broderzon*, 28.

44. Reles, *Di yidish-sovetishe shrayber fun Vaysrusland*, 47. Eli Kahan and Hirsh Berezkin, mentioned in chapter 1, were arrested with Akselrod.

45. Zeltser, *Evrei sovetskoi provintsii*, 152. Soviet census data from 1939 lists 77,173 Jews in the Vitebsk oblast, 89.3 percent of whom lived in urban areas (cited in Zeltser, *Evrei sovetskoi provintsii*, 152).

46. Elias Rubinstein, Melbourne, Australia, 5 Oct. 1997, interview code 35876, USC Shoah Foundation.

47. Grosman, *In farkishuftn land fun legendarn Dzshugashvili*, 27–28.

48. Feigenbaum interview, USC Shoah Foundation. Lucien Feigenbaum's time in Vitebsk was short. Three months after his arrival, he was deported to a gulag in the Kotlas region of the Arkhangelsk Oblast. With the release of Polish prisoners in late 1941, he migrated to Samarkand in Uzbekistan. Feigenbaum made his way to the West after the war, obtaining a visa for Switzerland and from there immigrating to South Africa.

49. Alexander Dimant, Vancouver, BC, Canada, 4 Dec. 1996, interview code 24025, USC Shoah Foundation. Dimant later worked as a metal fabricator in Makhachkala on the western shore of the Caspian Sea. At the end of the war, he migrated from Poland to Canada.

50. Feigenbaum interview, USC Shoah Foundation.

51. Kurinets interview, USC Shoah Foundation.

52. Raisa (Gendelev) Gringauz, Casper, WY, 10 Mar. 2000, interview code 50727, USC Shoah Foundation. Raisa recalled that the Yiddish schools in Leningrad closed around 1939—or she did not remember the few that still may have remained in the city thereafter.

53. Hanna Davidson Pankowsky, *East of the Storm: Outrunning the Holocaust in Russia* (Lubbock: Texas Tech Univ. Press, 1999), 46.

54. Rubinstein interview, USC Shoah Foundation; Feigenbaum interview, USC Shoah Foundation; Kurinets interview, USC Shoah Foundation.

55. Pankowsky, *East of the Storm*, 40–41.

56. Harvard Project on the Soviet Social System, schedule A, vol. 1, case 9, p. 83, at http://pds.lib.harvard.edu/pds/view/5040837?n=86.

57. Harvard Project on the Soviet Social System, schedule A, vol. 4, case 46, p. 15, at http://pds.lib.harvard.edu/pds/view/5155966?n=15.

58. Harvard Project on the Soviet Social System, schedule A, vol. 23, case 468, p. 6, at http://pds.lib.harvard.edu/pds/view/5357625?n=6.

59. "Dos yor 1941" [The Year 1941], *Oktyabr* (Minsk), 1 Jan. 1941. In October 1939, the Soviets forced mutual-aid and trade agreements, including permission to establish Red Army bases in Estonia, Latvia, and Lithuania. These three nations fell with barely a shot fired in June 1940 as the Soviets imposed Soviet-style governments in Tallinn, Riga, and Kaunas. The same pattern emerged there as had occurred in western Belarus and western Ukraine the previous year: newly elected and Communist-only "People's Assemblies" approved requests for annexation. By early August 1940, three new republics officially joined the Soviet Union. Concurrent with the final seizure of the Baltic states, the Soviets demanded of Romania the cession of Bessarabia and Northern Bukovina. The former subsequently became the Moldavian Soviet Socialist Republic, and the latter was annexed by the Ukrainian SSR.

60. Chris Bellamy, *Absolute War: Soviet Russia in the Second World War* (New York: Vintage Books, 2007), 78.

61. Harvard Project on the Soviet Social System, schedule A, vol. 4, case 46, p. 14, at http://pds.lib.harvard.edu/pds/view/5155966?n=14.

62. Gringauz interview, USC Shoah Foundation.

63. Markelis-Domnin interview, USC Shoah Foundation.

64. Dimant interview, USC Shoah Foundation.

65. Albert Weeks, *Stalin's Other War: Soviet Grand Strategy, 1939–1941* (Lanham, MD: Rowman and Littlefield, 2002), 85.

66. Timothy Johnston, *Being Soviet: Identity, Rumour, and Everyday Life under Stalin, 1939–1953* (New York: Oxford Univ. Press, 2011), 7.

67. "Unutrypalitychnaye stanovishcha va Frantsyi" [Internal Situation in France], *Chyrvonaya zvyazda* (Vitebsk), 22 Aug. 1940, f. 2289, op. 2, d. 131, GAVO.

68. Johnston, *Being Soviet*, 9.

69. "Angla-Germanskaya vaina—Germanskiya pavedamlenni" [Anglo-German War—German Reports], *Vitsebski rabochy* (Vitebsk), 7 Sept. 1940, f. 2289, op. 2, d. 132, GAVO.

70. "Tsvishnfelkerlekher iberzikht" [Cooperation between Peoples], *Oktyabr* (Minsk), 29 Mar. 1941.

71. "Di milkhome in Eyrope un in Afrike" [The War in Europe and Africa], "Amerikaner korespondentn vegn Marshals aroystretung" [American Correspondents on Marshal's News Conference], "Shiler vern tsugetsoygn tsu landvirtshaftlekhe arbetn in England" [Students Sought for Agricultural Work in England], "Fargreserung fun di Englishe luft-kreftn" [Increases in English Air Power], "Amerikaner bombardirer vern aribergevorfn in Singapur" [American Bombers Used against Singapore], "Produktsie fun di Frantsoyzishe konservn-zavodn far der

Daytshisher armey" [Production from French Canned-Goods Factories for the German army], *Oktyabr* (Minsk), 23 Feb. 1941.

72. Harvard Project on the Soviet Social System, schedule A, vol. 34, case 380/(NY) 1460, p. 46, at http://pds.lib.harvard.edu/pds/view/5605044?n=46. The Belarusian man was thirty-two at the time of his interview in 1951.

73. Malanowski, "Sociological Aspects of the Annexation of Poland's Eastern Provinces," 82.

74. Among other sources on rumor during the 1930s in the Soviet Union, see Fitzpatrick, *Everyday Stalinism*; Davies, *Popular Opinion in Stalin's Russia*; and Johnston, *Being Soviet.*

75. Fitzpatrick, *Everyday Stalinism*, 183.

76. For a brief overview of these "apocalyptic" rumors spread during the 1930s, see Mark Edele, *Stalinist Society, 1928–1953* (New York: Oxford Univ. Press, 2011), 152–54.

77. Blumstein, *A Little House on Mount Carmel*, 17.

78. Hannah Arkin to Leon Arkin, 12 Feb., 7 Mar., 24 May, and 24 June 1940; 15 and 23 May 1941, Record Group 230, Leon Arkin Papers, box 1, YIVO. Hannah Arkin's messages contain no substantive information about conditions under the Soviet occupation other than that her son's letters and packages were arriving via the Soviet postal system. Her primary concern was to encourage her son to write to her more frequently.

79. Hollander interview, USC Shoah Foundation.

80. One surviving example is Katharine Novak, Kraków, to the mayor of Białystok, 8 July 1940, f. 292, op. 1, d. 45, l. 9, 10, and 10 ob., GAGO. In the letter, the writer asks the mayor of Białystok for help in finding her husband.

81. Martel interview, USC Shoah Foundation.

82. Avraham Zak wrote that he sent a letter to his wife, who stayed behind in Warsaw, and that he received a reply; he did not, however, state how the letters were sent (Zak, *Knekht zenen mir geven*, 1:190). Hanna (Davidson) Pankowsky, a refugee from Warsaw living in Orsha in 1940 and early 1941, remembered that her parents received a letter from a relative in the Warsaw ghetto. In response, Hanna's parents sent a package of food and soap, later receiving a letter from the Warsaw relation acknowledging that the package arrived (Pankowsky, *East of the Storm*, 44–45). Max Markiewitz received several letters from his parents in Warsaw (Martel interview, USC Shoah Foundation). Dora Huze reported that even after she was deported to a Soviet labor camp, she received letters from her father in the Łódź ghetto as well as letters from her brother in Yalta. She even remembered that her brother sent a parcel from Soviet territory to his parents in the Łódź ghetto (Huze interview, USC Shoah Foundation). When Alexander Dimant migrated to Makhachkala north of

the Caucasus, he received a letter from his parents in the Warsaw Ghetto (Dimant interview, USC Shoah Foundation).

83. Yosef Govrin, *The Jewish Factor in the Relations between Nazi Germany and the Soviet Union, 1933–1941* (Portland, OR: Vallentine Mitchell, 2009), 76.

84. "Mosmitlen fun der Frantsoyzisher regirung tsu bazorgn Parizsh mit shpayz-produktn" [Measures of the French Government to Provide Paris with Food Products], *Oktyabr* (Minsk), 11 Jan. 1941; "In oysland" [Abroad], *Oktyabr* (Minsk), 11 Jan. 1941.

85. "Rede fun Ruzveltn" [Speech of Roosevelt], *Oktyabr* (Minsk), 1 Jan. 1941.

86. The Communist Party–sanctioned Yiddish newspaper *Kamf* (Struggle, published in Riga) advertised screenings of *Alexander Nevsky* in its first issue (1 July 1940), microfilm at Dorot Jewish Division, New York Public Library.

87. Zak, *Knekht zenen mir geven*, 1:111.

88. Kurinets interview, USC Shoah Foundation.

89. Zibert interview, USC Shoah Foundation.

90. Gringauz interview, USC Shoah Foundation.

91. Bornstein-Bielicka, *One of the Few*, 96.

92. Zandman, *Never the Last Journey*, 30–31.

93. Blumstein, *A Little House on Mount Carmel*, 17.

94. Until the 1990s, historians agreed that Stalin accepted an alliance with Nazi Germany to buy time to rebuild the Soviet armed forces and was looking toward a defensive or offensive war no earlier than 1942. Vladimir Bogdanovich Rezun, a member of the Soviet General Staff, argued under the pen name "Viktor Suvorov" in *Icebreaker: Who Started the Second World War?* (London: Hamish Hamilton, 1990) that the Soviet military was preparing a preemptive strike timed for as early as July 1941. However, several historians have dismissed this assertion. The British historian Chris Bellamy examines the critiques of and variations on Suvorov's thesis, concluding that a Soviet offensive was not practicable in the summer of 1941 (*Absolute War*, 113–17).

95. Blumstein, *A Little House on Mount Carmel*, 19.

96. Blumstein, *A Little House on Mount Carmel*, 28.

97. "Di armey un dos folk" [The Army and the People], *Oktyabr* (Minsk), 23 Feb. 1941.

98. Rubinstein interview, USC Shoah Foundation.

99. *If There Is War Tomorrow* was certainly not screened in newly annexed cities such as Grodno during the period of Nazi–Soviet rapprochement.

100. *Oktyabr* (Minsk), 4 Feb. 1941.

101. Sergey Vladimirovich Mikhalkov, "Di Royte armey" [The Red Army], *Oktyabr* (Minsk), 18 Feb. 1941.

102. Zelik Akselrod, "Lager" [Camp], in *Ordentregerishe Vaysrusland*, ed. Akselrod and Kamenetski, 240.

103. Hirsh Reles, "Afn grenets" (On the Border), in *Onheyb*, n.p.

104. Yosif Rubinsteyn, "Mayn land" [My Country], *Oktyabr* (Minsk), 1 Jan. 1941.

105. Siemaszko, "Mass Deportations of the Polish Population to the USSR," 218.

106. Lazar interview, USC Shoah Foundation.

107. Klovsky, *The Road from Grodno*, 14–15.

108. Rubinstein interview, USC Shoah Foundation.

109. Gordon interview, USC Shoah Foundation.

110. *Oktyabr* (Minsk), 1 Jan. 1941.

111. *Oktyabr* (Minsk), 12 Jan. 1941.

112. *Oktyabr* (Minsk), 12 Jan. 1941.

113. "Far undzere kinder" [For Our Children], *Oktyabr* (Minsk), 18 Feb. 1941.

114. *Chyrvonaya zvyazda* (Vitebsk), 22 Aug. 1940, f. 2289, op. 2, d. 131, GAVO.

115. "Stalinskaya aviyatsyya" [Stalinist Aviation], *Chyrvonaya zvyazda* (Vitebsk), 22 Aug. 1940, f. 2289, op. 2, d. 131, GAVO. The Battle of Khalkhin Gol began on 11 May 1941 when Imperial Japanese forces entered a disputed region on the Mongolian–Manchurian border. The victory of the Red Army and Mongolian military forces over the Japanese in August 1941 permitted Stalin to concentrate on defending Soviet interests in the West—and to occupy eastern Poland the following month.

116. F. Voronin, "Di mekhtike armey funem land from sotsializm" [The Powerful Army of the Land of Socialism], *Oktyabr* (Minsk), 23 Feb. 1941.

117. Some of the recent studies of the Soviet military and intelligence situation during the pact period include Bellamy, *Absolute War*; Gabriel Gorodetsky, *Grand Illusion: Stalin and the German Invasion of Russia* (New Haven, CT: Yale Univ. Press, 1999); Ian Kershaw, "Moscow, Spring–Summer 1941: Stalin Decides He Knows Best," in *Fateful Choices: Ten Decisions That Changed the World, 1940–1941* (New York: Penguin Press, 2007), 243–97; David Murphy, *What Stalin Knew: The Enigma of Barbarossa* (New Haven, CT: Yale Univ. Press, 2005); and Constantine Pleshakov, *Stalin's Folly: The Tragic First Ten Days of World War II on the Eastern Front* (New York: Houghton Mifflin, 2005).

118. "Postanovlenie" [Order], 17 May 1941, Vitebskii oblastnoi komitet Kommunisticheskoi partii Belorussii [Vitebsk Regional Committee of the Communist Party of Belarus], f. 1-P, op. 1a, d. 8, l. 113, GAVO. Drysa, located on territory that was part of the pre-1939 Polish Republic, has been known as Verkhnedvinsk since 1962.

119. "Postanovlenie," 26 May 1941, f. 1-P, op. 1a, d. 8, l. 120–21, GAVO.

120. Bellamy, *Absolute War*, 67.

121. Pankowsky, *East of the Storm*, 48–49.

122. Shulman, "Ostrov Relesa," 248.

123. Mikhalkov, "Di Royte armey."

124. Gringauz interview, USC Shoah Foundation.

125. Fleish interview, USC Shoah Foundation.

126. Mikhail Ryvkin and Arkadii Shulman, *Chronik der furchtbaren Tage: Die Tragödie des Witebsker Getto* [Chronicle of Terrible Days: The Tragedy of the Vitebsk Ghetto], trans. F. Thomas Gatter (Minsk, Belarus: Medisont, 2007), 4–5.

127. Paczynski interview, USC Shoah Foundation; Utianski interview, USC Shoah Foundation; Bornstein-Bielicka, *One of the Few*, 96; Blumstein, *A Little House on Mount Carmel*, 28.

128. Leib Reizer, *In the Struggle: Memoirs from Grodno and the Forests*, trans. Haike Beruriah Wiegand (Jerusalem: Yad Vashem, 2009), 17. Reizer wrote the manuscript for his memoirs in Yiddish in 1948.

5. Invasion and Holocaust

1. "Togbukh fun Sore Fishkin" [Diary of Sarah Fishkin], in *Yizkhor-bukh Rubizivitsi*, ed. Sztokfisz, 183–84.

2. Pleshakov, *Stalin's Folly*, 51.

3. Pleshakov, *Stalin's Folly*, 126.

4. Testimony of Borys Grajneman (Boris Grayneman), 20 June 1947, No. 301/4766, pp. 1–5, Reference 301, Zbiór relacji Żydów Ocalałych z Zagłady [Collection of Holocaust Survivor Testimonies, Recorded by the Central Historical Commission of the Central Committee of the Jews in Poland], Żydowski Instytut Historyczny [Jewish Historical Institute], Warsaw (ZIH).

5. Quoted in Blumstein, *A Little House on Mount Carmel*, 45.

6. Utianski interview, USC Shoah Foundation.

7. Blumstein, *A Little House on Mount Carmel*, 41–42.

8. Klovsky, *The Road from Grodno*, 19.

9. Bornstein-Bielicka, *One of the Few*, 99.

10. Bornstein-Bielicka, *One of the Few*, 99.

11. Ekstein interview, USC Shoah Foundation.

12. Kremer interview, USC Shoah Foundation.

13. Lazar interview, USC Shoah Foundation.

14. Paczynski interview, USC Shoah Foundation, emphasis in original.

15. Chakin interview, USC Shoah Foundation.

16. Utianski interview, USC Shoah Foundation.

17. "Grodno: The German Occupation," in *Lost Jewish Worlds*, ed. Spector and Freundlich, 108; Bornstein-Bielicka, *One of the Few*, 41.

18. "Der umkum fun Grodner kehilah," in *Grodne*, ed. Rabin, 679.

19. Bialo interview, USC Shoah Foundation.

20. Blumstein, *A Little House on Mount Carmel*, 42, 52.

21. Grozalsky interview, USC Shoah Foundation.

22. "Der umkum fun Grodner kehilah," 679.

23. Bornstein-Bielicka, *One of the Few*, 100.

24. Testimony of Borys Grajneman, Reference 301, ZIH, 5–8.

25. Klovsky, *The Road from Grodno*, 19.

26. Utianski interview, USC Shoah Foundation.

27. Reizer, *In the Struggle*, 18–19, 21.

28. Shlomo Bromberg, Rehovot, Israel, 31 July 1996, Russian language, interview code 18113, USC Shoah Foundation.

29. Reizer, *In the Struggle*, 25.

30. Blumstein, *A Little House on Mount Carmel*, 58–60.

31. The historian Andrzej Żbikowski has identified sixty-seven separate localities where elements of the Gentile population engaged in anti-Jewish violence in the northeastern regions of the former Polish Republic ("Pogroms in Northeastern Poland: Spontaneous Reactions and German Instigations," in *Shared History—Divided Memory: Jews and Others in Soviet-Occupied Poland, 1939–1941*, ed. Elazar Barkan, Elizabeth A. Cole, and Kai Struve [Leipzig: Leipziger Universitätsverlag, 2007], 316).

32. David W. Wildermuth, "Who Killed Lida's Jewish Intelligentsia? A Case Study of Wehrmacht Involvement in the Holocaust's 'First Hour,'" *Holocaust and Genocide Studies* 27, no. 1 (Spring 2013): 5–6.

33. Bellamy, *Absolute War*, 168, 223–25.

34. Testimony of Grigorii Isaakovich Lesin, n.p., n.d., in *Ya pomnyu: Vocpominaniya veteranov VOV* [I Remember: Memoirs of Soviet Veterans of the Great Patriotic War], at http://iremember.ru/mediki/lesin-grigoriy-isaakovich.html.

35. Fleish interview, USC Shoah Foundation.

36. Fleish interview, USC Shoah Foundation.

37. Gringauz interview, USC Shoah Foundation.

38. Ryvkin and Shulman, *Chronik der furchtbaren Tage*, 5–8.

39. Testimony of Grigorii Isaakovich Lesin, in *Ya pomnyu*.

40. Testimony of Grigorii Isaakovich Lesin, in *Ya pomnyu*.

41. Rebecca Manley, *To the Tashkent Station: Evacuation and Survival in the Soviet Union at War* (Ithaca, NY: Cornell Univ. Press, 2009), 24–5, 33.

42. Dov Levin, "The Fateful Decision: The Flight of the Jews into the Soviet Interior in the Summer of 1941," *Yad Vashem Studies* 20 (1990): 127.

43. Manley, *To the Tashkent Station*, 52–53.

44. The effectiveness of Soviet evacuations improved over the course of the summer, although Jews were never accorded a higher priority even when the first reports of mass killings of Jews reached Moscow. Nonetheless, the Germans noted that most Jews had evacuated from the urban areas of western Russia captured during Operation Typhoon in October 1941. Historically, this region had considerably fewer Jews than in Belarus (Manley, *To the Tashkent Station*, 58; Ben-Cion Pinchuk, "Was There a Soviet Policy for Evacuating the Jews? The Case of the Annexed

Territories," *Slavic Review* 39, no. 1 [Mar. 1980]: 44; "Operational Situation Report USSR No. 123; Einsatzgruppe B," 25 Oct. 1941, in *The Einsatzgruppen Reports*, ed. Yitzhak Arad, Shmuel Krakowski, and Shmuel Spector, trans. Stella Schossberger [New York: Holocaust Library, 1989], 203).

45. Kurinets interview, USC Shoah Foundation.

46. Markelis-Domnin interview, USC Shoah Foundation.

47. Gringauz interview, USC Shoah Foundation.

48. Fleish interview, USC Shoah Foundation.

49. Kurinets interview, USC Shoah Foundation.

50. Testimony of Grigorii Isaakovich Lesin, in *Ya pomnyu*.

51. Markelis-Domnin interview, USC Shoah Foundation.

52. Ryvkin and Shulman, *Chronik der furchtbaren Tage*, 48–52.

53. Zeltser, *Evrei sovetskoi provintsii*, 418. The total Jewish population in Vitebsk on 22 June 1941 was probably somewhat greater than 37,000 because of the presence of refugees who fled German-occupied Poland after September 1939. The number of refugees was likely only a few thousand because the Soviets had maintained the pre-1939 frontier as an internal border to control the refugee presence.

54. Christian Gerlach, "German Economic Interests, Occupation Policy, and the Murder of the Jews in Belorussia, 1941–43," in *National Socialist Extermination Policies: Contemporary German Perspectives and Controversies*, ed. Ulrich Herbert (New York: Berghahn Books, 2000), 214; Jeff Rutherford, "The Radicalization of German Occupation Policies: The *Wirtschaftsstab Ost* and the 121st Infantry Division in Pavlovsk, 1941," in *Nazi Policy on the Eastern Front, 1941*, ed. Alex J. Kay, Jeff Rutherford, and David Stahel (Rochester, NY: Univ. of Rochester Press, 2012), 134.

55. Ryvkin and Shulman, *Chronik der furchtbaren Tage*, 61.

56. Vsevolod Rod'ko (or Ŭsevalad Rodz'ko in a transcription from Belarusian) was born an ethnic Belarusian in 1920 in Pinsk. A soldier in the Polish army in 1939, he became a POW and joined a group of Belarusian nationalists in German-occupied Warsaw. He arrived in Vitebsk three days after the Germans took the city under SS patronage. The Germans appointed Rod'ko *Bürgermeister* in early August because, with his Belarusian identity, they could thus appear to be advocates of the local population. An utter political opportunist, he later joined the secret Belarusian Independent Party, suppressed because the Germans had no intention of ever giving the Belarusians independence. By 1944, Rod'ko was no longer *Bürgermeister* in Vitebsk but was acting as the chief of an anti-Soviet saboteurs' school in East Prussia. The Soviets put him on trial after the war (Ryvkin and Shulman, *Chronik der furchtbaren Tage*, 134–36; Leonid Rein, *The Kings and the Pawns: Collaboration in Byelorussia during World War II* [New York: Berghahn Books, 2011], 136, 178).

57. The son of an Imperial Russian diplomat and a wealthy mother, Lev Georgievich Brandt grew up in St. Petersburg (Leningrad) but was expelled from there

in 1936 as a "class enemy." Why the Soviets permitted him to resettle in Vitebsk, relatively close to the border, is unclear, but we know he made his living as a music teacher. His origins among the disenfranchised elites made Brandt just the sort of person the Germans could use. Lev Brandt and his wife were killed by an unknown assailant on the night of 29–30 January 1942 (Ryvkin and Shulman, *Chronik der furchtbaren Tage*, 137–38).

58. Christian Gerlach, *Kalkulierte Morde: Die deutsche Wirtschafts- und Vernichtungs-politik in Weißrußland, 1941 bis 1944* [Calculated Murder: German Economic and Destruction Politics in Belarus, 1941 to 1944] (Hamburg, Germany: Hamburger Edition, 1999), 522.

59. Kommandant in Weissruthenien, Wehrmachtbefehlhaber Ostland, *Lagebericht den Kommandanten in Weissruthenien in der Zeit von 1.10.41 bis 15.10.41, Minsk, 19.10.1941* [Commandant in Belarus, Wehrmacht Commander in Ostland, Situation Report in Belarus in the Time from 1 October to 19 October 1941], Accession 1996.A.0169, Holocaust-Related Records from European Archives Collected by Yad Vashem, reel 11, United States Holocaust Memorial Museum), Washington, DC (USHMM).

60. Max von Schenckendorff, der Befehlshaber des rückw. Heeresgebietes Mitte, "Verwaltungs-Anordnungen Nr. 2," 13 July 1941, in Dan Michman, *The Emergence of Jewish Ghettos during the Holocaust*, trans. Lenn J. Schramm (New York: Cambridge Univ. Press, 2011), 108–9, fig. 17. Similar patterns have been identified in Ukraine. The historian Wendy Lower has identified the response of field commanders under General Karl von Rocques, chief of the Rear Occupied areas of Army Group South in Ukraine, which included orders for the handling of Jewish property, the marking of Jews, exploitation of Jews' labor, and registration of the Jewish population. Ghettoization was not among these initial set of instructions because Nazi leaders felt assured of victory in about six weeks. A few field commanders, as in Vitebsk, created ghettos because of alleged security concerns. The fate of the ghettos in Ukraine ran parallel to their fate in Vitebsk. Lack of food and proper shelter led to starvation and disease and rendered the confined in no condition to provide forced labor. In both contexts, the SS and the Order Police annihilated the ghetto population (Wendy Lower, "Facilitating Genocide: Nazi Ghettoization Practices in Occupied Ukraine, 1941–1942," in *Life in the Ghettos during the Holocaust*, ed. Eric J. Sterling [Syracuse, NY: Syracuse Univ. Press, 2005], 122–31).

61. Schenckendorff, "Verwaltungs-Anordnungen Nr. 2," 108–9, fig. 17.

62. Daniel Romanovsky, "Vitebsk," in *Encyclopedia of Camps and Ghettos, 1933–1945*, vol. 2: *Ghettos in German-Occupied Eastern Europe*, part B, ed. Martin Dean (Bloomington: Indiana Univ. Press, 2012), 1745–46. Schenckendorff's decree mandated that Jewish councils have ten members in towns and settlements with less than 10,000 Jews and twenty-four members in cities with more than 10,000 (Schenckendorff,

"Verwaltungs-Anordnungen Nr. 2," 108–9, fig. 17). The exact number of Judenrat members in Vitebsk is unclear, but many accounts state that there were ten.

63. Ryvkin and Shulman, *Chronik der furchtbaren Tage*, 58–59; testimony of Yankev Sheinin, file 265, p. 4, Record Group O.33, Testimonies, Diaries, and Memoirs Collection, Yad Vashem.

64. Hirsch, *Empire of Nations*, 294.

65. "Aufzeichnung über den Verlauf der Besprechung am 29.Jan.1942 im Reichsministerium für die besetzten Ostgebiete" [Record of the Proceeding of the Meeting on 29 January in the Reich Ministry for the Occupied Eastern Territories], RG-18.002M, Selected Records from the Latvian Central State Historical Archive, reel 2 (Latvian State Archive, f. R-69, op. 1a, d. 6), USHMM.

66. "Ereignismeldung UdSSR Nr. 34" [Incident Report USSR No. 34], 26 July 1941, in *Die "Ereignismeldungen UdSSR" 1941: Dokumente der Einsatzgruppen in der Sowjetunion* [The "Dispatches USSR" 1941: Documents of the Einsatzgruppen in the Soviet Union], ed. Klaus-Michael Mallmann, Andrej Angrick, Jürgen Matthäus, and Martin Cüppers (Damstadt, Germany: Wissenschaftliche Buchgesellschaft, 2011), 188.

67. Ryvkin and Shulman, *Chronik der furchtbaren Tage*, 59.

68. Wolfgang Curilla, *Die deutsche Ordnungspolizei und die Holocaust im Baltikum und im Weissrussland, 1941–1944* [The German Order Police and the Holocaust in the Baltic Region and in Belarus, 1941–1944] (Paderborn, Germany: Ferdinand Schöningh, 2006), 845. Sonderkommandos 7a and 7b of Einsatzgruppe B were assigned the field army rear areas, where they sought population records and targeted killings of Bolsheviks, partisans, and other perceived security risks (Alex J. Kay, "Transition to Genocide, July 1941: Einsatzkommando 9 and the Annihilation of Soviet Jewry," *Holocaust and Genocide Studies* 27, no. 3 [Winter 2013]: 413).

69. "Protokol doprosa" [Record of Interrogation], NKGB, 27 Sept. 1944, Viktoria Danikovna Orlova, born 1908, file 23, pp. 57–60, Record Group O.53, Ludwigsburg USSR Collection, Yad Vashem; "Protokol doprosa svidetelya" [Record of Witness Interrogation], NKGB, 24 Mar. 1945, Petr Kuzmich Babochkii, born 1894, RG-22.002M, Selected Records of the Extraordinary State Commission to Investigate German-Fascist Crimes Committed on Soviet Territory, 1941–45, reel 8 (f. 7021, op. 84, d. 3, l. 146–146 ob., Gosudarstvennyi arkhiv Rossiiskoi federatsii [GARF, State Archives of the Russian Federation]), USHMM.

70. Ryvkin and Shulman, *Chronik der furchtbaren Tage*, 56.

71. "Protokol doprosa" [Record of Interrogation], NKGB, 29 Aug. 1944, Vasily Ivanovich Butrimovich, born 1897, RG-22.002M, reel 8 (f. 7021, op. 84, d. 3, l. 132, GARF), USHMM. The Germans drowned another 150 Jews in the river on 2 September 1941 when they placed the large group onto a barge and sank it (Ryvkin and Shulman, *Chronik der furchtbaren Tage*, 102).

72. "Protokol doprosa" [Record of Interrogation], NKGB, 27 Sept. 1944, Foma Tikhonovich Pankov, born 1927, file 23, pp. 61–64, Record Group O.53, Yad Vashem.

73. Mikhail Ryvkin and Arkadii Shulman], "Vitsebskaye geta" [Vitebsk Ghetto], in *Pamyats': Vitsebsk*, 1:440.

74. Lfd. nr. 643a, Massenvernichtungsverbrechen durch Einsatzgruppen [Crimes of Mass Murder by Einsatzgruppen], LG Essen, 22 Dec. 1966, 29 Ks 2/65, in *Justiz und NS-Verbrechen: Sammlung deutscher Strafurteile wegen nationalsozialistischer Tötungsverbrechen, 1945–1999* [Justice and Nazi Crimes: Collection of German Criminal Convictions for Nazi Homicides, 1945–1999], vol. 25 (Amsterdam: Univ. Press Amsterdam, 2001), 277.

75. Ryvkin and Shulman, "Vitsebskaye geta," 440; Curilla, *Die deutsche Ordnungspolizei und die Holocaust*, 845.

76. "Protokol doprosa," 27 Sept. 1944, Foma Tikhonovich Pankov–.

77. Ryvkin and Shulman, "Vitsebskaye geta," 440.

78. Testimony of Yankev Sheinin, file 265, p. 1, Record Group O.33, Yad Vashem.

79. "Poimennoi spisok, rasstrelyannykh, poveshennykh, zamuchennykh gr-n SSSR, Oktyabrskaya raion, g. Vitebsk" [List of Names, Shot, Lynched, Tortured Citizens of the USSR, Oktyabrskaya District, City of Vitebsk], n.d., RG-22.002M, reel 8 (f. 7021, op. 84, d. 3, l. 41–104, GARF), USHMM.

80. Romanovsky, "Vitebsk," 2:1746.

81. Romanovsky, "Vitebsk," 2:1746; Ryvkin and Shulman, *Chronik der furchtbaren Tage*, 62.

82. Polina Moisheevna Frumson's story is recounted in Ryvkin and Shulman, *Chronik der furchtbaren Tage*, 64–65.

83. Mikhail Ryvkin and Arkadii Shulman give the impression in *Chronik der furchtbaren Tage* that Ghetto II was formed in early August 1941 (75–77). In an entry for Vitebsk in *Encyclopedia of Camps and Ghettos, 1933–1945* (ed. Martin), Daniel Romanovsky places the date for the formation of Ghetto II in early September (Romanovsky, "Vitebsk," 2:1746).

84. Ryvkin and Shulman, *Chronik der furchtbaren Tage*, 76.

85. Ryvkin and Shulman, *Chronik der furchtbaren Tage*, 76. The Soviet Constructivist-style Metal Workers' Club was repaired after the war. The building survives, although it was vacant as of 2008. A monument commemorating the victims of the Vitebsk ghetto was placed near the entrance in the 1990s.

86. "Akt nr. 9, Po ustanovleniyu i rassledovaniyu zlodeyanii nemetsko-fashistskikh zakhvatchikob i ikh soobshchnikov na territorii Zheleznodorozhnovo raiona goroda Vitebska BSSR" [Act no. 9, On Establishing and Investigating Crimes of the German-Fascist Aggressors and Their Accomplices on the Territory of the Railway District of the City of Vitebsk, Belarusian Soviet Socialist Republic], n.d. [c. 1945], RG-22.002M, reel 8 (f. 7021, op. 84, d. 3, GARF), USHMM.

87. "Fota vitsebskava geta pradali na avktsyonye" [Photo of Vitebsk Ghetto Sold at Auction], *Narodniya naviny Vitsebska*, 28 Nov. 2011, at http://news.vitebsk.cc /2011/11/28/fota-vitsebskaga-geta-pradali-na-awktsyiyone/. This online news story describes the sale on Ebay.com of a photograph showing the sign.

88. Ryvkin and Shulman, *Chronik der furchtbaren Tage*, 137.

89. "Bobruysk," "Borisov," and "Polotsk," in *The Yad Vashem Encyclopedia of the Ghettos during the Holocaust*, ed. Guy Miron and Shlomit Shulhani (Jerusalem: Yad Vashem, 2009), 61, 68, 609.

90. Yuri Zaretski's story is told in Ryvkin and Shulman, *Chronik der furchtbaren Tage*, 75.

91. "Protokol doprosa," Vasily Ivanovich Butrimovich, RG-22.002M, reel 8 (f. 7021, op. 84, d. 3, l. 132, GARF), USHMM.

92. Markelis-Domnin interview, USC Shoah Foundation.

93. Ryvkin and Shulman, *Chronik der furchtbaren Tage*, 62, 74.

94. Ryvkin and Shulman, *Chronik der furchtbaren Tage*, 76.

95. Markelis-Domnin interview, USC Shoah Foundation.

96. "Operational Situation Report USSR No. 124; Einsatzgruppe B," 25 Oct. 1941, in *The Einsatzgruppen Reports*, ed. Arad, Krakowski, and Spector, 206.

97. "Akt nr. 9, Po ustanovleniyu i rassledovaniyu zlodeyanii nemetsko-fashistskikh zakhvatchikob."

98. "Protokol oprosa svidetelya" [Record of Witness Interview], NKGB, 31 Mar. 1945, Timofey Korneyevich Okunyev, born 1928, RG-22.002M, reel 8 (f. 7021, op. 84, d. 3, l. 172–172 ob., GARF), USHMM; "Akt nr. 9, Po ustanovleniyu i rassledovaniyu zlodeyanii nemetsko-fashistskikh zakhvatchikob."

99. "Akt nr. 9, Po ustanovleniyu i rassledovaniyu zlodeyanii nemetsko-fashistskikh zakhvatchikob." After liberation, Soviet investigators found 70 separate large mass graves and nearly 300 smaller ones in which bodies, mostly POWs but also civilian women, children, and the elderly, were dumped haphazardly. The larger mass graves measured approximately 7 meters by 8 meters by 4 meters deep; smaller graves were 2½ by 2 by 3 meters deep (NKGB Commission Report, Vitebsk, 26 Sept. 1944, RG-22.002M, reel 8 [f. 7021, op. 84, d. 3, l. 15, GARF], USHMM).

100. Gerlach, *Kalkulierte Morde*, 507.

101. Ryvkin and Shulman, *Chronik der furchtbaren Tage*, 76.

102. Markelis-Domnin interview, USC Shoah Foundation.

103. Inessa Gdalievna (Aronson) Ivanova, "My Shtetl," "Project 'Voices of Jewish Settlements: Vitebsk Region,'" n.d., at http://shtetle.co.il/Shtetls/vitebsk/ivanova_eng.html.

104. Markelis-Domnin interview, USC Shoah Foundation.

105. NKGB witness Vasily Butrimovich told investigators after the war that at least 5,000 Jews died of hunger in the ghetto ("Protokol doprosa," Vasily Ivanovich

Butrimovich, RG-22.002M, reel 8 [f. 7021, op. 84, d. 3, l. 132, GARF], USHMM). Based on a variety of sources, the historian Christian Gerlach has estimated that 5,000 to 10,000 starved to death in the Vitebsk ghetto (*Kalkulierte Morde*, 596).

106. "Grodno: The German Occupation," 110; "Der umkum fun Grodner kehilah," 679–80. The Germans later demanded the increase of the Grodno Judenrat to twenty-four members.

107. "Grodno: The German Occupation," 131.

108. Lazar interview, USC Shoah Foundation.

109. Reizer, *In the Struggle*, 103.

110. "Grodno: The German Occupation," 111.

111. "Operational Situation Report USSR No. 10; Einsatzgruppe C [B]," 2 July 1941, in *The Einsatzgruppen Reports*, ed. Arad, Krakowski, and Spector, 3; "Operational Situation Report USSR No. 13; Einsatzgruppe C [B]," 5 July 1941, in *The Einsatzgruppen Reports*, 9; "Operational Situation Report USSR No. 17; Einsatzgruppe C [B]," 7 July 1941, in *The Einsatzgruppen Reports*, 14; Blumstein, *A Little House on Mount Carmel*, 63.

112. Curilla, *Die deutsche Ordnungspolizei und die Holocaust im Baltikum und im Weissrussland*, 606; Gerlach, *Kalkulierte Morde*, 544–55, 545n251.

113. Alexandre Blumstein remembered decades later that this occurred around 10 July, the date of his older brother's birthday (*A Little House on Mount Carmel*, 66).

114. "Grodno: The German Occupation," 112.

115. Bornstein-Bielicka, *One of the Few*, 100.

116. Zandman, *Never the Last Journey*, 41.

117. Blumstein, *A Little House on Mount Carmel*, 66.

118. Blumstein, *A Little House on Mount Carmel*, 69–70. Blumstein recalled that this occurred in August 1941.

119. Klovsky, *The Road from Grodno*, 21.

120. Blumstein, *A Little House on Mount Carmel*, 64–65.

121. "Der umkum fun Grodner kehilah," 679; "Grodno: The German Occupation," 111.

122. "Beachtung" (Notice), 14 Oct. 1941, RG-53.004M, Selected Records from the Grodno Oblast Archive, reel 1 (Grodnenskii uyezdnyi komissar Grazhdaiskovo upravleniya Belostokskovo okruga, g. Grodno [Grodno County Commissar for (German) Civilian Control Białystok District, City Grodno], f. 1, op. 1, d. 15, GAGO), USHMM.

123. Harold Gordon [Hirshl Grodzienski], *The Last Sunrise: A True Story* (Salinas, CA: H&J, 1989), 37.

124. Blumstein, *A Little House on Mount Carmel*, 75.

125. Anna (Kovitzka) Kaletska, interview by David P. Boder, Wiesbaden, Germany, 26 Sept. 1946, Yiddish language (trans. David P. Boder), Voices of the

Holocaust, Paul V. Galvin Library, Illinois Institute of Technology, Chicago, at http://voices.iit.edu/interview?doc=kaletskaA&display=kaletskaA_en.

126. Bornstein-Bielicka, *One of the Few*, 102.

127. Grozalsky interview, USC Shoah Foundation.

128. "Grodno: The German Occupation," 130.

129. Kaletska interview by Boder, Voices of the Holocaust.

130. Paczynski interview, USC Shoah Foundation.

131. Reizer, *In the Struggle*, 102.

132. "Der umkum fun Grodner kehilah," 679; Reizer, *In the Struggle*, 101.

133. Klovsky, *The Road from Grodno*, 21.

134. Blumstein, *A Little House on Mount Carmel*, 71.

135. Zandman, *Never the Last Journey*, 42.

136. Paczynski interview, USC Shoah Foundation.

137. Reizer, *In the Struggle*, 65–89, 107–8.

138. Blumstein, *A Little House on Mount Carmel*, 84.

139. "Der umkum fun Grodner kehilah," 681.

140. Zandman, *Never the Last Journey*, 34–39; Felix (Shraga Feliks) Zandman, Bala Cynwyd, PA, 19 Dec. 1997, interview code 36736, USC Shoah Foundation.

141. Zandman, *Never the Last Journey*, 42.

142. Paczynski interview, USC Shoah Foundation.

143. "Grodno: The German Occupation," 109. The civilian administration of the Białystok District was organized along similar lines as a Prussian government district. A local governor (*Regierungspräsident*) headed the governmental structure over seven regions (*Kreiskommissariate*) and numerous subregions (*Amtskommissariate*). A district councilor (*Landrat*) headed the local administration in each region, with civil servants typically assigned from East Prussia working in various levels of government management. Poles and others from the local population served in municipal administrations at the Germans' favor ("The People vs. Kurt Wiese and Heinz Errelis, Accused of Murder, Verdict and Judgment, Cologne District Court, Federal Republic of Germany, June 27, 1968," in *Documents Concerning the Murder of 29,000 Jews of Grodno by the Germans, 1941–1943: Ghetto and Deportations to Death Camps: Cologne and Bielefeld Trials*, ed. Serge Klarsfeld, trans. Bill Templer [Ramat-Gan, Israel: Grodner Association of Israel, 1989], 18).

144. E. S. Yarmusik, "Ekanamichnaya, religiinaya i natsyianal'naya palityka akupantav" [Economic, Religious, and National Occupation Policies], in *Pamyats': Grodna*, 369.

145. Kreiskommissar des Kreises Grodno [Grodno regional commissar] to the Herrn Oberpräsident, Zivilverwaltung für den Bezirk Bialystok in Bialystok [head of the Białystok District Civil Administration], 29 Nov. 1942, RG-53.004M, reel 2 (f. 1, op. 1, d. 181, GAGO), USHMM.

146. "Sitzung der Amtskommissare und Amtsbürgermeister am Donnerstag den 23 Oktober 1941" [Meeting of the Commissars and Mayors on Thursday, 23 Oct. 1941], RG-53.004M, reel 1 (f. 1, op. 1, d. 15, GAGO), USHMM.

147. Richard J. Evans, *The Third Reich at War* (New York: Penguin Books, 2008), 31–33.

148. "Passtechnische Regelung des Verkehrs mit dem Bezirk Bialystok" [Pass Requirements for the Białystok District], der Reichsführer-SS und der Chef der Deutschen Polizei im Reichsministerium des Innern [the Reichsführer-SS and the head of the German police in the Ministry of the Interior], 22 June 1942, pp. 1–4, RG-53.002M, Selected Records of the Belarus Central State Archives, Minsk, reel 4 (f. 393, op. 1, d. 1, NARB), USHMM. The Germans also maintained a police border, requiring special passes, between the Białystok District and Reichkommissariat Ostland, Reichkommissariat Ukraine, and the General Government.

149. "Sitzung der Amtskommissare und Amtsbürgermeister am Donnerstag den 23 Oktober 1941."

150. Gordon, *The Last Sunrise*, 35.

151. "Einsatzgruppe A Gesamtbericht vom 16. Oktober 1941 bis 31. Januar 1942; Anlage nr. 6, Sonderbericht, Volkstum in Weissruthenien" [Einsatzgruppe A General Report of 16 October 1941 to 31 Jan. 1942; Enclosure No. 6, Special Report, Ethnic Identity in Belarus], pp. 15–16, RG-11.001M.01, Reichssicherheitshauptampt (RSHA)-SD, Berlin, reel 14 (f. 500, op. 4, d. 91, Osobyi Archive, Moscow), USHMM.

152. "Einsatzgruppe A Gesamtbericht vom 16. Oktober 1941 bis 31. Januar 1942; Allgemeine Lage in grundsätzlicher Hinsicht, Stimmungsbericht" [Einsatzgruppe A General Report of 16 October 1941 to 31 Jan. 1942; General Situation in Fundamental Respects, Mood Report], p. 16, RG-11.001M.01, reel 14 (f. 500, op. 4, d. 91, Osobyi Archive, Moscow), USHMM.

153. "An Herrn Stadtkommissar Grodno, Bericht von 13.X.1941" [To the City Commissioner of Grodno, Report of 13 October 1941], RG-53.004M, reel 1 (f. 1, op. 1, d. 33, GAGO), USHMM.

154. "An Herrn Landrat in Grodno" [To the District Representative], 13 Oct. 1941, RG-53.004M, reel 1 (f. 1, op. 1, d. 33, GAGO), USHMM.

155. "Der Befehlshaber des rückw. Heeresgebietes Mitte" [The Commander of the Rear Army Group Center], 24 July 1941, RG-53.004M, reel 1 (f. 1, op. 1, d. 33, GAGO), USHMM.

156. "An Herrn Feldkommandant im Grodno" [To the Field Commander in Grodno], 25 July 1941, RG-53.004M, reel 1 (f. 1, op. 1, d. 33, GAGO), USHMM.

157. Kommandant in Weissruthenien, Wehrmachtbefehlhaber Ostland, *Lagebericht den Kommandanten in Weissruthenien in der Zeit von 1.10.41 bis 15.10.41, Minsk, 19.10.1941.*

158. "Operational Situation Report USSR No. 50," 12 Aug. 1941, in *The Einsatzgruppen Reports*, ed. Arad, Krakowski, and Spector, 83.

159. "An die Feldgendarmerie" [From the Military Police], 1 Aug. 1941, RG-53.004M, reel 1 (f. 1, op. 1, d. 33, GAGO), USHMM.

160. "An Herrn Stadtkommissar Grodno, Bericht von 13.X.1941."

161. Kreiskommissar des Kreises Grodno [Grodno Regional Commissar] to the Bürgermeister [Grodno], 29 Jan. 1942, RG-53.004M, reel 2 (f. 1, op. 1, d. 181, GAGO), USHMM.

162. "Sitzung der Amtskommissare und Amtsbürgermeister am Donnerstag den 23 Oktober 1941."

163. Sergiusz Mojnicz to the Landrat Grodno, 11 Dec. 1941, RG-53.004M, reel 1 (f. 1, op. 1, d. 2, GAGO), USHMM.

164. "Der umkum fun Grodner kehilah," in *Grodne*, ed. Rabin, 681–82.

165. Bornstein-Bielicka, *One of the Few*, 104.

166. Blumstein, *A Little House on Mount Carmel*, 106.

167. Grozalsky interview, USC Shoah Foundation.

168. Blumstein, *A Little House on Mount Carmel*, 62, 84, 106.

169. Bornstein-Bielicka, *One of the Few*, 105.

170. Blumstein, *A Little House on Mount Carmel*, 105.

171. Blumstein, *A Little House on Mount Carmel*, 109.

172. Bornstein-Bielicka, *One of the Few*, 104.

173. Blumstein, *A Little House on Mount Carmel*, 107.

174. Klovsky, *The Road from Grodno*, 24–26.

175. Blumstein, *A Little House on Mount Carmel*, 108–9.

176. Examples of such images include: "Poland, Jews Deported to Grodno Ghetto by the German Police" (2982/218); "Grodno, Poland, Jews Deported to the Ghetto, 1942 [*sic*]" (3745/72); "Grodno, Poland, Deportation to the Ghetto" (3403/7); and "Grodno, Poland, Jews Moving to the Ghetto, 1942 [*sic*]" (3745/70), all in the Yad Vashem Photo Archive. The original sources for these images include the Belarusian State Archives in Minsk as well as private donors. Similar images are available in the photo collections of the United States Holocaust Memorial Museum.

177. Kaletska interview by Boder, Voices of the Holocaust.

178. Bornstein-Bielicka, *One of the Few*, 105–6.

179. Zandman, *Never the Last Journey*, 43–44.

180. Gordon interview, USC Shoah Foundation.

181. Blumstein, *A Little House on Mount Carmel*, 69.

182. Bialo interview, USC Shoah Foundation.

183. Zandman, *Never the Last Journey*, 44.

184. Bornstein-Bielicka, *One of the Few*, 105; Klovsky, *The Road from Grodno*, 26; Grozalsky interview, USC Shoah Foundation.

185. Klovsky, *The Road from Grodno*, 26.

186. Fleish interview, USC Shoah Foundation.

187. Lfd. nr. 540, Massenvernichtungsverbrechen durch Einsatzgruppen [Crimes of Mass Murder by Einsatzgruppen], LG Berlin, 22 June 1962, 3 PKs 1/62, in *Justiz und NS-Verbrechen: Sammlung deutscher Strafurteile wegen nationalsozialistischer Tötungsverbrechen, 1945–1966* [Justice and Nazi Crimes: Collection of German Criminal Convictions for Nazi Homicides, 1945–1966], vol. 18 (Amsterdam: Univ. Press Amsterdam, 1978), 620 (540 a-16).

188. Kay, "Transition to Genocide," 413.

189. Lfd. nr. 540, Massenvernichtungsverbrechen durch Einsatzgruppen, in *Justiz und NS-Verbrechen*, 18:623 (540 a-19); Curilla, *Die deutsche Ordnungspolizei und die Holocaust*, 906.

190. Eugen Kogon, Hermann Langbein, and Adalbert Rückerl, eds., *Nazi Mass Murder: A Documentary History of the Use of Poison Gas*, trans. Mary Scott and Caroline Lloyd-Morris (New Haven, CT: Yale Univ. Press, 1993), 58 (Kogon, Langbein, and Rückerl are identified as the editors of this volume, but they seem to be its authors). Yankev Sheinin reported in his written testimony given to Yad Vashem that the Germans followed up mass shootings in Vitebsk by introducing gas vans (he uses the Russian word *dushegubkes*), trucks modified to induct their exhaust into the airtight cargo area (Sheinin testimony, file 265, pp. 6–7, Record Group O.33, Yad Vashem).

191. Leonid Smilovitsky, *Holocaust in Belorussia, 1941–1944* (translation of *Katastrofia Evreev v Belorusii 1941–1944* [Tel Aviv: n.p., 2000]), at http://www.jewishgen.org/yizkor/belarus/bel178.html.

192. Markelis-Domnin interview, USC Shoah Foundation.

193. Ryvkin and Shulman, *Chronik der furchtbaren Tage*, 76.

194. For the evolution of the killing of women and children on occupied Soviet territory, see Christopher R. Browning, with Jürgen Matthäus, *The Origins of the Final Solution: The Evolution of Nazi Jewish Policy, September 1939–March 1942* (Lincoln: Univ. of Nebraska Press, 2004), 260–61, 277–89.

195. Kay, "Transition to Genocide," 424–26.

196. Leonid Rein, "The Radicalization of Anti-Jewish Policies in Nazi-Occupied Belarus," in *Nazi Policy on the Eastern Front, 1941*, ed. Kay, Rutherford, and Stahel, 228.

197. "Operational Situation Report USSR No. 67; Einsatzgruppe B," 29 Aug. 1941, in *The Einsatzgruppen Reports*, ed. Arad, Krakowski, and Spector, 117–18.

198. "Operational Situation Report USSR No. 73; Einsatzgruppe B," 4 Sept. 1941, in *The Einsatzgruppen Reports*, ed. Arad, Krakowski, and Spector, 124.

199. "Operational Situation Report USSR No. 92; Einsatzgruppe B," 23 Sept. 1941, and "Operational Situation Report USSR No. 108; Einsatzgruppe B," 9 Oct. 1941, in *The Einsatzgruppen Reports*, ed. Arad, Krakowski, and Spector, 153, 177–79.

Further afield from Vitebsk, German reports from October cite suspected partisan activity by marooned Red Army soldiers. In Velikiye Luki, a town 125 kilometers north of Vitebsk, partisans reportedly carried out nineteen separate attacks. Those responsible were believed to disperse successfully among the local village population. Partisans allegedly carried out other attacks in the region. Near Demidov, 75 kilometers east of Vitebsk, five partisans were captured after allegedly killing fourteen German soldiers. Twenty-seven partisans were captured and shot near Velizh, 70 kilometers northeast of Vitebsk ("Tätigkeits- und Lagebericht Nr. 6 der Einsatzgruppen der Sicherheitspolizei und des SD in der UdSSR [Berichtszeit vom 1.–31.10.1941]" [Activity and Situation Report No. 6 of the Einsatzgruppen of the Security Police and the Security Service in the USSR, 1–31 October 1941], file 3, pp. 8–10, Record Group O.53, Yad Vashem, document originals held in the Bundesarchiv, Ludwigsburg, Germany.

200. "Operational Situation Report USSR No. 124; Einsatzgruppe B," 25 Oct. 1941, 206.

201. "Operational Situation Report USSR No. 92; Einsatzgruppe B," 23 Sept. 1941, 152.

202. "Operational Situation Report USSR No. 67; Einsatzgruppe B," 29 Aug. 1941.

203. "Protokol doprosa," NKGB, 14 Aug. 1944, Mifodiya Yegorovich Fedosenko, born 1902, RG-22.002M, reel 8 (f. 7021, op. 84, d. 3, l. 118–19, GARF), USHMM.

204. Gerlach, *Kalkulierte Morde*, 569.

205. Markelis-Domnin interview, USC Shoah Foundation.

206. "Protokol, Kvartira, 8.9.1941, perevod sa nemetakovo" [Memo, Headquarters, 8 Sept. 1941, translated from German], RG-06.025*43, Central Archives of the Federal Security Services (former KGB) of the Russian Federation, Records Relating to War Crime Trials in the Soviet Union, 1939–1992, USHMM. The German-language original of Gefreitor Kilhorn's statement is not among the documents in RG-06.025.

207. "Protokol, Kvartira, 8.9.1941, perevod sa nemetakovo."

208. Ryvkin and Shulman, "Vitsebskaye geta," 445; Smilovitsky, *Holocaust in Belorussia*; "Protokol doprosa," NKGB, 29 July 1944, Yevgenia Nikolaevna Bavtuto, born 1916, RG-22.002M, reel 8 (f. 7021, op. 84, d. 3, l. 128–128 ob., GARF), USHMM.

209. "Operational Situation Report USSR No. 124; Einsatzgruppe B," 25 Oct. 1941.

210. Gerlach, *Kalkulierte Morde*, 596–97; Jörn Hasenclever, *Wehrmacht und Besatzungspolitik in der Sowjetunion: Die Befehlshaber der rückwärtigen Heeresgebiete, 1941–1943* [Wehrmacht and Occupation Policy in the Soviet Union: The Commanders

of the Rear Army Areas] (Paderborn, Germany: Ferdinand Schöningh, 2010), 504. Gerlach is more tentative in linking Schenckendorff's visit to the shootings on 8–10 October 1941, but Hasenclever presents additional circumstantial evidence to connect these two events.

211. Zupkevich's story is told in Ryvkin and Shulman, *Chronik der furchtbaren Tage*, 130.

212. "Protokol oprosa svidetelya," NKGB, 31 Mar. 1945, Aleksandr Stepanovich Solenik, RG-22.002M, reel 8 (f. 7021, op. 84, d. 3, l. 168–168 ob., GARF), USHMM.

213. "Protokol doprosa," NKGB, 28 July 1944, Anna Nikolaevna Tereshchenko, born 1911, file 23, pp. 29–33, Record Group O.53, Ludwigsburg USSR Collection, Yad Vashem.

214. "Protokol oprosa svidetelya," NKGB, 28 Mar. 1945, Anna Andreyevna Solodukhinya, RG-22.002M, reel 8 (f. 7021, op. 84, d. 3, l. 148–148 ob., GARF), USHMM.

215. "Protokol doprosa," Yevgenia Nikolaevna Bavtuto, RG-22.002M, reel 8 (f. 7021, op. 84, d. 3, l. 128 ob.–129, GARF), USHMM.

216. Lfd. nr. 540, Massenvernichtungsverbrechen durch Einsatzgruppen, in *Justiz und NS-Verbrechen*, 18:623 (540 a-19). Filbert was recalled to Berlin on 20 October 1941 to face a Reichssicherheitshauptampt (Reich Security Main Office) investigation for fraud and embezzlement. He received two years house arrest as punishment but by the spring of 1943 was employed by the criminal police—ironically in a division investigating economic offenses. He hid under a false identity after the war but reassumed his own name in 1950 under an amnesty. Subsequent West German investigations uncovered his involvement with Einsatzkommando 9, and he was arrested in 1959 (Lfd. nr. 540, Massenvernichtungsverbrechen durch Einsatzgruppen, in *Justiz und NS-Verbrechen*, 18:607 [540 a-3]). Sentenced to life imprisonment in 1962, Filbert was released in 1973 and died in 1990.

217. "Protokol doprosa," Mifodiya Yegorovich Fedosenko, RG-22.002M, reel 8 (f. 7021, op. 84, d. 3, l. 118–19, GARF), USHMM.

218. "Protokol doprosa," Yevgenia Nikolaevna Bavtuto, RG-22.002M, reel 8 (f. 7021, op. 84, d. 3, l. 128 ob.–129, GARF), USHMM. Based on her statement, Bavtuto did not keep the notebook.

219. "Zayavlenie" [Declaration], Extraordinary State Commission, 30 Aug. 1944, Maria Ignat'yevna Prokhorova, RG-22.002M, reel 8 (f. 7021, op. 84, d. 3, l. 195–195 ob., GARF), USHMM.

220. Markelis-Domnin interview, USC Shoah Foundation, ellipses indicating a pause.

221. Markelis-Domnin interview, USC Shoah Foundation, ellipses indicating a pause.

222. "Operational Situation Report USSR No. 124; Einsatzgruppe B," 25 Oct. 1941.

223. "Operational Situation Report USSR No. 148; Einsatzgruppe B," 19 Dec. 1941, in *The Einsatzgruppen Reports*, ed. Arad, Krakowski, and Spector, 264.

224. "Protokol doprosa," Mifodiya Yegorovich Fedosenko, RG-22.002M, reel 8 (f. 7021, op. 84, d. 3, l. 118–19, GARF), USHMM; "Protokol doprosa," NKGB, 14 Aug. 1944, Nikolai Ivanovich Bavtuto, born 1881, RG-22.002M, reel 8 (f. 7021, op. 84, d. 3, l. 114–15, GARF), USHMM; "Protokol doprosa," Vasily Ivanovich Butrimovich, RG-22.002M, reel 8 (f. 7021, op. 84, d. 3, l. 132, GARF), USHMM.

225. "Protokol doprosa," Yevgenia Nikolaevna Bavtuto, RG-22.002M, reel 8 (f. 7021, op. 84, d. 3, l. 128 ob.–129, GARF), USHMM.

226. "Protokol doprosa," NKGB, 29 July 1944, Yevgenia Ivanovna Mudriyenko, born 1924, RG-22.002M, reel 8 (f. 7021, op. 84, d. 3, l. 122–23, GARF), USHMM.

227. "Protokol doprosa," NKGB, 15 July 1944, Ivan Averyanovich Porubova, born 1915, RG-22.002M, reel 8 (f. 7021, op. 84, d. 3, l. 109, GARF), USHMM.

228. Martin Dean, *Robbing the Jews: The Confiscation of Jewish Property in the Holocaust, 1933–1945* (Cambridge: Cambridge Univ. Press, 2008), 194–96.

229. Similar invasive measures occurred in Bobruisk, 250 kilometers to the south, where the local *Bürgermeister* sought permission from the regional Wehrmacht commander to enter private homes to locate Jewish property (Adam Stankevich [*Bürgermeister*] to Supreme Commandant, 6 Dec. 1941, RG-53.006M, Mogilev Oblast Archive records, 1941–45, reel no. 4 (f. 858, op. 1, d. 18, l. 132), USHMM.

230. "Verzeichnis" [Register], 13 Feb. 1942, Vitebskaya gorodskaya uprava [VGU, Vitebsk City Council], f. 2073, op. 3, d. 20, l. 64, GAVO.

231. [Vitebsk City Council, Housing Department, to Finance Department] (orig. not given), 12 Sept. 1941, VGU, f. 2073, op. 3, d. 118, l. 7, GAVO.

232. A. M. Maslenko to Housing Department, 18 Nov. 1941, VGU, f. 2073, op. 3, d. 65, l. 27, GAVO.

233. I. I. Kovalenko to housing auditor, 2nd Vitebsk District, 25 Oct. 1941, VGU, f. 2073, op. 3, d. 65, l. 33, GAVO.

234. Laisukhovai, "Zayavlenie" [Declaration], 17 Sept. 1943, VGU, f. 2073, op. 3, d. 9, l. 25, GAVO.

235. Konstantya Petrovna Popsuyevich, "Prashenie" and "Gesuch" [Request], 15 Sept. 1941, VGU, f. 2073, op. 3, d. 19, l. 136 and 136 ob., GAVO.

236. Kurinets interview, USC Shoah Foundation.

237. Khvat interview, USC Shoah Foundation.

238. Markelis-Domnin interview, USC Shoah Foundation.

239. Klovsky, *The Road from Grodno*, 19.

240. Kremer interview, USC Shoah Foundation.

241. Blumstein, *A Little House on Mount Carmel*, 106–7.

242. Markelis-Domnin interview, USC Shoah Foundation.

243. Fleish interview, USC Shoah Foundation.

6. Exploitation and Annihilation

1. "From the Diary of Sarah Fishkin," 1 Nov. 1941, trans. Eva Zeitlin Dobkin, in Jacob Fishkin, *Heaven and Earth: The Diary of Sarah Fishkin* (N.p.: Pollack Graphics, 2005), 151.

2. Chakin interview, USC Shoah Foundation.

3. Zandman interview, USC Shoah Foundation.

4. Kurt Wiese was born 4 September 1914 in Schleusenau in Bromberg, a region ceded to Poland under the Treaty of Versailles. The son of a railway employee, Wiese completed elementary school in 1929 in Stargard in Pomerania (after 1945, Stargard Szczeciński, Poland) and subsequently received vocational training as a barber. He worked intermittently until October 1934, when he joined the Reichsheer (National Army) and served in the infantry. Wiese joined the SS in early 1937 and was assigned various guard postings around Berlin. He transferred to the SS Frontier Police in April 1939 and subsequently was posted to several towns in East Prussia. After the invasion of Poland, he carried out interrogations of persons who had illegally crossed the new border with Soviet-occupied territory in the Białystok District. Wiese was transferred to Białystok in November 1941 and to Grodno the following month. Upon assignment in Białystok, he was also made a member of the Gestapo ("The People vs. Kurt Wiese and Heinz Errelis, Accused of Murder: Verdict and Judgment, Cologne District Court, Federal Republic of Germany, June 27, 1968," in *Documents Concerning the Murder of 29,000 Jews of Grodno by the Germans, 1941–1943*, ed. Klarsfeld, 2–4). Otto Streblow's origins are far less clear. According to the historian Tikva Fatal-Knaani, Streblow was killed in the war ("After the War," Grodno Online, n.d., at http://www.grodnoonline.org/lost_worlds/section_4f_test.html). Alexandre Blumstein recalled that Streblow was in his midtwenties (*A Little House on Mount Carmel*, 149).

5. Blumstein, *A Little House on Mount Carmel*, 149–50.

6. "The People vs. Kurt Wiese and Heinz Errelis," in *Documents Concerning the Murder of 29,000 Jews of Grodno*, ed. Klarsfeld, 6. Born in West Prussia on 12 May 1912, Heinz Errelis was the son of a forester who was killed in the first year of World War I. His mother moved Heinz and his older sister to Flatow (and then after 1945 to Złotów, Poland), on the German border with Poland when most of West Prussia was incorporated into Poland under the terms of the Treaty of Versailles. Errelis completed his *Gymnasium* education in 1932 and worked as an unpaid trainee in a bank until he joined the local police force in Flatow in early 1933. He had joined the Nazi Party and the SS the previous year. Errelis rose through the ranks of the criminal police until he trained for a posting in the Gestapo in 1937. With the outbreak of war

in 1939, he was transferred to Flatow, Allenstein (April 1940), and then to Grodno (December 1941) ("The People vs. Kurt Wiese and Heinz Errelis," 5–6).

7. Karl Rinzler was an ethnic German from Romania (Krzysztof Bielawski, "Kiełbasin, O. Sołomowej St.: Former Nazi Transit Camp," Virtual Shtetl, n.d., at http://www.sztetl.org.pl/en/article/grodno/13,sites-of-martyrdom/34493,kielbasin-o-solomowej-st-former-nazi-transit-camp/).

8. "Verhandlungsniederschrift" [hearing transcript], Michael Kremer, 9 Feb. 1966, in *Documents Concerning the Destruction of the Jews of Grodno, 1941–1944*, 5 vols., ed. Serge Klarsfeld (N.p.: Beate Klarsfeld Foundation, n.d.), 1:160–61.

9. Bornstein-Bielicka, *One of the Few*, 111.

10. Bornstein-Bielicka, *One of the Few*, 113.

11. Reizer, *In the Struggle*, 114.

12. Zandman, *Never the Last Journey*, 44–45.

13. Bornstein-Bielicka, *One of the Few*, 124.

14. "Di tragedie fun grodner Yidn" [Tragedy of the Grodno Jews], journal, 11–28 Mar. 1943, p. 12, folder 58, Reference 204, Podziemne Archiwum Getta Białostockiego (Archiwum Mersika-Tenenbauma), 1941–43 [Underground Archives of the Białystok Ghetto (Mersik-Tenenbaum Archive)], ZIH.

15. Reizer, *In the Struggle*, 114.

16. Sylvia (Mydler) Kersh, Miami, FL, 23 May 1995, interview code 2797, USC Shoah Foundation.

17. Rabin interview, USC Shoah Foundation.

18. Bornstein-Bielicka, *One of the Few*, 108–9.

19. Shulman interview, USC Shoah Foundation.

20. Blumstein, *A Little House on Mount Carmel*, 113.

21. Reizer, *In the Struggle*, 112–14.

22. Utianski interview, USC Shoah Foundation.

23. Rantz interview, USC Shoah Foundation.

24. Kaletska interview by Boder, Voices of the Holocaust.

25. Blumstein, *A Little House on Mount Carmel*, 117.

26. Chakin interview, USC Shoah Foundation.

27. "Der umkum fun Grodner kehilah," in *Grodne*, ed. Rabin, 684.

28. Stadtkommandantur Grodno, Standortbefehl Nr. 16 [Standard Order], 12 Nov. 1941, RG-53.004M, reel 6 (f. 1, op. 1, d. 3, GAGO), USHMM; Geheime Staatspolizei, Dienststelle Bialystok [Gestapo] to Herren Landräte des Bezirks Bialystok [district councilors in the Białystok District], 16 Jan. 1942, RG-53.004M, reel 1 (f. 1, op. 1, d. 54, GAGO), USHMM; Der Kreiskommissar [regional commissar, Grodno] to Herrn Bürgermeister a.O.P.B. and Herren Amtskommissare [local mayors and Grodno commissar], 9 Feb. 1942, RG-53.004M, reel 1 (f. 1, op. 1, d. 53, GAGO),

USHMM; Grodno Judenrat, inventories of electrical appliances, n.d. [c. 1942], RG-53.004M, reel 2 (f. 1, op. 1, d. 150, GAGO), USHMM.

29. Reizer, *In the Struggle*, 114.

30. Abba Tarlovski, "Grodne Yudenrat" [Grodno Judenrat], in *Kovets Grodna* [Collection Grodno] (Tel Aviv: n.p., 1958), 27, Record Group 996, United Grodner Relief, folder "Grodner Awake," YIVO.

31. Chaika Grossman, "Provn fun vidershtand in Grodner geto" [Uprising Attempts in the Grodno Ghetto], in *Grodner opklangen*, 4.

32. Sitzung der Amtskommissare und Amtsbürgermeister am 30 Oktober 1941 [Meeting of the Commissars and Mayors on 30 October 1941], RG-53.004M, reel 1 (f. 1, op. 1, d. 15, GAGO), USHMM; Oberpräsident der Provinz Ostpreussen [head of the civil administration of East Prussia], *Verordnung* [regulation], 18 Sept. 1941, RG-53.004M, reel 1 (f. 1, op. 1, d. 65, GAGO), USHMM; wages for Jewish craftsmen working in the Construction Department, 1942, RG-53.004M, reel 5 (Grodnenskii burgomistr Grazhdaiskovo upravleniya Belostokskovo okruga, g. Grodno [Grodno Municipality for (German) Civilian Control Białystok District, City Grodno], f. 2, op. 1, d. 62, GAGO), USHMM; wages for non-Jewish Construction Department employees in specific projects, RG-53.004M, reel 6 (f. 2, op. 1, d. 72, GAGO), USHMM.

33. "Der umkum fun Grodner kehilah," 686.

34. Bialo interview, USC Shoah Foundation.

35. Kremer interview, USC Shoah Foundation.

36. Rabin interview, USC Shoah Foundation.

37. Zandman, *Never the Last Journey*, 63–64.

38. Bornstein-Bielicka, *One of the Few*, 110.

39. Kaletska interview by Boder, Voices of the Holocaust.

40. Bornstein-Bielicka, *One of the Few*, 116.

41. Kremer interview, USC Shoah Foundation.

42. Lazar interview, USC Shoah Foundation.

43. Zandman, *Never the Last Journey*, 45.

44. Bornstein-Bielicka, *One of the Few*, 122.

45. Gordon interview, USC Shoah Foundation.

46. "Der umkum fun Grodner kehilah," 684.

47. "Der umkum fun Grodner kehilah," 685–86.

48. Rantz interview, USC Shoah Foundation.

49. Bornstein-Bielicka, *One of the Few*, 120, 162.

50. Chakin interview, USC Shoah Foundation.

51. Lazar interview, USC Shoah Foundation.

52. Der Kreiskommissar des Kreises Grodno [regional commissar of Grodno County] to Herrn Oberpräsidenten der Provinz Ostpreussen, Zivilverwaltung für

den Bezirk Bialystok [head of the province of East Prussia, civil administration for the Białystok District], 13 Oct. 1942, RG-53.004M, reel 1 (f. 1, op. 1, d. 58, GAGO), USHMM.

53. Der Kreiskommissar des Kreises Grodno, Kreiswirtschaftsamt [regional Commissar of Grodno County, regional economic office], "Fragebogen" [Questionnaire], n.d. [c. Nov. 1942], RG-53.004M, reel 2 (f. 1, op. 1, d. 180, GAGO), USHMM.

54. Der Kreiskommissar des Kreises Grodno, Kreiswirtschaftsamt [regional commissar of Grodno County, regional economic office], memo correcting worker census of 5 Nov. 1942, 11 Nov. 1942, RG-53.004M, reel 2 (f. 1, op. 1, d. 180, GAGO), USHMM.

55. Die Deutsche Arbeitsfront, Bezirk Bialystok, Gauwaltung Ostpreussen [German labor front, Białystok District, Gau Administration East Prussia] to Kreiskommissar in Grodno [regional commissar in Grodno], 9 Dec. 1942, RG-53.004M, reel 2 (f. 1, op. 1, d. 180, GAGO), USHMM.

56. Der Kreiskommissar des Kreises Grodno, Kreiswirtschaftsamt [regional commissar of Grodno County, regional economic office] to Herrn Oberpräsident Zivilverwaltung in Bialystok [head of the civil administration in Białystok], 9 Dec. 1942, RG-53.004M, reel 2 (f. 1, op. 1, d. 180, GAGO), USHMM.

57. Der Kreiskommissar des Kreises Grodno [regional commissar of the Grodno county] to Herrn Oberpräsident der Provinz Ostpreussen, Zivilverwaltung für den Bezirk Bialystok [head of the civil administration in Białystok], 10 Dec. 1942, RG-53.004M, reel 2 (f. 1, op. 1, d. 276, GAGO), USHMM.

58. "Togbukh fun Yidishn tsar un peyn" [Diary of Jewish Sorrow and Pain], after 29 Jan 1943, p. 15, folder 21c, Reference 204, ZIH.

59. Klovsky, *The Road from Grodno*, 29; Rabin interview, USC Shoah Foundation.

60. Reizer, *In the Struggle*, 115.

61. Zandman interview, USC Shoah Foundation.

62. Zandman interview, USC Shoah Foundation; Bornstein-Bielicka, *One of the Few*, 112.

63. Bialo interview, USC Shoah Foundation.

64. Der Kreiskommissar, Kreisbauernführer [regional commissar, regional farm leader] to Kommandeur des Res. Pol. Batl. 91, Herrn Hauptmann Faust [commander of Reserve Police Battalion 91, Herrn Hauptmann Faust], 11 Mar. 1942, RG-53.004M, reel 1 (f. 1, op. 1, d. 54, GAGO), USHMM.

65. Gendarmen Posten Grandzicze, Kreis Grodno [Police Post Grandzicze, Grodno region] to Herrn Kreiskommissar in Grodno [regional commissar in Grodno], 21 Oct. 1942, RG-53.004M, reel 2 (f. 1, op. 1, d. 167, GAGO), USHMM.

66. Gendarmen Posten Grandzicze [Police Post Grandzicze], witness statements of Jankel Wassermann and Isak Grandzicki, 20 Oct. 1942, RG-53.004M, reel 2 (f. 1, op. 1, d. 167, GAGO), USHMM.

67. Der Kreiskommissar [regional commissar] to Standgericht Bialystok [State Court in Białystok], 20 Nov. 1942, RG-53.004M, reel 2 (f. 1, op. 1, d. 167, GAGO), USHMM; Transport Order, 9 Dec. 1942, RG-53.004M, reel 2 (f. 1, op. 1, d. 167, GAGO), USHMM.

68. Zandman, *Never the Last Journey*, 50.

69. Blumstein, *A Little House on Mount Carmel*, 118–19.

70. Reizer, *In the Struggle*, 143.

71. Reizer, *In the Struggle*, 125.

72. Zandman, *Never the Last Journey*, 62–63.

73. Reizer, *In the Struggle*, 126.

74. Bialo interview, USC Shoah Foundation.

75. Blumstein, *A Little House on Mount Carmel*, 129.

76. Rantz interview, USC Shoah Foundation.

77. Bialo interview, USC Shoah Foundation.

78. Bialo interview, USC Shoah Foundation.

79. Rabin interview, USC Shoah Foundation.

80. Blumstein, *A Little House on Mount Carmel*, 172.

81. "Der umkum fun Grodner kehilah," 688; Blumstein, *A Little House on Mount Carmel*, 122; Zandman interview, USC Shoah Foundation; Chakin interview, USC Shoah Foundation.

82. Zandman interview, USC Shoah Foundation; Zandman, *Never the Last Journey*, 47.

83. Shulman interview, USC Shoah Foundation.

84. Bornstein-Bielicka, *One of the Few*, 117.

85. Bornstein-Bielicka, *One of the Few*, 134.

86. Bornstein-Bielicka, *One of the Few*, 128, 131.

87. Hehalutz and Dror had merged in 1938. Organization members are referred to in this chapter according to either how they are identified in the historical literature or how they later self-identified.

88. Bornstein-Bielicka, *One of the Few*, 128.

89. Yehuda Bauer, *Rethinking the Holocaust* (New Haven, CT: Yale Univ. Press, 2001), 120. Bauer provides this characterization in the context of his discussion of *amidah*, a term that encompasses a broad range of deliberate armed and unarmed acts meant to defy the Germans' policies of oppression.

90. Nechama Tec, *Resistance: Jews and Christians Who Defied the Nazi Terror* (New York: Oxford Univ. Press, 2013), 4–5.

91. Tec, *Resistance*, 15.

92. "Der umkum fun Grodner kehilah," 689; Yitzhak Arad, *Ghetto in Flames* (New York: Holocaust Library, 1982), 224. Bella Chazan (born 1922) returned to Grodno several times in early 1942, setting up a "safe house" in the city for use by other

couriers. She traveled with fake identity papers with the name "Bronia Limanowska." She was arrested in April 1942 while transporting two guns back to Warsaw. The Gestapo took her false identity to be genuine, and she was deported as a Gentile first to Pawiak Prison in Warsaw and later to Auschwitz-Birkenau. Only after liberation (at the Malchow concentration camp, a subcamp of Ravensbrück, in April 1945) did Chazan discard her false Polish identity (Sara Bender, "Bela Ya'ari Hazan," Jewish Women's Archive Encyclopedia, n.d., at http://jwa.org/encyclopedia/article/hazan-bela-yaari).

93. Grossman, "Provn fun vidershtand in Grodner geto," 3.

94. Hashomer Hatzair leader Tosia Altman (1918–43) had fled Warsaw for Vilna with other group members in the first days of the war in 1939. Posing as a Gentile with false "Aryan" papers, Altman spent the next two years carrying messages to coordinate activities of youth groups in ghettos across Poland. She added weapons acquisition to her activities, smuggling guns, ammunition, and explosives into the Warsaw ghetto in the last months of 1942. Altman was engaged in the fighting during the Warsaw Ghetto Uprising of April–May 1943, leading a group of fighters through the sewers in the last days of the revolt. She was captured when her hiding place on the "Aryan" side of Warsaw caught fire. Suffering from horrible burns, Altman was handed over to the Germans by the Polish police. She was hospitalized but not treated. She died two days later, on 26 May 1943 (Ziva Shalev, "Tosia Altman," Jewish Women's Archive Encyclopedia, n.d., at http://jwa.org/encyclopedia/article/altman-tosia).

95. Bornstein-Bielicka, *One of the Few*, 137.

96. Bornstein-Bielicka, *One of the Few*, 136; see also Grossman, "Provn fun vidershtand in Grodner geto," 5.

97. "Der umkum fun Grodner kehilah," 689.

98. "Grodno: Youth Movements and Underground Activities," in *Lost Jewish Worlds*, ed. Spector and Freundlich, 171.

99. Bornstein-Bielicka, *One of the Few*, 155.

100. "Der umkum fun Grodner kehilah," 691.

101. Gordon interview, Univ. of California at Los Angeles.

102. "Der umkum fun Grodner kehilah," 689.

103. Grossman, *The Underground Army*, 99.

104. Bornstein-Bielicka, *One of the Few*, 149.

105. Bornstein-Bielicka, *One of the Few*, 138.

106. Bornstein-Bielicka, *One of the Few*, 137–38.

107. Bornstein-Bielicka, *One of the Few*, 138.

108. Kaletska interview by Boder, Voices of the Holocaust.

109. "Grodno: Liquidation of the Ghettos and the Deportations to the Camps (November 2, 1942–March 12, 1943)," in *Lost Jewish Worlds*, ed. Spector and Freundlich, 144.

110. Reizer, *In the Struggle*, 127. Reizer wrote that these events occurred in October, but the events described here followed the deportations and ghetto liquidation beginning in November 1942.

111. Reizer, *In the Struggle*, 127; "Der umkum fun Grodner kehilah," 692.

112. Reizer, *In the Struggle*, 127.

113. Kaletska interview by Boder, Voices of the Holocaust.

114. Yitzhak Arad, *The Holocaust in the Soviet Union*, trans. Ora Cummings (Lincoln: Univ. of Nebraska Press, 2013), 258.

115. Der Oberpräsident Zivilverwaltung für den Bezirk Bialystok [head of the civil administration of the Białystok District] to Herren Kreiskommissars des Bezirks und den Herrn Polizeipräsidenten in Bialystok [regional commissars and the head of the police in Białystok], 31 Aug. 1942, f. 1, op. 1, d. 44, l. 14 and 20, GAGO. For Grodno, these German civilian administrators collected six sets of natal and marital rolls from Catholic and Orthodox churches, one recording births as far back as 1713, along with the Soviet registry from 1 January 1940 to 21 June 1941. The records from the Jewish community extended back to 1885.

116. "Der umkum fun Grodner kehilah," 688.

117. "Grodno: Liquidation of the Ghettos and the Deportations to the Camps," 147.

118. Blumstein, *A Little House on Mount Carmel*, 168–69.

119. "Grodno: Liquidation of the Ghettos and the Deportations to the Camps," 146.

120. Gordon interview, USC Shoah Foundation; Gordon interview, Univ. of California at Los Angeles.

121. Reizer, *In the Struggle*, 128–29.

122. Blumstein, *A Little House on Mount Carmel*, 149.

123. "Pokazaniya" [Deposition], Petra Yul'yanovna Pavlovska, 11 July 1945, RG-22.002M, reel 8 (f. 7021, op. 84, d. 3, GARF), USHMM; "Svidetel'skoye pokazaniye" [Witness Testimony], Ivana Vladislavovna Kachan, 20 Aug. 1944, RG-53.002M, reel 5 (f. 845, op. 1, d. 8, NARB), USHMM; Chakin interview, USC Shoah Foundation; Blumstein, *A Little House on Mount Carmel*, 128.

124. *Zemlyanki* at Kielbasin consisted of an excavated floor approximately one-and-a-half meters deep, lined with rough planks to form bunks along the sides. This sunken shelter was covered with a pitched roof built from tree trunks, branches, and an earthen layer.

125. Bielawski, "Kiełbasin, O. Sołomowej St."

126. "Grodno: Liquidation of the Ghettos and the Deportations to the Camps," 147.

127. Utianski interview, USC Shoah Foundation.

128. Rantz interview, USC Shoah Foundation; Utianski interview, USC Shoah Foundation; Danuta Czech, *Auschwitz Chronicle, 1939–1945* (New York: Holt, 1990), 270.

129. "Der umkum fun Grodner kehilah," 693; Czech, *Auschwitz Chronicle*, 272.

130. Czech, *Auschwitz Chronicle*, 276, 281.

131. Bialo interview, USC Shoah Foundation.

132. Bornstein-Bielicka, *One of the Few*, 147.

133. "Verhandlungsniederschrift" [Hearing Transcript], Michael Kremer, 9 Feb. 1966, in *Documents Concerning the Destruction of the Jews of Grodno*, ed. Klarsfeld, 1:161.

134. Blumstein, *A Little House on Mount Carmel*, 151, 155.

135. Blumstein, *A Little House on Mount Carmel*, 171.

136. Reizer, *In the Struggle*, 133.

137. Bornstein-Bielicka, *One of the Few*, 141; "Der umkum fun Grodner kehilah," 692.

138. "Protokoll Zeugenvernehmung" [Protocol of Witness Interrogation; German-language translation of Polish-language statement], Vladimir Glembozski, 27 Feb. 1965, in *Documents Concerning the Destruction of the Jews of Grodno*, ed. Klarsfeld, 1:430.

139. Bornstein-Bielicka, *One of the Few*, 142; Zandman, *Never the Last Journey*, 59–60.

140. Chakin interview, USC Shoah Foundation.

141. Reizer, *In the Struggle*, 144–45; Lejb Rajzer (Leib Reizer), Łódź, 1945, No. 301/555, Reference 301, ZIH.

142. Blumstein, *A Little House on Mount Carmel*, 152–54.

143. Shulman interview, USC Shoah Foundation.

144. "Grodno: Youth Movements and Underground Activities," 174.

145. Grossman, "Provn fun vidershtand in Grodner geto," 6.

146. Bornstein-Bielicka, *One of the Few*, 137; Gordon interview, USC Shoah Foundation.

147. Grossman, "Provn fun vidershtand in Grodner geto," 3.

148. Bornstein-Bielicka, *One of the Few*, 140.

149. Grossman, "Provn fun vidershtand in Grodner geto," 6.

150. Bornstein-Bielicka, *One of the Few*, 159; Grossman, "Provn fun vidershtand in Grodner geto," 7.

151. Zandman, *Never the Last Journey*, 64–73.

152. "Grodno: Liquidation of the Ghettos and the Deportations to the Camps," 155.

153. Blumstein, *A Little House on Mount Carmel*, 174.

154. "Togbukh fun Yidishn tsar un peyn," after 29 Jan. 1943, p. 10. How the Jews in the Grodno ghetto learned of Anthony Eden's statement is unclear; perhaps someone in the ghetto had an illegal radio receiver.

155. "Grodno: Liquidation of the Ghettos and the Deportations to the Camps," 155.

156. "Grodno: Liquidation of the Ghettos and the Deportations to the Camps," 156.

157. "Togbukh fun Yidishn tsar un peyn," after 29 Jan. 1943, p. 12.

158. "Verhandlungsniederschrift" [Hearing Transcript], Michael Kremer, 9 Feb. 1966, 1:161–62.

159. "Grodno: Liquidation of the Ghettos and the Deportations to the Camps," 157.

160. Czech, *Auschwitz Chronicle*, 309–12. The "Deportation of the 10,000" arrived at Auschwitz-Birkenau over the course of five days: approximately 2,000 each on 20 and 21 January 1943; 3,650 on 22 January; approximately 2,000 each on 23 and 24 January (Czech, *Auschwitz Chronicle*, 309–12).

161. "Grodno: Liquidation of the Ghettos and the Deportations to the Camps," 156.

162. Reizer, *In the Struggle*, 133–36.

163. Gordon interview, Univ. of California at Los Angeles.

164. Blumstein, *A Little House on Mount Carmel*, 177–78.

165. Blumstein, *A Little House on Mount Carmel*, 183.

166. "Togbukh fun Yidishn tsar un peyn," after 29 Jan. 1943, p. 5.

167. "Togbukh fun Yidishn tsar un peyn," after 29 Jan. 1943, pp. 13–14.

168. "Grodno: Liquidation of the Ghettos and the Deportations to the Camps," 158.

169. "Grodno: Liquidation of the Ghettos and the Deportations to the Camps," 158.

170. Chakin interview, USC Shoah Foundation.

171. Gordon interview, Univ. of California at Los Angeles.

172. Bornstein-Bielicka, *One of the Few*, 149–50.

173. Bornstein-Bielicka, *One of the Few*, 150. The Germans killed the remaining eleven escapees after Polish informers reported that they were sleeping in a barn. The timing (February 1943) of a revolt on the disembarkation ramp at Treblinka indicates that perhaps some of the participants in the failed Great Synagogue uprising carried out the action. The deportation train from Grodno, which arrived in the middle of the night, was met by the usual contingent of SS, Ukrainians, and Sonderkommando forces. A group of young Jews slashed the camp personnel with knives and broken bottles. The resisters and anyone else nearby were gunned down where they stood.

Treblinka Sonderkommando member Samuel Willenberg recalled, "When we came out of the hut in the morning, we saw bodies strewn between the rags and bundles, with a thin layer of wonderful, pristine white snow covering everything" (Samuel Willenberg, *Surviving Treblinka*, ed. Władysław T. Bartoszewski, trans. Naftali Greenwood [New York: Blackwell, 1989], 63).

174. B. Borowski, "Der lebn fun di letste 1,000 Yidn in Grodne" [Life of the Last 1,000 Jews in Grodno], Mar. 1943, p. 8, folder 23, Reference 204, ZIH.

175. Klovsky, *The Road from Grodno*, 48–50; Bornstein-Bielicka, *One of the Few*, 148.

176. Kremer interview, USC Shoah Foundation.

177. Bürgermeister [of Grodno] to Kreiskommissar des Kreises Grodno, Kreiswirtschaftsamt [regional commissar of Grodno County, regional economic office], 6 Nov. 1943, RG-53.004M, reel 3 (f. 1, op. 1, d. 371, GAGO), USHMM.

178. The Reich declared that it held title to all "abandoned" items in the Białystok District through a trust controlled by Oberpräsident der Provinz Ostpreussen Erich Koch. Regional *Oberpräsident* Dr. Lalla clarified this point for the commissars under his authority: "The entire assets of the Jews, who were concentrated in camps [*sic*] during the current action falls to the German Reich." In the same statement, dated 13 November 1942, Lalla ordered the removal of property from ghettos for assessment, inventory, and storage for subsequent reuse (Der Oberpräsident, Zivilverwaltung für den Bezirk Bialystok [head of the civil administration for the Białystok District] to Herrn Kreiskommissars des Bezirk, Herrn Stadtkommissar in Bialystok [district commissars and Białystok city commissar], 13 Nov. 1942, RG-53.004M, reel 2 [f. 1, op. 1, d. 121, GAGO], USHMM).

179. "Auszug aus der Amtskommissar—Dienstbesprechung vom 6.11.1942" [Statement from the Commissar's Office, Service Meeting, 6 November 1942], 19 Nov. 1942, RG-53.004M, reel 4 (f. 1, op. 1, d. 365, GAGO), USHMM.

180. Bürgermeister [of Grodno], *Rundschreiben nr. 29 an die Wehrmachts- und Zivildienststellen und die in Grodno tätigen Reichsdeutechen* [Circular no. 29 to the Wehrmacht, Civil Authorities, and Reich Germans in Grodno], 25 Feb. 1943, RG-53.004M, reel 4 (f. 1, op. 1, d. 342, GAGO), USHMM. According to this document, the Ghetto II region was cleared of usable property by February 1943.

181. Bürgermeister [of Grodno] to Kreiskommissar des Kreises Grodno, 14 Sept. 1943, RG-53.004M, reel 3 (f. 1, op. 1, d. 371, GAGO), USHMM.

182. Rabin interview, USC Shoah Foundation.

183. Zandman, *Never the Last Journey*, 85–90.

184. Shulman interview, USC Shoah Foundation.

185. Blumstein, *A Little House on Mount Carmel*, 190–93.

186. Blumstein, *A Little House on Mount Carmel*, 226.

187. Blumstein, *A Little House on Mount Carmel*, 223, 229.

188. Rajzer Lejb, Łódź, 1945, No. 301/555, Reference 301, ZIH; Reizer, *In the Struggle*, 146–47, 150–51. Others in the ghetto learned of Reizer's theft and subsequent escape. A Grodno Jew deported to Białystok reported to the underground archive that "one group that left for the forest helped themselves to guns and uniforms from the [German] military hospital arsenal" (Eliezer, "Di reynikung-aktsie in Grodner geto fun 13 bizn 16 Februar 1943" [Cleansing Actions in the Grodno Ghetto from 13 to 16 February 1943], 23 Feb. 1943, p. 1, folder 13, Reference 204, ZIH.

189. "Grodno: Attempts at Flight and Rescue, Fighting in the Underground and with the Partisans' Units," in *Lost Jewish Worlds*, ed. Spector and Freundlich, 179.

190. Grossman, "Provn fun vidershtand in Grodner geto," 7.

191. Bornstein-Bielicka, *One of the Few*, 161–63, 163–64.

192. Borowski, "Der lebn fun di letste 1,000 Yidn in Grodne," 8.

193. Dovid Katz, "Der letster 'khashid' fun Grodne" [The Last "Hasid" of Grodno], Algemeiner.com, 14 July 2006, at http://www.algemeiner.com.

194. Gordon interview, Univ. of California at Los Angeles.

195. Gordon interview, Univ. of California at Los Angeles.

196. Gordon interview, USC Shoah Foundation.

197. Chakin interview, USC Shoah Foundation.

198. Chakin interview, USC Shoah Foundation. In addition to Zelda (Grodzienska) Gordon and Vivian Chakin (Vichna Sidranska), Linda Penn (Luba Kremer) was selected that day at the women's undressing barrack at Treblinka and transferred to Majdanek. Mrs. Penn survived the war and gave testimonies that are available through the Fortunoff Video Archive for Holocaust Testimonies at Yale University Libraries and the USC Shoah Foundation. See Linda Penn (Luba Kremer), Houston, TX, 24 Jan. 1992, T-1962, Fortunoff Video Archive of Holocaust Testimonies, Yale Univ., New Haven, CN, and Linda Penn (Luba Kremer), Houston, TX, 11 Jan. 1998, interview code 38042, USC Shoah Foundation.

7. Survival

1. "From the Diary of Sarah Fishkin," 1 Apr. 1942, trans. Eva Zeitlin Dobkin, in Fishkin, *Heaven and Earth*, 194. Sarah Fishkin's younger brother, Jacob, received the diary from their maternal aunt Rokhl after the war at Fernwald displaced persons camp. Rokhl retrieved the manuscript from its hiding place in Rubiezewicze before she and her family fled to a partisan family camp in the forests (Fishkin, *Heaven and Earth*, 74, 124–25).

2. Fishkin, *Heaven and Earth*, 94; "Togbukh fun Sore Fishkin," in *Yizkhor-bukh Rubizivitsi*, ed. Sztokfisz, 182–83.

3. The Jewish women selected at Treblinka arrived at Majdanek on 28 February 1943. Additional transports of forced laborers from France and the Netherlands selected at Sobibor reached the camp in March (Tomasz Kranz, *Extermination of*

Jews at the Majdanek Concentration Camp [Lublin, Poland: Państwowe Muzeum na Majdanku, 2007], 24).

4. Yitzhak Arad, *Belzec, Sobibor, Treblinka: The Operation Reinhard Death Camps* (Bloomington: Indiana Univ. Press, 1987), 159. The processing depot, a component of Aktion Reinhard commanded by SS and Police Leader Odilo Globocnik, was designated the Altsachenverwaltungsstelle der Standortverwaltung Lublin (Used Things Utilization Plant of the Garrison Administration in Lublin) in March 1943 (Kranz, *Extermination of Jews at the Majdanek Concentration Camp*, 33–34).

5. Gordon interview, Univ. of California at Los Angeles; Gordon interview, USC Shoah Foundation.

6. Chakin interview, USC Shoah Foundation; Penn interview, USC Shoah Foundation.

7. Gordon interview, Univ. of California at Los Angeles.

8. Arad, *Belzec, Sobibor, Treblinka*, 154–55.

9. Chakin interview, USC Shoah Foundation.

10. Penn interview, Fortunoff Video Archive of Holocaust Testimonies.

11. Chakin interview, USC Shoah Foundation.

12. Gordon interview, Univ. of California at Los Angeles.

13. "Bliżyn," in *Der Ort des Terrors: Geschichte der nationalsozialistischen Konzentrationslager* [The Place of Terror: History of the National Socialist Concentration Camp], vol. 7: *Niederhagen-Wewelsburg, Lublin-Majdanek, Arbeitsdorf, Herzogenbusch (Vught), Bergen-Belsen, Mittlebau-Dora*, ed. Wolfgang Benz and Barbara Distel (Munich: Beck, 2008), 85–86.

14. Gordon interview, USC Shoah Foundation.

15. Gordon interview, USC Shoah Foundation.

16. Gordon interview, Univ. of California at Los Angeles.

17. Reichsführer-SS Heinrich Himmler ordered the action to forestall another Jewish uprising as had occurred at the Warsaw and Białystok ghettos as well as at the Treblinka and Sobibor annihilation camps.

18. Gordon interview, Univ. of California at Los Angeles.

19. Chakin interview, USC Shoah Foundation. Trawniki served several functions, one of which was as a forced-labor camp, with Jewish prisoners producing clothing and other items for the Wehrmacht. Approximately 6,000 Jewish laborers and their families were being held in the camp at the time of its liquidation ("Trawniki," in *Der Ort des Terrors*, ed. Benz and Distel, 7:99).

20. Chakin interview, USC Shoah Foundation. Vichna was probably among the prisoners who arrived at Birkenau on 28 July 1944. Of the more than 1,000 prisoners, Jews and non-Jews, who were marched on foot from Majdanek on 22 July, 229 male Jews and 156 female Jews were tattooed with numbers after selection at Birkenau and

admitted into the camp. An additional 452 non-Jewish prisoners, male and female, were admitted as well (Czech, *Auschwitz Chronicle*, 569).

21. A transport of male and female Jewish prisoners from Bliżyn arrived at Birkenau on 31 July 1944. From this transport, 1,614 male Jews and 715 female Jews were admitted into the camp and tattooed with numbers (Czech, *Auschwitz Chronicle*, 674).

22. Gordon interview, USC Shoah Foundation.

23. Gordon interview, USC Shoah Foundation.

24. Gordon interview, USC Shoah Foundation.

25. Chakin interview, USC Shoah Foundation.

26. Andrzej Strzelecki, "The History, Role, and Operation of the 'Central Camp Sauna' in Auschwitz II–Birkenau," in *The Architecture of Crime: The "Central Camp Sauna" in Auschwitz II–Birkenau*, ed. Teresa Świebocka, trans. William Brand (Oświęcim, Poland: Auschwitz-Birkenau State Museum, 2001), 12–13.

27. Bialo interview, USC Shoah Foundation.

28. Bialo interview, USC Shoah Foundation.

29. Chakin interview, USC Shoah Foundation.

30. Gordon interview, Univ. of California at Los Angeles.

31. Kremer interview, USC Shoah Foundation.

32. Klovsky, *The Road from Grodno*, 69–73.

33. Kremer interview, USC Shoah Foundation; Klovsky, *The Road from Grodno*, 75–77.

34. Klovsky, *The Road from Grodno*, 79.

35. The Białystok transport arrived at Birkenau on 12 January 1944 with some 1,000 male and female Jewish prisoners from Stutthof. From the total number, 120 men and 134 women were admitted into the camp. The remaining prisoners (386 men and 360 women) were killed in the gas chamber (Czech, *Auschwitz Chronicle*, 569).

36. Daniel Klovsky recalled little of his first hours in Birkenau until decades later, when he met again with Moishe Kremer and they discussed their shared experiences (Klovsky, *The Road from Grodno*, 87).

37. Klovsky, *The Road from Grodno*, 86–89.

38. Kremer interview, USC Shoah Foundation.

39. Klovsky, *The Road from Grodno*, 100.

40. Chakin interview, USC Shoah Foundation.

41. Gordon interview, USC Shoah Foundation.

42. Bialo interview, USC Shoah Foundation. The Germans' official name for the Jaworzno subcamp was SS Arbeitslager (Labor Camp) Neu-Dachs. The labor-deployment roster for Jaworzno-Neu-Dachs in September 1943 lists 2,394 prisoners, including 258 skilled workers (Czech, *Auschwitz Chronicle*, 674).

43. Bialo interview, USC Shoah Foundation.

44. Gordon interview, Univ. of California at Los Angeles.

45. Gordon interview, Univ. of California at Los Angeles; Gordon interview, USC Shoah Foundation.

46. Chakin interview, USC Shoah Foundation.

47. Gordon interview, Univ. of California at Los Angeles.

48. Chakin interview, USC Shoah Foundation.

49. Gordon interview, Univ. of California at Los Angeles; Gordon interview, USC Shoah Foundation.

50. Chakin interview, USC Shoah Foundation.

51. Klovsky, *The Road from Grodno*, 122.

52. Kremer interview, USC Shoah Foundation.

53. Kremer interview, USC Shoah Foundation.

54. Kremer interview, USC Shoah Foundation.

55. Blumstein, *A Little House on Mount Carmel*, 206–24.

56. Zandman, *Never the Last Journey*, 88–99.

57. Blumstein, *A Little House on Mount Carmel*, 262.

58. Blumstein, *A Little House on Mount Carmel*, 241, 217.

59. Zandman, *Never the Last Journey*, 112–13.

60. Blumstein, *A Little House on Mount Carmel*, 255.

61. Zandman, *Never the Last Journey*, 103.

62. Zandman, *Never the Last Journey*, 101.

63. Zandman, *Never the Last Journey*, 47.

64. Blumstein, *A Little House on Mount Carmel*, 240, 277.

65. Markelis-Domnin interview, USC Shoah Foundation.

66. Markelis-Domnin interview, USC Shoah Foundation.

67. Fleish interview, USC Shoah Foundation. Lev Fleish did not say where his meeting with Morozov took place, although from some other remarks he made, it likely occurred when he had slipped out of the ghetto in search for food.

68. Fleish interview, USC Shoah Foundation.

69. Fleish interview, USC Shoah Foundation.

70. Markelis-Domnin interview, USC Shoah Foundation.

71. Markelis-Domnin interview, USC Shoah Foundation.

72. Fleish interview, USC Shoah Foundation.

73. Fleish interview, USC Shoah Foundation.

74. See chapter 6, "Labor Deployment instead of Annihilation: Policy on Foreigners, 1942," in Ulrich Herbert, *Hitler's Foreign Workers: Enforced Foreign Labor in Germany under the Third Reich* (New York: Cambridge Univ. Press, 1997), esp. 143–76.

75. Fleish interview, USC Shoah Foundation.

76. "Die Daimler-Benz Motoren GmbH Genshagen," in *Zwangsarbeit in Genshagen: Dokumentierte, Erinnerungen, Betroffener* [Slave Labor in Genshagen: Documents, Remembrances, Aftereffects], ed. Martina Dietrich (Potsdam, Germany: Brandenburgische Landeszentrale für politische Bildung, 1996), 16–19. In the last months of 1944, the SS constructed a subcamp in nearby Genshagen to quarter an additional 1,100 slave laborers, mostly adult women but also adolescents and children, drawn from the inmate population of Ravensbrück concentration camp. Although the Genshagen subcamp had women prisoners from Ravensbrück, it was administered as a subcamp of Sachsenhausen (Stephan Jegielka, *Das KZ-Aussenlager Genshagen: Struktur und Wahrnehmung der Zwangsarbeit in einem Rüstungsbetrieb 1944–45* [The KZ-Subcamp Genshagen: Structure and Experience of Slave Labor in an Armaments Plant, 1944–45] [Marburg, Germany: Tectum, 2005], 38, 57).

77. Fleish interview, USC Shoah Foundation.

78. Fleish interview, USC Shoah Foundation.

79. Markelis-Domnin interview, USC Shoah Foundation.

80. One of the largest POW camp in the German-occupied east, Stalag 319 consisted of four camps labeled A, B, C, and D. Fivel Markelis did not name the one in which he was held, but his description suggests it was 319A.

81. Andrzej Henryk Rybak, *Stalag 319: Międzynarodowy obóz jeniecki w Chełmie w latach 1941–1944* [Stalag 319: International Prisoner Camp in Chełm in the Years 1941–1944] (Che*ł*m, Poland: Stowarzzyszenie Rocznik Chełmski, 2009), 277, fig. 3.

82. Rybak, *Stalag 319*, 43–48.

83. Christian Streit, "Soviet Prisoners of War in the Hands of the Wehrmacht," in *War of Extermination: The German Military in World War II, 1941–1944*, ed. Hannes Heer and Klaus Naumann (New York: Berghahn Books, 2000), 88.

84. Markelis-Domnin interview, USC Shoah Foundation.

85. Markelis-Domnin interview, USC Shoah Foundation.

86. The Germans established several subcamps and forced-labor camps in the Danzig region, but the only one large enough to fit Fivel's description would have been the Stutthof concentration camp (Markelis-Domnin interview, USC Shoah Foundation).

87. Markelis-Domnin interview, USC Shoah Foundation.

88. Markelis-Domnin interview, USC Shoah Foundation; "Königsberg (Kaliningrad)," in *Der Ort des Terrors: Geschichte der nationalsozialistischen Konzentrationslager* [The Place of Terror: History of the National Socialist Concentration Camp], vol. 6: *Natzweiler*, *Gross-Rosen*, *Stutthof*, ed. Wolfgang Benz and Barbara Distel (Munich: Beck, 2007), 668.

89. Markelis-Domnin interview, USC Shoah Foundation.

90. Between 1,000 and 1,500 exhausted Jewish prisoners were killed along the road during the first days of the death march. The journey ended on the beach at

Palmnicken on the Baltic. Some 3,000 camp inmates were shot from the hillside with automatic weapons; only about 200 escaped and successfully hid in buildings abandoned by fleeing Germans (Daniel Blatman, *The Death Marches: The Final Phase of Nazi Genocide*, trans. Chaya Galai [Cambridge, MA: Harvard Univ. Press, 2011], 117–24).

91. Markelis-Domnin interview, USC Shoah Foundation.

92. Bornstein-Bielicka, *One of the Few*, 178.

93. Bornstein-Bielicka, *One of the Few*, 194.

94. Bornstein-Bielicka, *One of the Few*, 165–71.

95. Bornstein-Bielicka, *One of the Few*, 172, 181.

96. Bender, *The Jews of Białystok*, 185–91.

97. Bender, *The Jews of Białystok*, 203.

98. Bender, *The Jews of Białystok*, 214.

99. Bornstein-Bielicka, *One of the Few*, 210.

100. Bender, *The Jews of Białystok*, 159; Bornstein-Bielicka, *One of the Few*, 194–97.

101. Lenore J. Weitzman, "Bronka Klibanski: 1923–2011," Jewish Women's Archive Encyclopedia, n.d., at http://jwa.org/encyclopedia/article/klibanski-bronka-bronia.

102. Bornstein-Bielicka, *One of the Few*, 206, 210.

103. Bornstein-Bielicka, *One of the Few*, 215–19.

104. Bornstein-Bielicka, *One of the Few*, 221.

105. Bender, *The Jews of* Białystok, 261, 268–69.

106. Bender, *The Jews of Białystok*, 274.

107. Bornstein-Bielicka, *One of the Few*, 224–25.

108. Bender, *The Jews of Białystok*, 295.

109. Bender, *The Jews of Białystok*, 240–41. Otto Busse had joined the Nazi Party in 1933 but left in 1935 owing to the escalating anti-Jewish policies. He rejoined the party in 1939 under pressure from local officials in East Prussia. Although a committed antifascist, his politics were not distinctly socialist or communist. Chasia Bielicka referred to him as a *Bibelforscher*, a term often applied to followers of Jehovah's Witness, although he does not appear to have been a member of the sect (see "The Righteous among the Nations: Otto Busse," Yad Vashem website, n.d., at http://db.yadvashem.org/righteous/family.html?language=en&itemId=4014199, and Bornstein-Bielicka, *One of the Few*, 236).

110. Bornstein-Bielicka, *One of the Few*, 251.

111. Bornstein-Bielicka, *One of the Few*, 257.

112. Reizer, *In the Struggle*, 147–57.

113. Neither Reizer's postwar memoir nor his testimony for the Central Historical Commission, both written in the immediate postwar years, provides detail about

his contributions to partisan fighting operations (Reizer, *In the Struggle*; Lejb Rajzer, Łódź, 1945, No. 301/555, Reference 301, ZIH).

114. Reizer, *In the Struggle*, 158–59.

115. Reizer, *In the Struggle*, 162.

116. Leib Reizer remembered the massacre as occurring in the middle of 1943, but the historian and Jewish partisan Yitzhak Arad places the event in October of that year (Reizer, *In the Struggle*, 163–64; Yitzhak Arad, *In the Shadow of the Red Banner* [Jerusalem: Gefen Publishing House, 2010], 286).

117. Reizer, *In the Struggle*, 163–64, 168–70, 170–74.

118. Klovsky, *The Road from Grodno*, 89–96.

119. Klovsky, *The Road from Grodno*, 96.

120. Members of the international left-wing resistance organization successfully placed several key functionaries in the camp secretarial pool, labor-assignment office, political department, and hospital at Monowitz. This underground movement was established by Jewish political prisoners from Germany, Austria, and Poland. Among them was Stefan Heymann, a German Jew and Communist who took a personal interest in the welfare of David and Daniel Klovsky (Henryk Świebocki, "The Establishment and Growth of the Clandestine Movement in the Camp," in *Auschwitz 1940–1945: Central Issues in the History of the Camp*, vol. 4: *The Resistance Movement*, ed. Wacław Długoborski and Franciszek Piper, trans. William Brand [Oświęcim, Poland: Auschwitz-Birkenau State Museum, 2000], 127–28). See Klovsky, *The Road from Grodno*, 95–166, for Daniel Klovsky's perspectives on the Communist resistance members, including group leader Stefan Heymann.

121. Irene Strzelecka, "The Hospitals at Auschwitz Concentration Camp," in *Auschwitz 1940–1945: Central Issues in the History of the Camp*, vol. 2: *The Prisoners—Their Life and Work*, ed. Wacław Długoborski and Franciszek Piper, trans. William Brand (Oświęcim, Poland: Auschwitz-Birkenau State Museum, 2000), 298.

122. Klovsky, *The Road from Grodno*, 99, 105, 108. Izik Klovsky was arrested and imprisoned by the Polish authorities in the late 1930s. He returned to Grodno after the Soviet occupation in 1939. Evacuated from Grodno with the Red Army on 22 June 1941, Izik was presumed killed during the Soviet retreat (Klovsky, *The Road from Grodno*, 16).

123. Klovsky, *The Road from Grodno*, 133–36.

124. Klovsky, *The Road from Grodno*, 62–65.

125. Bialo interview, USC Shoah Foundation.

126. Zavgorodnev interview, USC Shoah Foundation.

127. Zavgorodnev interview, USC Shoah Foundation.

128. David Dodin, St. Petersburg, Russia, 5 Apr. 1998, Russian language, interview code 41093, USC Shoah Foundation.

129. Aleksandr Erofimov (Isaak Erukhimov), St. Petersburg, Russia, 16 Jan. 1996, Russian language, interview code 8494, USC Shoah Foundation.

130. The smaller number of survival accounts from young Jewish women might suggest that fewer women from Vitebsk survived. This is perhaps somewhat true because young women were less likely to abandon family members before the arrival of the Wehrmacht or during the first weeks of German occupation. Affecting such a calculation, however, was the deployment of young men in the armed forces as well as the greater number of young women who fled with their parents and younger siblings to escape the German military advance.

131. Zibert interview, USC Shoah Foundation.

132. Kurinets interview, USC Shoah Foundation; Daniel Romanovsky, "Liozno," in *Encyclopedia of Camps and Ghettos, 1933–1945*, ed. Dean, 2:1700.

133. See Albert Kaganovitch, "Stalin's Great Power Politics, the Return of Jewish Refugees to Poland, and Continued Migration to Palestine, 1944–1946," *Holocaust and Genocide Studies* 26, no. 1 (Spring 2012): 59–83.

134. Although Grodno remained within the Soviet Union, Białystok and its environs were returned to Poland in September 1944.

135. Gordon interview, Univ. of California at Los Angeles.

136. Chakin interview, USC Shoah Foundation.

137. Klovsky, *The Road from Grodno*, 149–51, 171–96, 273–74.

138. Klovsky, *The Road from Grodno*, 284.

139. Reizer, *In the Struggle*, 177.

140. Betty (Reizer) Broit, afterward to Reizer, *In the Struggle*, 179–80.

141. Bornstein-Bielicka, *One of the Few*, 277–89.

142. Y. Rapoport, "Grodner meydlekh" [Grodno Girls], *Eynikayt*, no. 4 (Apr. 1946), 25, microfilm serial 1977-Y-1072, YIVO.

143. Markelis-Domnin interview, USC Shoah Foundation.

144. Fleish interview, USC Shoah Foundation.

145. Erofimov interview, USC Shoah Foundation.

146. Gennadi Kostyrchenko, *Out of the Red Shadows: Anti-semitism in Stalin's Russia* (Amherst, NY: Prometheus Books, 1995), 14–19.

147. Shulman, "Ostrov Relesa," 253; Reles interview by Kellman, Brandeis Univ.

148. Reles, *Di yidish-sovetishe shrayber fun Vaysrusland*, 48; Alexander Statiev, *The Soviet Counterinsurgency in the Western Borderlands* (New York: Cambridge Univ. Press, 2010), 55.

149. Gennady Estraikh, *Yiddish in the Cold War* (London: Legenda, 2008), 41; Ioffe, "Patriarkh evreiskoi literaturi v Belarusi," 6.

150. Mikhail Gerchik, "Yevreiskaya Atlantida: Razmyshleniya nad knigoi G. Relesa" [Jewish Atlantis: Reflections on the Work of G. Reles], *Mishpokha* 20 (2007): 157.

151. Reles, *Di yidish-sovetishe shrayber fun Vaysrusland*, 70.

152. Arkadii Shulman, "Pokoleniye Relesa: Pamyati pisatalya" [Reles's Generation: The Writer Remembered], *Aviv* (Minsk), Oct.–Nov. 2004, 20; Reles interview by Kellman, Brandeis Univ.

153. Gringauz interview, USC Shoah Foundation; Alexander Kruglov, "Usviaty," trans. Steven Seegel, in *Encyclopedia of Camps and Ghettos*, ed. Dean, 2:1833.

154. Gringauz interview, USC Shoah Foundation.

155. Estraikh, *Yiddish in the Cold War*, 64.

156. Hirsh Reles, "In yenem vinkele" [In Every Corner], *Sovetish Heymland* (Jan. 1973): 130.

Bibliography

Archives

Belarus

Gosudarstvennyi arkhiv Grodnenskoi oblasti [State Archive Grodno Oblast] (GAGO)

Fond 1, Grodnenskii uyezdnyi komissar Grazhdaiskovo upravleniya Belostokskovo okruga, g. Grodno [Grodno County Commissar for (German) Civilian Control Białystok District, City Grodno]

Fond 2, Grodnenskii burgomistr Grazhdaiskovo upravleniya Belostokskovo okruga, g. Grodno [Grodno Municipality for (German) Civilian Control Białystok District, City Grodno]

Fond 56, Grodnenskaya yevreiskaya religioznaya obshchina [Grodno Jewish Religious Community] (GERO)

Fond 219, Chastnaya yevreiskaya uchitel'skaya seminariya obshchestva "Tarbut" [Grodno Private Jewish Teachers' Seminary "Tarbut"]

Fond 242, Upravleniye sel'skovo stroitel'stva, ispolnitel'novo komiteta Grodnenskovo oblastnovo, Soveta deputatov trudyashchikhsya [Management of Rural Construction, Executive Committee Grodno Oblast, Council of People's Deputies]

Fond 292, Ispolnitel'nyi komitet Belostokskogo gorodskogo Soveta deputatov trudiashchikhsia, g. Belostok [Executive Committee, Białystok Municipal Council of Workers Deputies]

Fond 1029, Komissariya po rassledovaniyo i ustanovleniyo zlodeyanii Nemetsko-fashistskikh . . . [Commission of Inquiry into the Atrocities of and the Damages Caused by the German-Fascist Invaders . . .]

Fond 1385, Upolnomochennyi Soveta no delam religioznykh kul'tov pri Sovete Ministrov SSSR po Grodnenskoi oblasti [Commissioner of the Council for Religious Affairs under the Council of Ministers of the USSR, Grodno Oblast]

Gosudarstvennyi arkhiv Vitebskoi oblasti [State Archive Vitebsk Oblast] (GAVO)

Fond 1-P, Vitebskii oblastnoi komitet Kommunisticheskoi partii Belorussii [Vitebsk Regional Committee of the Communist Party of Belarus]

Fond 102-P, Fondi mestnikh organov Kommunisticheskoi partii Belorussii, Gorodskiye komiteti KPb, Vitebskii [Records of Local Communist Party Organizations of Belarus, Vitebsk]

Fond 905, Vitebskoye evreiskoye pedagogicheskoye uchilishche [Vitebsk Jewish Pedagogical School] (VEPU)

Fond 1439-P, Upolnomochennyi Soveta no delam religioznykh kul'tov pri Sovete Ministrov SSSR po Grodnenskoi oblasti [Commissioner of the Council for Religious Affairs under the Council of Ministers of the USSR, Vitebsk Oblast]

Fond 2073, Vitebskaya gorodskaya uprava [Vitebsk City Council] (VGU)

Fond 4029-P, Upolnomochennyi Soveta no delam religioznykh kul'tov pri Sovete Ministrov SSSR po Grodnenskoi oblasti [Commissioner of the Council for Religious Affairs under the Council of Ministers of the USSR, Vitebsk Oblast]

Fond 7045-P, Fondi mestnikh organov Kommunisticheskoi partii Belorussii, Gorodskiye komiteti KPb, Glubokskii [Records of Local Communist Party Organizations of Belarus, Glubokie]

Fond 7046-P, Kommunisticheskoi partii Belorussii, Gorodskiye komiteti KPb, Dokshytsy [Records of Local Communist Party Organizations of Belarus, Dokshitzy]

Israel

Yad Vashem

Record Group M.41, Archives in Belarus

Record Group O.33, Testimonies, Diaries, and Memoirs Collection

Record Group O.53, Ludwigsburg USSR Collection

Poland

Żydowski Instytut Historyczny [Jewish Historical Institute], Warsaw (ZIH)

Reference 204, Podziemne Archiwum Getta Białostockiego (Archiwum Mersika-Tenenbauma), 1941–43 [Underground Archives of the Białystok Ghetto (Mersik-Tenenbaum Archive)]

Borowski, B. "Der lebn fun di letste 1,000 Yidn in Grodne" [Life of the Last 1,000 Jews in Grodno]. Mar. 1943. Folder 23.

Eliezer. "Di reynikung-aktsie in Grodner geto fun 13 bizn 16 Februar 1943" [Cleansing Actions in the Grodno Ghetto from 13 to 16 February 1943]. 23 Feb. 1943. Folder 13.

"Togbukh fun Yidishn tsar un peyn" [Diary of Jewish Sorrow and Pain]. N.d. [after 29 Jan. 1943]. Folder 21c.

"Di tragedie fun grodner Yidn" [Tragedy of the Grodno Jews]. Journal, 11 to 28 Mar. 1943. Folder 58.

Reference 301, Zbiór relacji Żydów Ocalałych z Zagłady [Collection of Holocaust Survivor Testimonies, Recorded by the Central Historical Commission of the Central Committee of the Jews in Poland]

Grajneman, Borys (Boris Grayneman). 20 June 1947. No. 301/4766.

Rajzer, Lejb [Leib Reizer]. Łódź, 1945. No. 301/555.

United States

American Jewish Joint Distribution Committee Archives, New York (JDC Archives)

File 338a, Organizations; Jewish Orphan Asylum, Grodno

File 354, Individual Yeshivot; Shaar Hatorah, Grodno, 1928–29

File 408, Countries and Regions; Poland: Localities, Chomsk to Jezierzany

File 486, Agro-Joint report, "Concerning Its Industrial Work, 1934"

File 506, USSR, Localities U–V; Vitebsk

File 833, Poland, Cultural and Religious, Yeshivot and Seminaries, Miscellaneous

File 874, Reports and Memos on Refugee Problems in Poland, 1934, 1937–39

National Archives and Record Administration, College Park, MD

T-175, Records of the Reich Leader of the SS and Chief of the German Police

T-454, Records of the Reich Ministry for the Occupied Eastern Territories, 1941–45

T-459, Records of the Reich Commissioner for the Baltic States, 1941–45
T-501, Records of German Field Commands: Rear Areas, Occupied Territories and Others, Microfilm Publication
United States Holocaust Memorial Museum Archives, Washington, DC (USHMM)
Accession 1996.A.0169, Holocaust-Related Records from European Archives Collected by Yad Vashem
RG-06.025*43, Central Archives of the Federal Security Services (former KGB) of the Russian Federation, Records Relating to War Crime Trials in the Soviet Union, 1939–92
RG-11.001M.01, Reichssicherheitshauptampt (RSHA)-SD, Berlin
RG-18.002M, Selected Records from the Latvian Central State Historical Archive
RG-22.002M, Selected Records of the Extraordinary State Commission to Investigate German-Fascist Crimes Committed on Soviet Territory, 1941–45
RG-22.028M, Records of the Jewish Anti-Fascist Committee from the Gosudarstvennyi arkhiv Rossiiskoi federatsii [State Archives of the Russian Federation] (GARF), Fond 8114, opis 1, 1942–48
RG-53.002M, Selected Records of the Belarus Central State Archives, Minsk
RG-53.004M, Selected Records from the Grodno Oblast Archive
RG-53.005M, Gomel Oblast Archive records, 1941–47
RG-53.006M, Mogilev Oblast Archive records, 1941–45
YIVO Institute for Jewish Research Archives, New York (YIVO)
Microfilm serial 1977-Y-1072, *Eynikayt.*
Record Group 4, Autobiographies of Jewish Youth
Anonymous autobiography ["Yankl"]. 1934. No. 3556.
Berkalt. "Oytobiografie" [Autobiography]. 1939. No. 3534.
"Oytobiografie" [Autobiography]. 1934. No. 3555.
"Oytobiografie fun Hanan L. in Grodne" [Autobiography of Hanan L. in Grodno]. 1934. No. 3553.
Żubawitsky, L. [Leib]. "Meyn oytobiografie" [My Autobiography]. 1939. No. 3554.
Record Group 104, Eyewitness Accounts of the Holocaust Period
Record Group 230, Leon Arkin Papers
Record Group 358, Joseph A. Rosen Papers

Record Group 996, United Grodner Relief
Record Group 1400, Bund Archives
Unaccessioned records
Sarah Fishkin diary

Contemporary Newspapers and Periodicals

Grodno

Grodner kurier (Yiddish); hard copies in GAGO, f. 56
Grodner lebn (Yiddish); microfiche at Biblioteka Narodowa, Warsaw
Grodner moment (Yiddish); hard copies in GAGO, f. 56; microfiche at Biblioteka Narodowa, Warsaw
Grodner shtime (Yiddish); hard copies in GAGO, f. 56
Kurier Grodzieński (Polish); microfiche at Biblioteka Narodowa, Warsaw

Minsk

Oktyabr (Yiddish); microfilm at YIVO Institute for Jewish Research, New York, and Dorot Jewish Division, New York Public Library
Shtern (Yiddish); microfilm at YIVO

Moscow

Der emes; microfilm at Dorot Jewish Division, New York Public Library
Eynikayt; microfilm serial 1977-Y-1072 at YIVO

New York

Forverts; hard copies at YIVO

Riga

Kamf; microfilm at Dorot Jewish Division, New York Public Library

Vitebsk

Chyrvonaya zvyazda (Belarusian); hard copies in GAVO, f. 2289, op. 2, d. 131
Vitsebski praletarii (Belarusian, Russian, Yiddish, and Polish); hard copies in GAVO, f. 2285, op. 2, d. 125
Vitsebski rabochy (Belarusian); hard copies in GAVO, f. 2289, op. 2, d. 132
Zarya zapada (Russian); *Vitebsker arbet* (Yiddish), biweekly supplement; hard copies in GAVO, f. 2289, op. 2, d. 118

Warsaw

Haynt (Yiddish); microfilm at Dorot Jewish Division, New York Public Library

INTERVIEWS

Fortunoff Video Archive of Holocaust Testimonies, Yale Univ., New Haven, CN

Kesselman, Rita (Rivke Altshuler). 13 Apr. 1989. Interview by the Holocaust Center of the Jewish Federation of the North Shore (Peabody, MA, 1989). HVT-1432.

Klibanski, Bronia (Winicka). 11 Apr. 1979. Interview by the Holocaust Survivors Film Project, Jerusalem, 1979. HVT-76.

Penn, Linda (Luba Kremer). Houston, TX, 24 Jan. 1992. T-1962.

Online Archives

Harvard Project on the Soviet Social System. At https://library.harvard.edu/collections/hpsss/index.html.

"My Shtetl." Project "Voices of Jewish Settlements: Vitebsk Region." At http://shtetle.co.il/shtetls/vitebsk_reg_eng.html.

Voices of the Holocaust. Interviews by David Boder. Paul V. Galvin Library, Illinois Institute of Technology, Chicago. At http://voices.iit.edu.

Kaletska, Anna (Kovitzka). Wiesbaden, Germany, 26 Sept. 1946. Interview by David P. Boder. Yiddish language.

Ya pomnyu: Vocpominaniya veteranov VOV [I Remember: Memoirs of Soviet Veterans of the Great Patriotic War]. At http://iremember.ru.
Lesin, Grigorii Isaakovich. N.p., n.d.

Other Oral History Interviews

Gordon, Zelda (Grodzienska). 6 Mar. 1984. Interview by Univ. of California at Los Angeles. At the 1939 Society website, http://www.the1939society.org/.

Reles, Hirsh. Minsk, Belarus, 2003. Interview by Ellen Kellman, Brandeis Univ.

USC Shoah Foundation, Univ. of Southern California, Los Angeles

Bialo, Leo (Leib). Lyndhurst, OH, 27 Jan. 1997. Interview code 25406.

Bromberg, Shlomo. Rehovot, Israel, 31 July 1996. Interview code 18113.

Ceder, Joseph. Far Rockaway, NY, 12 May 1996. Interview code 15128.
Chakin, Vivian (Vichna Sidranska). Los Angeles, 21 Nov. 1995. Interview code 7457.
Dimant, Alexander. Vancouver, Canada, 4 Dec. 1996. Interview code 24025.
Dodin, David. St. Petersburg, Russia, 5 Apr. 1998. Interview code 41093.
Ekstein, Elka (Fomin). North Borwin, Australia, 21 Oct. 1996. Interview code 21518.
Erofimov, Aleksandr (Isaak Erukhimov). St. Petersburg, Russia, 16 Jan. 1996. Interview code 8494.
Feigenbaum, Lucien. White Plains, NY, 11 June 1996. Interview code 16030.
Fleish, Lev. Rishon LeZiyyon, Israel, 12 June 1997. Interview code 30205.
Goldenberg, Frida (Fruma Rabinovich). Lincolnwood, IL, 1 Dec. 1997. Interview code 26584.
Gordon, Zelda (Grodzienska). Beverly Hills, CA, 15 July 1994. Interview code 15.
Gringauz, Raisa (Gendelev). Caspar, WY, 10 Mar. 2000. Interview code 50727.
Grozalsky, Sima (Kapulska). Hollywood, FL, 20 Mar. 1997. Interview code 27452.
Hollander, Ruth (Rozalia Herbshteyn). Phoenix, AZ, 6 Jan. 1996. Interview code 33260.
Huze, Dora (Blum). Melbourne, Australia, 13 June 1997. Interview code 32477.
Kersh, Sylvia (Mydler). Miami, FL, 23 May 1995. Interview code 2797.
Khvat, Dmitri. Jaffa, Israel, 20 Sept. 1996. Interview code 19847.
Kremer, Michael (Moishe). Hollywood, FL, 16 Mar. 1997. Interview code 27415.
Kurinets, Vera (German). Penza, Russia, 5 July 1997. Interview code 33813.
Lazar, Ann (Lewin). [No city], CA, 6 Mar. 1997. Interview code 27890.
Markelis-Domnin, Efim (Fivel Markelis). Tallinn, Estonia, 1 May 1997. Interview code 31115.
Martel, Max (Markiewitz). Los Angeles, 7 Feb. 1995. Interview code 817.
Paczynski, Liliana (Goldsopl). Ottawa, Canada, 25 Sept. 1996. Interview code 20082.
Penn, Linda (Luba Kremer). Houston, TX, 11 Jan. 1998. Interview code 38042.
Pototskaia, Elizaveta (Gurevich). Odessa, Ukraine, 27 May 1998. Interview code 46371.

Rabin, Yehuda (Rabinovich). Melbourne, Australia, 4 Feb. 1997. Interview code 26578.

Rantz, Fenia (Muller). [No city], FL, 14 Oct. 1996. Interview code 22686.

Rubinstein, Elias. Melbourne, Australia, 5 Oct. 1997. Interview code 35876.

Shulman, Bella (Ilin). Melbourne, Australia, 30 Nov. 1997. Interview code 35750.

Sisun, Sidney. Woodmere, NY, 8 Oct. 1996. Interview code 20823.

Utianski, Mina (Muller). North Miami Beach, FL, 17 July 1996. Interview code 17402.

Zandman, Felix (Shraga Feliks). Bala Cynwyd, PA, 19 Dec. 1997. Interview code 36736.

Zavgorodnev, Stepan. Kiev, Ukraine, 15 Apr. 1998. Interview code 43514.

Zbar, Iosif Moisevich. Grodno, Belarus, 24 Oct. 1997. Interview code 50572.

Zibert, Elena (Choukmazova). Vitebsk, Belarus, May 1998. Interview code 49456.

Photographs in Archives

American Jewish Joint Distribution Committee Archives, New York (JDC Archives)

NY 01787, NY 01789, NY 01796, NY 01798, and NY 01839 through NY 01848, Pogrom damage, Grodno, June 1935.

Yad Vashem Photo Archive

1366/405, Grodno, Poland, broken windows of a store mistakenly believed to be owned by Jews, 7 June 1935.

1366/406, Grodno, Poland, display window shattered in a pogrom, 7 June 1935.

2982/218, Poland, Jews deported to Grodno ghetto by the German police, [1 Nov. 1941].

3403/7, Grodno, Poland, deportation to the ghetto, [1 Nov. 1941].

3745/70, Grodno, Poland, Jews deported to the ghetto, [1 Nov. 1941].

3745/72, Grodno, Poland, Jews deported to the ghetto, 1942 [*sic*] [1 Nov. 1941].

Published Sources

Agresja sowiecka 17 września 1939 roku na Kresach Wschodnich i Lubelszczyźnie [Soviet Aggression 17 September 1939 in the Eastern Borderlands and the Lublin Region]. Vol. 1. Edited by Tomasza Rodziewicza. Lublin, Poland: Towarzystwo przyjaciół Grodna i Wilna, 2011.

Akselrod, Zelik. "Lager" [Camp]. In *Ordentregerishe Vaysrusland* [Belarus, the Common Porter], ed. Zelik Akselrod and Hirsh Kamenetsky, 238–40. Minsk, Belarus: Melukhe-farlag fun Vaysrusland, 1939.

———. *Oyg af oyg* [Eye to Eye]. Minsk, Belarus: Melukhe-farlag fun Vaysrusland, 1937.

Akselrod, Zelik, and Hirsh Kamenetsky, eds. *Ordentregerishe Vaysrusland* [Belarus, the Common Porter]. Minsk, Belarus: Melukhe-farlag fun Vaysrusland, 1939.

Allworth, Edward, ed. *Soviet Nationality Problems.* New York: Columbia Univ. Press, 1971.

Altshuler, Mordechai. "The Distress of Jews in the Soviet Union in the Wake of the Molotov-Ribbentrop Pact." *Yad Vashem Studies* 36, no. 2 (2008): 73–114.

———. *Religion and Jewish Identity in the Soviet Union, 1941–1964.* Translated by Saadya Sternberg. Lebanon, NH: Brandeis Univ. Press, 2012.

———. *Soviet Jewry on the Eve of the Holocaust: A Social and Demographic Profile.* Jerusalem: Center for Research of East European Jewry, Hebrew Univ., 1998.

Anderson, Barbara A., and Brian Silver. "Demographic Analysis and Population Catastrophes in the USSR." *Slavic Review* 44, no. 3 (Autumn 1985): 517–36.

———. "Tautologies in the Study of Excess Mortality in the USSR in the 1930s." *Slavic Review* 45, no. 2 (Summer 1986): 307–13.

Arad, Yitzhak. *Belzec, Sobibor, Treblinka: The Operation Reinhard Death Camps.* Bloomington: Indiana Univ. Press, 1987.

———. *Ghetto in Flames.* New York: Holocaust Library, 1982.

———. *The Holocaust in the Soviet Union.* Translated by Ora Cummings. Lincoln: Univ. of Nebraska Press, 2013.

———. *In the Shadow of the Red Banner.* Jerusalem: Gefen, 2010.

Arad, Yitzhak, Shmuel Krakowski, and Shmuel Spector, eds. *The Einsatzgruppen Reports.* Translated by Stella Schossberger. New York: Holocaust Library, 1989.

Aronson, Gregor, Jacob Lestschinsky, and Avraham Kihn. *Vitebsk amol: Geshikhte, zikhroynes, hurbn* [Lost Vitebsk: History, Memoirs, Destruction]. New York: Waldon Press, 1956.

Aviram, Tzevi (Hershl Abramovich). "Epizodn un refleksn" [Episodes and Reflections]. In *Grodner opklangen* [Grodno Echoes], 17–21. Buenos Aires: n.p., Sept. 1975.

Barabik, Berachah (Friedman). "Gviet adot" [Testimony]. In *Sefer Sokolkah: Dos bukh fun Sokolke* [Book of Sokolka], edited by Ester Miszkinski, David Yardeni, Ben-Zion Hasid, and Yekutiel Chinski, 525–30. Jerusalem: n.p., 1968.

Barkai, Avraham. "Jewish Life under Persecution." In *German-Jewish History in Modern Times*, vol. 4: *Renewal and Destruction, 1918–1945*, edited by Michael A. Meyer, 231–57. New York: Columbia Univ. Press, 1998.

Bauer, Yehuda. *The Death of the Shtetl.* New Haven, CT: Yale Univ. Press, 2009.

———. *Rethinking the Holocaust.* New Haven, CT: Yale Univ. Press, 2001.

"Belarusian Homer." N.d. At http://www.democraticbelarus.eu/node/5810.

Bellamy, Chris. *Absolute War: Soviet Russia in the Second World War.* New York: Vintage Books, 2007.

Bemporad, Elissa. *Becoming Soviet Jews: The Bolshevik Experiment in Minsk.* Bloomington: Indiana Univ. Press, 2013.

Bender, Sara. "Bela Ya'ari Hazan." Jewish Women's Archive Encyclopedia, n.d. At http://jwa.org/encyclopedia/article/hazan-bela-yaari.

———. *The Jews of Białystok during World War II and the Holocaust.* Translated by Yaffa Murciano. Lebanon, NH: Brandeis Univ. Press, 2008.

Benz, Wolfgang, and Barbara Distel, eds. *Der Ort des Terrors: Geschichte der nationalsozialistischen Konzentrationslager* [The Place of Terror: History of the National Socialist Concentration Camp]. Vol. 6: *Natzweiler, Gross-Rosen, Stutthof.* Munich: Beck, 2007.

———, eds. *Der Ort des Terrors: Geschichte der nationalsozialistischen Konzentrationslager* [The Place of Terror: History of the National Socialist Concentration Camp]. Vol. 7: *Niederhagen-Wewelsburg, Lublin-Majdanek, Arbeitsdorf, Herzogenbusch (Vught), Bergen-Belsen, Mittlebau-Dora.* Munich: Beck, 2008.

Berkhoff, Karel C. *Harvest of Despair: Life and Death in Ukraine under Nazi Rule.* Cambridge, MA: Belknap Press of Harvard Univ. Press, 2004.

Bielawski, Krzysztof. "Kiełbasin, O. Sołomowej St.: Former Nazi Transit Camp." Virtual Shtetl, n.d. At http://www.sztetl.org.pl/en/article/grodno/13,sites-of-martyrdom/34493,kielbasin-o-solomowej-st-former-nazi-transit-camp/.

Blatman, Daniel. *The Death Marches: The Final Phase of Nazi Genocide*. Translated by Chaya Galai. Cambridge, MA: Harvard Univ. Press, 2011.

Blitstein, Peter A. "Nation-Building or Russification? Obligatory Russian Instruction in the Soviet Non-Russian School, 1938–1953." In *A State of Nations: Empire and Nation-Making in the Age of Lenin and Stalin*, edited by Ronald Grigor Suny and Terry Martin, 253–74. New York: Oxford Univ. Press, 2001.

Blumstein, Alexandre. *A Little House on Mount Carmel*. London: Valentine Mitchell, 2002.

Bornstein-Bielicka, Chasia, with Neomi Izhar. *One of the Few: A Resistance Fighter and Educator, 1939–1947*. Translated by Naftali Greenwood. Jerusalem: Yad Vashem, 2009.

Brandon, Ray, and Wendy Lower, eds. *The Shoah in Ukraine: History, Testimony, Memorialization*. Bloomington: Indiana Univ. Press, 2008.

Broderzon, Sheyne Miriam. *Mayn laydns-veg mit Moishe Broderzon: Di milkhome hot gedoiert far undz zibetsn yor* [My Road of Suffering with Moishe Broderzon: For Us the War Lasted Seventeen Years]. Buenos Aires: Tsentral-farband fun Poilishe Yidn in Argentine, 1960.

Broit, Betty (Reizer). Afterward to Leib Reizer, *In the Struggle: Memoirs from Grodno and the Forests*, translated by Haike Beruriah Wiegand, 179–84. Jerusalem: Yad Vashem, 2009.

Brown, Kate. *A Biography of No Place: From Ethnic Borderland to Soviet Heartland*. Cambridge, MA: Harvard Univ. Press, 2004.

Browning, Christopher R., with Jürgen Matthäus. *The Origins of the Final Solution: The Evolution of Nazi Jewish Policy, September 1939–March 1942*. Lincoln: Univ. of Nebraska Press, 2004.

Brubaker, Rogers. *Nationalism Reframed: Nationhood and the National Question in the New Europe*. New York: Cambridge Univ. Press, 1996.

———. "Nationhood and the National Question in the Soviet Union and Post-Soviet Eurasia: An Institutionalist Account." *Theory and Society* 23 (1994): 47–78.

Cała, Alina. "The Social Consciousness of Young Jews in Interwar Poland." In *Polin*, vol. 8: *Jews in Independent Poland, 1918–1939*, 42–65. Portland, OR: Littman Library of Jewish Civilization, 1994.

Chapnik, Lisa. "The Grodno Ghetto and Its Underground: A Personal Narrative." In *Women in the Holocaust*, edited by Dalia Ofer and Lenore J. Weitzman, 109–19. New Haven, CT: Yale Univ. Press, 1998.

Chiari, Bernhard. *Alltag hinter der Front: Besatzung, Kollaboration, und Widerstand in Weissrussland, 1941–1944* [Everyday Life behind the Front: Occupation, Collaboration, and Resistance in Belarus,1941–1944]. Düsseldorf: Droste, 1998.

Cholawsky, Shalom. *The Jews of Bielorussia during World War II.* Amsterdam: Harwood Academic, 1998.

Conquest, Robert. *The Great Terror: A Reassessment.* New York: Oxford Univ. Press, 1990.

———. *The Great Terror: Stalin's Purge of the Thirties.* New York: Macmillan, 1968.

———, ed. *Soviet Nationalities Policy in Practice.* New York: Praeger, 1967.

Corning, Amy D. "Emigration, Generation, and Collective Memories: The Presence of the Past for Emigrants from the Former Soviet Union." *Social Psychology Quarterly* 73, no. 3 (Sept. 2010): 223–44.

Curilla, Wolfgang. *Die deutsche Ordnungspolizei und die Holocaust im Baltikum und im Weissrussland, 1941–1944* [The German Order Police and the Holocaust in the Baltic Region and in Belarus, 1941–1944]. Paderborn, Germany: Ferdinand Schöningh, 2006.

Cymet, David. "Polish State Antisemitism as a Major Factor Leading to the Holocaust." *Journal of Genocide Research* 1, no. 2 (1999): 169–212.

Czaykowski, Bogdan. "Soviet Policies in the Literary Sphere: Their Effects and Implications." In *The Soviet Takeover of the Polish Eastern Provinces, 1939–41*, edited by Keith Sword, 102–30. New York: St. Martin's Press, 1991.

Czech, Danuta. *Auschwitz Chronicle, 1939–1945.* New York: Holt, 1990.

Davies, Sarah. *Popular Opinion in Stalin's Russia: Terror, Propaganda, and Dissent, 1934–1941.* Cambridge: Cambridge Univ. Press, 1997.

Dean, Martin. *Collaboration in the Holocaust: Crimes of the Local Police in Belorussia and Ukraine, 1941–44.* New York: St. Martin's Press, 2000.

———, ed. *Encyclopedia of Camps and Ghettos, 1933–1945.* Vol. 2: *Ghettos in German-Occupied Eastern Europe*, part A and part B. Bloomington: Indiana Univ. Press, 2012.

———. *Robbing the Jews: The Confiscation of Jewish Property in the Holocaust, 1933–1945.* Cambridge: Cambridge Univ. Press, 2008.

Deportation of Polish Citizens from Western Ukraine and Western Belarus in the Year 1940. Moscow: Federal Security Service of the Russian Federation, Ministry of Internal Affairs; Warsaw: Republic of Poland Institute of

National Remembrance, Commission for Prosecution of Crimes against the Polish Nation, 2003.

Dietrich, Martina, ed. *Zwangsarbeit in Genshagen: Dokumentierte, Erinnerungen, Betroffener* [Slave Labor in Genshagen: Documents, Remembrances, Aftereffects]. Potsdam, Germany: Brandenburgische Landeszentrale für politische Bildung, 1996.

Dimanstein, Semion Markovich, ed. *Yidn in FSSR: Zamlbukh* [Jews in the USSR: Anthology]. Moscow: "Mezhdunarodnaya niga" un Farlag "Emes," 1935.

Dobroszycki, Lucjan, and Jeffrey S. Gorock, eds. *The Holocaust in the Soviet Union: Studies and Sources on the Destruction of the Jews in the Nazi-Occupied Territories of the USSR, 1941–1945*. Armonk, NY: M. E. Sharpe, 1993.

Dubson, Vadim. "Toward a Central Database of Evacuated Soviet Jews' Names, for the Study of the Holocaust in the Occupied Soviet Territories." *Holocaust Genocide Studies* 26, no. 1 (Spring 2012): 95–119.

Dwork, Debórah. *Children with a Star: Jewish Youth in Nazi Europe*. New Haven, CT: Yale Univ. Press, 1991.

Edele, Mark. *Stalinist Society, 1928–1953*. New York: Oxford Univ. Press, 2011.

Ekstein, Elka. *Chutzpe un Draystkayt: A Teenager with Chutzpah and Tenacity in the Holocaust*. Victoria, Australia: Makor Jewish Community Library, 2006.

Engerman, David C. *Know Your Enemy: The Rise and Fall of America's Soviet Experts*. New York: Oxford Univ. Press, 2009.

Estraikh, Gennady. *In Harness: Yiddish Writers' Romance with Communism*. Syracuse, NY: Syracuse Univ. Press, 2005.

———. "Pyrrhic Victories of Soviet Yiddish Language Planners." *Eastern European Jewish Affairs* 23, no. 2 (Winter 1993): 25–37.

———. *Yiddish in the Cold War*. London: Legenda, 2008.

Etiudn tsu der alt-yidisher geshikhte [Studies in Ancient Jewish History]. Adapted by A. Yuditski from A. Ranovitsh, *Etiud iber der geshikhte fun der alt-yidisher religie* [Historical Overview of the Ancient Jewish Religion]. Moscow: Melukhe-farlag "Der emes," 1940.

Evans, Richard J. *The Third Reich at War*. New York: Penguin Books, 2008.

Fatal-Knaani, Tikva. "After the War." Grodno Online, n.d. At http://www.grodnoonline.org/lost_worlds/section_4f_test.html.

———. *Zo lo otah Grodnoh: Ḳehilat Grodnoh u-sevivatah ba-milḥamah uva-Sho'ah, 1939–1943* [Grodno Is Not the Same: Jewish Community of

Grodno and Vicinity during the War and the Holocaust]. Jerusalem: Yad Vashem, 2001.

Figes, Orlando. *The Whisperers: Private Life in Stalin's Russia*. New York: Metropolitan Books, 2007.

Finkel, Evgeny. *Ordinary Jews: Choice and Survival during the Holocaust*. Princeton, NJ: Princeton Univ. Press, 2017.

Fishkin, Jacob. *Heaven and Earth: The Diary of Sarah Fishkin*. N.p.: Pollack Graphics, 2005.

Fitzpatrick, Sheila. *Everyday Stalinism: Ordinary Life in Extraordinary Times, Soviet Russia in the 1930s*. New York: Oxford Univ. Press, 1999.

Fleischhauer, Ingeborg. *Das Dritte Reich und die Deutschen in der Sowjetunion* [The Third Reich and the Germans in the Soviet Union]. Stuttgart: Deutsche Verlags-Anstalt, 1983.

"Fota vitsebskava geta pradali na avktsyonye" [Photo of Vitebsk Ghetto Sold at Auction]. *Narodniya naviny Vitsebska*, 28 Nov. 2011. At http://news.vitebsk.cc/2011/11/28/fota-vitsebskaga-geta-pradali-na-awktsyiyone/.

Gankina, Inyessa. "Portret na fonye veka" [Portrait against the Background of the Century]. *Aviv* (Minsk), Apr.–May 2001, 24.

Gaunt, David, Paul A. Levine, and Laura Palosuo, eds. *Collaboration and Resistance during the Holocaust: Belarus, Estonia, Latvia, Lithuania*. New York: Peter Lang, 2004.

Gerasimova, Inna. "Evreiskoye obrazovaniye v Belarusi v 20–30-kh godakh" [Jewish Education in Belarus in the 1920s and 1930s]. In *Evrei Belarusi*, vol. 2, edited by Inna Gerasimova, 58–72. Minsk, Belarus: PKP "ARTIFEKS," 1998.

Gerchik, Mikhail. "Yevreiskaya Atlantida: Razmyshleniya nad knigoi G. Relesa" [Jewish Atlantis: Reflections on the Work of G. Reles]. *Mishpokha* 20 (2007): 154–58.

Gerlach, Christian. "German Economic Interests, Occupation Policy, and the Murder of the Jews in Belorussia, 1941–43." In *National Socialist Extermination Policies: Contemporary German Perspectives and Controversies*, edited by Ulrich Herbert, 210–39. New York: Berghahn Books, 2000.

———. *Kalkulierte Morde: Die deutsche Wirtschafts- und Vernichtungs-politik in Weißrußland, 1941 bis 1944* [Calculated Murder: German Economic and Destruction Politics in Belarus, 1941 to 1944]. Hamburg, Germany: Hamburger Edition, 1999.

Getty, J. Arch. *Origins of the Great Purges: The Soviet Communist Party Reconsidered, 1933–1938*. New York: Cambridge Univ. Press, 1985.

Gitelman, Zvi. *A Century of Ambivalence: The Jews of Russia and the Soviet Union, 1881 to the Present*. 2nd ed. Bloomington: Indiana Univ. Press, 2001.

———. *Jewish Nationality and Soviet Politics: The Jewish Sections of the CPSU, 1917–1930*. Princeton, NJ: Princeton Univ. Press, 1972.

Goldhagen, Erich, ed. *Ethnic Minorities in the Soviet Union*. New York: Praeger, 1968.

Goldman, Wendy Z. *Inventing the Enemy: Denunciation and Terror in Stalin's Russia*. New York: Cambridge Univ. Press, 2011.

———. *Women at the Gates: Gender and Industry in Stalin's Russia*. Cambridge: Cambridge Univ. Press, 2002.

———. *Women, the State, and Revolution: Soviet Family Policy and Social Life, 1917–1936*. Cambridge: Cambridge Univ. Press, 1993.

Gordon, Harold [Hirshl Grodzienski]. *The Last Sunrise: A True Story*. Salinas, CA: H&J, 1989.

Gorodetsky, Gabriel. *Grand Illusion: Stalin and the German Invasion of Russia*. New Haven, CT: Yale Univ. Press, 1999.

Govrin, Yosef. *The Jewish Factor in the Relations between Nazi Germany and the Soviet Union, 1933–1941*. Portland, OR: Vallentine Mitchell, 2009.

Grabowski, Jan. *Hunt for the Jews: Betrayal and Murder in German-Occupied Poland*. Bloomington: Indiana Univ. Press, 2013.

Greenbaum, Alfred A. "Soviet Jewry during the Lenin–Stalin Period." *Soviet Studies* 16, no. 4 (Apr. 1965): 406–21.

Gregory, Paul R. *Terror by Quota: State Security from Lenin to Stalin (an Archival Study)*. New Haven, CT: Yale Univ. Press, 2009.

Grodner opklangen [Grodno Echoes]. Buenos Aires: n.p., Sept. 1975.

Grosman, Moishe. *In farkishuftn land fun legendarn Dzshugashvili: Mayne zibn yor lebn in Ratnfarband, 1939–1946* [In the Enchanted Land of the Legendary Jugashvili: My Seven Years in the Soviet Union]. Paris: Emes un Frayhayt, 1950.

Gross, Jan T. *Neighbors: The Destruction of the Jewish Community in Jedwabne, Poland*. Princeton, NJ: Princeton Univ. Press, 2001.

———. *Revolution from Abroad: The Soviet Conquest of Poland's Western Ukraine and Western Belorussia*. Exp. ed. Princeton, NJ: Princeton Univ. Press, 2002.

Grossman, Chaika. "Provn fun vidershtand in Grodner geto" [Uprising Attempts in the Grodno Ghetto]. In *Grodner opklangen* [Grodno Echoes], 3–11. Bueno Aires: n.p., July 1961.

———. *The Underground Army: Fighters of the Białystok Ghetto*. Edited by Sol Lewis. Translated by Shmuel Beeri. New York: Holocaust Library, 1987.

Gutman, Yisrael. "Polish Antisemitism between the Wars: An Overview." In *The Jews of Poland between Two World Wars*, edited by Yisrael Gutman, Ezra Mendelsohn, Jehuda Reinharz, and Chone Shmeruk, 97–108. Hanover, NH: Univ. Press of New England, 1989.

———. "Youth and Resistance Movements in Historical Perspective." Interview by Daniel Blatman. *Yad Vashem Studies* 23 (1993): 1–71.

Hagenloh, Paul. *Stalin's Police: Public Order and Mass Repression in the USSR, 1926–1941*. Baltimore: John Hopkins Univ. Press, 2009.

Harris, James. *The Great Fear: Stalin's Terror in the 1930s*. New York: Oxford Univ. Press, 2016.

Hasenclever, Jörn. *Wehrmacht und Besatzungspolitik in der Sowjetunion: Die Befehlshaber der rückwärtigen Heeresgebiete, 1941–1943* [Wehrmacht and Occupation Policy in the Soviet Union: The Commanders of the Rear Army Areas]. Paderborn, Germany: Ferdinand Schöningh, 2010.

Heer, Hannes. "Killing Fields: The Wehrmacht and the Holocaust in Belorussia, 1941–42." In *War of Extermination: The German Military in World War II, 1941–1944*, edited by Hannes Heer and Klaus Naumann, 55–79. New York: Berghahn Books, 2000.

"Henekh Shvedik (1914–1942)." *Sovetish Heymland* 10 (Oct. 1988): 168.

Herbert, Ulrich. *Hitler's Foreign Workers: Enforced Foreign Labor in Germany under the Third Reich*. New York: Cambridge Univ. Press, 1997.

Hirsch, Francine. *Empire of Nations: Ethnographic Knowledge and the Making of the Soviet Union*. Ithaca, NY: Cornell Univ. Press, 2005.

———. "Race without the Practice of Racial Politics." *Slavic Review* 61, no. 1 (spring 2002): 30–43.

Holmes, Larry E. *The Kremlin and the Schoolhouse: Reforming Education in Soviet Russia, 1917–1931*. Bloomington: Indiana Univ. Press, 1991.

Hundert, Gershon David, ed. *The YIVO Encyclopedia of Jews in Eastern Europe*. 2 vols. New Haven, CT: Yale Univ. Press, 2008.

Ioffe, Emmanuel. "Patriarkh evreiskoi literaturi v Belarusi" [Patriarch of Jewish Literature in Belarus]. Introduction to Grigorii [Hirsh] Reles,

V krayu svetlykh beryoz [In the Country of Bright Birches], 3–11. Minsk, Belarus: Izdatel E. S. Gilperin, 1997.

Ioffe, Grigory. "Understanding Belarus: Belarusian Identity." *Europe–Asia Studies* 55, no. 8 (Dec. 2003): 1241–72.

———. "Understanding Belarus: Questions of Language." *Europe–Asia Studies* 55, no. 7 (Nov. 2003): 1009–47.

Iwanow, Mikołaj. "The Byelorussian of Eastern Poland under Soviet Occupation, 1939–1941." In *The Soviet Takeover of the Polish Eastern Provinces, 1939–41*, edited by Keith Sword, 253–67. New York: St. Martin's Press, 1991.

Jacobs, Jack. *Bundist Counterculture in Interwar Poland*. Syracuse, NY: Syracuse Univ. Press, 2009.

Jegielka, Stephan. *Das KZ-Aussenlager Genshagen: Struktur und Wahrnehmung der Zwangsarbeit in einem Rüstungsbetrieb 1944–45* [The KZ-Subcamp Genshagen: Structure and Experience of Slave Labor in an Armaments Plant, 1944–45]. Marburg, Germany: Tectum, 2005.

Jeśmanowa, Teresa, ed. *Stalin's Ethnic Cleansing in Eastern Poland: Tales of the Deported, 1940–1946*. London: Association of the Families of the Borderland Settlers, 2000.

Johnston, Timothy. *Being Soviet: Identity, Rumour, and Everyday Life under Stalin, 1939–1953*. New York: Oxford Univ. Press, 2011.

Jolluck, Katherine R. *Exile and Identity: Polish Women in the Soviet Union during World War II*. Pittsburgh: Univ. of Pittsburgh Press, 2002.

Justiz und NS-Verbrechen: Sammlung deutscher Strafurteile wegen nationalsozialistischer Tötungsverbrechen, 1945–1966 [Justice and Nazi Crimes: Collection of German Criminal Convictions for Nazi Homicides, 1945–1966]. Vol. 18. Amsterdam: Univ. Press Amsterdam, 1978.

Justiz und NS-Verbrechen: Sammlung deutscher Strafurteile wegen nationalsozialistischer Tötungsverbrechen, 1945–1999 [Justice and Nazi Crimes: Collection of German Criminal Convictions for Nazi Homicides, 1945–1999]. Vol. 25. Amsterdam: Univ. Press Amsterdam, 2001.

Kaganovitch, Albert. "Stalin's Great Power Politics, the Return of Jewish Refugees to Poland, and Continued Migration to Palestine, 1944–1946." *Holocaust and Genocide Studies* 26, no. 1 (Spring 2012): 59–83.

Kahan, Sore. *In veg* [In the Path]. Minsk, Belarus: Melukhe-farlag fun Vaysrusland, 1934.

Kaplan Appel, Tamar. "Esther Frumkin, 1880–1943." Jewish Women's Archive Encyclopedia, n.d. At https://jwa.org/encyclopedia/article/frumkin-esther.

Karu, Baruch, ed. *Vitebsk*. Tel Aviv: n.p., 1957.

Kassow, Samuel D. *Who Will Write Our History? Rediscovering a Hidden Archive from the Warsaw Ghetto*. New York: Vintage Books, 2009.

Katz, Dovid. "Der letster 'khashid' fun Grodne" [The Last "Hasid" of Grodno]. Algemeiner.com, 14 July 2006. At http://www.algemeiner.com/generic.asp?id-1953.

Katzenlenberg, Leah. "Af dem vaynt mayn hartz" [From the Cry of My Heart]. In *Disnah: Sefer zikaron li-kehilah* [Disna: Memorial Book of the Community], edited by Dov Bernsthayn (Shalom Tsirlin), 139–54. Tel Aviv: Irgun yots'e Disnah be-Yiśra'el uve-Ar. ha-B., 1969.

Kay, Alex J. *The Making of an SS Killer: The Life of Colonel Alfred Filbert, 1905–1990*. New York: Cambridge Univ. Press, 2016.

———. "Transition to Genocide, July 1941: Einsatzkommando 9 and the Annihilation of Soviet Jewry." *Holocaust and Genocide Studies* 27, no. 3 (Winter 2013): 411–42.

Kelly, Catriona. *Children's World: Growing Up in Russia, 1890–1991*. New Haven, CT: Yale Univ. Press, 2007.

Kershaw, Ian. *Fateful Choices: Ten Decisions That Changed the World, 1940–1941*. New York: Penguin Press, 2007.

Kharik, Dina. "Eto svetly obraz" [This Bright Visage]. *Mishpokha* 7 (2000): 55–63.

Kharik, Izi. *Af a fremder khasene* [At a Stranger's Wedding]. Minsk, Belarus: Melukhe-farlag fun Vaysrusland, 1936.

———. *Finf poems* [Five Poems]. Minsk, Belarus: Melukhe-farlag fun Vaysrusland, 1936.

Klarsfeld, Serge, ed. *Documents Concerning the Destruction of the Jews of Grodno, 1941–1944*. 5 vols. N.p.: Beate Klarsfeld Foundation, n.d.

———, ed. *Documents Concerning the Murder of 29,000 Jews of Grodno by the Germans, 1941–1943: Ghetto and Deportations to Death Camps: Cologne and Bielefeld Trials*. Translated by Bill Templer. Ramat-Gan, Israel: Grodner Association of Israel, 1989.

Klibanski, Bronia. "In the Ghetto and in the Resistance: A Personal Narrative." In *Women in the Holocaust*, edited by Dalia Ofer and Lenore J. Weitzman, 175–86. New Haven, CT: Yale Univ. Press, 1998.

Klovsky, Daniel. *The Road from Grodno*. Samara, Russia: n.p., 2003.

Kogon, Eugen, Hermann Langbein, and Adalbert Rückerl, eds. *Nazi Mass Murder: A Documentary History of the Use of Poison Gas*. Translated by Mary Scott and Caroline Lloyd-Morris. New Haven, CT: Yale Univ. Press, 1993.

Korbonski, Andrzej. "The Polish Communist Party 1938–1942." *Slavic Review* 26, no. 3 (Sept. 1967): 430–44.

Korey, William. "The Origins and Development of Soviet Antisemitism: An Analysis." *Slavic Review* 31, no. 1 (Mar. 1972): 111–35.

Korzec, Paweł, and Jean-Charles Szurek. "Jews and Poles under Soviet Occupation (1939–1941): Conflicting Interests." In *From Shtetl to Socialism: Studies from Polin*, edited by Antony Polonsky, 385–406. Washington, DC: Littman Library of Jewish Civilization, 1993.

Kostyrchenko, Gennadi. *Out of the Red Shadows: Anti-semitism in Stalin's Russia*. Amherst, NY: Prometheus Books, 1995.

Kotkin, Stephen. *Magnetic Mountain: Stalinism as a Civilization*. Berkeley: Univ. of California Press, 1995.

Kotlerman, Ber Boris. *In Search of Milk and Honey: The Theater of "Soviet Jewish Statehood" (1934–49)*. Bloomington, IN: Slavica, 2009.

——— [Boris (Ber) Kotlerman]. "'Why I Am in Favour of Birobidzhan': Bergelson's Fateful Decision (1932)." In *David Bergelson: From Modernism to Socialist Realism*, edited by Joseph Sherman and Gennady Estraikh, 222–35. London: Modern Humanities Research Association and Maney, 2007.

Kranz, Tomasz. *Extermination of Jews at the Majdanek Concentration Camp*. Lublin, Poland: Państwowe Muzeum na Majdanku, 2007.

Krivut, V. I. *Molodyozhniye organizatsii no territorii zapadnoi Belarusi (1929–1939 gg.)* [Youth Organizations in Western Belarus (1929–1939)]. Minsk: Belarusskaya nauka, 2008.

Krupa, Władysław. "Osada Budowla, District Grodno." In *Stalin's Ethnic Cleansing in Eastern Poland: Tales of the Deported, 1940–1946*, edited by Teresa Jeśmanowa, 731–42. London: Association of the Families of the Borderland Settlers, 2000.

Kuromiya, Hiroaki. *The Voices of the Dead: Stalin's Great Purges in the 1930s*. New Haven, CT: Yale Univ. Press, 2007.

Lederman, David. *Fun yener zayt forhang* [From Those Times Past]. Buenos Aires: Tsentral-farband fun Poylishe Yidn in Argentine, 1960.

Le Foll, Claire. "The 'Belorussianisation' of the Jewish Population during the Interwar Period: Discourses and Achievements in Political and Cultural Spheres." *Eastern European Jewish Affairs* 38, no. 1 (Apr. 2008): 65–88.

Lestschinsky, Jacob. "The Jews in the Cities of the Republic of Poland." In *East European Jews in Two Worlds: Studies from the YIVO Annual*, edited by Deborah Dash Moore, 103–24. Evanston, IL: Northwestern Univ. Press, 1990.

———. "Der yidisher handl inem kleynem shtetl fun Poyln" [Jewish Trade in the Small Towns of Poland]. *Di yidishe ekonomik* 1 (May 1937): 7–18.

Levin, Dov. "The Fateful Decision: The Flight of the Jews into the Soviet Interior in the Summer of 1941." *Yad Vashem Studies* 20 (1990): 115–42.

———. *The Lesser of Two Evils: Eastern European Jewry under Soviet Rule, 1939–1941*. Translated by Naftali Greenwood. Philadelphia: Jewish Publication Society, 1995.

Linder, Menachem. "Der hurbn funem yidishn handl in Białystoker Raion" [The Destruction of Jewish Trade in the Białystok District]. *Di yidishe ekonomik* 1 (June 1937): 13–33.

Lipovski, Isaiah. "Der yidisher handl in tsofn-mizrekh-Poyln" [Jewish Trade in Northeastern Poland]. *Di yidishe ekonomik* 4–6 (Apr.–June 1939): 210–25.

Litvak, Yosef. "The Plight of Refugees from the German-Occupied Territories." In *The Soviet Takeover of the Polish Eastern Provinces, 1939–41*, edited by Keith Sword, 57–70. New York: St. Martin's Press, 1991.

———. "Polish-Jewish Refugees Repatriated from the Soviet Union to Poland at the End of the Second World War." In *Jews in Eastern Poland and the USSR, 1939–46*, edited by Norman Davies and Antony Polonsky, 227–39. New York: St. Martin's Press, 1991.

Lobodenko, Gleb. "Girsh Reles: 'Nadeyus uspet' . . . '" [Girsh Reles: "I Hope to Have Time"]. *Aviv* (Minsk), Mar.–Apr. 2003, 2–3.

Lower, Wendy. "Facilitating Genocide: Nazi Ghettoization Practices in Occupied Ukraine, 1941–1942." In *Life in the Ghettos during the Holocaust*, edited by Eric J. Sterling, 120–44. Syracuse, NY: Syracuse Univ. Press, 2005.

———. *Nazi Empire Building in Ukraine*. Chapel Hill: Univ. of North Carolina Press, 2007.

Lubachko, Ivan S. *Belorussia under Soviet Rule, 1917–1957*. Lexington: Univ. Press of Kentucky, 1972.

Malanowski, Jan. "Sociological Aspects of the Annexation of Poland's Eastern Provinces to the USSR in 1939–41." In *The Soviet Takeover of the Polish Eastern Provinces, 1939–41*, edited by Keith Sword, 71–85. New York: St. Martin's Press, 1991.

Mallmann, Klaus-Michael, Andrej Angrick, Jürgen Matthäus, and Martin Cüppers, eds. *Die "Ereignismeldungen UdSSR" 1941: Dokumente der Einsatzgruppen in der Sowjetunion* [The "Dispatches USSR" 1941: Documents of the Einsatzgruppen in the Soviet Union]. Damstadt, Germany: Wissenschaftliche Buchgesellschaft, 2011.

Manley, Rebecca. *To the Tashkent Station: Evacuation and Survival in the Soviet Union at War.* Ithaca, NY: Cornell Univ. Press, 2009.

Marakov, Leanid. *Akhvyary i karniki* [Victims and Criminals]. Minsk, Belarus: Vydavets Zmitser Kolas, 2007.

Margolis, O. *Viazoy lebn Yidn in Sovetnland* [How Jews Live in the Soviet Union]. Moscow: Melukhe-farlag "Der emes," 1940.

Martin, Terry. *The Affirmative Action Empire: Nations and Nationalism in the Soviet Union, 1923–1939.* Ithaca, NY: Cornell Univ. Press, 2001.

McLoughlin, Barry, "Mass Operations of the NKVD, 1937–8: A Survey." In *Stalin's Terror: High Politics and Mass Repression in the Soviet Union*, edited by Barry McLoughlin and Kevin McDermott, 118–52. New York: Palgrave Macmillan, 2003.

Megargee, Geoffrey P. *War of Annihilation: Combat and Genocide on the Eastern Front, 1941.* Lanham, MD: Rowman and Littlefield, 2007.

Meltser, David, and Vladimir Levin. *The Black Book with Red Pages: Tragedy and Heroism of Belorussian Jews.* Cockeysville, MD: VIA Press, 2005.

Melzer, Emanuel. "Antisemitism in the Last Years of the Second Polish Republic." In *The Jews of Poland between Two World Wars*, edited by Yisrael Gutman, Ezra Mendelsohn, Jehuda Reinharz, and Chone Shmeruk, 126–37. Hanover, NH: Univ. Press of New England, 1989.

Memorial [Organization]. "List of Purge Victims" (in Russian). N.d. http://lists.memo.ru.

Mendelsohn, Ezra. *The Jews of East Central Europe between the World Wars.* Bloomington: Indiana Univ. Press, 1983.

Merridale, Catherine. *Ivan's War: Life and Death in the Red Army, 1939–1945.* New York: Metropolitan Books, 2006.

Michlic, Joanna Beata. *Poland's Threatening Other: The Image of the Jew from 1880 to the Present.* Lincoln: Univ. of Nebraska Press, 2008.

———. "The Soviet Occupation of Poland, 1939–41, and the Stereotype of the Anti-Polish and Pro-Soviet Jew." *Jewish Social Studies*, n.s., 13, no. 3 (Spring–Summer 2007): 135–76.

Michman, Dan. *The Emergence of Jewish Ghettos during the Holocaust.* Translated by Lenn J. Schramm. New York: Cambridge Univ. Press, 2011.

Miron, Guy, and Shlomit Shulhani, eds. *The Yad Vashem Encyclopedia of the Ghettos during the Holocaust.* Jerusalem: Yad Vashem, 2009.

Mitsel, Mikhail. "The Final Chapter: Agro-Joint Workers—Victims of the Great Terror in the USSR, 1937–40." *East European Jewish Affairs* 39, no. 1 (Apr. 2009): 79–99.

Murphy, David. *What Stalin Knew: The Enigma of Barbarossa.* New Haven, CT: Yale Univ. Press, 2005.

Naimark, Norman M. "The Nazis and 'The East': Jedwabne's Circle of Hell." *Slavic Review* 61, no. 3 (Autumn 2002): 476–82.

Pamyats': Vitsebsk [Memory: Vitebsk]. Vol. 1. Minsk: Belaruskaya entsyklapedyya, 2002.

Pankowsky, Hanna Davidson. *East of the Storm: Outrunning the Holocaust in Russia.* Lubbock: Texas Tech Univ. Press, 1999.

Pazniak, Zianon, and Yauhen Shmyhalou. "Kurapaty—the Road of Death." In *Kurapaty*, edited by V. Bagdanovich, 78–92. Minsk, Belarus: "Tekhnalogiya," 1994.

Petrov, Nikita, and Arsenii Roginskii. "The 'Polish Operation' of the NKVD, 1937–8." In *Stalin's Terror: High Politics and Mass Repression in the Soviet Union*, edited by Barry McLoughlin and Kevin McDermott, 153–93. New York: Palgrave Macmillan, 2003.

Pinchuk, Ben-Cion. "Jewish Refugees in Soviet Poland, 1939–1941." *Jewish Social Studies* 40, no. 2 (Spring 1978): 141–58.

———. *Shtetl Jews under Soviet Rule: Eastern Poland on the Eve of the Holocaust.* Cambridge, MA: Blackwell, 1990.

———. "Sovietization and the Jewish Response to Nazi Policies of Mass Murder." In *Jews in Eastern Poland and the USSR, 1939–46*, edited by Norman Davies and Antony Polonsky, 124–37. New York: St. Martin's Press, 1991.

———. "Was There a Soviet Policy for Evacuating the Jews? The Case of the Annexed Territories." *Slavic Review* 39, no. 1 (Mar. 1980): 44–55.

Piotrowski, Tadeusz. Introduction to *The Polish Deportees of World War II: Recollections of Removal to the Soviet Union and Dispersal throughout the*

World, edited by Tadeusz Piotrowski, 1–14. Jefferson, NC: McFarland, 2004.

———. *Poland's Holocaust: Ethnic Strife, Collaboration with Occupying Forces, and Genocide in the Second Republic, 1918–1947.* Jefferson, NC: McFarland, 1998.

Pipes, Richard. *The Formation of the Soviet Union: Communism and Nationalism.* Rev. ed. Cambridge, MA: Harvard Univ. Press, 1964.

Pipkin, Marx. "Istoriya odnovo apkhiva" [History of One Archive]. *Mishpokha* 20 (2007): 121–24.

Pleshakov, Constantine. *Stalin's Folly: The Tragic First Ten Days of World War II on the Eastern Front.* New York: Houghton Mifflin, 2005.

Podlipskii, Arkadii. *Evrei v Vitebsk* [Jews in Vitebsk]. Vitebsk, Belarus: UPP "Vitebskaya oblastnaya tipografiya," 2004.

———. *Evrei v Vitebsk* [Jews in Vitebsk]. Vol. 2. Vitebsk: UPP "Vitebskaya oblastnaya tipografiya," 2012.

Pohl, Dieter. "The Robbery of Jewish Property in Eastern Europe under German Occupation, 1939–1942." Translated by Charlotte Kreutzmüller. In *Robbery and Restitution: The Conflict over Jewish Property in Europe*, edited by Martin Dean, Constantin Goschler, and Philipp Ther, 68–80. New York: Berghahn Books, 2007.

Polonsky, Antony. *The Jews in Poland and Russia.* Vol. 3: *1914 to 2008.* Portland, OR: Littman Library of Jewish Civilization, 2012.

Protko, Tatiana Sergeievna. *Stanovleniye sovetskoi totalitarnoi sistemy v Belarusi (1917–1941 gg.)* [Creation of the Soviet Totalitarian System in Belarus (1917–1941)]. Minsk, Belarus: Tesei, 2002.

Prusin, Alexander V. *The Lands Between: Conflict in the East European Borderlands, 1870–1992.* New York: Oxford Univ. Press, 2010.

Rabin, Dov, ed. *Grodne.* Jerusalem: Hevrat Entsiklopedyah shel galuyot, 1973.

Rayak, Mikhal, and Tzevi Rayak. *Khurbn Glubok, Sharkoystsene, Dunilovitsh, Postav, Droye, Kazan* [Destruction of Glubokie, Szarkowszczyzna, Dunilowicze, Postawy, Druja, and Kaziany]. Buenos Aires: n.p., 1956.

Rein, Leonid. *The Kings and the Pawns: Collaboration in Byelorussia during World War II.* New York: Berghahn Books, 2011.

———. "The Radicalization of Anti-Jewish Policies in Nazi-Occupied Belarus." In *Nazi Policy on the Eastern Front, 1941*, edited by Alex J. Kay, Jeff Rutherford, and David Stahel, 220–39. Rochester, NY: Univ. of Rochester Press, 2012.

Reizer, Leib. "Grodner bildlekh" [Grodno Images]. In *Grodner opklangen* [Grodno Echoes], 33–35. Buenos Aires: n.p., Sept. 1975.

———. *In the Struggle: Memoirs from Grodno and the Forests.* Translated by Haike Beruriah Wiegand. Jerusalem: Yad Vashem, 2009.

Reles, Hirsh. "Afn tish a bintl blumen" [On a Table a Bunch of Flowers]. *Shtern*, no. 2 (Feb. 1936): 20.

———. "Fun shtetl" [From a Shtetl]. *Shtern*, no. 1 (Jan. 1938): 15.

———. *Iber Vaysrusishe shtetlekh* [Over Belarusian shtetlekh]. Moscow: Farlag "Sovetski pisatel," 1983.

———. "In lazaret" [In Hospital]. *Shtern*, no. 1 (Jan. 1938): 16.

———. "In yenem vinkele" [In Every Corner]. *Sovetish Heymland*, Jan. 1973, 130.

———. "Kakim mnye zapomnilsya" [From What I Remember]. *Berega*, July 2001.

———. "Maydl komiugistke" [Komsomol Maiden]. *Shtern*, no. 7 (July 1935): 74.

———. *Onheyb* [Beginning]. Minsk, Belarus: Melukhe-farlag fun Vaysrusland, 1939.

——— [as Grigorii Reles]. *V krayu svetlykh beryoz* [In the Country of Bright Birches]. Minsk, Belarus: Izdatel E. S. Gilperin, 1997.

———. *Di yidish-sovetishe shrayber fun Vaysrusland* [The Yiddish-Soviet Writer from Belarus]. Minsk, Belarus: I. P. Logvinov, 2004.

Reyzin, Ruve. *Durkh mi un pratse* [Through Toil and Labor]. Minsk, Belarus: Melukhe-farlag fun Vaysrusland, 1934.

"The Righteous among the Nations: Otto Busse." Yad Vashem website, n.d. At http://db.yadvashem.org/righteous/family.html?language=en&itemId=4014199.

Ro'i, Yaacov, ed. *Jews and Jewish Life in Russia and the Soviet Union.* Portland, OR: Frank Cass, 1995.

Rosefielde, Steven. "Excess Deaths and Industrialization: A Realist Theory of Stalinist Economic Development in the 1930s." *Journal of Contemporary History* 23, no. 2 (Apr. 1988): 277–89.

———. "Excess Mortality in the Soviet Union: A Reconsideration of the Demographic Consequences of Forced Industrialization, 1929–1949." *Soviet Studies* 35, no. 3 (July 1983): 385–409.

Rossino, Alexander B. "Polish 'Neighbors' and German Invaders: Anti-Jewish Violence in the Białystok District during the Opening Weeks in Operation Barbarossa." In *Polin*, vol. 16: *Focusing on Jewish Popular Culture in Poland and Its Afterlife*, 431–52. Portland, OR: Littman Library of Jewish Civilization, 2003.

Rozshanski, Shmuel, ed. *Oysgeklibene shriftn: Dovid Hofshteyn, Izi Kharik, Itsik Fefer* [Collected Works: Dovid Hofshteyn, Izi Kharik, Itsik Fefer]. Buenos Aires: Literatur-gezelshaft beym YIVO in Argentine, 1962.

———, ed. *Oysgeklibene shriftn: Moishe Kulbak* [Collected Works: Moishe Kulbak]. Buenos Aires: Literatur-gezelshaft beym YIVO in Argentine, 1976.

Rubenstein, Joshua, and Ilya Altman, eds. *The Unknown Black Book: The Holocaust in the German-Occupied Soviet Territories*. Bloomington: Indiana Univ. Press, 2010.

Rubenstein, Joshua, and Vladimir P. Naumov, eds. *Stalin's Secret Pogrom: The Postwar Inquisition of the Jewish Anti-Fascist Committee*. Translated by Laura Esther Wolfson. New Haven, CT: Yale Univ. Press, 2001.

Rudling, Per Anders. *The Rise and Fall of Belarusian Nationalism, 1906–1931*. Pittsburgh: Univ. of Pittsburgh Press, 2015.

Rutherford, Jeff. "The Radicalization of German Occupation Policies: The *Wirtschaftsstab Ost* and the 121st Infantry Division in Pavlovsk, 1941." In *Nazi Policy on the Eastern Front, 1941*, edited by Alex J. Kay, Jeff Rutherford, and David Stahel, 130–54. Rochester, NY: Univ. of Rochester Press, 2012.

Rybak, Andrzej Henryk. *Stalag 319: Międzynarodowy obóz jeniecki w Chełmie w latach 1941–1944* [Stalag 319: International Prisoner Camp in Chełm in the Years 1941–1944]. Chełm, Poland: Stowarzzyszenie Rocznik Chełmski, 2009.

Ryvkin, Mikhail, and Arkadii Shulman. *Chronik der furchtbaren Tage: Die Tragödie des Witebsker Getto* [Chronicle of Terrible Days: The Tragedy of the Vitebsk Ghetto]. Translated by F. Thomas Gatter. Minsk, Belarus: Medisont, 2007.

———. "Vitsebskaye geta" [Vitebsk Ghetto]. In *Pamyats': Vitsebsk* [Memory: Vitebsk]. Vol. 1. Minsk: Belaruskaya entsyklapedyya, 2002.

Sakwa, Richard, ed. *The Rise and Fall of the Soviet Union, 1917–1991*. London: Routledge, 1999.

Schulman, Elias. *A History of Jewish Education in the Soviet Union*. New York: KTAV Publishing House, 1971.

Selimenev, Viacheslav, and Arkadii Zeltser. "The Jewish Intelligentsia and the Liquidation of Yiddish Schools in Belorussia, 1938." *Jews in Russia and Eastern Europe* 43, no. 3 (2000): 78–97.

———. "Kolyshki—a Shtetl in the Late 1930s." *Jews in Russia and Eastern Europe* 45, no. 1 (2001): 48–72.

———. "The Liquidation of Yiddish Schools in Belorussia and Jewish Reaction." *Jews in Russia and Eastern Europe* 41, no. 1 (2000): 74–111.

Shalev, Ziva. "Tosia Altman." Jewish Women's Archive Encyclopedia, n.d. At http://jwa.org/encyclopedia/article/altman-tosia.

Shapiro, Josef. "In geto Dokshitz" [In Dokshitzy Ghetto]. In *Sefer-Yizkor Dokshitz-Parafyanov* [Memorial Book Dokshitzy-Parafianow], 209–17. Tel Aviv: n.p., 1970.

Shearer, David R. *Policing Stalin's Socialism: Repression and Social Order in the Soviet Union, 1924–1953*. New Haven, CT: Yale Univ. Press, 2009.

Sherman, Joseph, and Gennady Estraikh, eds. *David Bergelson: From Modernism to Socialist Realism*. London: Modern Humanities Research Association and Maney, 2007.

Shestakov, V. "Viazoy es hot zikh geshafn fer lernbukh fun geshikhte fun FSSR" [How the Textbook for the History of the USSR Was Created]. *Shtern*, no. 9 (Sept. 1937): 82–91.

Shneer, David. *Yiddish and the Creation of Soviet Jewish Culture, 1918–1930*. Cambridge: Cambridge Univ. Press, 2004.

Sholem Izraelit [pseud.]. "Farayn fun medtuer, luftert oys ayere reyen!" (Union of Medical Personnel, Air Out Your Ranks!). *Vitebsker arbet*, supplement to *Zarya zapada*, 12 Jan. 1929.

Shternshis, Anna. *Soviet and Kosher: Jewish Popular Culture in the Soviet Union, 1923–1939*. Bloomington: Indiana Univ. Press, 2006.

Shulman, Arkadii. "Evreiskii Gorodok" [Jewish Gorodok]. In *Mesto yevo uzhe ne uznaet evo* [Places That No Longer Know Them], 102–30. Minsk, Belarus: Medisont, 2007.

———. "Ostrov Relesa" [Isle of Reles]. In Girsh [Hirsh] Reles, *Yevreiskie sovetskie pisateli Belorussii* [Jewish Soviet Writers of Belarus], 221–82. Minsk, Belarus: Izdatel' D. T. Kolas, 2006.

———. "Pokoleniye Relesa: Pamyati pisatalya" [Reles's Generation: The Writer Remembered]. *Aviv* (Minsk), Oct.–Nov. 2004, 20.

Shvedik, H. *Lider* [Poems]. Minsk, Belarus: Melukhe-farlag fun Vaysrusland, 1939.

Siekierski, Maciej. "The Jews in Soviet-Occupied Eastern Poland at the End of 1939: Numbers and Distribution." In *Jews in Eastern Poland and the*

USSR, 1939–46, edited by Norman Davies and Antony Polonsky, 110–15. New York: St. Martin's Press, 1991.

Siemaszko, Z. S. "The Mass Deportations of the Polish Population to the USSR, 1940–1941." In *The Soviet Takeover of the Polish Eastern Provinces, 1939–41*, edited by Keith Sword, 217–35. New York: St. Martin's Press, 1991.

Siemiński, Jan. *Grodno Walczące: Wspomnienia harcerza* [Grodno Fighters: Memories of Scouts]. Białystok, Poland: Towarystwo Literackie im. Adam Mickiewicza, Oddział Białstocki, 1992.

Skerpan, Alfred A. "Aspects of Soviet Antisemitism." *Antioch Review* 12, no. 3 (Autumn 1952): 287–328.

Slezkine, Yuri. "The USSR as a Communal Apartment, or How a Socialist State Promoted Ethnic Particularism." *Slavic Review* 53, no. 2 (Summer 1994): 414–52.

Smilovitsky, Leonid. *Holocaust in Belorussia, 1941–1944*. Tel Aviv: Biblioteka Motveya Chernogo, 2000. At https://www.jewishgen.org/yizkor/belarus/Belarus.html.

———. "Izi Kharik: Pevets i zhertva epokhi" [Izi Kharik: Singer and Victim of the Epoch]. *Mishpokha* 2 (1996): 53–58.

———. "Jewish National School in Belorussia, 1920–1930." *Shvut* 4 (1996): 59–78.

Snyder, Timothy. *Bloodlands: Europe between Hitler and Stalin*. New York: Basic Books, 2010.

———. *Sketches from a Secret War: A Polish Artist's Mission to Liberate Soviet Ukraine*. New Haven, CT: Yale Univ. Press, 2005.

Spector, Shmuel, and Bracha Freundlich, eds. *Lost Jewish Worlds: The Communities of Grodno, Lida, Olkieniki, Vishay*. Jerusalem: Yad Vashem, 1996.

Starks, Tricia. *The Body Soviet: Propaganda, Hygiene, and the Revolutionary State*. Madison: Univ. of Wisconsin Press, 2008.

Statiev, Alexander. *The Soviet Counterinsurgency in the Western Borderlands*. New York: Cambridge Univ. Press, 2010.

"The Story of the Poet, Moshe Kulbak (Recollections by Raya Kulbak)." N.d. At http://www.eliatgordinlevitancom/kurenets/k_pages/kulbak.html.

Streit, Christian. "Soviet Prisoners of War in the Hands of the Wehrmacht." In *War of Extermination: The German Military in World War II*,

1941–1944, edited by Hannes Heer and Klaus Naumann, 80–91. New York: Berghahn Books, 2000.

Strzelecka, Irene. "The Hospitals at Auschwitz Concentration Camp." In *Auschwitz 1940–1945: Central Issues in the History of the Camp*, vol. 2: *The Prisoners—Their Life and Work*, edited by Wacław Długoborski and Franciszek Piper, translated by William Brand, 291–346. Oświęcim, Poland: Auschwitz-Birkenau State Museum, 2000.

Strzelecki, Andrzej. "The History, Role, and Operation of the 'Central Camp Sauna' in Auschwitz II–Birkenau." In *The Architecture of Crime: The "Central Camp Sauna" in Auschwitz II–Birkenau*, edited by Teresa Świebocka, translated by William Brand, 11–93. Oświęcim, Poland: Auschwitz-Birkenau State Museum, 2001.

Strzembosz, Tomasz. "Armed Resistance in the North-eastern Provinces of the Polish Republic, 1939–41." In *The Soviet Takeover of the Polish Eastern Provinces, 1939–41*, edited by Keith Sword, 149–81. New York: St. Martin's Press, 1991.

Suvorov, Viktor [Vladimir Bogdanovich Rezun]. *Icebreaker: Who Started the Second World War?* London: Hamish Hamilton, 1990.

Świebocki, Henryk. "The Establishment and Growth of the Clandestine Movement in the Camp." In *Auschwitz 1940–1945: Central Issues in the History of the Camp*, vol. 4: *The Resistance Movement*, edited by Wacław Długoborski and Franciszek Piper, translated by William Brand, 63–137. Oświęcim, Poland: Auschwitz-Birkenau State Museum, 2000.

Sword, Keith. "Soviet Economic Policy in the Annexed Areas." In *The Soviet Takeover of the Polish Eastern Provinces, 1939–41*, edited by Keith Sword, 86–101. New York: St. Martin's Press, 1991.

———, ed. *The Soviet Takeover of the Polish Eastern Provinces, 1939–41*. New York: St. Martin's Press, 1991.

Szawłowski, Ryszard. "The Polish–Soviet War of 1939." In *The Soviet Takeover of the Polish Eastern Provinces, 1939–41*, edited by Keith Sword, 28–43. New York: St. Martin's Press, 1991.

Sztokfisz, Dovid, ed. *Yizkhor-bukh Rubizivitsi, derevne un svive* [Memorial Book Rubiezewicze, the Village and Surroundings]. Tel Aviv: n.p., 1968.

Tarlovski, Abba. "Grodne Yudenrat" [Grodno Judenrat]. In *Kovets Grodna* [Collection Grodno], 27–28. Tel Aviv: n.p., 1958.

Tec, Nechama. *Resistance: Jews and Christians Who Defied the Nazi Terror*. New York: Oxford Univ. Press, 2013.

Tomaszewski, Jerzy. "The Role of Jews in Polish Commerce, 1918–1939." In *The Jews of Poland between Two World Wars*, edited by Yisrael Gutman, Ezra Mendelsohn, Jehuda Reinharz, and Chone Shmeruk, 141–57. Hanover, NH: Univ. Press of New England, 1989.

Trevor-Roper, Hugh. *History and Imagination*. Oxford: Clarendon Press, 1980.

Vakar, Nicholas P. *Belorussia: The Making of a Nation*. Cambridge, MA: Harvard Univ. Press, 1956.

Volfson, S. "Di rasn-teories fun fashizm un der klasnkamf" [The Racial Theories of Fascism and the Class Struggle]. In *Afn visnshaftlekhn front* [On the Scientific Front], 3–30. Biuleten fun Institut far Yidisher Proletarisher Kultur ba der Vaysrusisher Visnshaft-Akademie, nos. 5–6. Minsk, Belarus: Institut far yidisher proletarisher kultur, 1934.

Walke, Anika. *Pioneers and Partisans: An Oral History of Nazi Genocide in Belorussia*. New York: Oxford Univ. Press, 2015.

Weeks, Albert. *Stalin's Other War: Soviet Grand Strategy, 1939–1941*. Lanham, MD: Rowman and Littlefield, 2002.

Weinreich, Max. *Der veg tsu undzer yugnt* [The Way to Our Youth]. Vilnius, Lithuania: Yidisher visnshaftlekher institut, 1935.

Weitz, Eric D. "Racial Politics without the Concept of Race: Reevaluating Soviet Ethnic and National Purges." *Slavic Review* 61, no. 1 (Spring 2002): 1–29.

Weitzman, Lenore J. "Bronka Klibanski: 1923–2011." Jewish Women's Archive Encyclopedia, n.d. At http://jwa.org/encyclopedia/article/klibanski-bronka-bronia.

———. "Living on the Aryan Side in Poland: Gender, Passing, and the Nature of Resistance." In *Women in the Holocaust*, edited by Dalia Ofer and Lenore J. Weitzman, 187–222. New Haven, CT: Yale Univ. Press, 1998.

Werth, Nicolas. "The NKVD Mass Secret National Operations (August 1937–November 1938)." SciencesPo, Mass Violence, and Resistance Research Network, 20 May 2010. At http://www.sciencespo.fr/mass-violence-war-massacre-resistance/en/document/nkvd-mass-secret-national-operations-august-1937-november-1938.

Wheatcroft, S. G. "A Note on Steven Rosefielde's Calculations of Excess Mortality in the USSR, 1929–1949." *Soviet Studies* 36 (1984): 277–81.

Wildermuth, David W. "Who Killed Lida's Jewish Intelligentsia? A Case Study of Wehrmacht Involvement in the Holocaust's 'First Hour.'" *Holocaust and Genocide Studies* 27, no. 1 (Spring 2013): 1–29.

Willenberg, Samuel. *Surviving Treblinka*. Edited by Władysław T. Bartoszewski. Translated by Naftali Greenwood. New York: Blackwell, 1989.

"Yakub Kolas: Personality and Work." N.d. At http://archives.gov.by/eng/index.php?id=109695.

"Yanka Kupala: Belarusian Treasure-Seeker." N.d. http://www.democraticbelarus.eu/node/5811.

"Yanka Kupala: Personality and Work." N.d. At http://archives.gov.by/eng/index.php?id=856629.

Yarmusik, E. S. "Ekanamichnaya, religiinaya i natsyianal'naya palityka akupantav" [Economic, Religious, and National Occupation Policies]. In *Pamyats': Grodna* [Memory: Grodno]. Minsk: Belaruskaya entsyklapedyya, 1999.

Zak, Avraham. *Knekht zenen mir geven* [We Were Slaves]. 2 vols. Buenos Aires: Tsentral farband fun Poylishe Yidn in Argentine, 1956.

———. *Oyf shlakhn fun hefker* [On the Road of Abandonment]. Buenos Aires: Farlag Yidnbukh, 1958.

Zakhari, Aaron. "Grodner tipn in mayn zikorn" [Grodno Characters in My Memory]. In *Grodner opklangen* [Grodno Echoes], 35. Buenos Aires: n.p., Sept. 1975.

Zandman, Felix [Feliks], with David Chanoff. *Never the Last Journey*. New York: Schocken Books, 1995.

Żbikowski, Andrzej. "Pogroms in Northeastern Poland: Spontaneous Reactions and German Instigations." In *Shared History—Divided Memory: Jews and Others in Soviet-Occupied Poland, 1939–1941*, edited by Elazar Barkan, Elizabeth A. Cole, and Kai Struve, 315–54. Leipzig: Leipziger Universitätsverlag, 2007.

Zeltser, Arkadii. *Evrei sovetskoi provintsii: Vitebsk i mestechki, 1917–1941* [Jews of the Soviet Provinces: Vitebsk and Surrounding Region, 1917–1941]. Moscow: Rossiiskaya politicheskaya entsiklopediya, 2006.

———. "Imaginary Vitebsk: The View from the Inside." *East European Jewish Affairs* 40, no. 3 (Dec. 2010): 217–35.

———. "Interwar Ethnic Relations and Soviet Policy: The Case of Eastern Belorussia." *Yad Vashem Studies* 34 (2006): 87–124.

Index

Italic page numbers denote illustrations.

Jeffrey Koerber is assistant professor of history at Chapman University. He holds a PhD in Holocaust history from Clark University as well as bachelor's and master's degrees in architecture from the University of Illinois at Urbana-Champaign. His research examines the relationships between place, historical actors, and events. He has received fellowships from Claims Conference, the University of Southern California Shoah Foundation Institute, the Holocaust Educational Foundation, the Tauber Institute for the Study of European Jewry, and the Fulbright Program.